Advances in Japanese Business and Economics

Volume 34

Advances in Japanese Business and Economics (AJBE) showcases the work of Japanese and non-Japanese scholars researching the Japanese economy and Japanese businesses. Published in English, the series highlights for a global readership the unique perspectives of Japan's most distinguished and emerging scholars of business and economics. It covers research of either theoretical or empirical nature, in both authored and edited volumes, regardless of the sub-discipline or geographical coverage, including, but not limited to, such topics as macroeconomics, microeconomics, industrial relations, innovation, regional development, entrepreneurship, international trade, globalization, financial markets, technology management, and business strategy. At the same time, as a series of volumes written by Japanese and non-Japanese scholars studying Japan, it includes research on the issues of the Japanese economy, industry, management practice, and policy, such as the economic policies and business innovations before and after the Japanese "bubble" burst in the 1990s.

AJBE endeavors to overcome a historical deficit in the dissemination of Japanese economic theory, research methodology, and analysis. The volumes in the series contribute not only to a deeper understanding of Japanese business and economics but to revealing underlying universal principles.

Overseen by a panel of renowned scholars led by Editor-in-Chief Professor Ryuzo Sato, AJBE employs a single-blind review process in which the Editor-in-Chief, together with the Managing Editors and specialized scholars designated by the Editor-in-Chief or Managing Editors, rigorously reviews each proposal and manuscript to ensure that every submission is a valuable contribution to the global scholarly readership.

All books and chapters in AJBE are indexed in Scopus.

Haruhito Takeda · Junko Watanabe
Editors

Rethinking Japanese Economic Policy at the Turn of the 21st Century

Springer

Editors
Haruhito Takeda
The University of Tokyo
Tokyo, Japan

Director at Mitsui Bunko
Tokyo, Japan

Junko Watanabe
Graduate School of Economics
Kyoto University
Kyoto, Japan

ISSN 2197-8859 ISSN 2197-8867 (electronic)
Advances in Japanese Business and Economics
ISBN 978-981-97-5511-0 ISBN 978-981-97-5512-7 (eBook)
https://doi.org/10.1007/978-981-97-5512-7

This Springer imprint is published by the registered company Springer Nature Singapore Pte Ltd.
The registered company address is: 152 Beach Road, #21-01/04 Gateway East, Singapore 189721, Singapore

Acknowledgments

This book, compiled on the basis of RIETI's research projects on the history of economic policy conducted from 2014 to 2021, owes a debt of gratitude to many people.

In particular, we would like to thank the METI bureaucrats and former government officials who were willing to be interviewed and provided behind-the-scenes stories of the policymaking process. We also had the opportunity to interview former senior Bank officials and well-informed people from private institutions, although the number of interviews was very small. With limited materials and information for research, interviews with individuals involved in policymaking were valuable research resources and memorable experiences for us.

RIETI provided significant support for this study. Former President Masayuki Morikawa, who has a deep understanding of policy history, has recognized the need for RIETI to conduct research on the history of industrial policy as a project and has always had our backs. We would also like to thank Mr. Yoichi Sekizawa, Mr. Masataka Saburi, and other RIETI Senior Fellows, and successive research directors for their appropriate and helpful advice. We received great support and assistance from Mr. Shigeru Yokoyama in collecting and organizing the research materials and data. Ms. Akiko Masugata and other staff members helped us with various procedures necessary for our research.

The RIETI staff members mentioned above also made significant contributions in arranging interviews and hearings with METI officials. This support was essential for our joint research activities, and we sincerely appreciate it. The publication of this book was made possible by a publication grant from RIETI and the support of Ms.Toko Tanimoto and Mr. Takehiro Watanabe, who are in charge of international and public relations.

In compiling some of the results of these projects into this book, we had several opportunities to receive advice and comments from Dr. Adam S. Posen, President at Peterson Institute for International Economics. We would also like to express our gratitude to Mr. Takayuki Sueyoshi (Daiwa Institute of Research Ltd.) for his advice and assistance in collecting and analyzing data on the Japanese economy.

It is our great pleasure and honor to publish this book as one of the Springer's book series "Advances in Japanese Business and Economics." We express our sincere gratitude to Professor Ruzo Sato, the supervisor of this series, for giving us the opportunity to present an overview of this book at the workshop he chaired, where we received valuable questions and comments from the participants and were able to fine-tune on the book's content. We also appreciate the assistance of Springer's editors and editorial staff, Ms. Juno Kawakami and Ms. Suganya Kothandaraman.

Tokyo and Kyoto
Spring 2024

Haruhito Takeda
Junko Watanabe

Contents

Contributors

W. Miles Fletcher III Department of History, The University of North Carolina, Chapel Hill, NC, USA

Kiyoto Ido Former Director-General of International Bureau, Ministry of Finance, Tokyo, Japan

Satoshi Kawamura Josai University, Saitama, Japan

Wataru Takahashi Osaka University of Economics, Osaka, Japan

Haruhito Takeda The University of Tokyo and Director at Mitsui Bunko, Tokyo, Japan

Takeshi Tashiro Research Institute of Economy, Trade and Industry, Tokyo, Japan; Peterson Institute for International Economics, Washington D.C., United States

Junko Watanabe Kyoto University, Kyoto, Japan

Introduction

Haruhito Takeda and Junko Watanabe

Abstract This chapter serves as an introduction to the book, providing background information such as an overview of the Japanese economy from the 1990s to the 2010s, and an outline of each chapter. Since the 1990s, Japan has experienced a prolonged period of recession following the bursting of the bubble economy and the financial crisis that began in 1997. The Japanese government faced a number of challenges during this period, including the implementation of economic stimulus measures in the context of fiscal rehabilitation, the disposal of non-performing loans, the stabilization of the financial system, and the revitalization of the industrial and corporate sectors. Additionally, the strengthening of their international competitiveness was a key objective. Some structural problems, such as declining birth rates and an aging and shrinking population, as well as institutional fatigue in the Japanese-style economic system, were associated with the recession-induced phenomenon.

The objective of this book is to enhance the comprehension of the historical evolution and contemporary state of the Japanese economy through an analysis of industrial, monetary, and other macroeconomic policies. Each chapter is written by scholars and current and retired bureaucrats, respectively, and provides a comprehensive analysis of the relevant policymaking process and its historical context.

We would like to express our gratitude toward the participants of the research seminar led by Dr. Ryuzo Sato and Dr. Yoshio Sasajima. Although we could not mention them all, their comments proved valuable in writing this chapter.

H. Takeda
The University of Tokyo and Mitsui Bunko, Tokyo, Japan

J. Watanabe (✉)
Kyoto University, Kyoto, Japan

H. Takeda and J. Watanabe (eds.), *Rethinking Japanese economic policy at the turn of the 21st century*, Advances in Japanese Business and Economics 34,
https://doi.org/10.1007/978-981-97-5512-7_1

1 Background

1.1 Japanese Economy at the Turn of the 21st Century

Around the year 2000, the terms "turn of the century" or "millennium" were often heard in Japan and around the world. Especially in Japan, these words seemed to not only describe the calendar year but also reflect the hopes and fears about the Japanese economy, particularly its recovery from the stagnation of the 1990s and its advancement through reforms in the 2000s and beyond.

After the bubble economy from 1988 to 1990 and the subsequent bubble burst after 1991, the Japanese economy sank into a prolonged recession. The 1990s also saw a business cycle that included a boom period, which faced another challenge because of the impact of the Asian currency crisis that began in the fall of 1997, as well as the financial crisis that developed within Japan. From 1997 to 1999, Japan experienced severe recession. This event was partly due to the various problems caused by the bubble burst not being fully dealt with until 1997 and partly due to the economy entering a downward phase. During the same period, the government undertook a major fiscal structural reform, which was ill-timed and spurred the recession.

Toward the end of the 1990s, the financial recovery legislation was passed as a series of laws requiring drastic measures to deal with non-performing loans, resolve bank failures, and restore the soundness of financial institutions to eliminate financial instability. In the wake of the withdrawal of funds from financial institutions following the disposal of non-performing loans, efforts had to be directed toward the consideration of the policy measures for the industrial sector, which was potentially threatened with a chain reaction of bankruptcies, even for companies with profitable management resources.

As for the global economy in the same period, corporate and industrial restructuring and the creation of new industries to strengthen international competitiveness were widespread, particularly in the United States and European countries. Meanwhile, Japan was in a state of stagnation and crisis. The impact of the Asian currency crisis in 1997–1998 on the global economy was less intense, partly because the Chinese market was rapidly growing while the global market was undergoing significant changes and expansion. To catch up to these changes in the environment surrounding Japan and return to a growth trajectory, the country had to integrate the implementation of financial and industrial revitalization. (For a detailed account of the developments during this period, refer to the chronology at the end of the chapter.)

In 2001, the central ministries were restructured and merged. The objectives of this reform included eliminating the negative effects of siloed administration, strengthening cabinet functions, and reducing and streamlining administrative operations. Thus, the "Prime Minister's Office-led" policies were promoted to revitalize the Japanese economy through centralized decision making and initiatives at the Prime Minister's Office.

As described above, the turn of the century was marked by turbulence and change in Japan. Meanwhile, various efforts were made to break away from the "lost decade."

The disposal of bad loans, consolidation of banks into megabanks, and industrial revitalization plans were almost complete in the mid-2000s, but deflationary trends continued in Japan. In addition, the country faced many challenges in strengthening industrial competitiveness, which were carried over into the "Abenomics" era of the 2010s along with the fiscal and monetary policies. In the meantime, as the phrase "lost two (or three) decades" emerges, the Japanese economy yet to show a stable growth trajectory. Its evaluation, including the assessment of Abenomics., has not yet been settled.

1.2 The Structural Problems

The transformation of the Japanese economy around 1990 was triggered by the collapse of the bubble. However, the dark turn from the 1980s, when Japan was regarded as an honor student of advanced industrial nations and praised for its "Japanese-style economic system," could not be attributed solely to the collapse of a temporary enthusiasm or business cycle recession. The assumption is that some structural problems are associated with these phenomena.

One issue is related to medium- to long-term factors, such as declining birth rates and an aging and shrinking population. The potential growth rate, which is the economic growth rate that could be achieved if the capital stock and labor force required for production activities were utilized without excesses or shortfalls, has been declining. Unless a bold change is made in the immigration policy, growth rates face natural constraints. Given the factors of capital, labor, and productivity as sources of economic growth, Japan has been promoting policies targeting productivity, especially in the last 20 years, but it has yet to achieve remarkable results. This case has been the subject of research and debate among domestic and international economists.

Another structural problem is the view that institutional fatigue exists in the Japanese-style economic system and that full-fledged economic growth will not be achieved until this system is reformed. From the 1960s to the early 1980s, when Japan was experiencing relatively high growth, this system was celebrated as an institutional factor that led to the country's extraordinary economic progress.

In the Japanese-style economic system, employment practices such as long-term employment, seniority systems, and company unions promoted workers' commitment to companies and their loyalty. In reality, these practices were limited to a segment of the male workforce in large companies. The workers were flexible in accepting responses to technological change as long-term employment was based on adjustments within companies through reassignments and transfers to remote locations. Peripheral segments around the core male workforce, such as women with part-time employment, male seasonal workers in factories, and small and medium enterprise workers serve as a buffer for overall employment adjustment.

However, the above-mentioned systems based on a pyramid-shaped demographic structure and the "division of roles" between men and women began to crumble within companies after the 1990s as women's social advancement proceeded and the demographic structure underwent major changes.

As for the financial system that constitutes the Japanese-style economic system, the so-called "convoy system," which is reflected in the relationship between the Ministry of Finance (MOF) and financial institutions, should be considered. This system guaranteed existing banks a certain amount of profit or *rents* through the MOF's regulation of bank entry and interest rates, which enabled these banks to support the financing needs of companies' strong capital investment.

In terms of government-business relations in the industrial sector, the industrial policy of the Ministry of International Trade and Industry (MITI) and other ministries has suggested a vision of the industrial structure that the Japanese economy should follow and various measures for industrial development.

The financial and industrial practices described above, which were formed during the period of rapid economic growth from 1960s to the 1980s, were effective to a certain extent during the development stage when the country was trying to catch up with Europe and the United States. This effectiveness was due to the fact that the goals to be attained were clear to some extent and that the government had a certain rationale behind its indirect involvement in allocating of the resources to achieve such goals.

However, as the catch-up phase ended, and the Japanese economy began to stand on the frontier of the world, the country lost sight of its vision for new industries and the economic systems it should pursue. The era of high investment, mainly in manufacturing, ended, and the industrial structure shifted toward service-oriented industrialization. In addition, increased economic activity at the global level limited the effectiveness of the economic policies that mainly targeted domestic firms and industries.

These factors led to "institutional fatigue" of the Japanese-style economic system, and the Japanese government believed that the solution was "deregulation." Deregulation has been a global trend since the 1980s, especially in Anglo-Saxon countries, such as the United States and the United Kingdom. After playing catch-up, Japan, being an advanced country, was expected to shift to an economy based on market mechanisms.

However, the complexities among nations should not be overlooked. The period between the 1980s and the 2000s saw a history of economic friction. (See the chronology at the end of the chapter.) In response to Japan's export growth until the early 1980s, the United States, which was suffering from "twin deficits," including a current account deficit, embarked on strengthening its own industrial competitiveness and demanded that Japan expand domestic demand and open its markets. Such demand included voluntary export restraints, the threats under Super 301 in industries such as automobile and semiconductor, and the opening of markets in the insurance and financial sectors.

The implementation of protectionist policies, government-led industrial competitiveness policies, and the banner of "deregulation" for market opening were intermingled bilaterally or probably multilaterally. Japan's stagnation since the 1990s contrasts with the condition of the United States, which enjoyed a golden age during the same period, reviving the international competitiveness of its existing industries while creating new industries such as information technology.[1] The book is concerned with how the Japanese government tried to manage its economy while dealing with its relationship with the United States and the evolving international environment.

2 Rethinking Japanese Economic Policy

2.1 RIETI's Research Projects

The purpose of this book is to review the history of the trials and errors of economic policies and to examine the problems they entailed, focusing mainly on the period from the 1990s to the 2010s. Some chapters extend the description to the periods before and after, attempting to place it in a broad mid- to long-term historical context.

This publication is based on two research projects conducted at the Research Institute of Economy, Trade and Industry (RIETI). One is the project titled "Historical Review of Economic and Industrial Policy: An International Perspective," which was conducted in 2014–2016 under the Policy History and Policy Evaluation Program. In this project, Satoshi Kawamura, W. Miles Fletcher III and Peter Von Staden, in addition to Haruhito Takeda and Junko Watanabe, wrote discussion papers as a part of the economic policy history research at the turn of the century.

The other project, titled "The Industrial Revitalization and the Role of Finance: The History of Japanese Economic Policies in the 1990s–2000s," was a joint research activity conducted in 2019–2021. The project was organized by inviting experts with deep knowledge of monetary policy, such as Kiyoto Ido, and Wataru Takahashi. It addressed the impact of the international financial environment on Japan's fiscal conditions and post-bubble monetary policies. This joint research benefited from the advice of internationally renowned Dr. Adam S. Posen (President of the Peterson Institute for International Economics).

Most discussion papers written for these two projects have been substantially updated or revised, and those written in Japanese have been translated into English for the current publication. The relevance of the first discussion papers to the chapters included in the book is described in the overview of each chapter.

[1] For an economic–historical perspective on the United States and global economies in the 1990s, see, for example, Rhode and Toniolo (eds.) (2006).

2.2 Transformation of Industrial Policies

Chapter 2 (Industrial Policy at the Turn of the Century) by Haruhito Takeda[2] reviews the long history of the policies of the MITI/METI since the mid-1970s and evaluates the changes in policy principles that occurred at the turn of the twenty-first century.

Several changes occurred during the study period. From the late 1980s through the 2000s, deregulation in various industrial sectors and fields was an issue in Japan, albeit belatedly, partly because of global trends. Furthermore, as the Japan–U.S. economic friction reached its peak as a result of the situation of Japan's current account surplus and the United States' deficit, the U.S. government demanded that Japan open its domestic market through deregulation.

Under external pressure from the United States and other countries or sometimes taking advantage of this external pressure, Japan introduced the ideas and methods of "deregulation" and "structural reform" not only at the industrial level but also in areas such as the labor market, social security system, and corporate system, all of which are all related to the institutional design of the Japanese economy. The author suggests that the key policy change was a shift in the direction of deregulation and structural reform. The policy had been to leave the self-efforts of the private sector or market mechanisms as much as possible. With the reorganization of the ministries in 2001, the MITI was renamed the METI, although it was reorganized with a slight expansion of its jurisdiction. METI's policy can be positioned as an extension of MITI's policy principles in the 1990s.

Additionally, during the recession of the 1990s and thereafter, structural reforms to restore economic vitality and place the Japanese economy on a growth trajectory emerged as policy issues. At the same time, Japan had to manage its domestic economy with consideration of foreign economic relations. In this context, MITI and its successor METI expanded the scope of their responsibilities and jurisdiction beyond their traditional focus on industry into the macroeconomic realm.

Chapter 3 (The End of the Industrial Adjustment Policy) and Chapter 4 (The Industrial Revitalization Policy in the 2000s) by Junko Watanabe[3] examine policy shifts at the industrial level in MITI/METI, as observed by Takeda in Chapter 2. Chapter 3 provides a historical retrospective of the policies that MITI had implemented since World War II, which can be summarized as "industrial adjustment policies." The

---

[2] The original paper is as follows but is revised as necessary for this book. Haruhito Takeda (2016) 'Seiki Tenkan-ki ni okeru Tsushō-Sangyō, Keizai-Sangyo Seisaku no Tenkan' [Transformation of Trade, Industry, and Economic and Industrial Policy at the Turn of the Century] RIETI Discussion Paper Series 16-J-026. https://www.rieti.go.jp/jp/publications/dp/16j026.pdf.

[3] The original paper is as follows but is revised as necessary for this book.

Junko Watanabe (2016) 'Tsusan-syō (Keisan-syō) no Sangyō Chōsei Seisaku' [MITI (METI)'s Industrial Adjustment Policy] RIETI Discussion Paper Series 16-J-033.https://www.rieti.go.jp/jp/publications/dp/16j033.pdf (copyright: the author).

Junko Watanabe and Haruhito Takeda (2021) 'Nisen-nendai no Sangyo Saisei Seisaku' [Industrial Revitalization Policies in the 2000s] RIETI Discussion Paper Series 21-J-030. https://www.rieti.go.jp/jp/publications/dp/21j030.pdf.

chapter also discusses the significance and impact of the end of these policies at the turn of the century.

The objective of the industrial adjustment policy was to promote the transformation of Japan's industrial structure to accommodate its international competitiveness and stabilize the growth path of the Japanese economy. To ensure that the restructuring of industries in a structural recession would proceed smoothly, policy measures were implemented for displaced workers and for regions suffering from exhaustion caused by the withdrawal of companies, in addition to the support for industries and companies. Given these factors, the social frictions in Japan, including the increased unemployment, were not as severe in some respects.

However, after the 1990s, this traditional industrial adjustment policy approach ended, and labor and social policies were separated from industrial policies. The policies related to industries were converted into industrial revitalization policies, which are analyzed in Chapter 4. These policies were implemented in the late 1990s and early 2000s under "integrated revitalization of the financial and industrial sectors." The METI drafted a plan to support the legal and incentive tax systems available to companies when restructuring their businesses.

In the mid-2000s, these government-supported restructuring was halted. The government gradually shifted its policy focus from a passive industrial revitalization policy in response to the aftereffects of the bubble economy to one that included more proactive growth strategies. During the Abenomics era in the 2010s, the policy succeeded and progressed in terms of legislation into an industrial competitiveness policy, which remain in place today.

Chapters 2, 3, and 4 all observe a trend in which the industrial policy principles and actual policies at the turn of the century became less colored by direct "policy intervention" and became more transparent and market driven. The authors recognize that this change is the result of the traditional industrial policy having completed a certain role in the development of Japan's economic history and evolving to adapt to new environmental changes.

At the same time, government intervention, whether good or bad, appears to persist in different ways. Especially with regard to policies to strengthen industrial competitiveness, this universal phenomenon is common not only in Japan but also in other countries, including those in Europe and the United States. Therefore, careful and in-depth analysis of industrial policy development process is necessary.

Chapter 5 (Standards Administration Policy in Japan between the 1980s and the 2000s) by Satoshi Kawamura[4] provides a historical analysis of why the standards certification administration has been emphasized as part of the economic growth policy since the late 1990s, when slow economic growth began to become the norm.

---

[4] The original paper is as follows but is revised as necessary for this book. Satoshi Kawamura (2016) '1980 nendai-2000 nenndai ni okeru Kijyun Ninshō Gyōsei: Seisaku Kadai to shiteno Keizai Seichō to Seihinkachi-kojyo-shisaku no Tenkai' [The Japanese Government's Initiative for Standards and Certifications in the 1980s-2000s: Economic Growth as a Policy Goal and Improvement of Product Value] RIETI Discussion Paper Series 16-J-045. https://www.rieti.go.jp/jp/publications/dp/16j045.pdf.

"Standards" for the quality of products, services, etc., was introduced in many countries for various legitimate purposes, including consumer, environmental, and health protection and quality requirements. However, the standards administration is a type of industrial policy that also affects international competitiveness as these domestic measures sometimes become trade restrictions for other countries. The international community, including the West, is ahead of Japan in this area, and governments and companies in each country are developing strategies for these matters.

As mentioned in Chapters 2 to 4, MITI, which had been retreating from the interventionist industrial policy, proceeded on a trial-and-error basis with policies that indirectly encouraged the development of enterprise strategies that utilized international standards.

2.3 *Various Macroeconomic Policies*

While Chapters 2 to 5 are mainly concerned with aspects of industrial policies, Chapters 6 to 8 focus on various aspects of the macroeconomic policy domain.

Chapter 6 (Changes in the Global Financial Environment Surrounding Japan in the 21st Century: Foreign Exchange Policy and International Financial Coordination) by Kiyoto Ido[5] provides an overview of the structural changes in the environment of international finance that have occurred in the two decades since 1990. The appreciation of the yen due to the Plaza Accord and the bubble triggered by the countermeasures against it, the financial liberalization and crisis that followed the collapse of the bubble, and the Asian currency crisis were all milestones that became major turning points in Japan's economic and financial system.

During this period, Japanese companies also made direct investments in Asian countries and established a division of labor in production, making these countries important partners in the international financial system. The Asian currency crisis catalyzed the development of financial cooperation in East Asia. The author, who was involved in policy formation as a bureaucrat in the MOF at the time, looks back on history and discusses how Japan's initiatives and responsibilities in Asia and the world have increased.

At present a wide range of themes, including the sustainable growth of the global economy and structural changes such as the aging of societies, are being addressed in international finance. The author notes that Japan plays a significant role in the international community.

[5] The original paper is as follows but is revised as necessary for this book. Kiyoto Ido (2019) '21Seiki Nihon wo meguru Kokusai Kinyū Kankyō no Henka: Kawase Seisaku to Kokusai Kinyū Kyochō' [Changes in the International Financial Environment Surrounding Japan in the 21st Century: Exchange Rate Policy and International Financial Cooperation] RIETI Discussion Paper Series 19-J-056. https://www.rieti.go.jp/jp/publications/dp/19j056.pdf.

Chapter 7 (Monetary Policy in Japan: A Review of the Heisei Period) by Wataru Takahashi[6] discusses Japan's monetary policy during the Heisei Period (1989–2019), which corresponds to approximately 30 years of the boost and bursting of the bubble economy and the subsequent deflationary period.

Regarding the monetary policy during the bubble period, this chapter introduces the hypothesis that expansionary monetary and fiscal policies were due to policy coordination after the Plaza Accord, as well as the hypothesis that the flow of funds from abroad affected the financial system.

The author points out that the policy of the Bank of Japan's (BOJ) might have focused on maximizing window guidance; however more fundamentally, the problem is that the BOJ failed to take measures from a medium- to long-term perspective. According to Chapter 7, the inadequacy of short-term monetary and fiscal policy responses to medium- and long-term structural changes in the economy is an important lesson that applies to subsequent policy responses during the deflationary period.

The monetary policy in the period of deflation is characterized as an expansion of "unconventional monetary policies," which is defined in this chapter as an expansion of the loosening of "monetary policy discipline." The author provides a brief summary of each non-traditional monetary policy, including forward guidance, inflation targeting, and quantitative and qualitative easing (QQE) policies. The relationship of these policies with inflation targets and to the fiscal policies is also discussed.

Since 1998, fiscal discipline has loosened with the suspension of the fiscal balance bill. This extraordinary monetary and fiscal easing continued for more than 10 years, but failed to achieve the inflation target and revitalize the Japanese economy. The author believes that to increase the effectiveness of the monetary policy and promote fiscal rehabilitation, the government and BOJ should conduct medium- to long-term policymaking aimed at increasing potential growth through higher productivity. The author also notes that BOJ's independence should be guaranteed and that it is expected to check the government's economic policies from non-political and long-term perspectives.

Chapter 8 (Policy Discussions on Output Gaps in Japan during the 1990s) by Takeshi Tashiro[7] discusses the issues surrounding the output gap based on his extensive research, policy analysis, and international experience. Tashiro, has authored numerous books and articles including Tashiro (2017), and is recognized as an expert in growth strategies and fiscal and financial problems.

This chapter examines the policy debates on the output gap (GDP gap) that emerged from the late 1990s to the 2000s, with a particular focus on the 1990s. As the output gap refers to the divergence between the economy's supply capacity (potential GDP) and aggregate demand, serving as a basic indicator for assessing

---

[6] The original paper is as follows but is revised as necessary for this book. Wataru Takahashi (2019) 'Nihon no Kinyū Seisaku: Heisei-jidai no Kaiko' RIETI Discussion Paper Series 19-J-055. https://www.rieti.go.jp/jp/publications/dp/19j055.pdf.

[7] The chapter is contributed to this book in its first published form.

price pressures and guiding the formation of economic policies. The estimations of the potential GDP and output gap are conducted by the Cabinet Office and BOJ, and their measurements are complex and challenging. While examining the controversies and debates surrounding this issue, the author emphasizes the need for cautious consideration when using the output gap in real-time policy making.

Moreover, the author states these controversies not only as statistical technicalities but also as crucial in identifying the root causes of the prolonged recession. This issue is now emerging in other countries, particularly in Europe and the United States. Given the common challenges faced by advanced economies, the author believes that lessons learned from Japan's economic policy debates hold significant value and warrant careful attention.

Chapter 9 (Redefining the Path to Economic Recovery and Prosperity: Keidanren, the Consumption Tax, and the Lost Decade of the 1990s in Japan) by W. Miles Fletcher III[8] is also a special contribution paper. The author has read and meticulously analyzed reports from Japanese economic organizations, newspapers, magazines, and other texts, and has successfully captured the historical turning point of the Japanese economy from a foreigner's perspective.

While economic policy by politicians and bureaucrats is one of the driving forces of the Japanese economy and is the focus of this book, another important entity behind it is intermediary groups such as Keidanren (Japan Federation of Economic Organizations). Keidanren, established in 1946 after World War II, was established to promote industrial policies for major industries such as the steel industry, as well as infrastructure policies such as the promotion of nuclear power projects, structural recession countermeasures such as industrial adjustment policies, and overall economic policies including recession countermeasures and fiscal policies, by maintaining close communication with the government and bureaucracy to ensure that the intentions of the business community. In this respect, it has assumed a significant role as a private-sector organization engaged in economic policies. In 2002, Keidanren and Nikkeiren merged to form the Japan Business Federation as a new comprehensive economic organization.

Chapter 9 analyzes the process of Keidanren's shift in attitude and policy and its role in the policy-making process, focusing on the issues of policy debate in Japan: the introduction of the consumption tax in the tax reform of the late 1980s and the consumption tax rate hike in the lost decade(s) of the 1990s and beyond.

The author suggests that the Keidanren's main motivation was to achieve its long-term goal of securing financial resources for an aging society, but this might have impeded its short-term goal of economic recovery and contributed to the prolonged deflationary recession.

---

[8] The original paper is as follows but is revised as necessary for this book. W. Miles FLETCHER III and TAKEDA Haruhito (2016) 'Keidanren, Consumption Tax, and the Lost Decade of the 1990s in Japan' RIETI Discussion Paper Series 16-E-043.
https://www.rieti.go.jp/jp/publications/dp/16e043.pdf.

3 Toward Better Policy Formation

Economists and researchers have contemporaneously engaged in various studies and debates about Japan's prolonged stagnation, known as the "lost decade(s)." In recent years, the post-1990s economy has also begun to be analyzed and evaluated not only from the perspective of the current situation in the same period but also from a historical, retrospective, or long-term perspective. Some English references have been made available.[9]

However, historical studies remain limited despite the period referred to as the lost decade(s) being marked by various policy discussions. A unique feature of this book is that it includes contributions from those who are or were in a position close to policy makers. By rethinking this era, many Japanese researchers and policy makers will be motivated to move toward a new era.

Many of the chapters in the book are based on primary sources not found elsewhere, including interviews with policymakers and a collection of policy documents, in addition to the authors' own analyses, views, and findings. They attempt to describe policymakers' struggles to exit the long-term recession after the collapse of the bubble economy, seeking to return to the trajectory of economic growth.

The issues presented in this book also contribute to the international understanding of policy efforts in Japan, which faces a frontier of high uncertainty. Japan's current and future experiences and challenges would be similar to those of developed countries.

Major Events Chronologies Associated with This Book: The 1980s–2010s

1980	
Spring	The economic friction between Japan and the Unites States became more serious. Negotiations continued, with the Unites States demanding that Japan implements voluntary export restraints (VER) and opens its domestic market
August	U.S. President Carter announced the "Economic Recovery Plan"
September	Outbreak of Iran-Iraq War
November	In the U.S. presidential election, Republican candidate Reagan defeated the incumbent President Carter. Inaugurated in January 1981
1981	
February	U.S. President Reagan announced the "Economic Recovery Plan"
May	The ASEAN-Japan Centre was established as an international organ zation based on an agreement between the governments of ASEAN member countries and Japan

(continued)

[9] See for example, Kitaoka (supervisor) and Komine (ed.) (2023).

(continued)

July	Establishment of Japan-ASEAN Investment Co., Ltd. (JAIC); the Private-sector-led economic cooperation plan launched
October	Economic friction with European countries:The economic delegation to Europe strongly requested the correction of trade friction and VER on the Japanese side
1982	
October	The unemployment rate in the United States exceeded 10%. The U.S. "twin deficits" worsening
November	Establishment of Nakasone Cabinet
1983	
February	The Japanese government decided on the outline of the Act on Teporary Measures for the Improvement of Specific Industrial Structures for Measures against Structurally Depressed Industries
October	The Japanese government implemented comprehensive economic measures aimed at reducing current account surpluses and increasing domestic demand
1984	
April	The Ministry of Finance released its outlook on financial liberalization
1985	
July	Establishment of Act on Securing the Proper Operation of Worker Dispatching Businesses and Protecting Dispatched Workers
September	Plaza Accord: The G5 agreed to strengthen intervention in the foreign exchange market to correct dollar appreciation
1986	
April	The "Study Group on Economic Structural Adjustment for International Cooperation" released a report (commonly known as the "Maekawa Report"). The Japanese government decided on comprehensive economic measures to expand domestic demand
October	"Recession caused by the strong yen": At that time, the rapid appreciation of the yen intensified the sense of recession
1987	
April	Japanese GNP per capita exceeds that of the United States
*This year, Japan's trade balance with the United States was a surplus of $56.8 billion (the United States had a trade deficit of $170 billion), and Japan-U.S. economic friction became serious	
1988	
December	Establishment of Consumption Tax Act of 1988
1989	
May	Japan - U.S. economic friction: The U.S. decided to identify Japan as an "unfair trade country" under Super 301
June	The OECD Ministerial Council adopted a joint statement indirectly criticizing Super 301
September	First Initial Meeting of the Japan-U.S. Structural Impediments Initiative to discuss improving "structural factors contributing to trade imbalances."

(continued)

(continued)

1990	
April	The U.S. President announced that Japan would be excluded from the Super 301 list of countries
June	The Japan-U.S. Structural Impediments Initiative were settled. Incorporating the arguments of the U.S. side, measures such as the implementation of public investment totaling 430 trillion yen over a 10-year plan starting in FY1991, shortening the patent examination period, revision of the Large-Scale Retail Store Law and the Antimonopoly Law were planned. The United States promised to make efforts to eliminate budget deficits
October	Share prices on the Tokyo Stock Exchange fell sharply. The collapse of the bubble economy to Collapse was imminent
1991	
January	Outbreak of the Gulf War
*Land prices began to fall this year, leading to the collapse of the bubble economy. A series of scandals in the financial and securities world have begun to expose the hidden realities	
1993	
February	U.S. President Clinton announced the "Economic RevitalizationPlan" with two generation goals of reducing the budget deficit and strengthening the competitiveness of U.S. industries.He also stated that the U.S. government would continue to pressure Japan on the "Japan problem."
1994	
March	U.S. President Clinton signed an executive order reinstating Super 301
1995	
January	The Great Hanshin-Awaji Earthquake occurred. More than 5,500 people died and more than 300,000 were evacuated
November	The Economic Council reported on the "Economic and Social Planfor Structural Reform," which aims to achieve 3.5% growth by promoting deregulation and other structural reforms
December	The OECD released a review report on the Japanese economy analyzing the fragility of the financial system (Japan Premium)
1996	
October	The Economic Structure Council recommends structural reforms in three areas: finance, employment information and communications
November	Japan's prime minister announced the "Japanese Big Bang."
December	Japan-US insurance talks were settled. It was agreed that non life insurance premium rates would be fully liberalized, and that the interests of foreign companies would be taken into consideration when entering fields such as personal accident and cancer insurance
1997	
January	A series of major corporate bankruptcies occurred
*Consumption tax was increased to 5%. Combined with the elimination of special tax reductions, the economy fell into a recession	
June	Amendments to the Bank of Japan Law promulgated (Enacted in April 1998)

(continued)

(continued)

1998	
June	The Financial System Reform Law, which provided the institutional basis for the Financial Big Bang, was passed
1999	
January	Eleven EU countries initiated a currency union which introduced a single currency, the euro
July	The Laws related to the reorganization of central ministries and agencies were enacted. It was reorganized into the Cabinet Office and 12 ministries in January 2001
August	The Industrial Revitalization Law was passed
September	The APEC Leaders' Meeting issued a statement welcoming the emergence from the Asian economic crisis and supporting the new round of the WTO
*This year was also known as the "first year of restructuring," as companies began to fully eliminate the three excesses of employment, equipment and debt in order to escape the worst postwar recession	
*Due to the recession and restructuring, the number of suicides among middle-aged and older adults increased, reaching a record high of more than 33,000 suicides per year	
2000	
March	The ASEAN Finance Ministers' Meeting confirmed the creation of an "Asian Monetary Fund" to prevent a currency crisis
April	The IT (dot-com) bubble burst, and stock prices on the Tokyo Stock Exchange plummeted
May	ASEAN + 3 Finance Ministers agreed to expand swap agreements to prevent a recurrence of the Asian currency crisis. (Chiang Mai Initiative, Thailand)
2001	
January	The Council on Economic and Fiscal Policy was established in the Cabinet Office to manage the economy and finances under the leadership of the Prime Minister's Office
March	The Bank of Japan initiated quantitative easing policy (until March 2006)
May	At the ASEAN + 3 Finance Ministers' Meeting, Japan agreed with South Korea, Malaysia, and Thailand on a bilateral swap agreement under the Chiang Mai Initiative
June	The Council on Economic and Fiscal Policy decided on the "Basic Policies for Economic and Fiscal Management" to guide structural reform
September	The September 11 attacks occurred in the United States
November	The WTO approved China's accession to the WTO
2002	
Spring	The total amount of nonperforming loans outstanding at the 13 major banks reached a record high of 26.7814 trillion yen (for the fiscal year ended March 2002)
May	*Keidanren* merged with *Nikkeiren* (the Japan Federation of Employers' Association) to form *Nippon Keidanren* (Japan Business Federation)

(continued)

(continued)

December	At the ASEAN + 3 Finance Ministers' Meeting, Japan proposed the establishment of the Asian Bond Market Development Initiative (ABF)
2003	
March	The United States and the United Kingdom launched Iraq War
June	The Chiang Mai Declaration, which called for promoting the Asian Cooperation Dialogue and creating an Asian bond market, was adopted.
September	The IMF issued a joint statement urging Japan to overcome deflation
2004	
May	The ASEAN + 3 Finance Ministers' Meeting agreed to promote intra-Asian financial cooperation
November	The ASEAN + 3 Summit adopted an action plan to create the ASEAN Community
2006	
March	The Bank of Japan lifted its quantitative easing policy
2008	
April	The Bank of Japan Deputy Governor Shirakawa was promoted to Governor
September	Lehman Brothers, an American securities firm, went bankrupt (the beginning of the Lehman Shock)
November	The first G20 summit confirmed that countries will respond to the financial crisis in a coordinated manner
December	ASEAN-Japan Comprehensive Economic Partnership Agreement comes into effect
	The zero-interest rate and quantitative easing policies were introduced in the U.S. for the first time in history
2009	
January	The Obama administration was inaugurated in the United States
July	Unemployment rate was 5.7%, the worst since the survey began in 1953
2010	
*China's GDP overtook that of Japan to become the world's second largest	
*The European debt crisis expanded	
2011	
March	The Great East Japan Earthquake occurred. The accident at the Fukushima Daiichi Nuclear Power Station of Tokyo Electric Power Company Holdings (TEPCO) became increasingly serious
November	The launch of Regional Comprehensive Economic Partnership (RCEP) negotiations was declared by ASEAN and Free Trade Agreement (FTA) partner countries
December	The second Shinzo Abe cabinet was inaugurated. To break out of the deflationary economy, Abenomics combined the "three arrows" of bold monetary easing, flexible fiscal policy, and a growth strategy to stimulate private investment

(continued)

(continued)

2013	
January	The government and the Bank of Japan issued a joint statement stating that they would work together on policy coordination to end deflation and achieve sustainable economic development
March	Mr. Haruhiko Kuroda, the newly appointed Governor of the Bank of Japan launched a bold monetary easing program, including large-scale purchases of long-term government bonds, with a 2% annual price target
April	The decision was made to introduce quantitative and qualitative monetary easing policies
2014	
April	The consumption tax rate rose from 5 to 8%
2016	
January	The introduction of the quantitative and qualitative monetary easing policy with negative interest rates was decided
June	The United Kingdom decided to leave the European Union (EU) by referendum
2017	
January	The Trump administration was inaugurated in the United States

Source: In addition to the literature listed below, the authors of this chapter drew from various sources, including the websites of the Nihon Keizai Shimbun, the Institute of Developing Economies, and the Japanese Bankers Association. Yabe Y ed.(2016) *Gendai Nihon Keizaishi Nenpyō* [*Chronological Table of Modern Japanese Economic History*]; Iwanami Shoten Henshu-bu [Iwanami Shoten Publishers, Editorial Department] (2001) *Kindai Nihon Sōgō Nenpyō* [*Comprehensive Chronological Table of Modern Japan, 4th edition*].

References

Kitaoka S (supervisor) and Komine T (ed.) (2023). *Examining Heisei Japan, Vol. III: Economy.* Tokyo: Japan Publishing Industry Foundation for Culture (JPIC).

Tashiro T (2017). *Nihon Keizai Saigo no Senryaku: Saimu to Seicho no Girenma wo Koete* [*The Last Strategy for Japan's Economy Beyond the Debt/Growth Dilemma*]. Tokyo: Nihon Keizai Shinbun Shuppannsha.

Rhode P and Toniolo G (ed) (2006), *The Global Economy in the 1990s: A Long-Run Perspective.* Cambridge: Cambridge University Press.

Haruhito Takeda is Professor Emeritus at Faculty of Economics at The University of Tokyo, Di-rector at Mitsui Bunko and former Faculty Fellow at RIETI. He is a authority in the field of economic policy history research, having authored many works and edited many collections of materials on the history of MITI/METI. His research interests include the history of "monopolies," including zaibatsu studies, and the history of the copper industry etc. He received the Japan Academy Prize in 2022 for his research.

Junko Watanabe is Professor of Economic History at Kyoto University and Faculty Fellow at RIETI. She has been in-volved in research on the economic policy history of MITI/METI for many years and has conducted numerous interviews with bureaucrats. She has also conducted research on pre- and postwar Sumitomo Group and history of industry such as textile, coal mining and others.

Industrial Policy at the Turn of the Century

Haruhito Takeda

Abstract The purpose of this chapter is to review the policies of the MITI/METI since the mid-1970s and to evaluate the changes in policy principles that occurred at the turn of the twenty-first century. The key policy change was a shift into the direction of deregulation and structural reform. Although MITI had policy jurisdiction over structural issues such as trade and industry, the environment, energy, and regional disparities since the mid-1970s, it has gradually adopted a restrained attitude toward the scope of its policy involvement. In other words, the policy has been to leave as much as possible to the self-efforts of the private sector or market mechanisms. METI's policy can be positioned as an extension of this policy. In addition, during the recession of the 1990s and thereafter, the structural reforms to restore economic vitality and put the Japanese economy on a growth trajectory emerged as a policy issue. At the same time, Japan had to manage its domestic economy in consideration of foreign economic relations. In these contexts, MITI and its successor METI expanded the scope of their responsibilities and jurisdiction beyond their traditional focus on industry into the macroeconomic realm.

1 Introduction

This chapter focuses on the period leading up to and following the 2001 launch of the Ministry of Economy, Trade and Industry (METI). It provides an historical examination of the key changes in the development of national trade and industrial policy from the mid-1970s on. In the last decades of the twentieth century, METI's precursor, the Ministry of International Trade and Industry (MITI), addressed structural policy issues in such areas as adjustment of the industrial structure, trade, the environment, energy, and regional disparities, while also responding to changes in the international economy. The wide-ranging nature of MITI's activities was the legacy of Japan's earlier industrial policy. With regard to structural issues, MITI began in the latter 1970s to adopt measures for a reduced role for national policy and

H. Takeda (✉)
The University of Tokyo and Mitsui Bunko, Tokyo, Japan

H. Takeda and J. Watanabe (eds.), *Rethinking Japanese economic policy at the turn of the 21st century*, Advances in Japanese Business and Economics 34,
https://doi.org/10.1007/978-981-97-5512-7_2

to foster an outlook favoring private-sector ingenuity and market mechanisms over MITI involvement. "*Keizai Kozou Kaikaku*" (structural economic reform), which complied new policy scheme by METI, meanwhile became a major task of policy as part of the effort to restore economic vitality after the long recession of the 1990s. The Ministry responded aggressively to this problem, viewing the effort to put Japan's economy on the path to renewed growth as its core mission. Thus, two successive stages are evident in the basic "philosophy" of industrial policy between the 1970s and the end of the century. These policy responses, while demonstrating the same flexibility of response that had characterized Japanese industrial policy historically, also called for significant changes to the process of determining which issues would be addressed by policy.

As described above, MITI's approach was to take up the policy issues relevant for a particular moment in time and formulate and promote prescriptions to address them. Because these prescriptions were justified in terms of the challenges facing the Japanese economy at any given time, they were not driven by a consistent set of principles. Rather, characteristic of industrial policy was its flexible response to changing times and its attempts through trial and error to develop prescriptive policies to resolve problems (Hashimoto 2001).

Although MITI's approach was characterized by this flexibility, it does not necessarily follow that its policies were simply ad hoc responses to different circumstances. Each era was characterized by major economic trends, such as declining growth rates or the severity of international economic friction, and the attendant changes in the underlying policy philosophy are clearly discernible in the industrial policies addressing these trends.

Looking back historically, it is evident that even after the controls of the postwar recovery era had been lifted in the 1960s MITI continued to adhere to the 1950s model, developing corrective market policy interventions as needed to promote the modernization and rationalization of the Japanese economy. Industrial policy aimed to rationalize key industries, nurture infant industries, and make adjustments for declining industries, and so on, while trade policy was designed to facilitate the orderly expansion of exports and controls on imports suitable for economic development under foreign currency constraints. The terms used to explain a policy's legitimacy were Japan's "economic backwardness," its "structural vulnerability," or its "ack of international competitiveness."

These policies engendered moves by domestic business for greater independence from the government, as reflected in the Draft Law on Temporary Measures for the Promotion of Specified Industries in 1963, as well as international criticism of the close ties between government and business, encapsulated in the term "Japan Inc." It was against this backdrop that MITI undertook a broad reconsideration of its policy aims and measures and shifted its sights to the establishment of an internationally open economic system. Its means were the liberalization of trade and foreign exchange, which began in the 1960s, and the capital liberalization that followed.

The need for policy change was expressed explicitly in the call for a "shift to a knowledge-intensive industrial structure" in the *1970s Vision for Trade and Industry Policy*, which MITI published in 1971. This position was based on the recognition that as its heavy and chemical industrialization progressed, Japan was becoming a mature industrial society like the other advanced economies and that it therefore needed to seek out new directions for industrial development. The limitations of the traditional policy framework were becoming evident as core industries became fully competitive internationally, and as independent corporate entities no longer needed government support, meaning that policy questions needed to be addressed from a broader perspective than before.

This policy shift also reflected the need to ascertain what policy measures could be used by way of support, given that liberalization was proceeding more smoothly than expected and that certain means of policy intervention were gradually being lost (the biggest among these being foreign currency allocation). In the 1970s, when Japan's status as an "economic power" became fully apparent, it was no longer sufficient in international eyes for Japan to prioritize its domestic interests as if it were still a backward and/or vulnerable "small country". Rather, Japan was called on to take responsibility for its influence on the world economy and to make changes to reflect its changing international status.

However, that same growth gave rise to domestic challenges where economic development intersected with people's lives: environmental conservation issues, urban overcrowding and rural depopulation, consumer issues such as the rise in consumer price problems emerged, among others. The limitations of policies directed at export expansion and at upgrading an industrial structure centered on heavy and large-scale industries became increasingly apparent, generating calls for a more "knowledge-intensive" industrial structure (greater knowledge intensity). At the same time, new and mounting problems in external affairs, including trade friction because of the nation's soaring balance of payments surplus, and charges for the excessive devaluing of the yen, required policy responses.

It was in this context that MITI launched the large-scale organizational reform that marks the starting point of the period under examination in this volume. The basic policy governing the organizational reform—"To achieve a comprehensive internal reorganization of this Ministry by utilizing the particular strengths of the bodies charged with design, planning, and implementation and coordinating policy among them for a well-balanced result"—was summarized by MITI as follows:

1. Unification of the trade policy bureaus. This meant reconfiguring the existing International Trade Bureau and Trade Promotion Bureau as the International Trade Policy Bureau and International Trade Administration Bureau.
2. Conversion of the existing Enterprise Bureau into the newly named Industrial Policy Bureau, in order to strengthen efforts toward cross-sector (horizontal) policy principles.
3. Establishment of the Industrial Location and Environmental Protection Bureau to engage actively in their namesake issues.
4. Reconfiguration of sector-specific organizations (vertical divisions). For this purpose, the various industries were reassigned according to shared organizational principles into the Basic Industries Bureau, the Machinery and Information Industries Bureau, and the Consumer Goods and Services Industries Bureau.

5. Last but not least, the establishment of the Agency of Natural Resources and Energy, charged with promoting a strong and comprehensive energy administration.[1]

These changes reconfigured the trade-related bureaus such that international economic policy planning would be undertaken in one bureau and trade policy—a unified administration of exports and imports, insurance matters, etc.—in another. The Industrial Policy Bureau was charged with the central task of coordinating shared policy areas, while its divisions focused on specific areas: the Price Policy Division concentrated on price problems, the Business Behavior Division "promoted appropriate corporate action", the Industrial Structure Division "advanced the knowledge intensification of the industrial structure", and the International Business Affairs Division "promoted industrial structure policies from an international perspective". With the establishment of the Industrial Location and Environmental Protection Bureau, the Departments related to industrial sites (previously in the Enterprise Bureau) and pollution protection were integrated into a single Bureau. Similarly, the Agency for Natural Resources and Energy was established as an affiliated agency that combined the former Mining and Coal Bureau and Public Utilities Business Bureau. The merger was based on the reasoning that "Comprehensive and powerful resource and energy administration is needed in order to advance policies in such areas as the securing of stable supplies of resources and energy, energy efficiency, the increasingly serious pollution problem, resource conservation, and energy conservation" (CHJTIP/RIETI 2020, pp. 4–5).

2 Toward a Shift in Industrial Policy

2.1 Attempts at Changing the Industrial Structure

In order to trace how policy trends changed based on the awareness described above, let us focus on the major issues as seen in the "New Policy" prepared each year by the Ministry of International Trade and Industry. The document's subtitle, "Industrial Policy Priorities", corresponds to the basic policy stance of the government. In the 1970s, this meant responding to the ruling Liberal Democratic Party's reconsideration of the high growth path and its shift to pledging to build a welfare society. The emphasis in domestic policy became the "improvement and enhancement of national welfare", and in foreign policy, the importance of international cooperation in areas like setting foreign exchange rates.

Under this framework, industrial policy from the mid-1970s on was, from the most basic level, addressing different policy problems than before, namely: (1) how to locate new industries and bring their development to fruition, and (2) how to fulfill

[1] Committee on the History of Japan's Trade and Industry Policy RIETI (CHJTIP/RIETI) 2020, p. 4. Original materials are found in Ministry of International Trade and Industry (1973).

Japan's responsibilities in the international community. The principal areas of focus listed in the "policy menus" published from 1976–1979 were "advancing industrial policy to realize Japan's economic recovery and stable development" (1976) and "new development of industrial policy under stable growth" (1977) (CHJTIP/RIETI 2020, p. 5).

The fact that industrial policy had reached a stage of seeking new directions and that contributing to the world economy had become a major priority, reflecting the international pledge made in 1979 by the Takeo Fukuda cabinet, is an indication that a major shift in policy principles had occurred. However, these new directions were not pursued in a clear and sustained way because of exogenously generated "shocks". As is well known, price and energy problems came to the fore intermittently during these years because of the abrupt transition to a floating exchange rate regime and the turbulent rise in crude oil prices. In the two years immediately after the first oil crisis in 1973, MITI found it necessary to prioritize price stabilization and improvements to consumer life, as evident in the "priority" policies of 1974 and 1975.

With regard to the threat of inflation, MITI's "Aggregate Demand Control Policy" produced results in a relatively short period, even as compared with other advanced economies. Energy conservation efforts began to penetrate, even as the issue rapidly lost its urgency with the relatively quick stabilization of oil prices. Moreover, the medium-range aim of decreasing Japan's dependence on fossil fuels was aided by the mid-1980s takeoff of nuclear power generation at light water reactors. It became the dominant view that this tailwind would help enable Japan to achieve both economic growth and a stable energy supply.

In this way, the Basic Direction of Trade and Industrial Policies as defined in the early 1970s emerged once again as a top priority concern. Construction of a "long-term development base" frequently appears in the New Policy subtitles, as illustrated in the priority policies of 1983–1985: (CHJTIP/RIETI 2020, p. 9).

1983 Promote industrial revitalization and technology development with a mid- and long-term perspective
1984 Form the foundations for creative development
1985 Build the foundations for technological development.

MITI's emphasis on technological development points to an expectation that the new technologies and systems would become the foundations for future industrial development. This was the case in the creation of new energy sources, developed against the backdrop of urgency in energy issues, in information processing and semiconductor technology, in factory automation (FA), the utilization of microelectronics technology (ME), and related to these, the area of space development. Fields like this require large-scale investment in research and development, making it hard to rely on voluntary action by private enterprises to assure sufficient investment. In other words, MITI sought policy involvement primarily in areas that could not be left entirely to market forces and began especially to take note of these as priority issues.

Nevertheless, with regard to pollution/environmental measures, which became policy priorities in this period, strict corporate emissions regulations were maintained based on environmental regulations. It is important to note that the stance of entrusting this oversight to the voluntary action of businesses and expecting that markets would adjust accordingly was not equivalent to the pursuit of a hands-off policy. Of course, MITI's position on this matter served as a counterweight to the strong regulatory bent of the Environment Agency by aiming toward preventing an excessive burden being placed on industrial enterprises. In the division of labor among ministries and agencies, MITI's position was in general to restrain interventions in the market. On the other hand, when it came to policy on industrial location, it was possible to help ease the concentration of industrial sites in the Pacific belt of Japan, the urbanized corridor on the Pacific coast, through financial and tax incentives. Pursuing the dispersion of the industrial sites into surrounding areas achieved some results (although no greater a range of diffusion than was originally sought), and MITI therefore did not hesitate to adopt policy measures to correct external diseconomies. In policy on small and medium-sized enterprises as well, traditional interventionist policy measures continued in much their original form.

Looking in aggregate at the measures that were aimed at new industrial development, on the other hand, it is clear that they could not be detached from policy authority over the information and communications industries at the core of that development. This situation continued to act as a constraint on the effort to develop an integrated industrial policy. Although the means of communication and information acquisition were expanded and diversified far beyond expectation in the data communications field (in areas such as VAN, or value-added networks), MITI's involvement in this field, beginning with the liberalization of the principal communication networks, was restricted by its need to share that role with other agencies granted jurisdiction by the government.

It would not be correct, however, to see MITI's inability to fulfill its own claims as only the result of disputes over authority. Information and communications technology made more progress in software than in hardware (such as technology development in the form of large-scale computers) that MITI had emphasized up to that point. As these technological advanments blended into the overall communications methods at production sites, a highly dispersed, guerilla-style development, accumulation, and transmission took on great significance. MITI was not necessarily able to find policy issues and take appropriate measures to respond flexibly to change in the information and communications sector, because it had little experience with policy intervention regarding consumer goods. Regardless, the continued restriction of the ministry's involvement in the information and telecommunications field made it hard for MITI to develop ideas about Japan's future industrial structure and to establish adjustment policies to address them. It should be noted that those restrictions were not removed even in the organizational reform of 2000.

2.2 *Emphasis on Free Trade and the Relaxation of Regulations*

The development of industrial technology was prioritized over international contributions in the early 1980s because Japan's trade surplus contracted temporarily with the soaring resource prices, especially that of crude oil. As a consequence, the subsequent recovery of Japan's trade surplus, which followed on the decline in crude oil prices, aroused criticism from the United States and Europe and resulted in serious trade friction. For this reason, MITI's emphasis also shifted to trade policy in the latter 1980s. This change is evident in the growing stress placed on what the MITI called "international harmonization" and Japan's contribution to the international economy as seen, for example, in the titles of the following reports: "Aiming for new dimensions of internationalization (1986)", "Promoting policies on industrial structure based on an international perspective (1987)", "Dedication to the international economic community (1989)", and "Correcting external imbalances and realizing an internationally harmonized economic structure and industrial activities (1990)" (CHJTIP/RIETI 2020, pp. 10–11).

Where these policies concerned international relations, the following points are notable. First, the demand from the U.S. and the EU that policies be considered for diplomatic reasons—namely to improve Japan-US relations—placed strong constraints on the policy options. Second, the policies were similar to the temporary export restraints previously promoted in the 1970s and 1980s, for the sake of implementing a strategy of "orderly exports". As a result, bilateral and bi-regional negotiations under these conditions were repeated endlessly, with only the trade items in question changing, and Japan was forced to make unilateral concessions.

Nevertheless, MITI continued to promote the development of the Japanese economy, while at the same time reaching a clear understanding of the new direction Japan would have to pursue in order to fulfill its international responsibilities. That is, rather than promoting measures that limited free trade, such as voluntary export restraints based on bilateral agreements, Japan would adopt policy solutions based on international rules agreed upon multilaterally. This was the shift in principle that MITI had been seeking since the 1970s.

In the negotiations that led to the WTO (World Trade Organization) agreement in 1995, Japan's response to international trade friction was to advocate "maintaining the free trade regime" and to limit the scope of issues handled either by single governments or by bilateral agreements between governments. In other words, Japan achieved better results in its negotiations with the outside world when it sought to avoid quantitative targets in trade and demands for preferential treatment by certain trading partners. Examples include the 1990s negotiations on steel, autos, and other sectors, which resulted in the elimination of the voluntary export restraints that had originally been established at the request of the US in the 1980s.

This approach in turn exposed the need to overhaul the myriad regulations that shaped industry and the relationships among industries domestically. Deregulation arose as a result not of foreign pressure but of internal pressures. To avoid raising corporate taxes, while at the same time overcoming the burden of government debt due to Japan's post-oil crisis macroeconomic recovery measures, the Second Extraordinary Administrative Research Council called for "small government," or administrative reform, in the early 1980s.[2]

MITI, ahead of other ministries and agencies, forcefully promoted deregulation as a measure for easing trade friction. In fact, combining promotion of import expansion with attention to the impact of imports on domestic industries represented a unique approach in international terms as well. It is not clear that it contributed to an actual expansion of imports; its significance was often only symbolic, but deregulation conveyed a clear message to the outside world that that the government was doing its best within the limits of its jurisdiction. At the same time, given the marked confrontation that had always characterized the relationship between industrial policy and the Antimonopoly Law of 1947. this new emphasis on deregulation raised the question of how government could engage in the competitive order shaped by the Antimonopoly Law. Previously, the Fair Trade Commission tried to enforce the Antimonopoly Law as strictly as possible to prevent cartels and foster competition among companies, whereas MITI often sought exemptions from the law to support cartels temporarily and help firms weather severe downturns.

It is apparent from the key industrial policy measures of this era that a major shift took place. The 1978 Law on Temporary Measures for Stabilization of Specified Depressed Industries and Industry Stabilization Law, the 1983 Temporary Measures Law for the Structural Adjustment of Specific Industries and Structural Improvement Law, the 1987 Law on Temporary Measures to Facilitate Industrial Structural Adjustment, the 1995 Law on Temporary Measures to Facilitate New Businesses, and the 1999 Law on Special Measures for Industrial Revitalization and Industrial Revitalization Law all suggest that the thrust of industrial policy was no longer one of seeking exemptions or "exclusions" from the Antimonopoly Law. Thus, the MITI's interventionist stance on industrial policy receded, and the long-standing conflict between MITI and the Japan Fair Trade Commission over cartel control was resolved.

This approach did not change significantly even after the collapse of the asset price bubble in the early 1990s. The subtitles of the Priority Measures cited above were frequently omitted or the wording changed due to policy fluctuations in the short-lived cabinets of the first half of the 1990s, but as discussed below, there was no perceived need for a major change in the framework of priorities established in the 1980s: (1) to achieve balanced trade through multilateral coordination, (2) to promote regulatory reforms limiting government involvement, and (3) to achieve both a stable supply of energy and economic growth.

---

[2] Regarding "domestic pressure," see Fletcher and Takeda (2016).

2.3 *Seeking Another Conceptual Shift at the End of the Century*

As the recession that began in 1990 dragged on, however, officials enacted regulatory reforms to reform the economic structure. They also envisioned deregulation as a comprehensive resolution to multiple policy issues, including the handling of non-performing loans, fiscal reconstruction, and economic recovery. These efforts indicate that industrial policy was once again seeking a new foundation. Because this process is still ongoing, caution is needed in making any definite assessments, but I will make a preliminary attempt to examine the "prospects for a shift and the direction it might take" (CHJTIP/RIETI, p. 13).

The principal measures of the latter half of the 1990s are given below. One of the keywords in the titles was the above-mentioned "economic structural reform," but the explicit macroeconomic goals were economic recovery and a return to the path of economic growth, as expressed in the priorities of "Acceleration of structural economic reform", "Strong promotion of structural economic reform" and "Pulling out of sluggish macro economy" which MITI listed in 1996, 1998, and 1999, respectively.

To further structural reform of the economy, MITI has shifted to a principle of promoting competition and undertaking comprehensive regulatory reform by, for example, attempting bold changes in its policies on small and medium enterprises to make firms take more responsibility for themselves. Trade policy has also changed somewhat due to Japan's long-term recession by adopting bilateral negotiations with the advancing industrialization of South Korea, China, and others, but overall, MITI has adhered to its emphasis on multilateral coordination.

However, faced with the need to focus on macro growth, MITI's stance on policy took on a new dimension. Although industrial policy prior to the early 1990s indeed led ultimately to economic growth, that does not mean that the aim of the policies was economic growth itself. Rather, the ministry was concerned with issues such as income distribution and with the distortions to the economic structure that were caused by the market economy. For example, MITI sought the modernization and rationalization of the small and medium-sized enterprises (SME) that were hindering economic development in the first half of the high-growth period in the 1950s and 1960s, because MITI concluded that policy intervention was the only way to resolve the problems posed by the dual economy. MITI's decision to address such issues as nurturing new industries or the friction arising with declining industries was also due to its judgment that its active intervention was needed in order to realize economic development in the medium term. In the latter half of the 1990s, however, when the long recession came to be viewed as a consequence of structural problems in the Japanese economy, MITI came to view not only structural reform but also economic growth itself as a policy concern. MITI has come to focus on eliminating factors that impede growth, rather than on structural problems that impede economic development.

3 Establishment of the Ministry of Economy, Trade and Industry (METI) and Prospects for Economic and Industrial Policy in the Twenty-First Century

3.1 Deliberations of the Administrative Reform Council

The government's administrative reorganization of 2001 clarified these changes in policy trends. In January of the same year, MITI was reorganized to become the Ministry of Economy, Trade and Industry. This was part of a central government reorganization that was the culmination of the administrative reforms that had begun in the early 1980s in the form of deregulation and was based on the 1997 "Final Report" of the Administrative Reform Council (CHJTIP/RIETI 2020, p. 309).[3]

Therefore, before discussing the content of the final report, it will be helpful to review the Administrative Reform Council's deliberations on trade and industrial policy.[4] The Administrative Reform Council, charged with "investigating and deliberating basic and comprehensive matters concerning the reorganization and integration of administrative organizations in the country necessary for flexibly and accurately dealing with complex administrative issues", discussed the underlying principles of reform and also sent questions to each ministry and agency and deliberated on the explanations received in response.

MITI submitted its "priority issues" to the Council on April 11, 1997, as summarized below.

MITI Priority Issues

1. To revitalize existing industries and create high value-added and new industries: an accurate grasp of the policy needs of each industrial sector and creation of a conducive environment through the strong promotion of deregulation, advanced information technology, and technological and human-resource development; improvement of intellectual infrastructure and effective and efficient development of social capital.
2. To facilitate an internationally appealing business environment: reform of institutions and practices such as the high-cost structure; of corporate systems through corporate organization; and of the labor and employment systems.
3. In a context of mounting constraints on the Japanese economy, such as a tightening energy supply and mounting global environmental problems: contributing to international efforts to resolve these issues; developing energy policies that simultaneously achieve stable supplies, are harmonized with the

[3] This description of the Administrative Reform Council's deliberations is based on the conference proceedings of and materials submitted to the "Administrative Reform Council", *Kantei* [Prime Minister's Official Residence]. website: http://www.kantei.go.jp/jp/gyokaku/#gaiyou.

[4] This description of the Administrative Reform Council's deliberations is based on the conference proceedings and materials submitted to the "Administrative Reform Council", *Kantei*. website: http://www.kantei.go.jp/jp/gyokaku/#gaiyou.

environment, and that improve efficiency; and overcoming these constraints by changing the approach of business itself to reduce environmental impact, including incorporating environmental considerations into all phases of business activity from the procurement of raw materials to manufacturing, use, and disposal.

4. To realize the full potential of Japanese industry: the development of a strategic trade policy to establish international rules, resolve international trade friction, form a favorable business environment abroad, etc., in bilateral and multilateral settings
5. To maintain and expand economic vitality, establish the appropriate direction for levels and types of public responsibility, and avoid economic confusion (recession, inflation, etc.) due to changes in external circumstances: flexible planning for economic measures based on real conditions in production, capital investment, inventory, etc.

Although these represented policy changes that were already underway as part of the effort to spur economic recovery, the Administrative Reform Council asked the following of MITI regarding these priorities:

1. Present the anticipated reform measures in light of the aims of the administrative reform.
2. What are your views on future approaches to industrial policy administration? What is your view on the need for vertically divided bureaus by industry and industry-specific administration?
3. What is your view on the relationship between MITI and the Foreign Ministry and other government agencies and on the organization of responsibilities with regard to trade policy and negotiations?
4. What is your view on unifying the organizations related to international economic cooperation?
5. What are your views on the future relationship between the administration of nuclear power and of energy, and between administration of science and technology and technological development by the Industrial Technology Institute, and how should they be organized?
6. How do you think research facilities should be organized, including the possibility of consolidating them with other research organs?
7. How should administrative organizations be organized to address the promotion of advanced information technology?
8. What are your views on making the Patent Office independent, on the privatization or independence of trade insurance, industrial standards, safety oversight of the mining, electricity and gas industries, and abolition of the alcohol monopoly system? (Item numbers are author's).

Questions 3 through eight address the reduction and simplification of administrative organization and confirmation of the relationships with other ministries. The answers were presented to the Administrative Reform Council on June 4 by MITI Director General Katsusada Hirose, Industrial Policy Bureau Director Osamu

Watanabe, Deputy Director General Yasuo Imai, and others. The written explanation submitted in response to Question 3 regarding "trade policy and negotiation" presented six points, including (1) guiding the formation of international rules and the harmonization of the international economic system in directions advantageous to the Japanese economy, (2) seeking appropriate solutions to trade friction based on real conditions in domestic industry, (3) asking other countries to rectify unreasonable institutions and practices on trade and investment. It also pointed out that "in order to develop effective trade policy and carry out trade negotiations, it was necessary to grasp the realities of domestic and overseas industries and to integrate these efforts with the coordination function in the domestic market".

The response to Question 4 on "unifying the organizations related to economic cooperation" addressed the same point of view and pointed out that there was a greater need for coordination than formerly thought between administration of science and technology and the Industrial Technology Institute for policy planning, implementation, and evaluation from the points of view of (1) cooperation with the private sector, (2) using methods related to industrial structural reform, (3) cooperation with trade policy, and (4) consideration of diverse approaches to economic cooperation. Regarding Question 5 on the relationship between administration of nuclear power and of energy, and Institute's administration of technological development, MITI's representatives explained that each MITI jurisdiction had its own value.

The answer to Question 6 differed from these in nuance: organizational reform of research facilities was already underway in this case, and the answer expressed a willingness to proceed with the reform including integrating research institutions as necessary. At the meeting itself, however, during the question and answer session, MITI's representatives expressed caution regarding integrated facilities "because at this time policy-aim-specific technological developments are already in process". The answers also stated the need for Japan to undertake basic research. These answers should not be taken to mean, however, that MITI expressed strong opposition to the simplification of administrative organization, and although there were other circumstances surrounding the later organizational reform, it appears likely that the groundwork for the abolition of the Industrial Technology Institute had already been laid. In that sense, MITI's stance was changing with regard to technology promotion policy, which had been regarded as a pillar of the "knowledge-intensive" industrial structure ever since MITI's formulation of its *1970s Vision*.[5]

The answers to Question 8 on making the Patent Office and other organs independent went no farther than acknowledging the importance of making this a basic aim and the need to respond to the issues that would arise in the process.

The answers to Question 7 on jurisdiction over advanced information technology, made clear that "responses to advanced information technology, technology development and infrastructure improvements continue to be necessary, but not only that, it is an urgent task to make full use of information and communications technology in every sector and thereby to overhaul society and the economy". The answers also stated that "in order to accelerate and improve on the use of advanced information

[5] For the background to the low priority of technology policy, see Sawai (2011).

technology going forward, MITI must promote information technology in a wide variety of fields, and while responding appropriately both to industry-specific issues and to issues shared by many sectors, and with those issues in mind, we must also enable the harmonious collaboration between users and information-related industries such as suppliers." Furthermore, MITI stressed that, since shifting to "advanced information" or "upgrading of information and communications" as an "approach of the government as a whole" would have a great impact, penetrating every aspect of citizens' lives and industrial activity, "the administrative agencies that have knowledge and responsibility in their administrative fields should also make it their task to advance the 'information' capability of their own sectors".

This could be read as an expression of MITI pride in its knowledge and burden of responsibility, but it can also be interpreted as MITI's effort to claim its turf leading to the eventual consolidation of the administration of information and communications. This attitude mirrors the other cases described above. Its pride in its "knowledge and responsibilities" notwithstanding, there was the sense that it would be hard for MITI to aggressively take on policy-making in this sector on its own: this was evident when, in response to a question suggesting that its policy had been inadequate in addressing the development of an information society, MITI was forced to acknowledge that "It was true that it had been slow to respond to this need".[6]

On issues directly involving organization, MITI essentially laid claim to its own turf,[7] but, obvious as that might seem, it also appears that MITI carefully refrained from saying anything that would throw a damper on reform. This attitude is evident, too, in MITI's response to Question 1 on the plans for "self-reform": MITI explained the results of its program of deregulation thus far and its plans going forward as well as its review of its organizational and personnel systems, giving the impression that it was already well along the path to meeting the Administrative Reform Council's aims.

There is not much record of the discussion on what kinds of policy would be part of MITI's post-reorganization mission. Regarding Question 2 about industrial administration in the future, the explanatory document of the ARC set out "the problems facing the Japanese economy heading into the twenty-first century" as follows: "in the international environment, economic globalization, the advent of an era of great competition, the emergence of Asia, and global issues of environment and energy, and in the domestic environment, the maturation of the economy, the

[6] At the 27th meeting of the Administrative Reform Council (August 21), committee members deliberating the "reorganization of the central ministries" "expressed the opinion that it should be made explicit that the Ministry of Industry's jurisdiction over information and communications was limited to the promotion of the industry itself". It is not clear what impact this statement had on the final opinion of the Council, but it may convey something of this atmosphere.

[7] Regarding organizational reform, committee members on June 4 asked about the possibility of consolidating environmental administration, and the response was: "We are being asked to take comprehensive responsibility in the future for environmental problems in everything from raw material procurement to manufacturing, sales and processing, so it is believed necessary to implement it as part of industrial administration." "As part of industrial administration" can be understood as implying opposition to consolidation and as indicating the idea that the existing division of responsibilities with the Environment Ministry would be maintained.

hollowing out of industry, falling birthrates and an aging society, deterioration of financial conditions, and others." Its most notable point was its statement about its standards for policy development, namely that: "While the globalization of the world economy will advance still further and that companies will be engaged in fierce international competition, the time is coming when companies will compare the economic systems of various countries and 'select the country' with the optimal environment for their activities" and that therefore, "We are promoting thoroughgoing improvements to our economic system to create an environment that is advantageous for business so that the competition among nations will prove advantageous to Japan."

The "aim of trade in industrial policy" regarding these types of policy issues was "maintenance and expansion of economic vitality" and the main items were those mentioned above under "MITI's priority issues." MITI argued to the Council that in order to pursue these aims, the ministry would need to cooperate and actively build ties not only within the ministry but with related sections of other ministries and agencies as well. It presented the example of the Action Plan for Structural Economic Change and Creation, which involved cooperation with 22 other ministries and agencies on the creation of new industries, improvement of a wide range of systems and practices, reduction of logistics and communications costs, and other areas.

It is likely that MITI's active stance on playing a central role in economic structural reform was also expressed in its proposals for enabling transparency in cross-ministerial discussions.[8] The other noteworthy point in the discussion was the response by members of the ARC to MITI's announcement that it was "working on improving the environment for the maintenance of economic vitality through deregulation and other means": the question was asked whether, given that MITI's jurisdiction included declining industries and low-productivity sectors, it was going too far in saying that the industries it administered were internationally competitive, and also whether MITI was not concerning itself only with its front-runners despite the fact that the nature of Japan's low-productivity sector would in future define the competitiveness of industry as a whole.

MITI responded with an explanation of the measures it had taken for the declining coal industry, while also showing its change in attitude with the remark that "because small retail/commerce, distribution, logistics, and other industries also face difficulties, policy is responsible not only for expanding growth industries but also for handling the discontinuance of declining sectors well." While we can take this answer

[8] A related question was asked as to whether MITI's proposal was aimed at "new legislation like the laws on administration and management", to which MITI replied: "(1) Although it is possible for the Cabinet to make adjustments even now, Article 3 of the Cabinet Law is comprehensive on the principle of shared control and it is undeniable that ministries and agencies are not permitted to speak to [issues under] each other's jurisdictions. (2) The binding is also important in the sense that the scope of coordination will be greater within the Ministry and it will become easier to achieve when we are organized under purpose-specific categories. (3) However, since the boundaries between ministries will not disappear even with the binding approach, it would be better to allow ministries to speak out on each other's policies." In addition, even at the time, the Act for Establishment of the Small and Medium Enterprise Agency made it able to speak to various ministries and agencies, and MITI explained that its proposal was intended to introduce such an approach.

as an explanation that policy responses were needed because of concerns about the social friction and other problems that accompany decline, its reference to SME problems in conjunction with "declining sectors" in need of a skillfully handled "discontinuance" represented a change in policy stance. That is, one of the pillars of the MITI's SME policy, based on theories of the dual economy (the coexistence in Japan of large and very small firms), had been to improve productivity in the SME sector in order to upgrade the economy as a whole The inclusion of these SMEs in the category of "declining sectors" was in effect an announcement that MITI would no longer pursue that approach. It is not clear whether this change in MITI's thinking was born of discussions within the ministry, but it was faithful to the direction called for by the Administration Reform Council. That is, it was the Council's "Criteria for Administrative Involvement" (December 16, 1996) that served as the starting point for the discussion of administrative reform, and Item 6 in this document, "Criteria relating to whether or not to pursue administrative involvement," made the aim of equal opportunity the first priority. This included the aims of reducing, in principle, those measures that had a strong income redistributive effect and of discontinuing income redistribution measures aimed at correcting for regional disparities and also included criteria regarding income redistribution among industries, as seen in the following examples[9]:

1. In principle, measures aimed at redistributing income among industries and for protecting industry will be discontinued.
2. Strong measures to preserve and extend the life span of declining industries will be discontinued. However, in cases of administrative intervention for emergency measures to encourage an industry's contraction so as to enable an effective utilization of resources to address changes in the economic environment, the reason for such involvement must be explained and the period of implementation must be limited and a schedule specified. Further, in such cases, extension of that time period is not permitted.
3. Policies aimed at nurturing specific industries will be discontinued. However, where such policies cannot be discontinued because they are necessary for productivity improvement in promising infant industries, for example, the reason for administrative involvement will be explained and the time period for the involvement will be limited and a schedule specified.

With these criteria as the premise for discussion, any clear statement that implementation of traditional SME and industrial location policy was policy tasks became difficult. Although there remain points that require further study (see Footnote 8), MITI's policies and the newly established METI's policy issues, thus clarified, led the way to the compilation of the Administrative Reform Council's Final Report, which provided the overall framework for the central government reorganization.

[9] Based on Administrative Reform Committee, "Criteria for Administrative Involvement" (December 16, 1996). http://www3.grips.ac.jp/~kanemoto/gyokaku/kijun.html.

3.2 The Administrative Reform Council's "Final Report"

The December 1997 "Final Report" of the Administrative Reform Council explained the "reasons for the need to undertake administrative reform" in terms of the "principles and aims of administrative reform," which it defined as: "to build on Japan's achievements thus far to reconstruct 'how this country does things', with the aim of forming a freer and fairer society". Specifically, it pointed out that the advances made by Japan's economy during rapid growth "had created the precious 'asset'of economic prosperity, but had also left a legacy of enormous debt, symbolized by a cumulative fiscal debt that had swelled to 400 or even 500 trillion yen. That stage is already retreating into the past." This development raised the following issues: "As a result of pursuing an effective but only copied industrial society over many years, Japan had become enveloped in an array of national regulations, conventions, and practices that have rendered society extremely uniform and rigid"; furthermore, "the steady growth of Japan's economy has come to an end, and the people's values have diversified as society has matured; thus, the same systems that in the past stimulated people's will to work hard and invigorated society, are today if anything promoting structures of dependence, reinforcing the sense that Japan is a closed society, and impeding the people's creative will and spirit of challenge." In short, what was being sought was "a revision of the postwar administrative system so as to create autonomous individuals, and a shift to a twenty-first century administrative system appropriate for forming a freer and fairer society." These critiques of existing conditions led to the establishment of the following goals. "In order to rebuild 'the way things are done in this country', what we need first and foremost is to reform government organizations, which have become over-enlarged and inflexible, and to realize a simple, effective, and transparent government suitable for effectively carrying out important national functions."

The Final Report thus called for reflection, in line with these goals, as to "whether the bureaucracy was not intervening excessively in the various aspects of people's lives". "The policies and regulations designed to guard the people's interest have become increasingly self-referential, inviting the result that they increasingly defend only the vested interests of certain people that conflicts and contradictions between different policy objectives are handled internally without transparency, or that resolutions to problems are simply put off". The Report concluded that in order to rectify this situation, the core of administrative reform must now focus on "the rigidity of the policy planning departments that were bound by the interests and constraints of a given project; inefficient implementation that neglected the convenience of the user; the unclear and closed policy-making process and the absence of an evaluative or feedback function; and the failure of the overall adjustment function due to an exclusive and inviolable system of jurisdictions in which ministries and agencies are divided vertically and are not permitted to speak out about areas in other administrative jurisdictions."

The Report recommended that the following mechanisms and characteristics be the goal of reform to build a "21st-century administrative system appropriate for forming a free and fair society". Specific prescriptions included: (1) For comprehensive and strategic policy-making, aim to strengthen drastically the functions of the Prime Minister's Official Residence and the Cabinet to include the planning and proposing of basic policies and to improve the capacity to carry out comprehensive coordination on important policies; (2) to separate the policy-making and implementation functions and to introduce a system of reorganization and mutual recommendations among groups of ministries and agencies divided along functional lines; (3) to ensure the transparency of administration; and (4) to ensure administrative efficiency by promoting a complete reexamination of projects by the joint undertaking of the public and private sectors and by utilizing private-sector capacity by establishing a system of independent administrative agencies.

3.3 METI's "Organization Plan"

A major reform of administrative agencies was thus carried out on January 6, 2001, reorganizing 22 ministries and agencies into 12, along with the establishment of the Cabinet Office and 10 Ministries (Ministry of Internal Affairs and Communications; Ministry of Justice; Ministry of Foreign Affairs; Ministry of Finance; Ministry of Education, Culture, Sports, Science and Technology; Ministry of Health, Labour and Welfare; Ministry of Agriculture, Forestry and Fisheries; Ministry of Economy, Trade and Industry (METI); Ministry of Land, Infrastructure and Transport (MLIT); Ministry of the Environment) along with the reorganization of the Prime Minister's Office and the existing 12. The Financial Reconstruction Commission and seven agencies were eliminated (the Management and Coordination Agency; Hokkaido Development Agency; Economic Planning Agency; Science and Technology Agency; Environment Agency; Okinawa Development Agency; and National Land Agency). Under the 1998 Basic Law on Central Government Reform, the "Organization Plan" (Article 21) of the newly established METI laid out the following aims[10]:

1. To promote economic structural reform
2. To develop industrial policy based on the following:

    a. To stop pursuing measures to promote specific industries or redistribute income among industries, or to reduce such practices and shift to policies that respect market principles.
    b. To focus on interdisciplinary policies such as the formulation and improvement of rules on economic transactions in the market, protection of industrial property rights, and policy-making across industry lines regarding technology development, and to promote the smooth transformation of the industrial structure.

---

[10] From the Basic Act on Central Government Reform (http://www.kantei.go.jp/jp/gyokaku/980303houan.html).

3. To actively contribute to the formation of a new international economic order through regional or multilateral frameworks on industrial and trade policy, and to develop measures for international coordination regarding industry.
4. To focus on reducing administration designed to protect SMEs or SME organizations, strengthening the role of regional bodies, and improving the environment to encourage the creation of new industries.
5. To strengthen the role of the region and to reduce the involvement of the central government in measures to promote regional economies and industries.
6. To develop energy policy based on the following:
   a. a focus on measures for energy conservation and new energy.
   b. the significant elimination or mitigation of regulations for adjusting supply-and-demand among business operators.
   c. the strengthening of crisis management and the links with environmental policy.
   d. determining directions for nuclear development and use to take.
7. To set government policy priorities regarding technological development.
8. With regard to the Economic and Fiscal Policy Advisory Council's deliberations on basic policy governing the operation of the economy as a whole, to participate in the planning necessary for that deliberation from the perspective of planning industrial policy, reform of the economic structure, and maintenance and strengthening of the vitality of the private sector.
9. To assume the functions of the former Ministry of International Trade and Industry [on] in regard to information and communications without any change to the functional division with the Ministry of Posts and Telecommunications.
10. The Fair Trade Commission will continue to be responsible for competition policy centered on antitrust policy, not to be taken over by the Ministry of Economy, Trade and Industry.
11. Regarding technological development through the Large-scale Project Program and other programs, the Ministry of Education, Science and Technology would be responsible chiefly for academic research and scientific research, and METI would be responsible chiefly for commercialization and practical applications of the results of that research.
12. Regarding technological development in nuclear power, the Ministry of Education, Science and Technology would be responsible for academic and scientific research, and METI would be responsible for areas related to energy use.
13. Regarding regulations to ensure the safety of using nuclear power for energy, the primary review would be conducted by METI and the secondary review by the Nuclear Safety Commission.
14. Based on changes in industrial policy, reviews would be conducted of the Ministry's internal organization, such as the sections responsible for promoting specific industries.

The major change from the point of view of MITI lay in the fact that "promotion of economic structural reform" headed the list of priorities of the organizational plan.

Structural reform of the general economy and of trade and industrial policy was therefore established as a major task of policy.

Previously, the Economic Planning Agency and the Ministry of Finance had jurisdiction over fiscal and monetary policy and focused on advancing macroeconomic responses to the economic cycle, while MITI promoted its policies with an eye to addressing structural problems in industry and business. This division was removed in the central government's organizational reform, and administration of economic policy as a whole became the priority task of METI when it replaced MITI. Given that there was little margin for fiscal approaches to economic stimulus because of the financial collapse which, after 1990, caused a decrease in tax revenue and an increase in non-performing loans in the financial sector the government decided that recovery from the long recession would come from the free and creative activities of business based on the rules of market competition established by the government. To that extent the only possible institution to take responsibility for policy development was MITI and then its successor METI, although MITI was not able to take the initiative on fiscal and monetary policies.

At the same time, in the section on industrial policy that followed, Clause 2, Item (a) called on the ministry to "stop pursuing measures to promote specific industries or redistribute income among industries, or to reduce the practice and shift to policies that respect market principles", which meant, for example, as cited in Clause 4, "reducing administration designed to protect SMEs or SME organizations." In other words, industrial policy to address social gaps or terminal care for declining industries was low on the list of METI policy priorities. Administrative Reform Committee standards were in this sense opposed to the reorganization plans. As economic growth was emphasized as a policy priority, policy areas that were not directly linked to economic growth were neglected, even though the problems of SMEs were not resolved.

Clauses 1–6 set out the main issues in economic and industrial policy, while the details are listed in 60 items in the Law for the Establishment of the Ministry of Economy, Trade and Industry, thus clarifying the extent of administrative authority. Trade and industry policy would be carried out based on laws rather than on former policy methods, such as the process of informal consultation called "administrative guidance," the legal basis of which was obscure. Here, too, the rules-based nature of government involvement going forward was clarified. Clauses 9 and beyond concern coordination with other ministries and agencies on policy for telecommunications, competition, technology, nuclear energy, nuclear energy safety, etc., but these did not constitute any major change from previous policies. With the clear statement that the jurisdictional divisions in telecommunications were to remain unchanged, restricting METI's involvement, there is no denying a certain lack of vision and thoroughness, given that the administrative reform's chief concerns were the positioning of the information industry in the prospects for and concepts of the economy and society of the future, and the promotion of economic structural reform as well.

3.4 Policy Development in Anticipation of Organizational Reform

Article 21 Paragraph 14 of the Basic Law on Reform of the Central Government Ministries and Agencies called for "reviews… of the Ministry's internal organization, such as the sections responsible for promoting specific industries", but this meant seeking the dissolution of the "window guidance" (informal advice by the Ministry to companies) that was so particular a feature of traditional industrial policy. The 1973 organizational reform had already taken this path to some extent, and industrial policy increasingly cut across specific industries, with the vertical, industry-specific form of organization increasingly seen as inapt for the purpose. Under these circumstances, as repeatedly pointed out above, "market-intervention industrial policy" became less and less the preferred solution to issues from the 1980s on, as the preference became "an approach to policy that respects and promotes the market mechanism". To that extent, the reform policy confirmed changes in policy issues and measures for resolving them that were already in fact underway.

A typical manifestation of the shift toward "respect for the market mechanism" was in the relationship with the Japan Fair Trade Commission, which began operation in 1947 to promote economic competition. Until the high growth period, MITI often conflicted with the FTC over the operation of the Antimonopoly Law; approvals of intra-industry collaboration were regarded as an important policy measure, and effective ways were therefore found for establishing exemption legislation, administrative guidance, and other measures.

This thinking changed dramatically in the first half of the 1980s, however, with a new emphasis in domestic industrial policy on promoting competition and a shift to leaving the question of facilities adjustment in expanding or contracting production capacity to the scope of voluntary action by companies. According to the 1978–83 Industry Stabilization Law (officially the Law on Temporary Measures for Stabilization of Specified Depressed Industries), facilities were supposed to be closed and companies merged under publicly authorized rules, to address the post-oil crisis issue of structurally depressed industries. The 1983–88 Structural Improvement Law (Temporary Measures Law for the Structural Adjustment of Specific Industries) that followed, however, took a different approach based on the "Six Yamanaka Principles" presented in its formulation: (1) (contraction and revitalization (2) mitigation of influence on employment and regional economies (3) implementation of comprehensive measures, (4) respect for private-sector autonomy, (5) focus on competition policy and adherence to open systems, (6) time-limit on policy responses). The new approach stressed (1) respect for the actual circumstances of the private sector (such that MITI would designate industries based on private-sector applications), (2) not regulating imports, and (3) undertaking preliminary negotiation with the FTC but not granting exemptions to the application of the Antitrust Law. The third of these represented a major change in the relationship of MITI's policies with the Antitrust Law, and from this time forward, policy shifted in the direction of supporting autonomous responses, including corporate mergers, at the company level.[11]

Thus, industrial policy came to focus less on industries than on the enterprise system and corporate organization. In the 1990s, MITI/METI no longer was directly engaged in advancing corporate mergers and combinations, but instead pursued "rule-based" policies, such as proposing the rules to govern policies on competition (such as reviewing the standards for examining mergers). This was evident in the June 1993 "interim compilation" (based on the deliberations of the Fundamental Issues Subcommittee of the Industrial Structure Council), which proposed institutional reform (for example, for relaxation of regulations on the establishment of pure holding companies, greater flexibility in the labor market, etc.) for a review of Japan's economic system. The revision of the Antimonopoly Act based on this recommendation was accomplished in 1997.

These changes were moreover supported by overseas criticism of Japan's industrial policy, and the fact that the Structural Impediments Initiative (SII) talks between Japan and the United States in 1989–90 attributed the closed nature of Japan's economy to industrial policy. The trade problems that lay in the background of these changes were raised beginning in the latter 1970s in terms of Japan's responsibility as an "economic superpower," and Japan's large trade surplus began to be perceived as a problem. Japan-US friction over Japanese textile products had already been an issue, but with friction arising over one sector after another, including steel, semiconductors, and automobiles, measures for resolving the bilateral trade imbalance often took the form of voluntary export restrictions by Japan. At the same time, countries in Europe and America seeking to export to Japan raised strong criticisms of the "closed nature" of the Japanese market, and demanded market opening and expansion of the import framework not only for manufactured goods but for primary products, particularly agricultural products, as well. In response, various government regulations of the domestic industrial sector that were pointed out as non-tariff barriers were relaxed and amended to comply with shared international rules.

The adoption of an import expansion policy to eliminate the excessive trade surplus was unprecedented in advanced industrialized countries. The fact that Japan's trade structure took the form of "processed trade," meaning imports of raw materials and exports of finished goods, came under criticism by developed countries. However, even if non-tariff as well as tariff barriers were pointed out and efforts were made to eliminate them, imports of goods from advanced economies did not noticeably expand.[12] Such efforts therefore failed to erase the political pressures from developed countries; it was also obvious that the numerical targets and other approaches to import expansion demanded by the US interfered with the free market economic system, and therefore they could not be acceded to.

---

[11] Regarding changes in policy on industrial adjustment, see Watanabe (2016).

[12] With the expansion of imports in the late 1980s, the Japanese trade structure weakened the structural features or so called "processed-trade model" that had characterized Japan's economy since the post-rapid-growth period. The import expansion did not come from industrialized countries, however, but was the result of Japanese companies' entry into East and Southeast Asia to manufacture products, which were them imported into Japan.

That regulatory reforms were implemented first in sectors involved with trade was the result of overseas pressure. Because industry relied heavily on exports it put a priority on preventing trade friction; thus, market opening in the mineral and industrial products sectors proceeded quite smoothly compared with that of the primary goods sectors. The expansion of deregulation more widely into areas unrelated to trade was in line with industry calls for fiscal rebuilding and demands for "small government".

However, these measures were transient and fundamentally inconsistent, given that voluntary restrictions on exports required policy involvement, on the one hand, while demands were made for minimal policy involvement regarding imports, on the other. Even in trade negotiations, therefore, industrial policy sought to address issues with rule-based approaches—that is, solutions based on rules agreed upon by multiple countries. Regarding unilateral measures taken in the course of bilateral coordination, Japan developed clear arguments to present at the World Trade Organization (WTO) that adhered to the principle of free trade, and took the policy stance, as a principle of trade negotiation, that the scope for government intervention was limited. For example, in the Japan-U.S. Steel negotiations, MITI, in accordance with the December 1991 draft of the international rules for trade negotiations submitted to the GATT Uruguay Round, decided that "the age of voluntary restraints has passed" and refused to extend its VERs on steel exports to the US. Similarly, in the negotiations on automobiles, it rejected the numerical targets requested by the William J. Clinton Administration and finally reached agreement based on its decision to bring the matter to the WTO for a ruling if necessary. Industrial policy thus shifted to a reliance on the market economy system, and, though later in coming, trade policy, too, began placing a greater emphasis on the market economic system. The fact that this strategy did not remain the ultimate landing point is touched on briefly at the end of this chapter (Abe 2013).

3.5 Changing Targets of Policy

The transformation of trade and industrial policy not only spread the general idea of relying on the market mechanism, but also changed the nature of each traditional policy task. An especially great change was seen in the policies on industry location and on SMEs, summarized in Clauses 4 and 5 of the Organization Plan cited above.

Industrial Location Policy, which had sought to correct regional disparities by dispersing factories in different localities, was until the 1980s based on such plans as the Comprehensive National Development Plan. Promoting industry relocation, it advanced regional development through such means as the Law for Accelerating Regional Development Based upon High-Technology Industrial Complexes (Technopolis Law, 1983), the Law to Promote the Group-Siting of Designated Types of Business Contributing to More Sophisticated Local Industrial Structures (Key Facilities' Siting Law, 1988), the Multi-Polar Pattern National Land Formation Promotion Law (1988), the Law for Comprehensive Development of Regional Core Cities with

Relocation of Office-Work Function (Regional Cores Law, 1992), the Office Arcadia Plan, and others. Where the main policy objectives of these measures concerned industrial location in the period of high economic growth through tax incentives and subsidies, the 1980s saw plans to form regional cores by advancing the service sector, premised on the *1980s Vision* (Trade and Industry Policy Vision in the 80s) of a shift to a more knowledge-intensive industrial structure.[13]

However, these policy approaches were in large part withdrawn in the latter 1990s. As explained above, Article 5 of METI's "reorganization plan" reduced the role of the national government, delegating more and more to regional localities; in 1998, the Technopolis Law and the Key Facilities' Siting Law were abolished and the Law for Facilitating the Creation of New Business was established, with support for new venture start-ups by individual business owners and SMEs in mind. Further, in 2001, METI abolished the New Industrial City Construction Promotion Law and the Law on the Promotion of the Development of Special Regions for industrial Development. As a result, METI has significantly diminished the interest in policy areas aimed at reducing regional disparities.

These ideas were clarified in the 1997 New Business Creation Promotion Act that replaced the Law on Temporary Measures for Activation of Specific Regional Industrial Agglomerations; in other words, it was spurred by the shift from the concept of conventional "industrial location" to that of "business creation." The "Law on Establishing Regional Industrial Clusters and Strengthening Them by Promoting Investment and Innovation" (Regional Industrial Revitalization Law), enacted in 2007, represented a distillation of this idea in policy form. Overall, the main policy change toward SMEs emphasized the creation of new businesses.

Similarly, the social policy perspective, including that of business and distribution policy, was also reversed with regard to the kind of SMEs referred to in Clause 4 ("reducing administration designed to protect SMEs or SME organizations, strengthening the role of regional bodies, and improving the environment to encourage the creation of new industries"). Regarding the SME sector, where the economic disparity with large companies became a problem in the high growth period, efforts were made, based on the Small and Medium Enterprise Basic Law of 1963, to eliminate significant gaps in productivity, corporate income, and wages, and to raise the stability and standard of living of SME owners and their workers. It was for that purpose, that policies to "modernize and upgrade the corporate structure of SMEs" and to "compensate for disadvantages in business activities" were adopted.

However, entering the 1990s, the controversy over the Large-Scale Retail Stores Law, which was one of the points at issue between Japan and the United States, led to a rethinking of the existing practice of protecting small scale businesses through restrictions on openings of large stores. Protective measures for SMEs underwent a transformation, as indicated by the Law's relaxation of restrictions on opening large stores and the emphasis on promoting local areas through the concentration of

[13] Regarding shifts in location policy, see Takeda (Tushō Sangō Seisaku-shi Hensan Iinkai [Committee for the Compilation of the History of International Trade and Industrial Policy] ed.) (2011), Part 1, Chapter 6.

commerce. The Large Store Law was abolished in 2000, a move that was in accord with the Administrative Reform Council's recommendation that the government's "excessive intervention" be reviewed.

With these changing expectations for the environment surrounding SMEs and for the SME role, correcting the disparities with large firms and between regions was no longer the aim of SME policy. Rather, based on hopes for growth potential in the SME sector, the nucleus of policy became to develop an environment in which SMEs would be able to fully exercise that potential. The Basic SME Law revision of 1999 demonstrated this new principle, as expressed in the statement that, "Conducting distinctive business activities in diverse business fields, providing opportunities for diverse employment, and providing opportunities for individuals to demonstrate their abilities and carry out their projects would form the foundation of our economy". Thus, the concepts underlying policy changed and with the new policy objective of creating "diverse and vibrant SMEs", the New Business Creation Promotion Law greatly changed the previous policies.

Even in policy on the textile industry, which had numerous SMEs, particularly among weavers, the registration system aimed at facilities adjustment—encouraging firms in declining industries to invest in new equipment so as to regain or maintain competitiveness—began to pursue a free trade structure. MITI, which was taking steps to rely on the market economy system and support voluntary activities by companies, abolished the Law on Extraordinary Measures for the Structural Improvement of the Textile Industries ("Textile Industries Law"), replaced it with a revised version, and ultimately abolished that as well in 1999. These measures marked the end of industrial adjustment policies targeting the coal and the textile industries to ease their decline meaning that at the end of the twentieth century, the curtain was falling on measures that had played such a large part in postwar industrial policy.[14]

The development of industrial technical policies followed a similar trajectory in terms of the withdrawal of national government involvement.[15] Industrial technology policy had leaned increasingly toward basic research since the 1980s, based on the Industrial Science and Technology Agency's "MITI National Research and Development Program" ("Large-Scale Projects"), and was promoting government-led large-scale projects as measures to secure international competitiveness through the development of original technology. Moreover, although the national new-energy development project, "Sunshine" and "Moonlight" projects, were promoted, R&D supported by the national government tended to focus more on basic research. In the late 1990s, however, the creation of new industries took on importance in the face of structural recession, and technological development shifted to projects with more practical applications. The November 1995 Science and Technology Basic Plan, which was based on the Basic Law on Science and Technology (July 1995), called for the strong promotion of R&D in response to social and economic needs, a

[14] Watanabe (2016).

[15] Regarding changes in technology promotion policies, see Sawai (Tsūshō Sangō Seisaku-shi Hensan Iinkai [Committee for the Compilation of the History of International Trade and Industrial Policy] ed.) (2011).

stance which also illustrates the shift to practical research, and greater stress was also placed on the role of private research institutions in R&D. Following the national administrative reorganization of January 2001, the National Academy of Sciences and Technology was renamed in Japanese and in April that year it changed organizationally as well, becoming the National Institute of Advanced Industrial Science and Technology (AIST), which became the largest research center in Japan.

Industrial policy regarding the information industry, a main focus of technology development, had originated and developed based on the 1956 Law on Temporary Measures for the Promotion of the Machine Industry ("Machine Industries Law") and the 1957 "Law on Temporary Measures for the Promotion of the Electronics Industry", but around 1990, the central issues shifted to the fusion of information management and telecommunications, and the development of human resources as the foundation for industry[16] However, although the new policy issues arising with the information-oriented society often required coordination among ministries and agencies across multiple jurisdictions, the 2001 reorganization of administration did not bring about the consolidation of these policy entities. As a result, despite growing calls for the creation of an advanced information and telecommunications society, many aspects requiring comprehensive policy promotion came to be entrusted to the Cabinet, and the twenty-first century began without the government determining an appropriate strategy.

Meanwhile, the intellectual property system emerged as a key policy issue due to intellectual property rights being negotiated in the Uruguay Round of the GATT (General Agreement on Tariffs and Trade). To further harmonize with overseas systems based on the 1994 Agreement on Trade-Related Aspects of Intellectual Property Rights ("TRIPS Agreement"), a series of revisions were made to the law and were appended to the 2002 Basic Law on Intellectual Property. This action represented a shift to a new framework. Through the formulation and implementation of an intellectual property promotion plan, intensive reforms aimed at realizing an intellectual property-oriented nation were promoted.

3.6 Policy Areas Focusing on New Issues

While there was retreat in some policy areas, there were others that attracted new attention. The most representative example was environmental issues.

Until the period of high growth, MITI had implemented regulations such as establishing the ratio of green areas to be preserved at the sites of industrial plants, based on the Factory Location Law. This policy reflected the viewpoint of environmental conservation. Subsequently, emissions regulations were implemented to prevent air pollution, for example, and MITI addressed the treatment of industrial waste and

[16] Regarding policy on the machinery and information industry, see Hasegawa (Tsūshō Sangō Seisaku-shi Hensan Iinkai [Committee for the Compilation of the History of International Trade and Industrial Policy] ed.) (2013).

other issues. As a result, environmental regulations had a considerable effect, and Japan, once described as "advanced in pollution" became "advanced in pollution control".

The movement to reduce greenhouse gas emissions bore fruit in the form of Japan's agreement to a six-percent emissions reduction in the 1997 "Third Conference of Parties to the Framework Convention on Climate Change" (Kyoto Conference on the Prevention of Global Warming, COP 3) agreement. Meanwhile, the Japanese government established a "Basic Law on the Environment" in 1993 and issued a Cabinet Decision on a Basic Environment Plan in 1994. In 1997, the "Environmental Impact Assessment Law" was enacted, and the system for environmental impact assessment, long a concern, was made consistent and improved. In the process, MITI sought to ensure maximum respect for corporate autonomy on environmental measures, and to take care that environmental regulation not restrict economic growth, such that both these features became part of policy on the environment. MITI's policy stance recognized that environmental efforts could become a springboard for economic progress and took a flexible approach to incorporating new policy issues.

The core issues of energy policy had to be redefined in relation to such environmental measures. The electricity industry underwent liberalization and regulations were relaxed concerning the petroleum industry: both cases illustrated the expectation that a virtuous cycle would be brought about by greater freedom in corporate activity, which viewpoint became a distinctive feature of planning production. The basic principle that had long governed energy policy namely, that of securing an abundant and low-priced supply of energy—was expected to be effective for introducing a competitive order by virtue of "being inexpensive"—while at the same time hopes were high for nuclear power generation on account of its being able to produce an "abundant" demand of energy. This was because dependency on fossil fuels had to be reduced to achieve compatibility between the increased supply of energy required for economic growth and the environmental demand for reduced greenhouse gas emissions.

METI's Basic Energy Plan of 2003 was thus based on the Basic Law on Energy Policy (October 2003), in which the three key issues were "ensuring stable supply", "adapting to the environment", and "utilizing the market principle". The Plan stated that METI would "continue to promote nuclear power generation as a main power source, with the promotion of safety as a major premise," and announced that it "planned to diversify energy sources," including "nuclear energy that is produced domestically". In this way, energy policies that included the aim of constructing new nuclear power plants were accelerated.

4 Conclusion

Among the various policies that METI has promoted since the turn of this century are some that are already requiring rethinking. The best illustration of this is energy policy. The accident at the Fukushima Daiichi Nuclear Power Plant in 2011 forced a change in the promotion of nuclear power, formerly a major pillar of energy policy. This is because the safety standards for nuclear power generation were removed from METI's jurisdiction and because of growing public opinion calling for a reduction of reliance on nuclear power. However, while the third Shinzo Abe Cabinet's "Fifth Basic Energy Plan" (July 3, 2018) set a goal of ending the reliance on coal and for the first time designated renewable energy Japan's "main energy source" of the future, it also positioned nuclear power generation as "a realistic non-coal option" and has not yet produced a map for departure from reliance on nuclear power. The interests of the electric utility industry make the LDP-led Administration reluctant to reduce nuclear power generation. As a result, Japan lags significantly behind European countries where technological innovations and cost reductions have enabled progress on the shift to renewable energy. Nevertheless, the outdated stress on nuclear policy, ignoring public opinion as it does, probably cannot be sustained for much longer.

The basic policy of emphasizing harmonization, cooperative relations with other nations based on multilateral rules governing trade policy also fluctuated in the early twenty-first century over policies on implementing APEC (Asia–Pacific Economic Cooperation), and this inconsistency too, represented a significant change. In particular, as regional trade liberalization had not necessarily proceeded smoothly, the fact that the idea of bilateral FTA (Free Trade Agreements, Free Trade Areas) attracted the attention of participating countries meant the need for different policy approaches than before. At the start of the twenty-first century, Japanese trade policy had to make the shift from complete commitment to "multilateralism" to the "joint pursuit of bilateral and multilateral agreements."

The TPP (Trans Pacific Pact) initiative is representative of such changes. Although they do not rely on uniform rules as the WTO does, agreements made among many countries based on multilateral rule can serve as a means for resolving trade issues. The emergence of the forceful protectionist policies of America's Trump Administration, however, makes the prospect for these approaches uncertain as well. China's actions add another element of instability to international agreements on trade. Wise policy choices will be needed to ensure that the world does not again become mired in the vicious cycle of 1930s-type tariff wars and bloc economies. However, it remains unclear what sort of role METI will play in developing concrete policy.

Needless to say, the issues facing economic society and economic development have changed with the times, and because of the need to address these issues, the focus of policy, viewed in the near term, has also changed and thus become a mirror reflecting the age. More important, however, is that the policy approaches, and the ideals supporting them, have themselves changed with the times.

That process of change does not mean, however, that it was immediately obvious what measures should be taken to address the challenges confronting Japan. As mentioned at the beginning of this essay, policy planning has been carried out in a trial-and-error manner with the aim of developing creative reforms that could break through existing conditions and produce solutions appropriate for the time. In the early twenty-first century, the basic direction of policy has been changing to become something universal that can be shared across national borders, premised on trust in the market economic system and a shift toward greater respect for corporate autonomy.

Since the late twentieth century, the international economy has been undergoing major structural change due to the rapid growth in Asia. Under these circumstances, it is necessary for trade, industrial, and economic policy to balance revitalization of the domestic economy with foreign economic relations based on market mechanisms (Hasegawa 2013, p. 591). The important point here is that the twenty-first century has seen a growing awareness of the inadequacy of the simple logic that MITI/METI policy could bring about economic recovery through broad guarantees of freedom of corporate action. That is, to the extent that a major element in macroeconomic policy continues to be market intervention measures for adjustment in order to respond to the cumulative vicious cycles that are inevitably a part of market economics, the need for another rethinking of the concepts underlying trade, economic, and industrial policy is becoming evident. Thus, in order both to stress growth promotion from a macroeconomic perspective and to allow for policy measures to counter the inevitable economic cycles, it is not sufficient merely to maintain the competitive order. Rather, what is now being sought is reform of the players in the market, namely the companies themselves, and therefore of corporate and labor systems, or in other words, reform of the economic structure itself. As a reform in line with this policy, the revision of labor-related laws and regulations was promoted in favor of management. At the same time, while Japan's external policy has been primarily to resolve conflicts through multilateral coordination, the moves to new regional and bilateral trade agreements mean that it is getting harder to maintain the single principle of "protecting the free-trade system." In that sense, the shift in economic and industrial policy should still be regarded as incomplete, with elements of uncertainty included in the very direction of the transformation that is underway.

References

Abe T (Tsūshō Sangō Seisaku-shi Hensan Iinkai [Committee for the Compilation of the History of International Trade and Industrial Policy] ed.) (2013) *Tsūshō Sangyō Seisaku-shi: 1980–2000 (2) Tsushō Bōeki Seisaku* [*History of International Trade and Industrial Policy: 1980–2000 (2): Trade Policy*]. Tokyo: Keizai Sangō Chōsakai.

Committee on the History of Japan's Trade and Industry Policy RIETI (CHJTIP/RIETI) (2020) Dynamics of Japan's Trade and Industrial Policy in the Post Rapid Growth Era (1980–2000). Springer Singapore, Open Access.

Fletcher W. M, Takeda H (2016) Keidanren, Consumption Tax, and the Lost Decade of the 1990s in Japan. RIETI Discussion Paper Series, 16-E-043.

Hasegawa S (Tsūshō Sangō Seisaku-shi Hensan Iinkai [Committee for the Compilation of the History of International Trade and Industrial Policy] ed.) (2013) *Tsūshō Sangyō Seisaku-shi: 1980–2000 (7) Sanghō Gijutsu Seisaku* [*History of International Trade and Industrial Policy: 1980–2000 (7): Machinery and Information Industry Policy*]. Tokyo: Keizai Sangō Chōsakai.

Hashimoto J (2001) *Sengo Nihon Keizai no Seichō Kozō* [The Structure of the Postwar Japanese Economic Growth]. Tokyo: Yūhikaku.

Ministry of International Trade and Industry (1973) *Tsūshō Sangyo Seisaku no Gaiyo* [*Overview of the Organizational Reform of the Ministry of International Trade and Industry*]

Sawai M (Tsūshō Sangō Seisaku-shi Hensan Iinkai [Committee for the Compilation of the History of International Trade and Industrial Policy] ed.) (2011) *Tsūshō Sangyō Seisaku-shi: 1980–2000 (9) Sanghō Gijutsu Seisaku* [*History of International Trade and Industrial Policy: 1980–2000 (9): Industrial Technology Policy*]. Tokyo: Keizai Sangō Chōsakai.

Takeda H (Tsūshō Sangō Seisaku-shi Hensan Iinkai [Committee for the Compilation of the History of International Trade and Industrial Policy] ed.) (2011) *Tsūshō Sangyō Seisaku-shi: 1980–2000 (5) Ritchi, Kankyō, Hoan Seisaku* [*History of International Trade and Industrial Policy: 1980–2000 (5): Location, Environment, and Safety Policy*]. Tokyo, Keizai Sango Chōsakai.

Watanabe J (2016) Tsūsan-shō (Keisan-shō) no Sangyo Chōsei Seisaku [MITI (METI)'s Policies of Industrial Adjustment in Postwar Japan]. RIETI Discussion Paper Series 16-J-033.

Haruhito Takeda is Professor Emeritus at Faculty of Economics at The Universi-ty of Tokyo, Director at Mitsui Bunko and former Faculty Fellow at RIETI. He is a authority in the field of economic policy history research, having authored many works and edited many collections of materials on the history of MITI/METI. His research interests include the history of "monopolies," including zaibatsu studies, and the history of the copper industry etc. He received the Japan Academy Prize in 2022 for his research.

The End of the Industrial Adjustment Policy

Junko Watanabe

Abstract This chapter takes a retrospective review of the policies for "industrial adjustment" conducted by the Ministry of International Trade and Industry (MITI) and its successor, the Ministry of Economy, Trade and Industry (METI), in postwar Japan, and examines the effects of their completion which occurred from the end of the 1990s to the beginning of the 2000s. The essentials of these policies are (1) adjustments of supply and demand at production or investment level in the depressed industries and (2) mitigation of unemployment problem or social conflicts. MITI had played the role of coordinator among various concerned interests as needed to reflect changing circumstances in successive periods. However, in the latter half of the 1990s and on, the conventional industrial adjustment policies were ended, and some parts of the policies related to the restructuring and industrial revival were inherited by the "industrial revitalization policy" which MITI (METI) established as one of the new lines of policies at that time. Although this policy was based on market mechanism in principle, the policy intervention on the industries, especially on the specific firms to protect them, persisted in different forms, whereas some aspects of the labor were excessively "marketized."

1 Introduction

1.1 Industrial Adjustment Policy: Definition and History

The aim of this chapter is to undertake a retrospective review of Japanese *industrial adjustment policy* in the post-World War II period, as implemented by the Ministry of International Trade and Industry (MITI), and to examine the significance and effects of their prima facie "demise" during the period at the turn of the century from the 1990s to the 2000s (overlapping with the January 2001 reorganization of

J. Watanabe (✉)
Kyoto University, Kyoto, Japan

H. Takeda and J. Watanabe (eds.), *Rethinking Japanese economic policy at the turn of the 21st century*, Advances in Japanese Business and Economics 34,
https://doi.org/10.1007/978-981-97-5512-7_3

government ministries transforming MITI into the Ministry of Economy Trade and Industry [METI]).[1]

First, the definitions of "industrial adjustment policy" and "industrial adjustment" are reviewed here. These definitions and concrete measures are a little complex given that they differ according to industry and vary with time. As will be explained in detail later, historically, certain policies, later labeled as industrial adjustment policies, began to be implemented in the textile and coal mining industries from the 1950s to the 1960s. Likewise, in the '70s–'80s, similar policies were implemented for the shipbuilding industry, and petrochemical and aluminum-smelting sectors of the materials industry; in the late 1980s to the beginning of the 1990s, the cement industry, as a type of materials industry, also became subject to such policies. Of these, the shipbuilding industry fell under the jurisdiction of the Ministry of Transport, but almost all the others were under the aegis of MITI.

Although there were commonalities and differences in the content of the measures according to industry, generally, they centered on matters relating to supply and demand adjustments, such as controls on over-investment and overproduction (e.g., curtailment of operations, halting or eliminating overcapacity) in so-called structurally-depressed industries. Apart from that, there were a range of measures, responding to industry characteristics and predicted future demand, including industrial revitalization measures, like equipment modernization and structural reforms, support measures to transform industries, unemployment measures, as well as regional measures and small/medium business measures. Since labor-related measures, such as unemployment countermeasures, fall under the jurisdiction of the Ministry of Labor (Ministry of Health, Labor and Welfare, from 2001), MITI implemented policy in conjunction with other ministries, such as the Ministry of Labor.

The terms "industrial adjustment policy" or "industrial adjustment" became established, with clear definitions from the latter half of the 1970s to the 1980s. In particular, since the OECD Positive Adjustment Policy (PAP) guidelines were summarized in '83, "International Industrial Adjustment" garnered attention in developed countries in terms of a direction to aspire towards, and even in Japan, "Industrial Adjustment" came to feature in policy terminology.[2] The idea of "International Industrial Adjustment" means that each country should undertake necessary adjustment of industrial structure depending on the "comparative advantage" not to revert to protectionism, although developed countries faced a structural crisis due to the two oil crises and the growth of newly industrializing countries in the 1970s.

---

[1] Takeda (2016), who carried out a panoptic retrospective of the MITI's post-war policy, highlighted that from the 1990s, MITI /METI policy changed focus to "Structural Reform," while such industrial policies as industrial adjustment policy and small and medium-sized enterprise policies in the traditional sense, met their "demise." As stated by Odaka K (2013, pp. 323–324), MITI /METI policies overall "changed into a rule-oriented policies" {that is, not direct interventions} and is akin to undergoing a "conversion of the industrial policy ideology" "to respecting market principles."

[2] Lobbying from Japan, which had faced the issue of industrial adjustment early on, also played a background role in the OECD formulating a direction.

During this period, the Law on Temporary Measures for Stabilization of Specified Depressed Industries (Industry Stabilization Law) was enacted in Japan in 1978 as a structurally depressed industry countermeasure. Moreover, "industrial adjustment" came to be clearly touted as the objective in the enactment of Temporary Measures Law for the Structural Adjustment of Specific Industries (Structural Improvement Law) of 1983 and Law on Temporary Measure to Facilitate Industrial Structural Adjustment of 1987, as successors to the aforementioned.

In the "MITI Policy Vision for the 1980s," published by the advisory body to the Minister of International Trade and Industry, the Industry Structure Council, "industrial adjustment" was defined as "reduction of specific industry sections and the transfer of content to other industry sections," which "usually, takes the form of an active response carried out individually by an old industry to develop into a new form." However, "in cases where friction from structural transformation is very large, a solution to the problem may be sought by temporary industrial adjustment measures." Thus, this can be considered a prima facie definition relating to industrial adjustment policy according to MITI. Similarly, "industrial adjustment" began to actively be taken up as a theme in the "White Paper on International Trade" and so forth during the 1980s.

Meanwhile, within Japan, theoretical approaches were tested by neo-classical economists, and MITI began to base industrial adjustment policy on logical arguments, rather than the heretofore ad hoc implementation practices. Speaking in economics terms, industrial adjustment is defined as "the transfer of production factors, such as labor or capital, from industries in decline to growth industries," however, it is mentioned that, "in the majority of cases, the transfer of these kinds of production factors does not occur smoothly." That is, "workers from declining industries are unable to easily find employment in the new industries, and the adjustment process often creates large numbers of unemployed." Therefore, the research also suggests the necessity of implementing temporary policies to reduce societal friction accompanying conversion, as an industrial adjustment measure to support industrial adjustment. At the time, MITI policymakers and economics scholars held a joint conference and council, sharing opinions and information, and from this, it can be seen that the above-mentioned views and policies of MITI underwent alignment.

Thus, in Japan, policies equivalent to industrial adjustment policies were being implemented from fairly early in the post-war era, and these were then given a theoretical rationale from the latter half of the 1970s through to the 1980s, while simultaneously receiving international authorization of sorts in terms of policy alignment with the OECD's policy direction. The purpose and definition of industrial adjustment policy and the relevant MITI policy directions can be said to have been clarified to a certain extent by this time.

It should be noted here that MITI, as well as the OECD and economics scholars, with whom it shared the same views, admitted that avoiding market failure relied upon the temporary policy intervention tackling social friction, and that justifiable industrial adjustment policy is basically a policy philosophy which treats market mechanisms as a principle. This direction was revealed even in the aforementioned "MITI Policy Vision for the '80s." As such, amid the regulation reform arising around

1990, policy intervention elements were gradually abating from industrial adjustment policy, and due to the increasing market-oriented nature, it would not have been all that unusual for the policy to have met its demise. Since expiring in 1996, further extension of the Law for Facilitating Transformation of Industrial Structure, which was enacted in 1997, has been denied.

1.2 Market Mechanism vs. Policy Intervention

However, the reasons this has been set as the subject of the chapter are as follows. To date, industrial policy has combined two aspects; one as a government policy measure dealing with industry and business, and another as a measure of labor, social and regional policy dealing with unemployment and the community. Since the 1990s, this has been characterized by the reorganization of the former into a different format, and the retraction of the latter.

In actuality, the situation that has developed since the 1990s has favored or emphasized the supply side. Since the '90s, traditional industrial adjustment has indeed disappeared, in general, METI policy is shifting to an increasingly market-oriented policy, and policy interventions dealing with industry and business continue to change form. Meanwhile, in terms of labor, the labor market has undergone rapid deregulation, with over "marketization" of some layers. As a result, income inequality and job insecurity, caused by the huge increase in non-regular employment, has become a concern during lost decades.

Policy favoring the supply side may bring improved production and corporate profits in the short term; however, in the long term, it becomes a significant destabilizing factor with regard to aspects such as future social security and development of human resources in the Japanese economy as a whole. For this reason, one cannot help but question the wisdom of allowing current policy to be carried out devoid of criticism, and without the need to investigate it from every possible angle.

Originally, the design of the Japanese economy should be carried out reflecting the long-term and overall perspective. However, while politicians appear to be making decisions from broader perspectives, their actual actions exhibit a tendency towards short-sighted, election-conscious behavior. While Japanese corporations are maintaining a characteristically Japanese management style to a certain extent, such as taking a long-term view of management, and employees, business partners and customers play a rather large role as stakeholders (Morikawa 2013), their actions are not for the sake of the Japanese economy as a whole, and in that sense are definitely being short sighted. While both the government and corporations may each have their own justifiable perspective, the result of this is that a "fallacy of composition" situation may arise in the future.

At this point, our hopes get pinned on the bureaucratic structure, thought to be basically neutral, maintaining a long-term, comprehensive view of the Japanese economy; however, what kind of a role did MITI (METI) play in the aforementioned policy transition? While keeping in mind the issues noted above, this chapter will analyze the transition of industrial adjustment policy by focusing on its position amid various related stakeholders, and the purposes of MITI policies.

The structure of this chapter is as follows. Section 2 will investigate industrial adjustment policy prior to the 1990s by dividing it into suitable sections based on industry and time period.[3] Section 3 will consider the '87 Law for Facilitating Transformation of Industrial Structure', and the ensuing industrial and corporate restructuring and policy development after the 1990s.

2 The Beginning of Industrial Adjustment Policy in Post-war Japan

2.1 Structural Improvement of the Textile Industry

The first industrial adjustment policy that was ever actually implemented in Japan was in the textile industry (cotton spinning and the woven cloth sectors). This section will confirm MITI's policy purpose, at the time, through a review of the implementation process.

The first measures were taken at the beginning of the 1950s, when curtailment was carried out under the guise of MITI offering "guidance" to the industry. While the 1950–1951 textile boom was due to the Korean War, post-1952, when the war had ended, the cotton-spinning and woven cloth sectors fell into over-production. It was the usual practice in the industry, since before the war, for production cartels to join together in carrying out curtailment, however, with the enactment of the 1947 Anti-Monopoly Act post-war, limiting production was prohibited as collusion between companies, thus under the guise of "government guidance" MITI to industry, it became well-known as "advisory" curtailment. In the case of the woven fabrics industry, given the overwhelming number of small/medium-sized traders, forming a cartel was a logistical impossibility. So, in August 1952, at the behest of the woven fabrics industry, MITI enacted the Small and Medium Enterprise Stabilization Law as a law exempt from prosecution under the Anti-Monopoly Act, carrying out a similar policy under the rationale of the same law.

The following measures, which were carried out in the early half of the 1950s as intervention measures according to the MITI supply-and-demand adjustment policy, were the first of the subsequent industrial adjustment policies, although at this stage, they had not been established as "industry adjustment policies." At the time, the textile industry was still an important export industry, with new entries and facility increases continuing. Since this led to the cut-throat competitiveness of the recession, and decreased export prices (dumping issue), MITI only carried out supply-and-demand adjustment for the purpose of "promoting exports."

[3] For detailed information on the textiles and coal industries, refer to Watanabe (2008, 2010).

However, from the latter half of the 1950s, the textile industry came to take on the appearance of being structurally depressed. While demand had peaked, overinvestment continued unabated, and overproduction, based on an excess of facilities and competition, brought about price reductions and instability. As a result, MITI continued with intermittent advisory curtailment, as well as the suppression of overinvestment, by enacting the 1956 Law on Temporary Measures for Textile Industry Equipment and Related Equipment (Old Textile Law), to restrict the addition of new equipment. This period is generally understood to be the beginning of industrial adjustment policies. This law was succeeded by the enactment of the '64 Law on Temporary Measures for Textile Industry Equipment and Related Equipment, the '67 Law on Temporary Measures for the Structural Improvement of Specified Textile Industry, and the '74 Law on Temporary Measures for the Structural Improvement of the Textile Industry. In accordance with these laws, equipment expansion was prohibited and equipment disposal was carried out. Meanwhile, the structural reforms policies were carried out by the implementation of modernized equipment.

Summarizing the above, the initial policy aim of MITI was merely the "promotion of exports," and the purpose was not necessarily to offer countermeasures to deal with structurally-depressed industries and industries in decline. However, since the latter half of the 1950s, this was transformed into industrial adjustment policy as countermeasures against structurally depressed industries, and the purpose of MITI policy is considered to have gradually changed content amid these circumstances.

Although the reasons and rationale for why MITI chose to commit to industrial adjustment policy, as a countermeasure for structurally-depressed industries and industries in decline, are unclear, one possible hypothesis is some type of "compensation principle."

During the post-war reconstruction period, the government and MITI encouraged production and promoted cotton exports for the purpose of foreign currency acquisition. However, it also had to implement policy, which ran counter to these aims. At the time, the synthetic textile development policy,[4] promoted by MITI, aiming for balance of payments equilibrium, was making inroads into the natural fiber markets of cotton products and so forth. Moreover, in light of the Japan-US textile trade frictions (trade friction in the '50s over cotton and sewn products, typified by the "$1 blouse" issue), which had become increasingly pronounced since the 1950s, Japan was forced to compromise by accepting production quantity restrictions under Japan-US bilateral agreements. As for MITI, settling the textile trade friction was intended to remove barriers for future trade export industries (heavy-chemical industries, such as steel and automotive). In this era, newly emerging industrial countries not only began production and export of textile products, but in addition to the domestic policies mentioned above, demand for Japanese cotton products had unavoidably peaked.

---

[4] While cotton product exports are a means to raise foreign currency, its merits as a method of raising trade revenue were severely limited by its dependence upon the import of 100% of the raw cotton.

It is thought that given these developments, MITI, that is, the textile bureau was forced to continue its commitment towards the textile industry. Out of deference to the declining textile industry, MITI treated it as a crucial national policy issue, carrying out reparations such as the synthetic textile development policy and compromises over the Japan-US textile trade frictions. In the event that there is enough profit for society as a whole to gain, despite compensating for the damages incurred by some companies (or people), such "compensation" is socially justified.

Meanwhile, it is also true that one of the reasons behind the implementation of such as policy was that there was industry-side lobbying by beneficiaries. Apart from the Japan Spinners Association, pressure groups, such as organizations of small/medium weaving companies and the Japan Textile Federation, created in January 1970, in response to the Japan-US textile trade friction compromise, proposed a range of demands to the Japanese government and MITI.[5] Moreover, at the time, there was a plan to have both ruling and opposition parties, such as the Liberal Democratic Party and the Socialist Party, incorporate these demands into policy.

However, from the 1980s, there were developments, such as the re-energizing of the textile industry, shift of large corporations to other industries (diversification) and business change/discontinuation of small/medium traders, so it is not as though there were no elements of industrial adjustment policy in terms of "active adjustment." The production and investment aspects of the government's support, for supply-and-demand adjustments and equipment disposal, softened the textile industry's pace of decline, and by preserving corporate strength, entailed an aspect of gradually progressing the transformation of labor and investment to other industries via corporate self-support endeavors.

On the whole, employment adjustment failed to present that much of an issue, due to the spinner industry's labor force being mainly females with few years of consecutive employment, although there were cases of serious labor disputes in small/medium-sized spinner companies. Furthermore, in Japan, amid the aforementioned gradual industrial adjustment, relatively moderate employment adjustment was also carried out, such as in the large spinner corporations which made efforts to respond to the shift within the corporation.

Industrial adjustment of the textile industry frequently comes under criticism for vested interests (especially of the small/medium textile traders), policy inertia and its prolonged nature, having continued from the 1950s to around the 80s–90s. In addition, there is an aspect of the government being dragged along by the demands of industry. Moreover, it cannot necessarily be said that the Japanese textile industry has

---

[5] The Japan Textile Federation was formed from a need to counter the American cotton import regulations beginning in the 1950s and increasing demands for import regulations on wool and synthetic fiber products, which became pronounced in the 1960s. The Japan Spinners' Association, Japan Chemical Fibers Association, Japan Wool Industry Association, Japan Cotton & Staple Fiber Weavers' Association are members, as well as various industry organizations from dyeing, processing and sewing sectors. From formation to the present day, it is involved in gathering various types of information regarding trade issues, submitting policy demands to government and carrying out exchange with related international organizations. Reference: Japan Textile Federation Homepage (accessed February 1, 2016).

made sufficient fashion-industry centered progress in terms of the "textile industry of developed countries" as was pursued by MITI from the '80s.

Overall, however, MITI industrial adjustment policy for the textile industry can be evaluated positively as having promoted policy that was concerned with national interests, while also surveying developments in other industries. Since the high growth period, carrying out policy measures (income transfer) toward the sacrificed textile industry, amid the increased income growth of other industries, was supported by it being relatively easy to accept from a societal perspective.

2.2 Regional Measures and Dislocated Worker Measures in the Coal Mining Industry

Industrial adjustment policies for the coal mining industry can be seen to begin in the 1950s, just as for the textile industry. Both textiles and coal mining were major industries of the post-war reconstruction period, and they shared a commonality that a rapid and vast supply-and-demand gap arose when the Japanese economy recovery was ending in the first half of the 1950s.

As mentioned previously, in the case of textiles, this was because, after the boom from the Korean War, demand wavered, export of textile products were suppressed due to Japan-US textile trade friction, developing countries began to catch up, and synthetic fibers increased. In the case of coal, production increase policies were carried out during wartime and in the immediate post-war period, and while supply capacity did increase enormously, at the beginning of the 1950s various post-war regulations were relaxed, a price difference with imported coal existed, and international competition was fierce, with further competition from petroleum due to the energy revolution; in terms of domestic coal. As with the textile industry, structural depression became prominent during the '50s–'60s. Government and MITI energy policy, which brought about an energy revolution by implementing petroleum use, despite its position as a competitor to coal, is similar in composition to the synthetic textile development policy for the textile industry.

Considered in this way, the circumstances for coal and textiles are of a similar type. Both were major industry leaders in the post-war reconstruction period, which shared the experience of being racked by a vast supply-and-demand gap brought about by policy factors, and the policies dealing with this point can thus be seen to take on a more compensatory hue.

Moreover, speaking of coal, the energy policy was seen to be unique, so for an ongoing period since the 1970s, the government and MITI continued conservative policies, with a view to securing energy, maintaining a certain level of domestic coal, while supply industries and the financial world (Japan Business Federation, etc.) also aligned themselves with this policy.

At the heart of the industrial adjustment policies for the coal industry is the streamlining of the coal mines as a prelude to supply-and-demand adjustment. The government and MITI enacted the Act on Temporary Measures Concerning the Rationalization of the Coal Mining Industry in 1955 and promoted a "scrap and build" coal mining policy. On the supply side, rationalization efforts were made to reduce costs, and supply-and-demand adjustment was carried out having secured the cooperation (domestic deals specifying a certain amount of coal) of the demand side (especially, the large demand industries of electricity and steel). These negotiations and adjustments were carried out with MITI shouldering the role of acting intermediary, where domestic coal production levels were planned, and prices were usually set at the coal mining council meetings.

However, this coal mining rationalization method produced sacrifices, such as closures, massive reorganization of personnel, resulting in frequent outbreaks of strikes, societal anxiety, and impoverishment of the coal-producing regions. In 1960, the Japan Coal Miners' Union changed from the conventional "fight against rationalization," to develop the "fight to change government policy," joining with the national center, the General Council of Trade Unions of Japan to pressure the government for a policy review. The Japan Business Federation also filed a petition regarding policy.

Against this background, at the beginning of the 1960s, there was a fundamental shift in policy principles, with industrial adjustment policy becoming established for the coal industry. Since the frequent occurrence of large-scale strikes accompanying the labor disputes reduced the production capacity, increased production costs for coal companies, and caused disruption to the stable supply of domestic coal, the government was forced to take action and these events become the reason for the policy shift. In 1961, the Law on Temporary Measures for Coal Mining Area Development was enacted, and along with the aforementioned Act on Temporary Measures Concerning the Rationalization of the Coal Mining Industry became the rationale for the industrial adjustment of the coal industry.

Following this, in 1962, the government created the coal mining industry survey group, instating Hiromi Arisawa as chairman, calling for opinions from coal company laborers, local governments and coal-related industries, with regard to new rebuilding measures for the coal mining industry. As a result, up until 2000, versions one to nine of the coal policies were carried out based on the recommendations of the group. Furthermore, a corresponding legal measure to the next policy was that the two previous laws survived as amendments. In the latter half of the 1960s, the decline of the coal mining industry could no longer be denied, and in the '68 coal mining council's report, "Coal Reconstruction Measures," it was determined that "autonomous rebuilding is undoubtedly difficult, and final closures should be facilitated," after which, emphasis was placed on smooth reduction through industrial adjustment.

The characteristics of the initial coal policy beginning in 1960 are as follows. Firstly, while it did continue in line with rationalization policies to date, competition with foreign coal and petroleum, as well as the economic aspects were abandoned, and the goal was to maintain the stability of the coal industry and the ongoing domestic supply of coal. Secondly, it was concerned with labor disputes.

The purpose of policy was not rationalization of the coal mining industry in order to compete with petroleum and overseas coal, but rather had shifted to be a "national issue," about "the effects the fall of the coal mining industry had on those involved, the deep shock it had caused regional society, and the desire to avoid a serious blow to the economy," or in other words, "a broad policy focusing on avoiding societal friction brought about by the fall of the coal mining industry." Coal mining policy was transformed into "seeking how to smoothly facilitate structural adjustment of the coal mining industry," while considering the effects on regional society, mining, employment and the coal producing regions' economies, amid the various conflicting interests and ideas (Coal Mining Policy History Editorial Committee 2002).

In terms of unemployment policy, in 1959 the government enacted the Law on Temporary Measures for Dislocated Workers in Coal Mines and also prepared a re-employment promotion system. Specifically, (1) in addition to employment insurance-based unemployment benefits, provision of employment promotion allowance for 3 years, (2) to carry out employment referrals and career advice through the job security and employment promotion agency, and (3) measures, such as employment incentives for companies to hire ex-workers. These measures are said to have ensured that approximately 200 thousand ex-coal mine workers were able to be re-employed. Compared with other subsequent eras, the employment climate of the high economic growth period was better, and so a certain number of ex-workers were absorbed into other sectors.

However, even in the 1980s, mine explosion accidents and closures continued. With the gradual suppression of the domestic coal production volume due to the coal miming policy, major coal mines closed, and tens of thousands of workers are thought to have been terminated. A temporary countermeasures division was set up within the labor ministry, formulating re-employment plans and gathering employment information, as well as opening career counseling centers in coal mining regions. Furthermore, the Law on Temporary Measures for Dislocated Workers in Coal Mines was extended twice in 1982 and 1987, and activities introducing employment over a wider range of regions, such as doubling financial support for relocation expenses and regional job-seeking activities expenses, were promoted as a means of encouraging re-employment outside of the local region.

As mentioned above, industrial adjustment policy for the coal industry focused on regional and labor measures. In the background to this were political parties supporting coal workers and coal mine labor movements, such as the Miike labor dispute. Since in the coal mining industry, the majority of workers were men with families, for whom transferring due to labor aspects was a particularly difficult issue, the policies definitely had an element of avoiding societal friction.

Given that from the high growth period to the stable growth period, other production industries were flourishing, while the coal mining industry was declining, income disparities between industries increased. Amid this, social, compensatory income redistribution measures for coal producing regions and ex-coal mine workers, that is, carrying out measures to narrow the gap, are thought to have been met with easy approval from the people of the nation.

Sawaki (2007) has taken a political-science approach to an analysis of the reasons why the coal policy has continued for tens of years and become affected by inertia.

Moreover, the reason for its long-term nature was a result of the "balance" of "interests" between the policy beneficiaries; the coal mine employers and employees, residents of the coal producing regions, demand industries, who bear the resource burden of the policy (electricity and steel), as well as the government, MITI and "political actors" such as political parties. He analyzes that the demand industries (particularly the electric power industry) were willing to take on the relatively high price of domestic coal, considering the social costs. The role of MITI was basically that of coordinating related interests.

However, as Sawaki and the majority of other commentators have somewhat critically noted, even though the "long-term" nature of the coal policy was the reality, closures and associated grave circumstances still continued during the 1980s–1990s, making the continuation of policy inevitable. MITI and the Agency for Natural Resources and Energy, joining with regional local governments and financial institutions, implemented mine closure-related anti-trust preventative measures, bankruptcy-preventative measures aimed at related local small/medium-sized enterprises, prioritizing coal-producing regions for public works projects, supporting the regional promotional activities of local government, and so forth. In addition, working with the Ministry of Labor to prepare for the dismissal of all workers, they planned countermeasures, such as a subsidy system for coal corporations to conduct reskilling of workers while they were still employed, through revision of the Law on Temporary Measures for Dislocated Workers in Coal Mines.

After the end of the industrial adjustment measures for the coal industry were announced in the Administrative Reform Council's 1997 final report, the MITI minister announced a policy direction at the coal-producing Region Promotion Council, [toward ending coal policy] "reforming the post-war government administrative system, into a new government administrative system suitable for the 21st century and based on the individual independence and formulation of a freer public society." In the end, the "Act on the Rearrangement of Relevant Acts Upon Completion of the Structural Adjustment of the Coal Mining Industry," was passed at the March 2000 plenary session of House of Councilors, signaling the demise of coal mining industry industrial adjustment policy.

To conclude, what has been described thus can be briefly summarized as follows. During the 1950s–1960s, as was the case with textiles, individual industry countermeasures for coal were planned primarily by MITI's Coal and Resource Bureaus (later changed to the Agency for Natural Resources and Energy, in the 1973 structural reforms), since coal was threatened with production adjustments due to increased coal production during the reconstruction period and the subsequent severe curtailment; acting as the secretariat for the councils and policy development, MITI is considered to have taken a fairly neutral position regarding the industrial adjustment policy for the coal mining industry, (particularly during the 1950s–1960s), in its efforts to develop and implement policy. Although the policy did include some aspects aimed at big corporations, it was characterized by "protecting the weaker-style" bailout measures aimed at coal-producing regions experiencing "societal friction," and ex-coal workers.

As mentioned previously, industrial adjustment policies for the coal mining industry have many commonalities with the textile industry situation. Meanwhile, as seen in the following section, in the '70s, the newly added industrial adjustment policy for the basic materials industry seemed to have become something different. While MITI's stance continued unchanged in terms of generally respecting the autonomy of the industry and corporations, and maintaining a secretariat-like role, the presence of the financial world, such as the Japan Business Federation, grew bigger due to the fact that corporations attached to the basic materials industry were powerful members of the Japan Business Federation, as well as due to the presence of huge corporations.

While it's not that the main targets of industrial adjustment policy in the seventies, the basic materials industry and the ship-building industry, didn't suffer from the situation of worldwide relative price fluctuations and rapid economic growth in Japan (for instance, reduced international competitiveness due to rising age costs) triggered by the oil crisis; measures aimed at these industries were much less colored by "societal policy" aspects such as "compensation" and "avoiding societal friction," seen in the labor intensive textile and coal industries. Instead, in a capital-intensive industry like the basic materials industry, relationships between government and corporations arising from capital (excess facilities and overinvestment) and its conversion, became even more acute. This will be further examined in the following section.

3 Expansion of Policies Toward Basic Materials Sector

3.1 Structural Recession in the Basic Material Industry

While differing in many respects from the nature of textile and coal mining industries, from the 1970s, basic materials industries, such as the aluminum smelting industry and petrochemical industry, became the target of industrial adjustment policy.

As seen in Fig. 3.1, reduction of the textile and coal mining industry are conspicuous (this reduction can be viewed as both a cause and effect of industrial adjustment); nevertheless, both industries can be said to have been characteristic of an industry in decline. In comparison, in the case of basic materials industries such as "chemicals," "pulp, paper and paper products," "ceramics, stone and clay products," "non-ferrous metals," apart from certain specialist sectors, such as aluminum smelting (non-ferrous metals), peak demand was broadly seen to hold an important position in the Japanese economy, even after the 1990s.

It is therefore possible to say that in the industrial adjustment policy, for the basic materials industries, the structural adjustment response to the temporary supply-and-demand gap from the oil crisis of the 1970s and the strong yen in the 1980s after the Plaza Accord and so forth, was a much bigger aspect.

In the 1970s, the majority of industries, and especially the basic material industries which were high-oil, high-electricity consuming industries, underwent a sudden

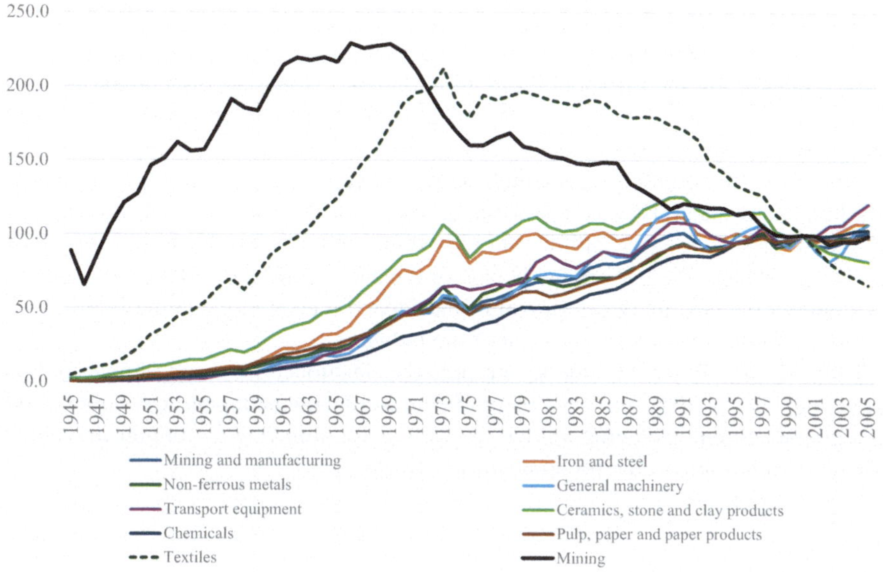

Fig. 3.1 Index of industrial production (value added weights, 2000=100). *Source* Sōmushō Tōkei Kyoku [Statistics Bureau of Japan] (2006) *Shin Chōki Tōkei Sōran* [*New Long-Term Statistical Compendium*], *Vol. 2*. Tokyo: NihonTōkei Kyokai, Tabel 8.16. The original source is *Koukougyo Sisū Nenpō* [*the Annual Report of Industrial Indices*] by Research and Statistics Department, Economic and Industrial Policy Bureau, Ministry of Economy, Trade and Industry

change from heretofore expansion, to experiencing a supply-and-demand gap, being troubled by excess facilities and went on to became "structural recession industries" because of increased oil prices (and oil-based electricity prices) during the oil crisis, the economic slump and developing countries catching-up under the strong yen.

Since naphtha prices were relatively higher compared to that of Western countries, the petrochemical industry faced a dramatic decline in international competitiveness. The aluminum smelting industry, a sector where electricity expenses make up 50% of production costs, experienced a huge reduction in international competitiveness and was forced to operate at a loss, due to vastly higher electricity costs, compared to the west and the strong yen. Furthermore, the shift to low economic growth and excessive competition intensified from the demand slump, and were the main reasons causing many industries to fall into a slump. In the paper and pulp sector, over 500 companies continued to fight for a share amid weak demand, and even in the electric furnace sector, approximately 60 companies continued to run at a deficit. In the shipbuilding industry, due to the long post-oil shock recession, there was an excess of vessels worldwide and orders decreased dramatically, bringing about a substantial excess capacity.

As described above, reasons for structural recession varied according to industry; however, MITI defined structural recession industries as below. Although in the course of the 1970s recession, the economy exhibited a moderate economic recovery, those "sectors which will not recover by economy promotion measures or temporary production price adjustment alone," and "sectors which experience increased fuel prices triggered by the oil shock, long term demand slump accompanying shift to stable growth, substantial excess capacity due to structural factors, such as reduced international competitiveness, due to developing countries catching up."

Moreover, "those enterprises which are on the very edge, which if left untreated, could endanger the very survival of the company or the sector, which could exert adverse effects on relate small/medium-sized enterprises, destabilize the supply of goods important to the lives of the people of the nation, and furthermore, threaten to vastly affect the healthy development of the Japanese economy and the recovery of regional economies, built on the core of the industry."

Thus, MITI policy goals can be interpreted as fashioned for responding to industries/companies, which exert a not insignificant weight on the Japanese economy, and on regional economies facing a crisis, as well as for adjusting to counter inevitable structural variations occurring domestically or abroad.

3.2 *Commitments by Various Agencies and Groups*

As a result of this kind of awareness, from around 1977, the government and MITI began working in earnest on structural recession industry countermeasures. At the time, the Japanese economy was slowly beginning its recovery from the serious blow dealt by the oil shock, there was stagnation focused on the extensive recession industries, and breakthrough solutions were still being sought.

In September 1977, the Ministerial Conference on Economic Measures decided on general economic measures to bring Japan out of recession and put the Japanese Economy on the path to stable economic growth, proposing structural recession industry countermeasures as a major tenet, along with measures to stimulate private demand and promote public investment. MITI set up an internal headquarters for structural recession industry countermeasures in order to carry out policy drafting, adjustments, and promotion.

The content of the measures were (1) overseeing production adjustment matters such as production reductions and disposal of excess facilities (implementation of the cartel based on the anti-monopoly law and the small/medium business organizations law), (2) facilitation of financial matters, such as borrowing of funds required for carrying out production adjustment, (3) enterprise shift measures (utilization of the enterprise shift lending system), enterprise shift through creation of an employment stabilization fund, (4) employment measures (employment adjustment etc.) and (5) carrying out price adjustment with the oil industry and increasing import quantity in terms of a petrochemical measure, to reduce the price of naphtha. In addition, carrying out a review of regular inspection and repair periods, as an aluminum smelting measure, to raise capacity utilization rates of electricity self-generation and joint-generation plants.

In order to systematically implement these measures, long-term supply-and-demand predictions were made, as was progress on the creation of structural reform plans at industrial adjustment councils for each industry. The directions measured here were envisioned from 1977 with the "Temporary Measures Law," and the 1978 "Temporary Measures Law for the Stabilization of Specified Depressed Industries," of the following year.

The types of discussions in the related organizations held up until the enactment of the 1978 "Temporary Measures Law for the Stabilization of Specified Depressed Industries" are explored as follows:

Firstly, looking at the activities of the MITI minister's advisory body, the Industry Structure Council, from February 1977 to May 1978, sub-meetings of the council (open-arc furnaces, aluminum, chemical industry, ferroalloy), and research groups formed under their jurisdiction submitted reports and responses to the MITI minister. All these emphasized the significance of the industries, the fact that they were struggling under the supply-and-demand gap, and the necessity of structural reform policies centered on the disposal of excess facilities.

Initially, the Japan Business Federation (JBF) and each sector were not positive toward exemptions to the Anti-Monopoly Act like the Industry Stabilization Law, desiring instead the reformation or flexible application of the Anti-Monopoly Act, however, the difficulty of the issue, along with the fact that MITI suggested and preached it, resulted in a position shift toward cooperating in the establishment of the Industry Stabilization Law. In this manner, public and private sectors came to share an awareness of the necessity of gaining a short-term production adjustment from the disposal of excess facilities and long-term industrial structural reform progress, thus working toward the implementation of a new scheme (legislative measures for the Industry Stabilization Law). To achieve this, the industry, MITI, the government and the LDP joined together to progress policy formation to this end.[6]

The JBF and each sector worked together to apply powerful pressure on the government, LDP, MITI and Ministry of Transport (MOT), regarding the individual industry policies. From June to August in 1977, the JBF individually invited various MITI and MOT Bureau chiefs in charge of each industry sector, to hear the government's views on the sectors within their jurisdiction. It is thought that the issues raised therein became the central themes of the structural recession industry measures.

One reason thought to be behind the JBF's strengthening of interest was the presence of numerous materials producers as powerful corporate members. Moreover, "materials industry as a fundamental industry, it was not just that their share of the Japanese economy was large, but also that the assembly and processing industry was dependent upon the supply of materials, and high quality, stable supply from the domestic materials industry had made a significant contribution to the nation's

[6] According to the private recollections of a Japan Business Federation associate, there is remorse over the fact that the Industry Stabilization Law essentially spoiled corporate self-help efforts and competitive principles. Adding, however, that at the time, the basic materials industry was suffering with excess facilities and since those sectors were in need of a policy, such as the Industry Stabilization Law, a law had to be passed. In this way, general opinion within the Japan Business Federation was also formed.

assembly and processing industry, as well as the development of the high tech industry, and thus the reliance of the Japanese economy overall on the existence of the materials industry was a critical issue."

In many cases, the chairman of the JBF himself took the lead in promoting specific measures for individual industries, such as aluminum smelting, petrochemicals and shipbuilding. In the case of the petrochemical industry, the JBF acted as an intermediary between the oil refining industry and the demand sectors of petrochemical, chemical fertilizer and synthetic fiber industry, facilitating price negotiations for naphtha, and so forth, and worked toward resolving these issues, while maintaining close contact with the government.

Consequently, naphtha import quotas increased, and by the first half of 1978, reached a level not dissimilar to western naphtha prices; moreover, in the petrochemical industry as well, the issue of unfavorable raw material prices was resolved overall. In order to reduce electricity costs, which were the reason for rising smelting expenses in the aluminum smelting industry, measures such as extending the timing of electricity-producing facilities' regular maintenance inspections, and the extended expansion of the tariff quota system for aluminum ingots bought by aluminum smelting companies, were being actively carried out.

In addition, although differing from that of the basic materials industry, measures were also taken for the ship-building industry. In the ship-building sector, especially among the small/medium ship-building companies, there had been hopes of facility disposal and land-sales, since there were some who were being forced out of business. However, due to support from the JBF, a purchasing agency was established based on government subsidies and survivor burden. Moreover, steps to reform the development bank's financing conditions and subsidize the scrap collection businesses were included in the 1979 budget.

As a result of the aforementioned efforts from the JBF and industry, demands from related sectors were also included in the Industrial Structure Council report. While industry and the JBF were heavily involved in policies regarding industry and corporations, mention was also made of employment issues; "It is desirable that this aspect be promoted through the early passage of laws related to measures for displaced workers and the utilization of employment stabilization funding as an excess employment measure." This was because employment adjustment could not be avoided if the production adjustment needed by corporations was to proceed.

4 Extension of Structural Recession Countermeasures

4.1 Enactment of the Law on Temporary Measures for Stabilization of Specified Depressed Industries

As noted above, causes of, and measures for structural recession differ according to each individual industry sector, however, the five-year Law on Temporary Measures for Stabilization of Specified Depressed Industries was enacted in May 1978 to deal with the issue of excess facilities, a basic problem common to all structural recession industries. This same law was enacted in light of the government's implementation of the general economic measures of the previous year, under which policy was proposed and implemented by the internal headquarters for structural recession industry measures, and after various subsequent measures for individual sectors had been taken, in order to carry out adequate measures on the structural recession industries.

The law was an exception to the anti-monopoly act, holding the voluntary efforts of the private sector as a premise, with the government in a complementary position, and as such, the main content involved promoting the processing of excess facilities and providing a surety on the necessary funds.

In addition, because facilities to be processed were held as collateral for bank loans, the disposal of excess facilities was not progressing. Therefore, with the cooperation and agreement of the JBF, a system was created where the Development Bank of Japan, among others, would provide surety on investment funds, when corporations had to borrow the necessary fund to carry out disposal of excess facilities.

Under the act, an industry would become specified if it met the recession requirements of having more than half of the companies in the sector running at a deficit. The number of specified industries reached 14, including open-arc furnaces, aluminum smelting, ammonia manufacture, urea, phosphoric acid, shipbuilding, synthetic fibers (four types: nylon, acrylic, polyester etc.), cotton spinning, worsted yarn spinning, ferrosilicon, and cardboard base-paper manufacturers, from which four industry cartels were formed, (ammonia manufacturing sector, etc.). Moreover, by providing administrative guidance such as production curtailment, MITI become involved in structural reform of the rubber footwear industry, which had been struggling under the proliferation of cheap imports from South Korea. As described above, while the act was focused on the basic materials industries, it dealt with a relatively wide range of industries, including small and medium-sized sectors.

4.2 Employment and Regional Measures

Along with the establishment of the aforementioned General Economic Measures in September 1977, came the formation of the Ministerial Advisory Council on

Employment Issues, under the direction of the Chief Cabinet Secretary, the Agriculture and Forestry Minister, International Trade and Industry Minister, Transport Minister, Labor Minister and the Secretary of the Economic Planning Agency. In December of the same year, the Law for Temporary Measures Regarding Ex-workers of the Specified Depressed Industries was passed as an act of parliament, and since the Labor Ministry pursued measures promoting reemployment of ex-workers from the specified depressed industries, in accordance with the act, measures were taken including creation of reemployment support plans, supply of training allowances, extension of employment insurance benefits (maximum of 90 days), as well as offering employment development benefits (50% of wages, and six month long, two-thirds wage subsidies for small and medium-sized businesses) to employers taking on ex-workers.

Industries specified in the law for ex-workers were decided by the Labor Ministry's central employment stabilization advisory committee but overlapped with those falling under the jurisdiction of MITI's Industry Stabilization Law. The number of specified industries, including those until June 1978, spanned 35 sectors (textiles, open-arc furnace, shipbuilding, non-ferrous metals, plywood, cardboard base-paper, ammonia manufacturing, rubber-soled cloth shoes etc.), with the number of employees reaching approximately 1,490,000.

Moreover, in November 1978, the Law on Temporary Measures for Small and Medium Enterprises in Specified Depressed Regions, the so-called Depressed Regions 2nd Act, and the Law on Temporary Measures for Those Unemployed in Specified Depressed Regions were passed. Thirty specified depressed regions were designated, and small/medium business measures were taken, including low-interest loans and subsidies to stabilize employment and lifestyle of unemployed from "company-towns."

4.3 *Brief Summary*

As outlined above, the appearance or policy system of the 1978 Law on Temporary Measures for Stabilization of Specified Depressed Industries is very much set up as an industrial adjustment policy. While it is true that industry, some labor groups and the mass media voiced criticism of and opposition to "bureaucratic control" regarding the enactment of the law, the MITI has taken the stance that while industry and companies should strive to help themselves, the MITI will provide lateral support to facilitate the transformation of the industrial structure in response to the changing environment.

For the main part, labor policies aimed to prevent further worsening of the recession, rather than being proactively involved in employment adjustment; however, the legal developments made to stabilize the lives of the unemployed and support re-employment were very significant.

An MITI appraisal of the law is as follows. The MITI itself positively evaluated policy objectives, policy instruments, and policy effects (Okazaki 2012, pp. 29–43).

Regarding the policy objectives, MITI was rational in recognizing certain factors: (1) excess facilities were a factor in decreased corporate profits (ROA); (2) rapid drop in employment in structurally depressed industries; and (3) these were social frictions (bankruptcies and job insecurity) that could occur in the long term due to the environmental conditions following the oil crisis, rather than individual company management problems, and adopted policy instruments to deal with these problems.

Even with respect to policy effects, the rate of goal attainment regarding facility processing was more than 95% and almost all industries experienced a reduction in company numbers (that is, the criticism that marginal enterprises were maintained is unfounded). Furthermore, this suggests that it may have increased industry profitability and productivity.

5 Toward the Continuation of the 1983 Law on Temporary Measures for Stabilization of Specified Depressed Industries

5.1 Movements in Related Industries

As a temporary legislation, the aforementioned Law on Temporary Measures for Stabilization of Specified Depressed Industries, was due to expire in June 1983, however in 1982, the year before the expiration, calls to extend the act in practice, strengthened in some industry sectors. Under the Law on Temporary Measures for Stabilization of Specified Depressed Industries, excess facility disposal goals were generally achieved, and some sectors saw improved supply and demand; thus, the law had a level of success, in terms of improving the overall structure of industry. Nevertheless, the second oil crisis arose in 1979, and in 1982 the economy, which had begun to improve, once again became sluggish, and the employment situation worsened.

Demands sought by industry and economic organizations, such as the Japan Business Federation (JBF) and the Tokyo Chamber of Commerce, were the reform or flexible application of the Anti-Monopoly Act, and overtures were made to the government, LDP, MITI, and Fair Trade Commission on the issue.[7] However, recognizing that this immediately would be difficult, because those organizations believed that a new law amending and strengthening the Law on Temporary Measures for Stabilization of Specified Depressed Industries should be enacted as a transitional or next best measure, and they were willing to cooperate for its enactment.

---

[7] Industry was unsatisfied with the strictness of conditions needed to be fulfilled for recognition as recession cartels under the Anti-Monopoly Act, and the limits on the rationalized cartels and their areas of use, demanding that it should operate in accordance with actual conditions regarding the requirements for recognition of a recession cartel and its duration, stock ownership, business transfers, mergers, and business alliances etc.

Even though the Law on Temporary Measures for Stabilization of Specified Depressed Industries is exempt from the Anti-Monopoly Act, its original form was inadequate. Therefore, the economic world urged that the proposed new law be not just capable of processing excess facilities but engage in enterprise consolidation (joint purchasing of raw materials, production consignment, and joint sales) based on industry cooperation, and also merger-based industry reshuffling, as a preemptive condition for conducting fundamental structural improvements, while also petitioning the necessity of making these combined actions immune from the Anti-Monopoly Law.

Initially, more so than industry, it was MITI that was positive toward the enactment of a new law (Nihon Keizai Shinbun, December 21, 1982). A senior MITI official urged the enactment of a new law, issuing the following "threat or request" to the leaders of the petrochemical industry, imploring them to support the new law: "If things continue as they are, only one-third of the petrochemical companies would survive, but if a new law is enacted and measures are taken accordingly, the industry as a whole would be able to survive." The petrochemical industry was also vulnerable because of the industry's prolonged recession.

The chairman of the JBF expressed the true feelings held in economic circles, proposing that "flexible application of the Anti-Monopoly Law is needed more than a new law," but then the MITI minister explained the necessity of the new law, and so the chairman reluctantly conceded. From then on, the chairman came to support the new law as "the next best thing."

However, whether the initiative was led by MITI or by industry and the JBF was a delicate matter, as it could not be attributed entirely to either. During this period, the ideas of MITI and the JBF were not that much different. At this point, sectors that desired the extension of the stabilization law (enactment of a new law) in practice were concentrated in the basic materials industry; for instance, aluminum smelting, petrochemicals, and nonferrous metals.

In the aluminum smelting sector, the effect of facility scrapping was not visible because imports exceeded expectations. In the ferroalloy sector, despite facility scrapping, the result was that marginal enterprises were maintained, and the over-competitive nature of the business did not improve. In addition, open-arc furnace and chemical fertilizer industries were very eager for the extension, and the petrochemical and pulp paper sectors desired new applications under a new law.

Meanwhile, the textile industry, including synthetic fibers and cotton spinning, and the shipbuilding industry were reluctant to extend the Law on Temporary Measures for Stabilization of Specified Depressed Industries, even though they were subject to it. Initially, the textile industry surprised interested parties by stating that it no longer wanted to be reliant on this law.

The industry was virtually prohibited from building new equipment under the Law, and production was subject to a recession cartel and coordinated production cutbacks in line with demand forecasts. But in the meantime, the industry was facing fierce competition from South Korea, Taiwan, and other countries, resulting in a decline in international competitiveness.

There was a judgment that it was no longer possible to overcome this problem by adjusting domestic supply and demand alone, but more than that, there was a growing awareness among industry leaders that the cartel structure had become so entrenched that if they remained in the lukewarm grip of the government, "they would never be able to escape from their spoiled structure," leading to declining in international competitiveness.

As international competitiveness was draining away bit by bit, they finally gained the power to debate structural improvements based on self-help measures. If they fell under the jurisdiction of the new law, being unable to purchase new equipment for a period of four years would be disadvantageous for industry.

The year after the Law on Temporary Measures for Stabilization of Specified Depressed Industries expired, the textile industry started planning business partnerships with other companies and increasing equipment purchases with other, mainly major, companies, in an attempt to enter a competitive era based on leveraging technological innovation. During this time, the "Textiles Vision for the '80s" was created in an effort to revitalize the textile industry based on the advice of the Textile Industry Council and the Industry Structure Council. Around this time, industry and companies had begun actively strengthening their international competitiveness and undertaking a technical revolution.

However, as mentioned previously, while the textile industry was initially not proactive toward the new law, after the further worsening of the market, they eventually shifted to a rather tenuous position of becoming involved based on the content.

While these are the trends in various industries, at the Ministerial Meeting on Economic Measures of October 1982, measures to deal with structural recession industries, like the basic materials industry, were included in the general economic measures. Around this time, from about the first half of 1982, MITI became involved in investigating the possibility of a new law to replace the Law on Temporary Measures for Stabilization of Specified Depressed Industries and began informal talks with industry.

5.2 *Enactment of the Law on Temporary Measures for the Structural Improvement of Specified Industries (Structural Improvement Law)*

As noted above, since the aluminum smelting, non-ferrous metals, petrochemical, and other industries were proactive in working toward the enactment of a new act, as a continuance of the Law on Temporary Measures for Stabilization of Specified Depressed Industries, policies for "basic materials industries" were at the forefront. In December 1982, the JBF compiled a set of recommendations titles, "The Importance of the Basic Materials Industries to National Economy," appealing for the reformation of the Anti-Monopoly Law and the enactment of a new law.

Following the enactment of the Structural Improvement Law, MITI defined the basic materials industries as "petrochemical, chemical fertilizer, aluminum, chemical fiber, paper, ferro alloy, and furnace sectors, located in the upper middle of the industry structure, and supplying the raw materials from primary industries upstream for refining and processing." These basic materials industries "have an important role in employment, related small/medium enterprises, regional economy and industry structuring, and taking into consideration the possible new, future developments in developing new materials, their transformation into an economically viable industry and long-term recovery of economic rationalism is desired."

That is, the theory was that structural reform was necessary for policy to reinvigorate the sector, because the basic materials industry was not necessarily a waning industry, but rather had an important future role to play in providing a high quality stable supply of materials to assembly-type industries. Japanese industrial structure was progressive in services, software, and information; however, the manufacturing industry was the basis of the Japanese economy, so in order to facilitate structural adjustment, industry adjustment of structural recession industries was necessary while maintaining a suitable balance between assembly-type industries and high-tech industries. These perceptions were formed by MITI while taking into account the requests of industry and the JBF.

From 1981, working toward the reform of the stabilization Law, MITI began deliberations at the Industrial Structure Council, presenting a final report in December 1982. This report is of enormous significance as it set the direction of the new law, in which the basic principles emphasized were (1) industry's stringent self-help efforts, (2) adherence to the open economy system, (3) temporary nature of the policy, (4) planned implementation according to the mid-/long-term vision, (5) lessening the impact on employment, (6) stabilization of related small-/medium-sized enterprises and the regional economy.

Based on these basic principles, MITI's drafting work was conducted, outlining a direction for industry which made "reduction and revitalization" pivotal—that is to say, facilitating as smooth a reduction as possible through equipment disposal of those sectors, which have no future or prospect of recovery and forfeiting the economic aspects, while simultaneously carrying out revitalization for the industries that had the potential to recover, through cost reduction of raw materials and energy, capital investment, technological development for high value-added, fuel conversion, and business partnerships.

In contrast, with respect to the prerequisite of "lessening the impact on employment and regional economy" and the reduction of inefficiency, the goal was to "aim for gentle employment adjustment," by being mindful of carrying out systematic excess equipment disposal and efforts to secure stable job opportunities through enterprise shift and revitalization.

As described above, the Structural Improvement Law clearly revealed its nature as a "Positive Adjustment Policy (PAP)."

5.3 *Industrial Adjustment for "Changing the Economic Structure"*

The Law on Temporary Measures for the Structural Improvement of Specified Industries was promulgated in May 1983. In the Law on Temporary Measures for Stabilization of Specified Depressed Industries, moves to increase disposal of excess equipment were limited to adjusting the Anti-Monopoly Law (making it an exception to the Anti-Monopoly Law), however, the Law on Temporary Measures for the Structural Improvement of Specified Industries was added to this establishing new regulations related to the business partnerships, including alliances and mergers, to make it possible to streamline costs across corporations. In addition, financial and tax measures were established to promote active investment, resulting in renewed investment to enhance facilities and promote technological development.

As mentioned previously, the government re-emphasized the importance of environmental preparations and support conducive to an autonomous industry response, which was at the core of this law, and it was a view shared by MITI, the council, industry and the corporate sector. Around 1982–1983, the terms, "industrial adjustment" and "aggressive industrial adjustment" were often seen even in Japanese Business Federation (JBF) Documents.

There was a definite learning effect from the time of the Law on Temporary Measures for the Structural Improvement of Specified Industries, and collaboration between the government, MITI, and industry is seen to have increased during the enactment of the Law on Temporary Measures for the Structural Improvement of Specified Industries.

Requests for support in the form of tax incentives and low-interest loans for equipment disposal, tax and financial incentives and other subsidies to promote capital investment and technological development, employment measures, and regional measures were also sought by the industry and JBF.

Around this period, another industry sector, not the JBF, proposed taking measures within Japan like those imposed by the US and the West, such as procedural improvement sanctions like the GATT-recognized safeguards, anti-dumping tariffs, off-set tariffs, conclusion of bilateral agreements (textiles), and application of the tariff quota system (aluminum smelting, etc.), because the proliferation of imports was impeding structural improvements.

However, MITI has indicated that its policy is to promote the international division of labor appropriately on the premise of an open economic system, rather than through protectionist measures such as import restrictions, demanding strict self-help efforts by the private sector. This was positioned as the embodiment of the development of a new industrial policy in the 1980s, along with the development of infrastructure to support advanced technology development.

The evaluation regarding the above is difficult due to ambivalence. There is a view that MITI's emphasis on market functions by introducing the concept of Positive Industry Adjustment Policy (PAP) is only a posture, and that "MITI is also trying to avoid the provocative expression of exempting depressed industries from the Anti-Monopoly Law when consolidating them. Since the Special Measures Law and the current Structural Reconstruction Law has been criticized."

5.4 Employment and Regional Measures

In light of the action by MITI outlined above, the Ministry of Labor began moves toward legal developments regarding the employment aspects. Taking into consideration the long-term recession at the time, the Labor Ministry predicted long-term difficulties, including high unemployment, and thus began working toward revising and strengthening the law.

From 1977 to 1978, the Law on Temporary Measures for the Unemployed in Specified Depressed Industries and the Law on Temporary Measures for Those Unemployed in Specified Regions were set to expire in June 1983, just like the Law on Temporary Measures for the Structural Improvement of Specified Industries. However, the Labor Ministry, aiming to ensure integral, flexible administration of policies regarding recession industries and regions, combined these laws, enacting the Law on Special Measures for Stable Employment in Specified Industries and Regions in July 1983. The content of the new law extended (up to 90 days) employment insurance (Unemployment Insurance), thereby continuing the policies of the previous two laws, while also including new measures such as those outlined below.

The first was the relaxing of the specified industries and regions, accompanied by flexible application. In the past, designation was strictly limited to industries where industrial policies (laws and budgetary measures) were invoked, such as joint disposal of equipment, but the new law removes this condition and allows for flexible designation from the perspective of employment policy.

According to the direction set by the Labor Ministry in discussion with the Central Employment Stability Council, the specification standards of the 1977–1978 recession industry law and recession region law continued to be employed. Furthermore, the specified period for reconsideration was newly set to two years, thereby allowing for reassessment of those sectors whose conditions were improving, and as such, the intention was to make it easier to specify new industries or regions that were even more severely affected by recession.

Under the new law, 34 industries were specified, with some of the original 40 excluded, such as the open-arc furnace sector, which had since died out. In addition to paper, pulp, oil refining, petrochemical, lumber, and cement, which had all been added with the Industry Structure Law, there were some, like the sugar industry, which had been added according to the Labor Ministry's own standards. Although there were originally 51 towns and cities, 39 regions (public employment stability office figures used on principle) were specified, including three new regions: Noshiro (Akita Prefecture), Ohtake (Hiroshima Prefecture), and Aki (Kochi Prefecture).

The second new measure included the expansion and strengthening of the employment adjustment subsidies (a national system to subsidize part of the leave benefits for company employees), which emphasized employment security. When company owners in the specified industries had to fire an employee anew, (1) wages were subsidized for six months in the event that re-employment training was carried out prior to the worker leaving, and (2) if re-employment mediation was carried out, the new employer was entitled to one year of wage subsidies. Moreover, company owners in specified recession regions received benefits for the promotion of regional employment and for ex-workers from specified recession industries, subsidies for re-employment, such as raising the amount of training and employment benefits, were strengthened.

The third new measure was to make countermeasures for subcontractors' ex-workers flexible to use. In the past, extension of employment insurance was not recognized for subcontractor employees, who were fired prior to the specification of the parent company's industry. However, the jurisdiction of the ex-worker policies was broadened to include subsidies for small-/medium-sized subcontracting enterprises in related industries, applied three months retroactively.

The above measures met with approval from industry, the business sector, the labor sector, as well as from the ruling and opposition parties.

Members of the business sector, such as the Japan Business Federation have stated that if the presumption was the maintenance of employment, "flexible, rational wage setting was needed," in line with labor market conditions to avoid cost inflation. The report also states that the employment system needs to be reexamined, along with a review of the wage system (seniority-based wages, etc.) through "labor-management cooperation."

However, in the mid-term, the dire employment situation continued, particularly in the structural recession industries, and the Japan Business Federation was aware that "high rates of unemployment are a concern, given future increasing industrial adjustment and limited economic growth."[8] Since there are limits to the extent that companies can shoulder the burden to maintain employment, there is a need for the government to implement suitable employment policy, such as optimization of the employment insurance system, improved efficiency of the job-training system, recruitment mediation, and income subsidization. In the case of structural recession, for industry companies withdrawing from the sector, there are "withdrawal support policies" which minimize the impact on regional society and employment.

The Japan Business Federation saw the issue of structural recession industries as "an issue to be resolved, while avoiding large societal friction," and believed that "it is essential ...in order to establish a foundation for stable growth of the Japanese economy." Therefore, "the government should also clarify its policy objectives, paying heed to societal friction, ensuring economic stability, long-term supply-and-demand balance, to carry out measures to implement smooth transition and withdrawal, through the efforts of the private sector."[9] What the JBF meant by "societal

[8] Japan Business Federation Economic Research Committee, "Issues for the Japanese Economy in the 1980s: Seeking to Unleash Corporate Vitality and Stable Growth."

[9] Japan Business Federation Economic Research Committee, "The Current State of the Japanese Economy and Mid-term Issues: Aiming to Unleash Corporate Vitality."

friction" is unclear; however, one aspect was the employment issues. The JBF report submitted to the government and LDP (Prime Minister Fukuda and MITI Minister Kawamoto) included employment measures.

Regardless of their stance to date, the opposition party, the Socialist Party, and the workers union were all in agreement with the new law. During the enactment of the Stabilization Law, the Socialist Party raised the issue of bureaucratic control, openly opposing MITI; however, their stance on the Industry Structure law was different. The MITI officials were surprised by the request from the Council of Labor Unions for Policy Promotion to "strengthen guidance and coordination with the Anti-monopoly Law, including regulations on outsiders," and were again surprised when they saw that the Socialist Party, together with the Democratic Socialist Party, had submitted a petition requesting the immediate implementation of the Industrial Structure Council's opinion report, which will serve as the basis for the new law.

As described above, from the Industry Stabilization Law of 1978 to the Structural Improvement Law of 1983, the intents of the basic materials industry and the JBF were strongly represented. But even so, a relatively broad range of industries, opposition parties, and labor unions lent their support, partly because of the consideration of measures for displaced workers.

MITI has taken the initiative in sharing information with the industry and coordinating with the Fair-Trade Commission (FTC) in enacting legislation exempting companies from the Anti-Monopoly Law, and to some extent has succeeded in maintaining its own value as a coordinator.

5.5 Industrial Adjustment Progression

The Structural Improvement Law produced considerable effects from its industrial adjustments. There were active overtures toward corporate restructuring and technological innovations within industry from before the promulgation of the Structural Improvement Law; however, it was the sectors which used the law to take a break from structural improvements that made progress in research and development organization and technological innovation.

In the spinning sector, closures and transitions of small-/medium-sized spinning enterprises continued unabated, while large corporations reduced their spinning departments, transitioned to textiles, and continued updating facilities. The cotton spinning industry filed its first dumping complaint for cotton yarn from South Korea and Pakistan, but no other instances of protectionism were seen.

In Western countries, imports from developing countries, based on the MFA as recognized by the GATT, were regulated to an extent under bilateral agreements, and the industry implored that Japan also undertake MFA bilateral agreements. However, considering the impact on other industries, it was a situation in which the government was unable to make any careless moves. Under these circumstances, the spinning industry was forced to undertake industrial adjustment through their own efforts. In the synthetic fiber industry, there were some instances, albeit limited in number, of restructuring due to the establishment of distributer alliances and groups. Amid this, the textile industry, mainly major spinning corporations and synthetic fiber manufacturers, made progress in new material technological innovations, such as carbon fiber, and attempted to conquer European and Southeast Asian markets.

Even in the petrochemical industry, reorganization, such as grouping, was taking place. Furthermore, each ethylene center corporation competed to introduce linear low-density polyethylene (LLDPE) technology, which used one-quarter of the energy costs required for the existing high-pressure polyethylene technology.

The facility capacity expansion race changed direction, and even in the paper, pulp industries, which were slow to enter the research and development race, there were moves to establish a serious research system to discover breakthrough energy-saving technology. Additionally, there were continual mergers in the paper and pulp industries. Furthermore, even in the cement industry, progress was made in high temperature firing techniques, which sped up the development of high quality, fine ceramics.

As described above, even in the basic materials and other related industries, which had traditionally experienced cut-throat competition over product differentiation, a new way forward materializing from research and development. Subsequently, technological innovation was used to leverage an industry shift, beginning a so-called new material revolution, and entry into the foreign market. Additionally, "technological innovation," "knowledge consolidation," and "service economy" became keywords in the MITI Industry Structure Council report, "Issues in Industry Structure Development of the '80s," presenting a positive outlook on industry structure.

MITI undertook a quantitative analysis of the policy effects of the Stabilization and Industry Structure laws (Okazaki 2012, pp. 43–57). According to which, the benefit of facility processing was seen to vary but had a positive effect on profitability and productivity.

6 Toward the Smooth Transition Law

6.1 Enactment of the Smooth Transition Law

With the expiration of the Structural Improvement Law of 1983, the Act on Temporary Measures for Facilitating Industrial Structure Transformation (Smooth Transition Law) was enacted in May 1987 as a temporary legislation for nine years until 1996, succeeding the Structural Improvement Law.

Developments such as the rapid appreciation of the yen, which triggered the Plaza Accord of '85 and the structural adjustment of the export industry were background to the enactment. Moreover, the "Maekawa Report" indicated the necessity of a shift to internationally coordinated industrial adjustment as a response to the trade imbalances that became prominent in the first half of the '80s. In December 1986, the

Industrial Structure Council report, "Development of practical measures for Industry Structure Adjustment," exhibited a pro-Smooth Transition Law direction.

The Smooth Transition Law, like the Structural Improvement Law, was a legislative means of conducting industrial adjustment; however, the former is characterized as emphasizing the measures to support the structural industry transition through market mechanisms even more than the latter did.

The law is comprised of two main tenets, measures for specified industries and measures for specified regions.

Since measures for specified industries were support measures, such as tax incentives and low-interest loans for facility processing and corporate shift/diversification, to save industries troubled by oversupply, an expanded industry infrastructure fund, "Industrial Structure Improvement Fund," was established. Twenty-five types of production facilities, including cement, steel, and textile, received designation as facilities specified for disposal.

Under the measures for specified regions, regions and industries with declining production and employment were recognized as "specified regions" and "specified enterprises," receiving support in terms of equity and debt guarantee from the Industrial Structure Improvement Fund, and low-interest loans from the Development Bank of Japan. Fifty-one regions were designated as specified regions. Nippon Steel's "Space World" in Kita-Kyushu and "Canadian World" in Hokkaido are two of the regional projects that were recognized under the Smooth Transition Law.

6.2 Industrial Reorganization Under the Smooth Transition Law

Under the Smooth Transition Law framework, reorganization of industry, companies and regions were undertaken from the end of the 1980s to the 1990s. The main target of Smooth Transition Law policy was said to be companies that were dealt a blow from appreciation of the yen; however, in reality, typical industries, like the automobile industry, which suffered under the strong yen, overcame the effects of the recession by their own efforts (passing the effects on to subcontractors).

Only a limited number of industries, such as the cement industry, took advantage of the Smooth Transition Law. The cement industry in 1987 was suffering from a chronic oversupply, then imports increased due to the strong yen, and there was a sense of crisis in the industry that the market could suffer further stagnation. Up until that point, there had been around 23 companies in the cement industry; however, there was already fierce competition due to the difficulty of product diversification in the industry. For this reason, the industry applied for specification under the Smooth Transition Law, in order to review the production system. However, after this, building demand grew in the bubble era, and since imports failed to increase as predicted, the domestic cement market subsequently increased. As such, in some respects, each company felt hobbled by the law.

The reorganization of the cement industry before and after the Smooth Transition Law was as follows.[10] Under the Structural Improvement Law and the Smooth Transition Law, the cement industry facilitated grouping and alliances between recession cartels and structure improvement enterprises three times and destroyed 30% of facilities under the Smooth Transition Law. Then, in 1991, after the Smooth Transition Law specification had been lifted, major corporate reorganizations took place in the form of continued large-scale mergers. The lifting of specifications meant the end of the incentive measures; however, instead they were able to freely engage in activities such as facility expansion. The five groups formed under the Smooth Transition Law were disbanded, while alliances and mergers continued. In particular, the formation in October 1998 of the Taiheiyo Cement Corporation ("Pacific Ocean Cement Corporation"), through the merger between Chichibu Onoda and Nihon Cement, created the company with the number one share domestically and the number two position world-wide, and a prominent example of a large-scale merger.

As described above, essentially, the cement industry underwent processing of excess facilities and grouping (large-scale mergers and cooperative sales), then the Smooth Transition Law measures ended, along with the industry adjustment policies.

In 1991, when the cement industry became unspecified, there were apparently discussions, even within MITI; however, the solution that was decided upon was that "increased demand due to the improved economy caused a positive shift in the management environment." There has been criticism and indications that the Smooth Transition Law's cooperative sales system had become a hotbed of unauthorized cartels from previous years. In addition, there were measures in the Japan-US Structural Impediments Initiative to deal with calls from the US to disband the cartel structures. Yet MITI said it would continue to provide administrative guidance to prevent excessive competition.

Furthermore, one could say that the mergers and reorganization of the cement industry reflected the intentions of the Fair-Trade Commission and MITI which demand to break out of the cooperative sales-based cartels. The merger between Mitsubishi Materials Corporation and Tohoku Development was an example of this.

As mentioned above, while the cement industry was reorganizing domestically, some companies were expanding overseas. In 1988, Onoda Cement was one of the first in the industry to enter the US market, buying the cement division of construction materials manufacturer, CalMat Co. (California). From 1992, Onoda Cement was running its own plant in China and carrying out production in joint ventures.

The only other industry to use the Smooth Transition Law to reorganize was the liquefied oxygen industry. Liquefied oxygen was struggling, not just from the effects of the post-Plaza Accord's rapid appreciation of the yen to its major demand industries, steel and shipbuilding but also because its other enterprises, nitrogen gas, and semi-conductors were also in semi-recession. Against this background, the liquefied oxygen industry became specified in October 1987, and until January

[10] Below, the description on industry restructuring is based on the website of the Cement Association etc.

1990, received approval for two business partnership plans and five business adaption plans to carry out facilities processing. Due to these equipment investment restrictions, excess competition had weakened and circumstances in the industry had improved. One example of a merger/reorganization is the January 1990 establishment of New Sagamihara Oxygen from the merger between Sagamihara Oxygen and Sanyo Oxygen.

In 1987, the same year that the Smooth Transition Law was enacted, the Law for the Promotion of Regional Employment Development was also enacted.

This involved measures to specify regions burdened with many structural recession industries due to yen appreciation and (1) provide subsidies to corporations in order to encourage the re-employment of middle-aged and older employees, and (2) cover some of the financial burden regarding corporate employment adjustment grants, such as temporary leave. Moreover, in April 1988 the government revised the Law on Temporary Measures Concerning Stabilization of Employment in Specified Depressed Industries, extending its term by seven years to June 1995. As outlined above, until the early 1990s, the employment measures and regional measures of the original industry adjustment policy were still being upheld to some extent.

"History of International Trade and Industrial Policy" analyzes policy efficacy, focusing on the effects of designation of specified regions due to the small number of cases of businesses specified under the Smooth Transition Law (Okazaki 2012, pp.70–73). Even here, the Smooth Transition Law is evaluated as having had an effect of increasing employment and production in the regions.

7 After the Demise of the Smooth Transition Law

7.1 From "Industrial Adjustment Policy" to "Industrial Revival Policy"

When the Smooth Transition Law was nearing its expiration in May 1996, there was a range of opinions within MITI; however, the law was essentially seen to have served its purpose and expired without extension. Nevertheless, as mentioned at the beginning, as one of the pillars of the Smooth Transition Law, the business measures still exist under another law with a different name.

After the Industry Innovation Law of 1995, the next was the 1999 Law on Special Measures for Industrial Revitalization; this was then extended in 2003 and 2007, before being revised in April 2009, with its name changed to Law on Special Measures concerning Industrial Revitalization and Innovation of Industrial Activities. In accordance with the Law, the "Restructuring Plan" for each company was formulated and personnel reductions were being made based on this plan. In January 2014, Act on Strengthening Industrial Competitiveness was enacted, subsuming the Revitalization Law.

The purpose of these laws is said to have been to improve the productivity and revitalization of the Japanese economy by taking measures to facilitate business-instigated rebuilding projects and revitalization, while being mindful of employment stability. The aim was to revive the Japanese economy through effective utilization of resources in economic society as a whole. In order to promote the revitalization of the "Revitalizing the Functioning of Industrial Activities," supportive policies, such as tax incentives and financial support measures for recognized activities, are being carried out by the Industry Revitalization Organization (from 2003 to 2007, and then by the revised Industry Innovation Organization from 2009). As illustrated here, elements of the original industrial adjustment are being partially maintained.

Furthermore, from the 1990s, rather than industrial adjustment, an even more aggressive "industry revival" policy came to the forefront. The main policy content involved the promotion of structural reform, through deregulation and so forth, in order to create new industry growth areas. In relation to this, industrial organization policies (including easing of restrictions on pure holding companies due to the revision of the Anti-Monopoly Law in 1997, reviewing large corporate stock holding regulations, and revision of the merger and split-up regulations due to the commercial law revision) to reduce the difficulty of industry reorganization, business reorganization, and reorganization of corporate structure were carried out successively. In December 1999, the Civil Rehabilitation Law was established to support rapid rebuilding and facilitate bankruptcy procedures for small/medium businesses, and various types of insolvency laws were revised and improved upon, such as the Corporate Rehabilitation Law.

As illustrated by these law reforms, the policy view of the Ministry of Economy, Trade and Industry (METI), shifted to emphasizing facilities for progressing the restructuring measures carried out according to corporate initiative, changing from measures for individual companies to a cross-sectional industry policy. In terms of emphasizing corporate initiative, this kind of policy system became the foundation upon which the aforementioned measures, such as the Industry Revitalization Law, were built.

Economic policies from the 1990s onwards are generally considered to show increased Prime Ministerial initiatives, particularly with respect to industry, as the Industrial Competitiveness Council, which was organized under the umbrella of the Japanese Economy Revival Headquarters set up in the Cabinet Office, took on a leadership position. The council is comprised of the Prime Minister and other cabinet ministers; MITI bureaucrats are also involved.

For example, at the time of the first meeting in March 1999, it was reported that "Even reaching this Industrial Competitiveness Council, a scenario was drawn up in which companies would appeal for the disposal of excess facilities, and tax and financial incentives would be given to those companies that comply with this appeal. In the Industrial Revitalization Bill being considered by MITI, it appears that there is a plan to compile disposal plans for individual industries and to force individual companies to submit management structure reform plans."

These traditional "disposal of excess facilities"-type orthodox policies plied by MITI (METI), which were not realized as is, continue directly and indirectly as individual industrial reorganization policy interventions. For example, METI's "Survey Report on Petrochemical Industry Structure (Survey Report based on Article 50 of the Industrial Competitiveness Enhancement Act)" (November 2014) outlines policy intervention regarding petrochemical industry market structure. In addition, METI also promoted mergers and consolidations in the oil industry. From 2012 to 2013, the Renesas Electronics Corporation was one example of a bailout in the semi-conductor industry. It is thought that concern over "the collapse of Japan's manufacturing base," caused by the flow of Japanese technology into overseas hands as a result of foreign funding, was behind METI's final decision on the issue.

Industry reorganization from the 1990s was unlike the previously seen post-war industrial adjustment policies based on government guidance "adjustment" models; it had the appearance of company-led, "industry-use" reorganization, which nevertheless included aspects of cabinet and prime minister leadership. In that sense, MITI/METI industry interventions still continued despite becoming localized.

Post-1990s, the policy system shifted toward trusting and utilizing market mechanisms as a whole. On the premise of using market mechanisms, a consensus was formed to identify which areas should undergo policy interventions. Of these, industry revival policies aiming to improve productivity and ensure smooth transition of industry structure were determined to be necessary policies for the resurgence of the Japanese economy. In other words, a new type of industrial policy—that is to say, a strategic industrial policy—incorporating a globally competitive perspective is being formed. Thus, as outlined above, "industrial adjustment policy" was transformed into "industrial revival policy."

Meanwhile, although there were regional calls for the continuation of the Smooth Transition Law, with respect to the structural shift of industrial cluster regions where manufacturing was concentrated, regional measures only went so far as changing to a specified industry cluster utilization loans system.

7.2 The Labor Market and Regional Reorganization After the 1990s

As described above, during the 1990s, large-scale reorganization occurred in some industries and employment adjustments progressed.

One of the background influences for this was the effect of the unified stance from industry on government policy. In May 1995, the then Japan Federation of Employers' Associations (which was later absorbed by the current Japan Business Federation in May 2002) published the report "Japanese Management for the Current Era: Directions to Aim for and Relevant Practical Measures" proposing a partial review of lifelong employment and the seniority system. Specifically, implementation of an efficient employment portfolio combined three types of employment, namely long-term accumulation capacity utilization model, highly specialized capacity utilization model, and flexible employment model, as well as implementation of a vocational qualifications system and a review of the seniority-based regular pay system. After the demise of the bubble economy, a reduction in wages and labor costs was pursued in order to escape the so-called three excesses (employment, facilities, and liabilities); however, this was said to be a trigger for the rapid mobilization of employment that followed. Around this time, labor deregulation progressed and employment mobilization was pursued under various amendments to the Worker Dispatch Act, the result of which is well known: high rates of non-regular employment.

However, the RENGO Soken (JTUC Research Institute for Advancement of Living Standards) Report featured a special edition entitled, "20 Years After the New Era of Japanese Management," which according to the recollection of a former executive chairman of the Japan Federation of Employers' Associations, stated that the report was well-received as in expressing a different direction to that of the Japan Federation of Employers' Association.

As far as the Japan Federation of Employers' Associations was concerned, it had intended to propose maintaining the good aspects of Japanese management while reorganizing the excessive portion. Yet, as a result, the worsening of the employment situation in the 1990s is said to be caused by worsening of the economic situation beyond projections due to the effects of yen appreciation (global competition), improper management of exchange rates by government monetary policy, and the Lehman shock. Moreover, since the mobilization of the workforce exceeded expectations, they were forced to be concerned about "employment degradation." These were comments made at the labor union (JTUC-RENGO; Japanese Trade Union Confederation), and given that at the time, the Japan Federation of Employers' Associations and the Labor Union had many opportunities to cooperate on proposals, one can assume that this is the truth.

At any rate, the employment situation deteriorated significantly, especially for certain groups. The labor share (total wages (W)/total value added (Y)) declined from the 1990s to the 2000s.

There are various theories regarding the indexes and measurement methods for the labor share, and there are several series of numerical data, however, the prevailing view is that despite being stable in the 1990s (some say it increased due to rising labor costs), it has declined since the 2000s (although it varies by period) as a result of employment adjustment in the 1990s and the rise in the unemployment rate. The most common view is that the labor share declined since the 2000s (although it varies from period to period).

Against the background of increased mobilization of employment and increased numbers of non-regular employee is a declining trend for the number of people joining the labor unions. Immediately after World War II, the percentage of total workers who were union members (proportion of organized workers) was over 50%; however, in the latter half of the 2000s, the figure had fallen to 18%. Subsequently, the Abe cabinet announced a "policy shift from an employment maintenance model to a labor mobility support model," as part of the 2013 Japan is Back (Japan Revitalization) Strategy.

Up until this point, the Employment Adjustment Subsidy System, established by the former labor ministry, had to a certain extent maintained progressive employment adjustment in Japan. This same system was designed to protect the wages/employment of workers in businesses forced into downsizing through recession, etc. In the case of businesses conducting temporary closures, training, or temporary loaning of employees, the government would subsidize some businesses with respect to wages and leave allowances, to prevent serious unemployment such as dismissal or early retirement. For small/medium sized businesses, there was an employment stabilization subsidy system, with expanded measures. Originally, it was industry-specific; however, with the 2001 revision, it became available for use regardless of industry.

Then, in 2008, in the wake of the rapid increase in dismissals and employment stoppages due to the Lehman shock, the government significantly relaxed employment adjustment subsidy requirements and raised the subsidy rate in order to prevent further worsening of employment. In December of the same year, the emergency employment stabilization subsidy for small-/medium-sized businesses was established anew.

However, against the background of some improvement, in the 2014 budget, the Ministry of Health, Labor and Welfare reduced employment adjustment subsidies, greatly increased labor mobility subsidies in the regions, and also made the system applicable to large corporations. The labor mobility subsidies were not just applicable to "business scale (business activity) downsizing" but also in the case of "business shift (shift/reorganization)." Subsidies were paid to employment introduction services providing re-employment support for workers forced into unemployment and to business owners who offered paid leave to those searching for work. This is said to have raised concerns regarding promotion of restructuring through the use of eviction posts (positions to which workers are promoted to force them to leave employment voluntarily) in large corporations.

The following quote is from an article about MITI's consideration of the aforementioned Industry Revitalization Law, published in the *Nihon Keizai Shimbun* (May 7, 1999).

> So, what do people with job insecurity due to disposal of facilities think? The government chants the mantra of creating new businesses, strengthening vocational training, and mobilization of the labor force through elimination of mismatches, but how much actual employment effect is there? Those bureaucrats who really honestly think that these constitute employment measures should definitely quit their job and try searching for employment.
>
> The best employment measure is for businesses to retain as many employees as possible, even when is difficult. Lower wages, business spin-offs, reshuffling, temporary transfers, whatever it takes, just do not throw them out on the streets. It would be better if more employers thought like this.
>
> However, there is an opinion within the Industrial Competitiveness Council to abolish the employment adjustment subsidies, which amounted to only 61.1 billion yen in the FY99 budget, on the grounds that it would hinder the mobility of the labor force. Instead, it would be better to raise it to around 1 trillion JPY.

> Without employment, there is no economy. The Japanese economy has overcome hardships this way numerous times.

It is somewhat surprising to see this kind of an article in the *Nihon Keizai Shinbun*. However, this criticism is not just leveled at economy bureaucrats but also at many politicians and members of the public.

Labor aspects came to be characterized by market principles after the 1990s; however, when government policy planners lack understanding of and empathy toward the associated problems, the effects of policy are called into question and are less convincing.

METI had awareness of the difficulties of employment adjustment and the resultant societal friction, showing a commitment, especially during the recession era, to plan and implement a range of economic policy. METI bureaucrats are well aware that labor (employment) adjustment, by its very nature, is a significantly more difficult issue than investment (facilities) adjustment. Nevertheless, the labor law and employment adjustment subsidy systems are largely outside of METI jurisdiction, and the policy stance of METI is that what they are capable of doing is contributing to the creation of new employment opportunities.

Additionally, on a fundamental level, the key to the societal issues of industrial adjustment/employment adjustment are to be found in resolution of the mismatch between labor market facilities and the labor market; however, this is a problem that requires a long-term commitment, such as human resource development, including education, and skill development. This exceeds the mandate of METI and is an issue that should be dealt with by Japan as whole.

8 Conclusion

The following is a summary of the issues presented in this chapter.

Firstly, the measures which fit the description of "industrial adjustment policy," focusing on the textiles and coal in 1950s and 1960s, the Stability Law of the 1970s, the '80s Structural Improvement Law and Smooth Transition Law, chronologically, as well as MITI's policy intentions (developments and background) as well as the stakeholders involved in the policy formation process were examined.

Individual industry measures for textile and coal exhibited numerous conceptual differences with the subsequently enacted Stabilization Law on one hand, while also sharing some aspects; thus, grasping and clearly expressing an overall understanding of the essential elements in terms of "industrial adjustment policy" is difficult. Nevertheless, it can be explained hypothetically as follows.

The first element is interventions to adjust supply-and-demand, where industry producers and facilities cartels are on the receiving end of government (MITI) support and MITI plays the role of adjuster, in coordination with the Fair Trade Commission. The target of supply-and-demand interventions are basically industries which are worthy of continuing to exist or produce in some form, cases where the private sector is not capable of resolving overproduction/excess facilities or the facility disposal costs are exceedingly high. Government policy's fiscal and financial assistance contributes to improvements in corporate profits, which is indirectly connected to regeneration of the industry concerned or industry transformation. Within industrial adjustment, the aspect of industrial transformation was initially only included in some policy, however, after the 1990s, the focus on industry transformation and the creation of new industries increased. "industry adjustment policy" was reincarnated as "industry regeneration policy."

If only this first element is extracted, it would be possible to gauge and evaluate, to a certain extent, the economic purpose and efficacy of industrial adjustment policy. The analysis and evaluation of industrial adjustment policy, after the enactment of the Stabilization Law from an economic viewpoint by Okazaki (2012) was as presented in this chapter. However, when viewed overall, it is not sufficiently clear what MITI and METI's own summary of "industrial adjustment policy" is.

The second element is the alleviation of industrial adjustment-induced societal friction. This involves government factors, labor policy, and social policy, which cannot be dealt with solely in terms of economic rationalism; however, taking a mid-/long-term view, it can be seen to be a contributing factor in reducing business adjustment costs. Again, in terms of a national economy perspective, the social consensus to avoid placing a heavy burden on just some of the working class could be considered to have been related to the subsequent stable growth of the Japanese economy. In this sense at least, it cannot be said to lack economic rationality.

As described above, in terms of the implementation of industrial adjustment policy, with its complex and multi-faceted nature, MITI (METI) is thought to have acted as the administrative headquarters, paying heed to a multitude of related aspects, accurately carrying out the role of coordinator. In particular, in sectors involving regional economies and small/medium corporations, such as coal and textiles, it played the role of paternalistic guide, yet, in international trade matters, it held a strategic position, keeping a mid-/long-term view and coordinating between industries to a certain extent.

In this sense, MITI could be broadly said to have been a supporter of industrial adjustment policy. MITI (METI) held the view that it was less about remedies for individual industries than about promoting a steady economic recovery in the midst of a difficult international environment, securing stable employment, the huge overarching goal and justification of continuing industrial adjustment/structural adjustment to place the Japanese economy on track to continued stable economic growth.

From around the time of the enactment of the Stabilization Law, there was high involvement by the business world, such as the Japan Business Federation, in government policymaking, and from the 1970s–1980s, there were considerable labor and regional concerns, and it appears that MITI consulted with the Ministry of Labor to carry out policy paying heed to a variety of aspects. However, during the period after the industrial regeneration of the 1990s, the voices of business and larger corporations increased even more, and policy steered toward overemphasizing the supply side.

After the 1990s, it is possible to determine to a certain extent that MITI and other regulatory agencies were continuing to carry out industrial/corporate reorganization sporadically, while traditional industrial adjustment policy had met its demise. Meanwhile, the "market utilization model" of labor was emphasized excessively and substantially implemented. Disparity reduction policies complementing market principles were scaled back and coupled with cuts to other social security policies, promoted the deterioration of the nation's labor and lifestyle and the intent in this chapter is not to argue that traditional industrial adjustment in which various aims and measures are combined and criticized domestic and internationally for being "controlling," and "opaque," should be reinstated out of nostalgic interest.

Rather, it would be desirable that undifferentiated aims and methods were refined, industry and business policies were clearly separated from labor and regional policies, and the stance was based on market principles. However, the question is the nature of this process, where the latter retreats and the former alone moves forward as a growth strategy. In industrial adjustment, business and labor are two wheels of the same car, thus the necessity of taking a mid-/long-term view and considering policy in order to get on the path to stable economic growth.

Post-war, the main targets of the industrial adjustment policy were industries such as textiles, coal, and basic materials, but by the beginning of the 1990s, almost all had finished the adjustment process, and the demise of industrial adjustment policy at the beginning of the '90s was perhaps natural.

Moreover, the pace of adjustment was originally rapid, that is, it was a period when economic growth was high, like during the post-war recovery period to the high-growth period, the oil shock of the '70s, or the rapid appreciation of the yen during the mid '80s. It was a short period when a large supply-and-demand gap arose, and policy support for industrial adjustment was carried out in difficult circumstances to ensure smooth adjustment of business and labor. Therefore, with the downturn in the growth rate, during the "lost 10–20 years," industrial adjustment policy could be thought of as being unnecessary.

However, considering the process to adjust the "excess," after the collapse of the bubble economy, especially the situation of electrical industry restructuring, financing/securities, and the building industry, even though the target industries had changed, one could not say that the necessity of policy support had disappeared. Despite this, there are many reasons why traditional industrial adjustment policy was not implemented, such as after the 1980s–90s; (1) opaque industrial policies faced criticism at home and abroad,[11] (2) prior to the 1990s, government finance was still secure, (3) MITI (METI) had changed the rationale behind its policy (the background here was the economist model, the number of neo-classical economics adherents in the bureaucracy had increased), (4) demands and pressure from industry (e.g., Japan Business Federation) were changed to a direction different to industrial adjustment

[11] Particularly the influence of anti-Japanese criticism from the US at the Japan-US Structural Talks was profound. In this chapter, little mention has been made of international aspects, such as US criticism of Japanese economic policy, however, it was one of the major issues to be considered as a background to industrial adjustment policy changes.

policy, (5) the number of organized workers had declined, due to structural changes to industry and work, and (6) it had become difficult for the voices of workers to reach the policy makers.

With the collapse of the bubble economy and the recession of the Heisei Era, the structural transition period approached, and from the 1990s, in a sense, almost all industries have become "losers." Meanwhile, one could say that, due to the government's deficit, there was a lack of financial resources available for industrial adjustment policy and policy measures. In any case, as outlined above, in order to avoid a fallacy of composition, there is a renewed necessity for a national consensus, including the working class, regarding reconsideration of policy roles and systems/policy design.

References

Morikawa M (2013) 'Business Restructuring of Japanese Firms: Structural Changes during the "Lost Decades,"' RIETI Discussion Paper Series, 13-E-083.

Odaka K (Tsūshō Sangō Seisaku-shi Hensan Iinkai [Committee for the Compilation of the History of International Trade and Industrial Policy] ed.) (2013) *Tsūshō Sangyō Seisaku-shi: 1980–2000 (1) Sōron [History of International Trade and Industrial Policy: 1980–2000 (1): General Remarks*]. Keizai Sangō Chōsakai, Tokyo.

Okazaki T (Tsūshō Sangō Seisaku-shi Hensan Iinkai [Committee for the Compilation of the History of International Trade and Industrial Policy] ed.) (2012) *Tsūshō Sangyō Seisaku-shi: 1980–2000 (3) Sanghō Seisaku [History of International Trade and Industrial Policy: 1980–2000 (3): Industrial Policy*]. Keizai Sangō Chōsakai, Tokyo.

Sawaki K (2007) 'Seisaku no Chō-ki Keizoku ni kansuru Youin Bunseki: Nihon no Sekitan Kogyō wo meguru Seisaku Katei wo Sozai-ni' [An Analysis of Factors Related to the Long-Term Continuity of Policy: A Case Study of the Japanese Coal Mining Industry] Tokyo Daigaku Sentan-ken Sentan Kokyō Seisaku Kenkyu-kai Series [Research Center for Advanced Science and Technology, The University of Tokyo. Advanced Public Policy Workshop Series], Vol. 1.

Shigen Enerugi Chō Shigen Nenryō-bu Sekitan-ka Kansyu / Sekitan Seisakushi Hensan Iinkai (ed.) (2002) [Coal Miming Policy History Editorial Committee (ed.); editorial supervision by Agency of Natural Resources and Energy]. *Sekitan Seisaku-shi. [Hintory of Coal Minig Policy*].

Takeda H (2016) 'Seiki Tenkan-ki ni okeru Tsushō-Sangyō, Keizai-Sangyo Seisaku no Tenkan' [Transformation of Trade, Industry, and Economic and Industrial Policy at the Turn of the Century]. RIETI Discussion Paper Series 16-J-026. https://www.rieti.go.jp/jp/publications/dp/16j026.pdf

Watanabe J (2008) 'Tsusanshō no Jukyū Chōsei Seisaku: Sen-i Sangyō no Jirei' [Supply and Demand Adjustment Policy by MITI: the Case of Textile Industry]. Kyoto University Working Paper, J-69.

Watanabe J (2010) *Sangyō Hatten Suitai no Keizaisi: Jūdai bo no Keisei to Sangyō Chosei. [History of Industrial Development and Declining: Japanese Cotton Textile Companies and Their Adjustment Process*]. Tokyo: Yuhikaku.

Junko Watanabe is Professor of Economic History at Kyoto University and Faculty Fellow at RIETI. She has been involved in research on the economic policy history of MITI/METI for many years and has conducted numerous interviews with bureaucrats. She has also conducted research on pre- and postwar Sumitomo Group and history of industry such as textile, coal mining and others.

The Industrial Revitalization Policy in the 2000s

Junko Watanabe

Abstract This chapter analyzes the policy formation process of the industrial revitalization policy implemented by the METI, which aimed to help companies promote restructuring and eventually to improve the international competitiveness of Japanese industries. The features revealed by the analysis are as follows. (1) In the process from the enactment of the law in 1999 to its revision in 2003, the "integrated revitalization of finance and industry" became an issue for the Japanese economy. It reflected the thought of policymakers from METI and business leaders, who had a sense of crisis that there were few counter measures for industries and companies, while measures to deal with the financial sector had proceeded. (2) When the issue of non-performing loans was settled in the mid-2000s, the priority of the industrial revitalization policy shifted toward institutional design for the formation of the Japanese business revitalization markets and innovation systems. Emphasis was placed on expanding the systems related to voluntary liquidations and bankruptcy legislation, and to new business creation measures. The method of increasing productivity through moving and revitalizing management resources is one of the sources of economic growth. The revision of the law in 2007 and 2009 can be interpreted from the above perspective.

1 Introduction

[1]This chapter clarifies the policy-making process of the Industrial Revitalization Policy implemented by the Japanese Ministry of Economy, Trade and Industry (MITI) from the end of the 1990s to the mid-2000s. After Japan's bubble economy burst,

[1] The original discussion paper is given below, but is revised and summarized as necessary for this book. The sources cited and contents of the interviews are diverse. Therefore, to avoid complication, the citations in this chapter have been kept to a minimum. Interested parties should refer to the following discussion paper for more details. Watanabe and Takeda (2021) 'Nisen-nendai no Sangyo Saisei Seisaku' [Industrial Revitalization Policies in the 2000s] RIETI Discussion Paper Series 21-J-030. https://www.rieti.go.jp/jp/publications/dp/21j030.pdf.

J. Watanabe (✉)
Kyoto University, Kyoto, Japan

H. Takeda and J. Watanabe (eds.), *Rethinking Japanese economic policy at the turn of the 21st century*, Advances in Japanese Business and Economics 34,
https://doi.org/10.1007/978-981-97-5512-7_4

industrial reconstruction became one of the central issues of Japanese economy in connection with the problem of non-performing loans of financial institutions and measures against deflation. The industrial reconstruction policy aimed to eliminate the "three excesses" of equipment, debt, and employment when the bubble economy came to an abrupt end, and to promote business restructuring with methods such as the "selection and concentration" of companies, which in turn would improve the international competitiveness of Japanese industry.

The industrial reconstruction policy started when the Industrial Revitalization Special Measures Law (hereinafter abbreviated to Industrial Revitalization Law) was passed in August 1999 and continued until it was abolished in January 2014. However, policy after the mid-2000s concentrated on industrial competitiveness; when the Act on Strengthening Industrial Competitiveness enacted in December 2013 it effectively inherited the function of the Industrial Revitalization Law.

The industrial reconstruction policy up to the end of 2000 was prescribed by Okazaki (2012), but no historical analysis has yet been edited or published regarding the records of this policy post-2001. A relevant study was conducted by Ishiguro (2003), a policymaker at the Ministry of Economy, Trade, and Industry (METI), where the background, purpose, content, and achievements of the revised 2003 law, including the situation of the Japanese economy, industry, and companies at that time, were discussed.

In this chapter, in addition to using publicly available material, interviews were conducted with policymakers who were involved at the time to understand the internal discussions and policy ideas.[2] The analytical viewpoints are as follows.

First, the scope of what can be viewed as an industrial revitalization policy is not limited to METI's measures but also covers developments in the Japanese economy, including the financial sector. "Financial revitalization," which includes the disposal of non-performing loans and the reorganization of the financial system, and "industrial revitalization," which includes the elimination of excess debt of companies and the promotion of business restructuring, are two sides of the same coin, as shown by the use of the term "finance-industry integrated revitalization" at the time.

Second, policymaking systems and policy management since the 2000s have had different characteristics than before. Since the 2000s, the industrial revitalization policy was carried out under "government-led" decision-making that included the Prime Minister's private advisory bodies, the Economic Strategy Council, the Industrial Competitiveness Council, and the Council on Economic and Fiscal Policy. The use of schemes such as the Industrial Revitalization Corporation of Japan (IRCJ), a public–private fund, was also introduced for the first time. These measures are

[2] The materials used are wide ranging and include a large number of articles in the Nihon Keizai Shimbun, but citation notes have been omitted in this chapter because all the references are only available in Japanese. See Watanabe and Takeda (2021), the source for this chapter, for more information. We would also like to extend our thanks to Norihiko Ishiguro, Daisuke Koriya, Masayuki Morikawa, Keita Nishiyama, Kazuhiro Wakatsuki, Ryuichi Yamashita, and Yutaka Yoshimoto (former policymakers affiliated to MITI/METI, in alphabetical order, titles omitted) for their collaboration with the interviews.

similar in that they utilized the vitality of the private sector and that other ministries and agencies were also involved in a coordination and collaboration capacity.

At the time of the reorganization of ministries and agencies in 2001, the Ministry of Economy, Trade, and Industry established the Economic and Industrial Policy Bureau with the aim of "promoting economic structural reform in consideration, not only of the industrial side, but also of the economic structure itself from both macro and micro perspectives." Policymakers have since been advancing institutional designs related to the utilization of market mechanisms not only at the abstract level of economic theory, but also in practice, and within such this policy stance, industrial revitalization policy expanded into being part of the economic structural reform.

When the disposal of non-performing loans was completed in the mid-2000s, the industrial revilalization policy thereafter shifted to a more universal system designed to create an innovation system and/or a turnaround market, focusing on expanding the voluntary liquidation system related to bankruptcy legislation (legal liquidation) and policies for creating new businesses. Methods of improving productivity included moving and utilizing management resources by business unit are a source of economic growth. The revisions to the Industrial Revitalization Law of 2007 and 2009 can also be seen from the above perspectives.

This chapter is structured as follows. In Sect. 2, the policy-making process leading up to the enactment of the Industrial Revitalization Law is traced. In Sect. 3, the content and effects of the law are examined. In Sect. 4, the policy-making process leading to the revision of the law in April 2003 is analyzed.

In the government's comprehensive deflationary measures of October 2002, a new proposal to establish the IRCJ based on the "integrated revitalization of finance and industry" policies emerged and it was packaged with the Industrial Revitalization Law, which was then about to be revised. In Sect. 5, the 2003 amendments to the law and the operation of the IRCJ are discussed. In Sect. 6, the prospects after the revision of the law in 2007 and 2009 are described. Finally, this chapter's findings are summarized.

2 Process of Enactment of the 1999 Industrial Revitalization Law

2.1 Japanese Economy at the End of the 1990s

At the end of the 1990s, due to the Asian currency crisis and Japan's financial system crisis following the fall of 1997, the Japanese economy was suffering from worsening deflation. The financial crisis also affected the production and employment sides of the business sector, which mentally depressed the households and businesses. The economic depression continued to deepen through a vicious cycle of weaker private demand. The real gross domestic product (GDP) growth in 1997 was the first negative value in 23 years since the oil crisis in the 1970s. The Japanese economy was in a difficult situation where negative growth was expected for the second consecutive year in 1998.

Ryutaro Hashimoto's cabinet had implemented several emergency economic measures to stimulate demand, but Keizo Obuchi, who had become prime minister in July 1998, prioritized the "Revitalization of the Japanese Economy."

2.2 Prime Minister Obuchi's Economic Revitalization Plan

In August 1998, Prime Minister Obuchi, as a measure to revitalize the Japanese economy, appointed the Economic Strategy Council, an advisory body under the direct control of the Prime Minister that was modeled after the Council of Economic Advisers of the United States. This council considered various recovery and revitalization measures for the Japanese economy in the short term as well as in medium- to long-term. Their mission was to examine economic and social structures in the twenty-first century and to express their opinions. The council was represented by members of both the business and academic communities.

During a meeting in September, Prime Minister Obuchi, as part of the revitalization measures for the Japanese economy, announced the "living space doubling strategic plan," a policy aimed at creating more living space for citizens, and the "industrial revitalization plan," a policy with the development of new businesses and the creation of new employment opportunities as its fundamental pillars. By presenting a vision of a "rich society," the aim was to eliminate the psychological deflationary factors within the Japanese economy and to create a catalyst for economic stimulation.

The outline of the plan that was being considered at this point was strongly associated with conventional economic measures: (1) support for opening and growing new businesses, (2) industrial revitalization centered on existing companies and support for in-house entrepreneurship, (3) deregulation and technological development in fields expected to show future growth, such as medical/welfare, distribution/logistics, biotechnology, aerospace, and housing, and (4) the facilitation of personnel transfer. After that, the Economic Strategy Council also discussed the industrial revitalization plan, but its content was limited to advocating employment measures such as unemployment insurance and the expansion of the skills training system and new-business support measures for small- and medium-sized enterprises (SMEs). The government intended to implement these measures as part of its stimulus package.

2.3 The Path to Japan's Economic Revival

Alongside these financial stimulus measures, in October 1998, Prime Minister Obuchi announced that financial institutions would take drastic measures to deal with non-performing loans in order to eliminate financial instability and restore their financial functions, by passing a bill related to financial reconstruction. In the Prime Minister's general policy speech in November 1998, the path to Japan's economic reconstruction was explained as follows.

The first path was to stabilize the financial system and take measures against the credit shortage. In the scenario that he proposed, as a result of the disposal of non-performing loans and the reorganization of financial institutions, trust in financial institutions would be restored and the factors that hindered the recovery of the real economy would be removed. He also said that, as the financial system reform progressed, he strongly expected corporate efforts such as strategic business restructuring and the termination of employee contracts.

The second path consisted of economic recovery measures and large scale financial expenditures aimed at restoring demand and creating employment. As a result, the mindset of households and companies would improve, leading to a situation where, "as a result of the recovery of the real economy and financial reconstruction creating a virtuous circle, the economic recovery has led to increased private demand, including capital investment, which would allow the economy to return to a stable growth trajectory." For the time being, the aim was to shift economic structural development gradually led by private demand through the recovery of private consumption, while trying to support the economy by focusing on public demand.

Prime Minister Obuchi also indicated that he would promote structural reforms with the twenty-first century in mind in order to link the economic recovery movement to stable growth over the medium- to long-term and that the living space doubling strategy plan and the industrial revitalization plan were also based on this idea.

The third path consisted of industrial revitalization and employment measures. The enhancement of public support measures, including venture to support the creation and growth of new businesses, the creation of a better environment for the reconstruction of existing businesses, and the development and spread of technology in 15 fields where growth was expected. This was based on the basic industry revitalization policy, which focused on ensuring employment by creating new businesses and increasing investments to improve productivity.

2.4 *Shift to Supply-side Policy*

As mentioned above, the initial industrial revatalization plan focused on fiscal mobilization to eliminate a deflationary mindset and emergency economic measures for the short term. In the medium- to long-term it was closely related to structural reforms, venture support, and new business creation for the twenty-first century, but it was basically an extension of conventional industrial policy.

However, its content started to change gradually from the beginning of 1999. At the end of December 1998, the MITI, in compiling the basic policy for industrial revitalization to be implemented from January 1999, strayed from the conventional route which emphasized an aggressive fiscal stimulus to create effective demand.

The MITI announced a focus shift toward supply-side reform through, for instance, the disposal of surplus production facilities.

Specifically, the minister envisioned tax measures associated with equipment disposal, the establishment of a real estate securitization system, a review of bankruptcy legislation in order to reduce the cost of liquidating and reducing non-performing assets—which could be considered the aftereffects of the bubble economy—and the deregulation of land use. Regarding employment, the aim was to support the reduction of surplus personnel held by companies by enhancing employees' ability to change jobs, such as the retraining and upskilling of lower-skilled office workers, who are generally less productive than those in Western companies. There were proposals for an employment adjustment system that prioritized subsidies for companies investing in capacity development. A task force was also set up to consider these policies and set up a concrete direction to follow.

2.5 Cabinet Decisions on the Industrial Revitalization Plan

The draft of the Industrial Revitalization Plan revealed in January 1999 clearly indicated a policy shift from economic management that aimed to create an effective demand through an aggressive fiscal mobilization to one that shifted the emphasis to structural reforms on the supply side, such as the disposal of surplus facilities, with the aim of improving corporate productivity.

The purpose of this plan was based on an understanding that "even if the fluctuation of the business cycle is reduced by measures on the demand side, it is the growth of the potential output capacity on the supply side that determines the long-term economic growth trend," and that rather than a short-term reduction in the supply and demand gap through demand-side measures, "the focus should be on medium-term policies aimed at the supply side in order to recover potential output (potential GDP) growth."

While the "camphor agent" of the 1999 budget plan, which included the issuance of government bonds of over 30 trillion yen and tax cuts of over 9 trillion yen, was in effect, the government begun reforming the supply-side structure, seen as the basis for a smooth transition of demand to the private sector and a way to solidify the foothold for economic reconstruction.

Specifically, the policy stance was to do away with the negative legacy of "excesses in terms of employment, funds/finance, and equipment" further as an aftereffect of investment during the bubble period, and to "recognize the fields in which each company is competitive in order to make the best possible use of human, financial, and technical resources."

Themes related to supply-side issues included: (1) a reform of economic systems such as the legal and public systems related to corporate economic activities, and practices within and between companies, (2) efficiency of corporate management funds, finance, and assets, (3) the smooth movement of human resources between companies and industries, (4) an improvement in the quality of the labor force by accumulating human capital by, for example, improving the vocational abilities of workers, and (5) improving the quality of capital stock through technological progress and innovation. However, despite these issues being considered targets for reform, only the measures that had been set up in the past ended up being mentioned.

The government's industrial revitalization plan was written based on this draft at the end of January had an almost identical content. In addition to creating effective demand through aggressive fiscal stimulus, the government formulated a policy to boost the economy by promoting structural reforms on the supply side, such as eliminating excessive equipment and human resources in the manufacturing industry. Although additional demand measures based on comprehensive economic measures had the effect of narrowing the demand–supply gap, this plan showed that strengthening the supply-side constitution was essential for maintaining the growth potential of the Japanese economy over the longer term.

The industrial revitalization plan, based on the judgment that an "improvement of corporate productivity is urgently needed to rebuild the Japanese economy," aimed to raise the economic growth rate by the contribution of total factor productivity (TFP), create new industries, improve international competitiveness in the manufacturing industry, and eliminate excessive equipment and human resources.

As mentioned above, the industrial revitalization plan, which was one of the highlights of the Obuchi cabinet, also known as the "economic revitalization administration," focused on the supply side, and the policy shift happened between the end of 1998 and the beginning of 1999. However, even at that point, it was still regarded that "this plan gives off a strong impression of being only a collection of conventional industrial policies, such as the creation of businesses in new industries," and that "the MITI has formed a research team within the ministry and has begun to hear further opinions from individual industries, but there still is no clear direction in sight."

2.6 *Actions of the MITI*

How did the MITI act in the meanwhile? It can be speculated that the Industrial Revitalization Plan had shifted the ministry's focus onto supply-side policies, as exemplified by the creation of the reviewing task force mentioned above.

Behind the emergence of these policies was a strong sense of crisis among policymakers and that the overcapacity accumulated after the bubble economy era had prolonged the recession. According to the estimates of the Economic Planning Agency, overcapacity in companies reached a record high of about 86 trillion yen in the period between July and September of 1998. The inability of companies to handle this overcapacity reduced the productivity of the industry as a whole and hindered new capital investment. There was also a growing awareness that "eliminating overcapacity is not the exclusive responsibility of the MITI, but an issue that the government as a whole should tackle" (Taichi Sakaiya, Director General of the Economic Planning Agency).

Another notable highlight from the MITI around December 1998 was the inclusion of special tax measures to promote the consolidation and abolition of oil facilities in the 1999 tax lineout. This measure exempted taxes on the gains on transfers generated when a company sells assets under certain conditions. This system allowed multiple oil companies to integrate equipment in pseudo-mergers, thus promoting industry-wide reform. This mechanism could also be used in the chemical, steel, and electrical industries, which had problems with overcapacity. The MITI positioned it as the "first step in structural reform on the supply side."

The MITI pressured the Liberal Democratic Party and the Ministry of Finance to realize this system. Around this time, it was widely acknowledged that supply-side reforms, such as eliminating excess equipment and employment, were essential for the Japanese economy to recover and regain its sustainable growth trajectory.

2.7 Financial and Industrial Revitalization

From the end of January to February 1999, the issue of treating financial and industrial revitalization as connected issues gathered attention even in newspapers. One of the background aspects was the Financial Revitalization Commission, a task commission established by the government in December 1998, with a 2-year time limit, to examine major banks for temporary nationalization and public fund injection. Even if a large amount of public funds were to be injected into a bank, the provision for a disposal of non-performing loans only has the effect of raising the capital adequacy ratio of the bank. Moreover, this type of financial revitalization will not lead to industrial revitalization, that is, the issue was seeing how these fund injections could eventually be connected with the debtor companies. The ratio of debt balance to annual operating income for non-financial corporations had almost doubled at this point since the bubble burst and non-performing loans included not only the ones that had become so directly because of the bubble bursting, but also the ones which had done so during the subsequent long-term recession.

It was under these circumstances that the connection between financial industrial revitalization came to the fore. In the editorials of the Nihon Keizai Shimbun, it was argued "whether or not financial and industrial reconstruction can be linked is the key to revitalizing the economy as a whole." In addition, there were various movements under the hood over the disposal of non-performing loans centered mostly around members of the Liberal Democratic Party.

Reflecting on this trend, the final report compiled by the Economic Strategy Council at the end of February 1999, stated that promoting the elimination of excess facilities and concurrent investment in growing industries was extremely important to develop "a new mechanism, system, and environmental improvements to promote the reorganization of financial institutions at the same time as practical measures are taken to dispose of non-performing loans," and, "a new framework for industrial reconstruction for revitalization and international competitiveness."

Around March 1999, the government decided to inject public funds into a subset of financial institutions and policy, which at first was simply trying to escape the recession and began to shift its focus to industrial revitalization. There was also an expectation that it would be discussed once again at the newly established Industrial Competitiveness Council.

2.8 Launch of Industrial Competitiveness Council

The draft of the Industrial Revitalization Plan mentioned above stated that the "means for comprehensively exchanging opinions will be set up as soon as possible, taking into account cooperation between the public and private sectors according to the division of their roles" in order to promote supply-side reform. This resulted in the establishment of the "Industrial Competitiveness Council" by the government and the business community. The practical measures of the industrial revitalization plan were to be discussed at this newly established council.

Takashi Imai, the chairman of the Japan Business Federation (JBF) (and chairman of Nippon Steel Corporation), proposed a plan that would lead to the establishment of the Industrial Competitiveness Council. It was officially proposed in the "JBF's Proposals for Strengthening Industrial Competitiveness" in December 1999. The proposal to set up this conference was modeled on the United States Presidential Industrial Competitiveness Committee, which was jointly established by the public and private sectors during the Reagan administration in the 1980s, with the aim of bringing the United States back to its former glory. It was also an unprecedented attempt to convey the voice of the top company executives to the public sector and discuss the division of roles between public and sectors on an equal footing.

In January 1999, a round-table conference was held between the leaders of the JBF and Kaoru Yosano, the Minister of International Trade and Industry, where they agreed on the establishment of the Industrial Competitiveness Council. After that, a talk was held at the Prime Minister's Office with Prime Minister Obuchi, the Minister of International Trade and Industry Yosano, and JBF Chairman Imai, who agreed that "strengthening competitiveness is a strategic issue which should be spearheaded by political leaders in developed countries." Furthermore, following the Cabinet's decision on the Industrial Revitalization Plan, the establishment of the Industrial Competitiveness Council was officially announced in order to reflect the opinions of the private sector when considering policies related to industrial revitalization. In March, the purpose of the council's establishment and its members were announced.[3]

The Economic Strategy Council, which had compiled its final report in February 1999, also played a role in presenting the recommendations of the private sector to

[3] Accessed online at Prime Minister's official website (https://www.kantei.go.jp/jp/singi/sangyo/990421kesai.html), on March 31, 2021.

There were 17 members from the private sector, including Japan Business Federation (JBF) Chairman Imai, Fujitsu CEO Naoyuki Akikusa, Sony CEO Nobuyuki Idei, NTT CEO Junichiro Miyazu, and other active corporate managers.

the public sector, but the scope of discussion had become wider, and now ranged from macroeconomic policy to pension issues. In addition, as the management of the Economic Strategy Council was led by scholars, there was a feeling that the business world was excluded. The Industrial Competitiveness Council would focus exclusively on industrial revitalization for a "narrow and deep" approach, unlike the "wide and shallow" approach of the Economic Strategy Council (Shimizu 2005).

2.9 Mechanism for Financial Institutions to Participate and Discuss

It is noteworthy that at this Industrial Competitiveness Council, ideas and requests to be incorporated into the Industrial Revitalization Law, which was later drafted by the MITI, were presented.

In the first meeting held on March 29, 1999, Minister of International Trade and Industry Yosano started by saying that "aiming to strengthen the competitiveness of industry, the public and private sectors will work together to tackle economic supply-side problems through a free exchange of opinions," and then said that, "I wish for the discussion to reach a conclusion before the end of the year regarding themes such as business reconstruction, employment, technological development, infrastructure, SMEs, the creation of new industries and new businesses, high-cost structures, and future leading industries."(First Meeting of the Industrial Competitiveness Council: Summary of Minutes, March 29,1999).[4]

JBF Chairman Imai, one of the core members of the Industrial Competitiveness Council, said that it was necessary to reform the supply structure in relation to issues such as overcapacity, overemployment, and excess debt in order to revitalize existing industries as well as foster leading industries and new industries. In order to eliminate overcapacity, he said it would be important to amend the commercial code, review tax measures, utilize and liquidate idle land, secure employment, and transfer labor.

During the exchange of opinions, after the members of the private sector presented their thoughts, Finance Minister Kiichi Miyazawa said, "Is it not possible to create a mechanism for financial institutions to participate in discussions on the issue of equipment disposal? I would like the Minister of International Trade and Industry to consider this possibility." He emphasized the importance of measures to mitigate the excess debt of companies undergoing management trouble in relation to the disposal of excess equipment, and proposed the creation of a framework to encourage financial institutions to waive their debts. As individual negotiations between companies could only go so far, industry and the financial world would have to discuss it in earnest, and the government would have to provide support from the sidelines. Within this context, the government also feared that, without reducing excess corporate debt, an "injection

[4] Unless otherwise noted, the following quotations are from this document.

of public funds into banks—in excess of 7 trillion yen—would not lead to industrial revitalization" (Hakuo Yanagisawa, Minister of Financial Revitalization) (*Nihon Keizai Shimbun*, March 29 and 30).

Finance Minister Miyazawa's statement set the tone for the meeting, confirming the policy of considering frameworks such as Debt Equity Swap (DES) as measures to reduce corporate debt (*Nihon Keizai Shimbun*, March 30). A DES is an acquisition by a financial institution of shares newly issued by a distressed company, for a portion of the loan receivable in exchange for waiving part of their debt. This exempted the company from paying a part of its debt. As a shareholder of the borrower company, the financial institution could monitor its management, and if this led to the reconstruction with mergers or reorganizations, the company's stock price could be expected to rise. In the United States, this same system was used in numerous reconstructions such as those of Chrysler, Trans World Airlines, and Macy's (*Nihon Keizai Shimbun*, March 30).

Financial institutions were wary of simply waiving debt, because, as a major bank executive stated, they were concerned that "if a borrower company forsakes payment of a loan without going legally bankrupt, and that loan has the potential to generate profits in the future, it may be subject to a shareholder derivative suit." In anticipation of this, JBF Chairman Imai have recommended the use of DES to Finance Minister Miyazawa. The industrial world had high expectations regarding the use of DES for waiving debt and banks also showed a positive attitude, stating, "this will expand our options for debt collection." "DES is just one part of the prescription," said Yosano, the Minister of International Trade and Industry, "rather, I would like to appreciate the fact that the JBF's initiative allowed a constructive dialogue between the financial and industry worlds to start." (*Nihon Keizai Shimbun*, March 30).

2.10 Examinations at the Industrial Competitiveness Council

Regarding Miyazawa's remarks at the first meeting, Yosano, the Minister of International Trade and Industry, consulted with Prime Minister Obuchi, Chief Cabinet Secretary Hiromu Nonaka, Finance Minister Miyazawa, the Chairman of the Financial Revitalization Commission Yanagisawa and Chairman Imai decided to hold a meeting of the top executives of the financial and industrial worlds to exchange opinions at the start of April. At the meeting, the industrial sector requested that financial institutions also cooperate in advancing supply-side reforms, and the financial representatives said that they would cooperate with individual financial institutions for a smoother processing of individual cases (The Second Meeting of the Industrial Competitiveness Council: Summary of Minutes, April 28, 1999).

Meanwhile, the JBF was consolidating the content of the industrial revitalization proposal related to tax reform from the second meeting of the Industrial Competitiveness Council. The content included: (1) an expansion of the deduction system for losses carried forward due to equipment disposal, (2) a drastic shortening of depreciation periods to encourage new investments, (3) a deferral of transfer profit taxation on in-kind investment, and (4) tax exemption measures for the transfer of assets, including registration and license tax and real estate acquisition tax.

While (1) promoted the liquidation of historical losses, it also required positive structural reforms such as (2), (3) and (4), and tax reforms that promoted capital investment. For example, (3) reduced the tax burden for a company proceeding with group reorganization and facilitated the creation of a flexible organization. Under the existing system, when a factory was moved to another company, if the market value was higher than the book value, the profit on the transfer would have to be taxed. Although there were some special measures, the JBF proposed to apply these mitigation measures on the whole industry. From the perspective of improving industrial competitiveness, most of the requests from the industry regarding employment issues related to industrial revitalization involved the development of a legal system for a smoother transfer of human resources.

Based on these discussions, Prime Minister Obuchi announced his intention to improve the existing laws promptly. The government, mainly led in this effort by the Ministry of International Trade and Industry, began to draft a bill that included policies to encourage corporate restructuring and the disposal of excess equipment, beginning with coordination with other governmental bodies such as the Ministry of Finance.

At the second meeting of the Industrial Competitiveness Council, Imai and other members of the private sector made the abovementioned requests and the Prime Minister stated, "I would like to receive concrete proposals regarding what the problematic laws and tax systems are from a private standpoint and how they should be fixed." Based on this, the JBF compiled "The First Recommendations for Strengthening the Competitiveness of Japanese Industry" on May 18, and Imai explained its content at the third meeting held on May 20, 1999 (The Second and Third Meetings of the Industrial Competitiveness Council: Summary of Minutes, April 28 and May 22, 1999).

The requests expressed in the abovementioned "First Recommendations" were large in scale and number, but what attracted the most attention was the fact that parts of the law and tax reforms regarding organizations and corporate groups, which would later be implemented in the Industrial Revitalization Law, were first proposed through these recommendations. For example, some of the recommendations regarding company-split legislation (revision of the Commercial Code) included the abolition of the inspector investigation in the case of in-kind contributions, property underwriting, and subsequent incorporation (as a general rule, the business code would allow for bulk transfer), deferral of transfer profit taxation on in-kind contributions (including business transfers) for the establishment of joint ventures, and the establishment of special provisions on registration and license tax related to asset transfers, for example.

The Prime Minister instructed the relevant ministers to put together measures by mid-June, focusing on the matters requested at the previous Industrial Competitiveness Council. Then, at subsequent meetings, the discussion shifted from industrial revitalization measures to themes more relevant for the future, such as the creation of new businesses and industries.

3 Contents and Effects of the Industrial Revitalization Law

3.1 Enactment of the 1999 Industrial Revitalization Law

"The Emergency Employment Measures and Industrial Competitiveness Enhancement Measures" decided on by the government in June 1999 incorporated the results of the examinations performed by the Industrial Competitiveness Council. In order to put the measures into practice as soon as possible, a bill was submitted to extend the session of the Diet, and the Act on Special Measures for Industrial Revitalization was enacted in August 1999 (The following is based on the Ministry of International Trade and Industry ed. 2000, including citations in quotes).

The first point to be confirmed is emphasis on the supply side approach. The premise of the law was that the long-term trend of economic growth was dependent on the potential growth rate of the supply side. Not only were labor and capital input not expected to grow in the future due to Japan's declining birthrate, aging population, and the decline in the savings rate, but there was also the fear that technological innovation, management innovation, and social system reform in relation to the TFP growth rate, would be too slow in Japan.

Based on these issues, the purpose of the Industrial Revitalization Law was "to prevent the excellent management resources existing in Japan from fleeing the country and to create new businesses and develop technologies through their re-evaluation, optimal placement, and optimal utilization and to promote the efforts of various companies through selection and concentration to shift management resources promptly and smoothly from low-productivity fields to high-productivity fields, while creating more of the latter through measures such as reconstruction."

Second, the MITI did not consider the burst of the bubble economy and having to escape the post-financial crisis as the only issues, but was also aware of the increase in global competition in the 1990s. Major American companies had made efforts to improve profitability through "selection and concentration" during the economic downturn that started in the late 1980s and continued into the early 1990s, and, as a result, American companies had dramatically improved productivity since the early 1990s and this had contributed to the recovery of the American economy. In countries in the European Union (EU) as well, international business restructuring and merge and acquisition (M&A) movements were accelerating in fields such as oil, automobiles, chemicals, and telecommunications.

However, looking at trends in Japanese companies, management resources were not being used effectively despite the growth in corporate assets and liabilities brought on by the economic bubble, and, as a result, return on assets (ROA) was significantly lower in Japan than in the United States, and Japan's rate of productivity increase was still lower than the average for countries in the Organization for Economic Cooperation and Development (OECD). Some of the major companies had been pioneering business restructuring with selection and concentration, but the overall situation did not allow for swift changes, and these issues could no longer be postponed in the face of changes in the global economic environment. The early 2000s were expected to lead to a financial "big bang" and major changes in accounting standards, with companies with low profitability in danger of not surviving.

Under these circumstances, it was explained that the aim of the Industrial Revitalization Law was to "promote selection and concentration" in Japanese companies and improve productivity drastically by organizing unprofitable assets and focusing management resources on their own areas of strength and new fields.

As seen above, the industrial revitalization policy began with an industrial revitalization plan that was mostly based on emergency economic measures and demand-stimulating measures by the government, but after discussions at the Industrial Competitiveness Council it was taken up in the Industrial Revitalization Law in a shape and form that reflected the demands of the JBF. The Industrial Revitalization Law, other than the issues that the MITI was already aware of, eventually took on a more universal approach to included supply-side measures (improvement of productivity), improvement of international competitiveness in the global environment, promotion and support of industry and business reorganization, and more.

3.2 Support for Business Restructuring and Industrial Revitalization Tax System

The specific policy packages are as follows. The basic concept of the Industrial Revitalization Law rested on two main pillars: special legal system measures and tax incentives to support corporate business restructuring (the Ministry of International Trade and Industry ed. 2000).[5] The application of both was subject to the approval of the designated minister for the business restructuring plan and submitted by the applicant.

Looking at the legal side, the bill focused on creating special measures for the commercial code, which posed institutional obstacles to business restructuring. The commercial code at the time provided uniform and strict procedures for organizational restructuring, which slowed down companies who wanted to restructure their business promptly in response to changes in the environment.

The following measures were aimed at promoting business restructuring by relaxing regulations: (1) the omission and simplification of inspector investigations related to in-kind investment and property underwriting due with the establishment of a new company or additional investments in an existing company, (2) simplification of the business transfer system (no need for the approval of the general meeting of shareholders), (3) expansion of the target- and upper-limit for granting stock options, (4) improvement of the environment associated with DES (expansion of the issuance limit for shares without voting rights), and more.

Tax incentives included a reduction in registration and license tax, an extension of the deferral period of deficit or selective application of unfreezing carryover refunds,

[5] There were other special support measures, including financial ones.

and the deferral of taxation of profit on the transfer of in-kind contributions to jointly owned subsidiaries.

Of these, the reduction of registration and license tax had been one of the traditional policy measures for the MITI as well. The registration license tax is a tax system peculiar to Japan and is inevitably incurred in organizational restructuring that involves capital movement (e.g., buying and selling of businesses, capital increases). In the case of the establishment of a company, the tax rate of 0.7% of the capital was reduced to 0.35%, and in the case of a merger, it was reduced from 0.15% to 0.1%. Large-scale business restructuring would normally have attracted a large amount of registration license tax; therefore, this exemption became an incentive for restructuring.

3.3 Policy Effects of the Industrial Revitalization Law

Under the Industrial Revitalization Law of 1999, 202 business restructuring plans were approved in the about 3.5 years before the revision of the law in April 2003.[6]

As for concrete examples of some of those businesses, it is known that they included[7] Sumitomo Metal Mining, Suzuki, Hino Motors, Fuji Heavy Industries, Toyota Motors, Nissan Motors, Mitsubishi Motors, Mitsubishi Chemicals, Mitsui Chemicals, Ube Kōsan (Ube Corporation), Idemitsu Petrochemicals, Dainippon Ink and Chemicals, Nippon Oil & Fats (Nihon Yu-shi), Glass Tech Ibaraki, Nihon Paper Industries and Daishowa Paper Industries, Tokyo Electron, Matsushita Electric Industrial, Jack and Nippon AM, Jack Holdings, Shiseido, Shiseido Fine Toiletry, Bandai, and Unitika Trading. These businesses came from a variety of industries, including metal, chemical, automotive, electronics, and more. One of the most notable measures, especially for the automobile industry, was the strengthening of sales functions through group reorganization by increasing capital through third-party allotments, the consolidation of assembly lines, and business reorganization of financial and sales subsidiaries.

The policy effects of the 1999 Industrial Revitalization Law were also related to the formulation of the 2003 Amendment Bill, which will be examined next, and the policy officials of the Ministry of Economy, Trade, and Industry (METI) studying all these cases in great detail. The results of their case studies were not published, but some are believed to have been cited in the response of Minister of International Trade and Industry Hiranuma in the deliberations regarding the 2003 Amendment Bill. In other words, by April 1, 2003, 11 of the 14 cases for which the planning period had ended had achieved their productivity improvement targets and about

[6] Based on the response of Minister of International Trade and Industry Takeo Hiranuma at the House of Councilors Economic and Industrial Committee, Minutes of the Diet (156th House of Councilors Economic and Industrial Committee No. 8) (April 1, 2003).

[7] This is based on the press releases of the department in the Ministry of Economy, Trade and Industry responsible for the approval of corporate business restructuring plans available from the National Diet Library Web Archiving Project.

60% of the 65 cases during the planning period showed at least some productivity improvement. As globalization was inevitable, it was necessary to reorganize the industry boldly through international business alliances and M&As, and there was an urgent need to develop corporate legislation to facilitate this. It could be said that competitive companies had improved their profitability by performing business restructuring while utilizing the support measures the Industrial Revitalization Law provided.

However, as subsequently explained in Minister Hiranuma's deliberation, the subsequent deterioration in the economic situation required the law to be amended to extend its effects. "ROA, which indicates the productivity of Japan's industry as a whole, started to grow after the enactment of the Industrial Revitalization Law but then began to decline again and we have to admit that there is no strong recovery trend in sight."

It can be said that the policy effect was achieved in that a certain number of global companies achieved the productivity improvements set as targets in their business restructuring plans by utilizing the Industrial Revitalization Law of 1999, but the situation changed in the early 2000s, giving rise to new challenges.

4 Process of Enactment of the 2003 Revision to the Industrial Revitalization Law and Industrial Activity Law

4.1 Review at the Council on Economic and Fiscal Policy

In the 2000s, although there were signs of recovery from the severe recession triggered by the financial crisis in the fall of 1997, the financial system was still unstable due to a vicious cycle of bad debts and deflation. Banks had to deal with non-performing debts, while businesses were suffering from excess debt. In some industries, inefficient equipment continued to operate and the whole structure continued to work at overcapacity. At that time, the Japanese economy was still in a state of stagnation after the bubble economy burst.

Furthermore, the problem of the "liquidation type non-performing loans" caused by end of the bubble economy was now paired with an increase in "depression-type non-performing loans" caused by worsened cash flows stemming from the prolonged recession and corporate bankruptcies (Ishiguro 2003). The demand for financial support for companies that were struggling because of the prolonged deflation was increasing rapidly. The number of loans that had to be carefully managed; the loans of companies that had obtained concessions in interest lending rates—reduction or exemption—exceeded 10 trillion yen at major banks alone.

The Junichiro Koizumi administration, which was inaugurated in April 2001, appointed Heizo Takenaka as the new Minister for Economic and Fiscal Policy to save the Japanese economy from this terrible situation. With the reorganization of ministries and agencies in January 2001, the revision of the government's policy-making system began in earnest, with the newly-established Council on Economic and Fiscal Policy in the Cabinet Office at its core.

The Council on Economic and Fiscal Policy was tasked to decide on the basic policies for economic and financial management. This shifted the responsibility for budgeting, which previously belonged to the Ministry of Finance, making it a politically led decision. The council was established during the Yoshiro Mori administration, but under the strong leadership of the Koizumi administration, which was established under the slogan "from the public to the private sector," the government created a mechanism for preparing economic policies and budgets based on the input of the private sector. Members included the Prime Minister and related ministers, the governor of the Bank of Japan, two economists as private experts, and Jiro Ushio (Chairman of Ushio, Inc.) and Hiroshi Okuda (Chairman of the Toyota Motor Corporation) as industry representatives.

The focus of their discussion was on a macro-economic level relating to economic measures and the Japanese economy in general (*List of Agenda Items of the 2001 Council on Economic and Fiscal Policy* and other sources), but they were also interested in areas related to industrial revitalization as a drastic solution to the problem of non-performing loans. The RCC (The Resolution and Collection Corporation)[8] was also discussed during the November 2001 meeting, and the material covered during those discussions included statements such as, "It is not feasible that the RCC should reconstruct a company that the banks have failed to reconstruct," and, "The Financial Services Agency (FSA) explained that the important distinction is not between legal and private liquidation, but between liquidation and reconstruction."

The final draft of the Council on Economic and Fiscal Policy, released in December 2001 stated that "by ensuring the final disposal of non-performing loans within the next few years while promoting structural reforms in other fields, the situation would be back to normal in no more than 3 years from now. As a result, economic growth will be achieved by (1) a recovery of financial intermediary function by improving bank profits, (2) an improvement in the problem of excess corporate debt through reorganization and reconstruction, and transitioning resources accumulated in low-productivity companies and industries into new growth industries, and (3) the positive impact on investment and consumption of a regained confidence in the financial system." These words were directly incorporated into the Cabinet decision of January 25, 2002 ("Structural Reform and the Medium-Term Outlook for the Economy and Public Finance").

Then, various financial measures were mentioned in the "Deflation Countermeasures to be Taken Immediately" document released by the government in February, however, the most important aspect in relation to the concept of establishing the IRCJ (Industrial Revitalization Corporation of Japan) was that, at the time, the RCC was

---

[8] RCC was a joint-stock company funded by the Deposit Insurance Corporation of Japan, established in 1999 by a merger between the Housing Loan Administration Corporation and the Resolution and Collection Bank.

expected to "aggressively purchase non-performing loans." In addition, the establishment of multiple corporate restructuring funds was supposed to accelerate corporate restructuring and the disposal of non-performing loans.

The related document following from this was the "Comprehensive Deflation Countermeasures," which included "Structural Reform Acceleration Measures for Financial, Industrial and Economic Revitalization" (October 2002).

To summarize, around the fall of 2001, the issue of non-performing loans was deliberated on by the Council on Economic and Fiscal Policy in relation to industrial revitalization, and the RCC was one of the focal points of their concrete measures to address it. The plan to use the RCC later changed into the plan to establish IRCJ.

4.2 Proposal to Establish IRCJ

The Industrial Revitalization Act of 1999 was a time-limited legislation that had a March 2003 deadline and a review clause. After the Ministry of International Trade and Industry was reorganized into the Ministry of Economy, Trade, and Industry due to the reorganization of ministries and agencies of 2001, the Industrial Structure Division of the newly-reorganized ministry started to review the revised bill. This review began in the fall of 2001 and the New Growth Policy Subcommittee of the Industrial Structure Council began deliberating in January 2002 (Ishiguro 2003).

In response to these developments, the Japanese Business Federation (JBF) stated in its "Proposals for Building a New Growth Base" (April 2002) that they wished for an extension and expansion of the support measures of the Industrial Revitalization Law, such as reduced taxation on closing, converting, and transferring businesses, as well as disposing of equipment, as these would promote the reduction of overcapacity. In October 2002, the JBF's statement of opinion included a request for "the early implementation of the financial system stabilization and deflation countermeasures," financial revitalization, which was the most urgent issue at the time, could not be realized unless integrated with measures for industrial revitalization and overcoming deflation. As a concrete measure, in addition to strengthening the corporate revitalization functions of the RCC, related legislation and tax systems were established to promote intra-industry business and industrial restructuring, inefficient equipment disposal, and the introduction of cutting-edge equipment. In addition, in their "Toward Industrial Revitalization" statement of opinion at the end of October, they requested a drastic expansion of the Industrial Revitalization Law. This once again resurfaced the importance of integration between industrial and financial revitalization.

Around the same time, Takashi Imai, the Honorary Chairman of JBF, proposed the establishment of an IRCJ (then a tentative name), as a receiving organization for non-performing loans. It seems that this suggestion was promptly taken up and implemented according to the following schedule.

The interim report on the government's comprehensive measures against deflation, compiled by Finance Minister Takenaka in October, focused on financial issues, but the ruling party's opposition put off the announcement of a plan for financial stabilization measures. In less than 24 h, Mr. Imai asked Prime Minister Koizumi to accept Takenaka's initiative, stating, "Is it really acceptable to just accelerate the disposal of non-performing loans and bankrupt companies?" Imai also met with Chief Cabinet Secretary Yasuo Fukuda and suggested the creation of an organization to support industrial revitalization.

Imai thought that Japan had few options to support corporate revitalization. The RCC, which was established as an institution to purchase and collect non-performing loans from financial institutions in order to promote their disposal, took on the collateral starting from the assumption that the company was bankrupt and many thus believed that it was not ideal for revitalization.[9] Unless a new organization able to receive them was created, all non-performing loans would go to RCC.

In response to Imai's proposal, the Ministry of Finance took the initiative by involving the METI, to realize the IRCJ establishment plan in little more than a week. According to newspaper reports, the Ministry of Finance (MOF) had secretly been considering the IRCJ establishment plan since around August. As RCC focused on debt collection, it was not considered suitable for industrial revitalization. The ministry believed not having to establish it the best option but they wanted to keep it as an ace up their sleeve in case the demand for budget financing increased.

Meanwhile, the FSA was considering a plan to have the IRCJ (or the RCC) work as subsidiaries of the Development Bank of Japan. However, the MOF was against it because they believed that it was not appropriate for the Development Bank of Japan to use their surplus accumulated over many years for high-risk financing that had a high probability of generating losses. The MOF consequently teamed up with the METI against the FSA proposal.

Finance Minister Masajuro Shiokawa insisted on the use of the Deposit Insurance Corporation of Japan. It was pointed out within the government that "the combination of the Deposit Insurance Corporation of Japan, whose purpose is protecting depositors, and the industrial revitalization is a strange one," but, owing to its financing mechanism, using the Deposit Insurance Corporation of Japan was going to turn out to be a good decision.

---

[9] The main business of the RCC was the collection of non-performing loans, but as it did not have any financing function, it could not properly fulfill its role in industrial revitalization. It has been pointed out that after selling RCC receivables to banks, borrowers could not receive additional loans and their cash flows suffered.

The revised Financial Revitalization Law, which came into effect in January 2002, expanded the functions of RCC and established an organization to support industrial revitalization. In addition, starting from the fall of 2002, it became possible to make new loans in partnership with the Development Bank of Japan, but this provision was limited in various ways: for example, these loans were limited to equipment investment by large companies.

4.3 The Preparatory Office for the Establishment of the IRCJ

Based on the above circumstances, the establishment of the IRCJ was described in the "Comprehensive Deflation Countermeasures" officially decided on by the government on October 30, 2002. Prime Minister Koizumi explained it as follows. (1) The Financial Revitalization Program announced on the same day by the FSA would be implemented immediately in order to achieve the goal of ending the non-performing loan problem by the end of fiscal year 2004. (2) By doing so, the non-performing loan ratio of major banks would be reduced to about half of the current level, thereby revitalizing the financial system. (3) In implementing this, the related ministries and agencies would work together to promote the early industrial revitalization. (4) The government would also strongly promote the establishment of a mechanism to ensure corporate revitalization and the drastic revision of the Industrial Revitalization Law, and strive for the reorganization and early revitalization of industry.

It was decided that details of the IRCJ proposal presented in the comprehensive deflationary measures would be summarized by the end of November 2002. The Preparatory Office for the Establishment of the IRCJ was created and Sadakazu Tanigaki was appointed as the minister in charge; in addition, a group of elite members of the MOF, the FSA, the METI, and the Ministry of Land, Infrastructure, Transport, and Tourism (MLIT) was selected to proceed with the formulation of a draft bill to be submitted to the ordinary session of the Diet in January 2003 (*Nihon Keizai Shinbun*, November 7 and 8, 2002).

At this point, the bill was expected to follow the following outline:

(1) IRCJ would be a public–private fund in which the government's public funds matched the investment of private companies (banks and other private corporations). The public fund portion would be invested by the Deposit Insurance Corporation of Japan and the Norinchukin Bank, and the IRCJ juxtaposed by the RCC as a subsidiary of the Deposit Insurance Corporation of Japan.
(2) The IRCJ would target the purchase of loans from companies that financial institutions had classified as "sub-performing," were being supported by the main bank as the bank and company had agreed on a reconstruction plan, and the IRCJ had itself considered capable of revitalization.[10]

The loans would be purchased from banks other than the main bank at a "reasonable price," and industrial revitalization would be supported in collaboration with the main bank. By discounting and purchasing the loans of non-main banks (including government-affiliated financial institutions) who wanted to withdraw loans, the only remaining large creditors would be the main bank and the IRCJ. For this reason, the adjustments that had until that point been impossible to make because of conflicts of interest between banks and difficult-to-create reorganization plans had now become easier to implement.

---

[10] Companies for which revitalization was judged to be difficult would be brought to the RCC and debt collection would be performed through the disposal of collateral. In principle, the RCC would deal with companies at least concerned about bankruptcy, thus differentiating it from IRCJ.

The following two points were considered the most urgent. The first was how to set the aforementioned "reasonable price." The second was the content of the operations to be performed by the IRCJ. At this point, their operations were limited to the purchase of debt and the selection of companies to support. They had no financing or investment functions. This is described again later.

4.4 Purchases at the Market Price

Regarding the first point, the issue was whether the reasonable price was the market value or the book value of the debt. If the market value were used—the actual price that the market was ready to pay for the debt—banks would hesitate to sell debt to IRCJ, as selling the debt would increase their losses. The most convenient option for banks was to sell the debt at their book value, or, in other words, at the principal price of the loan receivable. In the past, the RCC generally bought debt at their market value, usually only about 10% of the book value, thus discouraging banks from selling.

However, representatives of the METI thought that the market value was a fair price. Representatives of the MOF and the METI had already started to prepare different draft bills even before the Preparatory Office for the Establishment of the IRCJ was officially established. The difference between the two proposals was essentially about whether to use the book value or the market value of the debt, but in the proposal submitted by the MOF, which used the book value, the newly created IRCJ risked being burdened with cheap non-performing loans. This would not have put an end to the problem of non-performing debt, so METI's representative was positive that it would never be allowed.

At the time, policy continued to keep interest rates low, making it difficult for "market discipline" mechanisms to work effectively, and financial institutions with many corporate debtors with excessive debt could not decide on how to act. The METI hoped that the situation would artificially keep companies alive without leading to the elimination of the oversupply structure. When Takenaka was appointed as the minister in charge of financing, he changed the financial administration policy, changing the balance sheet from a soft-landing one to a hard-landing one. The METI was convinced that the framework to accept loans had to be able to sort companies between those that could be revitalized and those that could not.

The government draft bill was revealed on November 20, 2002, and was a method of purchasing receivables at the "real book value," that is, the book value minus an allowance for doubtful accounts, subject to a strict calculation of reserves. Under the circumstances at that time, the real book value was expected to be higher than the market value.

At that time, newspapers asked, "Will this strategy of aiming for two birds with one stone, revitalizing industry and stabilizing finance at the same time, work?" Purchasing non-performing loans from banks with an emphasis on stabilizing the financial system had the potential to create easy relief for sub-performing companies.

Conversely, if the purchase conditions were too strict, it would take more time for banks to dispose of their non-performing loans. Setting a balance between financial and industrial revitalization was a difficult challenge, which some people at the time described as a "stick and carrot" situation.

As a "carrot" for financial institutions to bring in the loans, the government draft included a plan to buy them at their "real book value," which was higher than the market value. Moreover, as a "stick," when calculating the real book value, the reserve funds would have to be strictly calculated using the discount cash flow (DCF) method.[11] When using the DCF method, some believed that major banks needed to increase their reserves by 1.5 to 2 times, while the real book value of their loans would, on average, be around 16% of the book value. In order to make it easier for banks to sell their loans, there were also proposals to operate the DCF method flexibly and raise prices.

In any case, unlike the RCC, the IRCJ targeted companies that were most likely to succeed at revitalization; so, even when buying receivables at a premium, the possibility of selling them to the market for a higher price in the future, thus making a profit, still remained. On the contrary, if the revitalization of the company did not proceed as expected, the receivables price would fall and the IRCJ would register a loss. In which case, it was assumed that the public and private sectors would bear the loss according to their shareholdings. "It is difficult to say that there will be no loss at all," said Minister of Industrial Revitalization Tanigaki, who considered filling the gaps with public funds.

Then, on December 11, 2002, the final draft of the IRCJ bill was revealed. The receivables purchase price was specified as the "appropriate market price" in consideration of how likely the company was to be revitalized. However, at a de facto level the price was to be set higher than if assuming the liquidation of the company and it was expected that it would be close to the "real book value" requested by the banking industry and proposed in the government's November draft. If there was a loss when the IRCJ was dissolved, the government could subsidize it, paving the way for future public funding.

The budget for the IRCJ to purchase receivables from banks was set at 10 trillion yen in early December 2002 and was included in the 2003 budget. Opinions were divided on whether 10 trillion yen was too much or too little, but the METI decided that it was sufficient for the time being.[12]

---

[11] The discount cash flow (DCF) method is a method of calculating the value of non-performing loans widely used by banks in the United States. It is a strict provision standard that estimates the future profit prospects of lenders and the income that would be obtained from the sale of their assets. Assessing assets using DCF would result in an even more pessimistic valuation of non-performing loans by major Japanese banks, making it necessary to increase reserves even more. Many Japanese banks used the method of mechanically calculating reserves based on past bankruptcy probabilities, but the financial revitalization program for comprehensive deflation measures required them to use the DCF method for loans of sub-performing companies.

[12] At the end of 2001, banks' sub-performing bonds were estimated at about 12 trillion yen, but the IRCJ purchased only the loans held by non-main banks, so the total was less than 10 trillion yen. However, if this calculation were expanded to all financial institutions with deposits, the total would

In the fiscal year 2003, the DCF method was announced to make asset assessment stricter. As a result, the amount of reserves required of banks was expected to increase significantly. Therefore, it was stipulated that banks short of capital would be injected with public funds.

4.5 *Financing/Investment Function*

As stated above, the second point for discussion, regarding the scope of the operations of the IRCJ, was whether it should include financing and investment functions.

The original concept was that that IRCJ would only buy and sell receivables. However, this risked creating a situation where banks would temporarily transfer their non-performing loans to the IRCJ just to inflate their balance sheets, or it could lead to IRCJ registering losses (which would ultimately be paid through citizens' taxes). The Preparatory Office for the Establishment of the IRCJ, especially the members coming from the METI, considered that it had to be more than this as an institution.

In the process of business restructuring performed by companies, which included equipment disposal, personnel reduction, and more, the necessary funds would temporarily increase due to the payment of, for example, retirement allowances. In order to supply such restructuring funds, it was important to add functions such as financing to the IRCJ.

As a result, with a financing function eventually added, the IRCJ became a de facto financial institution that could implement additional financing and investment, debt guarantees, trusts, and other support measures in order to facilitate corporate restructuring. In cooperation with the main bank, the IRCJ was now able to promote the partial exemption of debt, value calculations using DES, and more, while utilizing the information, know-how, funds (connecting funds and new money) and human resources of the main bank to rebuild the management of companies.

Thus, in the end, the IRCJ, that at first was only meant to shoulder non-performing debt instead of the banks, became closer to an organization performing a turnaround function for companies. Of course, if the IRCJ wanted to implement revitalization projects through private funds, it would be required to turn a profit. This is because performing revitalization at a loss would be the same as simply handing out funds. For this purpose, it was necessary to create a framework where IRCJ would take on risky investments and subsequently reap a return in order to maintain discipline. Based on this recognition, the Preparatory Office for the Establishment of the IRCJ focused on creating investment rules.[13]

---

be closer to 19 trillion yen, and if the IRCJ were to purchase all loans held by local banks that lent to SMEs and loans other than sub-performing bonds, 10 trillion yen was expected not to be enough. Around this time, one of the focal points was whether to include SMEs in the IRCJ purchases.

[13] According to an interview with a representative of the METI in the Office, these rules were created by taking the United States as an example, where revitalization projects were carried out

In its policy proposal "Regarding the Formulation of the Basic Guidelines for Corporate and Industrial Revitalization" from early December 2002, the JBF said that "the role of the government is only to support the individual efforts of companies through the Industrial Revitalization Law and other laws that create the necessary environment and an appropriate tax system. The government should not be expected to rate companies and to lead their revitalization efforts."

In light of these intentions of the business community, the government's "Basic Guidelines for Corporate and Industrial Revitalization" were officially formulated in mid-December 2002 and emphasized that their approach would be based on market mechanisms. In addition, because there were criticisms that the use of public funds would hinder fair competition between private companies, the IRCJ was established as a time-limited organization with a lifespan of 5 years and the debt purchase period was limited to the end of March 2005.

5 The 2003 Industrial Revitalization Law and the IRCJ

5.1 The 2003 Revision

The revised bill for the Industrial Revitalization Law was enacted in April 2003 and the law was extended until the end of March 2008. The Industrial Revitalization Corporation Act was also drafted and passed, and IRCJ was established based on it.

At the same time as the revision of the Industrial Revitalization Law, the METI underwent a reform, and from April 2003, in order to "establish a system to create new companies and revitalize existing companies in an integrated manner," an Industrial Revitalization Division was created within the Economic and Industrial Policy Bureau. In this way, the ministry's reorganization was implemented to promote the industrial revitalization policies.

The revised law was based on the efficient use of management resources in order to increase productivity. Its aim was, just as with the 1999 law, the prompt revitalization of the industry, but it focused more on management resources. As a concrete measure, the focus was on increasing the types of business restructuring plans that could be certified and expanding the policy tools. Under the Industrial Revitalization Law of 1999, the "Business Restructuring Plan" was the only acceptable restructuring plan, but the 2003 revision added the following three types.

The "Joint Business Restructuring Plan" was "a plan for multiple businesses to jointly consolidate, eliminating or reducing oversupply in order to increase efficiency," and was used for two or more companies to jointly perform restructuring. Examples include consortiums, business transfers, and business exchanges (transferring business X from company A to company B and business Y from company B to company A).

---

on a private basis. This was based on running the organization not only by buying receivables, but also by including equity in expectation of revitalization in order to eventually gain a return.

The Industrial Revitalization Law of 1999 was expected to promote business and industry restructuring of Japanese companies, but the METI believed that there were still too many companies operating the same business was too large, and there was an "oversupply" or "overcapacity" situation). Therefore, it sent out a policy message that reorganization would be promoted not only through mergers, but also through a new type of reconstruction involving the transfer of individual business departments.

The "Management Resource Reutilization Plan" was "a plan to improve the efficiency of the business field by utilizing the management resources that are not being effectively utilized by existing companies." It was a measure to make full use of excellent management resources used by companies with excess debt, through the purchase of debt.

The "Innovative Equipment Introduction Plan" was "a plan to establish a manufacturing base in Japan for R&D-integrated first-demonstration equipment." It was also a measure to encourage capital investment and R&D to avoid hollowing out of domestic industry.

As described above, the number of possible effective choices (plan types) for industrial revitalization had been increased to four and the plans approved based on these four types received the same treatment as those described by the 1999 Industrial Revitalization Law, with the same legal and tax incentives. From the revision in April 2003 to March 2008 there were 116 approved applications, including Mitsubishi Motors, Maruzen, and Sanyo Electric.

The "Joint Business Restructuring Plan," the "Management Resource Reutilization Plan," and the "Business Restructuring Plan" types involved business mergers and combinations, but the government's "Basic Guidelines for Corporate and Industrial Revitalization" mentioned above stated that "all possible policy measures should be applied in a consistent manner by all interested parts" in order to achieve corporate and industrial revitalization. The Fair Trade Commission decided to implement additional measures such as expediting the examination of business mergers for cases related to the Industry Revitalization Law (The Fair Trade Commission 2003).

5.2 Special Provisions for Commercial Code

Another point of the revised law was the expansion of special provisions for the commercial code. This flowed in part from the 1999 law and it included, (1) investigation of inspectors, (2) simple organizational restructuring, (3) dividends of subsidiary shares, (4) flexibility of merger considerations, (5) company split notifications, and (6) capital reductions. All of these measures were aimed at promoting business restructuring by making the process less complex and less restrictive.

If the commercial code itself were to be amended to include these deregulation measures, as a general rule, the deliberation by the Legislative Council would require nearly a year to conclude its deliberations. The special commercial code exceptions of the Industrial Activity Law were not so important, but they were a way to relax regulations which, in consideration of the environment at the time, were unreasonably strict. They were also a way to test possible revisions to the commercial code itself.

Although the commercial code exceptions were not actually applied in many cases, most of them were incorporated as general rules in the subsequent amendments to the commercial code and the Companies Act (the Companies Act was alienated from the commercial code in 2005), thus making them a significant measure for law improvement.

5.3 Expansion of the Industrial Revitalization Tax System

With the revision of the Industrial Revitalization Law, tax incentives had also been expanded (see *Ministry of Economy, Trade and Industry Annual Report*). In addition to measures to reduce registration and license taxes, further expansions were implemented to promote intra-company business and industrial restructuring, disposal of inefficient equipment, and introduction of cutting-edge equipment. In addition, the calculation method for the debt exemption gain generated when receiving debt exemption from a bank had been reviewed, and its application would lead to a significant tax cut. This revision made it possible to formulate reconstruction plans with debt exemption, and was expected to facilitate business revitalization with debt waivers.

Although the revised Industrial Revitalization Law and the IRCJ bill were superficially not related, in terms of operation they were related through the scheme of this debt exemption offset system. For example, in many cases such as Daiei, IRCJ's work on the project was approved as a business restructuring plan under the Industrial Revitalization Law. From this perspective, the Industrial Revitalization Law and IRCJ had effectively been integrated.

This debt exemption gains offset system had traditionally required approval by the National Tax Agency notification in the case of legal liquidation based on the Corporate Reorganization Law and the Civil Rehabilitation Law. In the case of legal liquidation, the court was involved in creating the rehabilitation or revitalization plan, so that the plan could be judged as appropriate from the perspective of a disinterested third party. Thus, it was judged that the debt exemption gains offset system could be applied to debt forgiveness based on such a plan.

Compared to the United States, where companies could be reformed or defaulted through Chapter 11 Bankruptcy, the practice of utilizing bankruptcy legislation had not yet taken root in Japan. The IRCJ scheme was also basically a private arrangement. In the case of private reorganization, as only some creditors would accept the waiving of the debt, from the viewpoints of equality and objectivity, it was possible for the abovementioned offsetting system of debt exemption gain based on the National Tax Agency (NTA) notification to be inapplicable.

However, when thinking of business revitalization, one of the problems was that companies were sub-performing because they lacked liquidity while at the same time, they had to pay a large amount of corporate tax if they were exempted from debt. In response to this situation, the METI suggested to the NTA that because the business restructuring plans based on the Industrial Revitalization Law were approved by the competent authorities, they should be treated in the same way as the legally arranged rehabilitation or revitalization plans. As a result, the NTA notifications included cases where the business restructuring plan was approved based on the Industrial Revitalization Law.

The abovementioned corporate tax debt exemption was the largest financial incentive under the Industrial Revitalization Law. For instance: the registration license tax (about 0.35% of the transfer of capital) would be 350 million yen even when transferring only 100 billion of capital. Meanwhile, in the debt-exemption gain-offset system, for a revitalization plan approved on the basis of the Industrial Revitalization Law, even when receiving debt exemption for 100 billion yen, corporate tax would be levied for 30 billion yen, but, based on the exemption gain and the result of the asset assessment, part of this tax could be canceled. This had an enormous impact on the liquidity of companies.

However, these benefits were limited to large-scale and drastic business restructuring through debt reduction. In many smaller cases, companies sought approval for their business restructuring plans to take advantage of reduced registration and license taxes rather than of corporate taxes.[14]

5.4 Operation of the IRCJ

The following section examines developments since the establishment of the IRCJ. As mentioned above, there was a conflict between the Ministry of Finance and the Ministry of Economy, Trade, and Industry on whether to use the book value of debt or the market value. Furthermore, possibly because the IRCJ did not include any members involved in the banking industry, it was not able to obtain the cooperation of banks immediately after starting its operations in May 2003. Effectively, the IRCJ could not start operations unless the banks (the main bank) brought a plan to them. As a result, the IRCJ remained inactive for a while, but, after its easy-to-use scheme came to be understood, banks started approaching it with several plans.

The responsibility of judging whether reconstruction was possible and ensuring the appropriateness of the reconstruction plan and purchase price, rested on the Industrial Revitalization Committee, which was set up within the IRCJ. The debts and shares purchased by the IRCJ would be sold to new sponsor companies, investment funds, and investors within 3 years. Support was terminated when the debt of the supporting company was paid off, after which the IRCJ would be dissolved.

As a final result, the IRCJ had approved to support the reconstruction of a total of 41 companies and groups in the 4 years until March 2005, the debt purchase deadline.

---

[14] The Industrial Revitalization Law did not distinguish between companies based on their size and it included SMEs, but, in terms of registration license tax and the debt-exemption gain-offset system, its main target was large enterprises. As a support measure for SMEs, a separate SME support council was set up in which the government cooperated with local financial institutions, lawyers, and certified accountants to support these companies by providing various advisory functions.

The target companies included Mitsui Mining Corporation, Kanebo, Daiei, Matsuya Denki, Dia Kensetsu, Daikyo, Misawa Homes Holdings, Skynet Asia Airlines, and spa hotels in Nikko and Kinugawa.

The IRCJ was originally established with a 5-year time limit, but as the disposal of non-performing debts happened earlier than originally planned, it disbanded a year earlier, in March 2007, and was liquidated in June of the same year. Residual assets at the end of liquidation were approximately 94,032 million yen, of which approximately 50,749 million yen was distributed to shareholders (Deposit Insurance Corporation of Japan and Norinchukin Bank), with the remaining approximately 43,282 million yen being paid to the national treasury. In addition, throughout its operations, the IRCJ paid a total of approximately 31.2 billion yen in national and local taxes (INCJ, Ltd. "About the completion of liquidation of IRCJ, Ltd," June 5, 2007)." Before the establishment of the IRCJ, it was assumed that public funds would have to be invested because of possible backwardation, at the expense of taxpayers, but IRCJ ultimately closed at a profit, completing its project 1 year ahead of schedule.

In certain cases, when financial institutions have large amounts of non-performing loans, the main bank system, which is a practice peculiar to Japan, has failed in its corporate revitalization support function. The IRCJ, a semi-public institution, intensively supported the restructuring of promising companies as a time-limited measure and is considered a successful demonstration of policy involvement.

The success of the IRCJ was the catalyst for the establishment of the corporate revitalization business in Japan. As 90% of IRCJ staff came from the private sector, such as finance, accounting, and legal affairs, it was able to realize the full potential of private sector rehabilitation business personnel and accumulate know/how. After its dissolution and liquidation, many members of the IRCJ became corporate revitalization professionals in the private sector.

6 The 2007 and 2009 Amendments and the Innovation Network Corporation of Japan

6.1 The Economic Situation in the Mid-2000s

In the mid-2000s, Japan headed for economic recovery and was in a long-term economic recovery phase until 2006. The factors that supported this economic recovery were a strong global economy and the structural adjustments that had been made as companies improved their internal structures through rationalization efforts. The disposal of non-performing loans was finally in sight for the major banks and the revitalization of large corporations that had fallen into excess debt had also achieved some results.

The "three excesses" of "employment, facilities, and debt," which had been pointed out in the 1999 edition of the "Economic White Paper" as negative legacies of the bursting of the bubble economy and long-term factors behind Japan's economic stagnation, were considered to have been largely resolved in the 2005 edition of the "Annual Report on the Japanese Economy and Public Finance (White Paper on Economy and Finance)."

From the 1999 Industrial Revitalization Law to its 2003 amendment, the industries that the Ministry of International Trade and Industry and the Ministry of Economy, Trade, and Industry envisioned as targets for business restructuring were the steel, electrical machinery, and chemicals industries. Some of them underwent revitalization through the Industrial Revitalization Law and voluntary reorganization efforts by the industry at large and individual companies, but some, like the electrical machinery industry, could not be said to have been sufficiently reorganized. However, for a variety of reasons, the METI did not seem particularly inclined to intervene in the restructuring of any specific industry.

Although this was not under the jurisdiction of the Ministry of Economy, Trade, and Industry, the Industrial Revitalization Law was used more frequently in the banking industry under the jurisdiction of the Ministry of Finance and in the construction industry under the jurisdiction of the Ministry of Land, Infrastructure, Transport, and Tourism, as these two sectors had suffered considerable damage when the bubble economy burst. Furthermore, having a very large monetary scale, the banking industry could be said to have been the industry that benefited the most from the reduction of the registration license tax and debt exemption gains. In fact, during this period, the banking industry was rapidly reorganized toward mega banking, ultimately making the industrial revitalization policy a major tool for bank restructuring.

The problem of major banks' non-performing loans had, to some extent, been resolved. The non-performing loan ratio of major banks dropped from 8.4% in March 2002 to 2.9% in March 2005 and 1.8% in March 2006. However, the disposal of non-performing loans by regional financial institutions was still a matter for future concern, as were efforts to revitalize local businesses and SMEs. Within the field of local businesses and SMEs this amounted to nothing more than the tip of the iceberg, but the IRCJ and other support measures were used to promote the revitalization of the bus companies, hotels, and spa resorts.

6.2 Challenges for Creating a Business Revitalization Market

When the emergency measures were completed in the early 2000s, building a private sector business revitalization market became the next challenge for the Japanese economy. As envisioned from the beginning of the Industrial Revitalization Act of 1999, enhancing the turnaround of management resources was indispensable for revitalizing the Japanese economy and enhancing Japan's industrial competitiveness.

In addition, considering the shift that business revitalization was to make towards a more local approach, even including rural areas, the system needed further development. As the disposal of non-performing loans and business revitalization, which had been an issue for more than 10 years, were being resolved, it was now important to develop a business revitalization mechanism focused on the private sector by making use of the practical experience gained so far.

Originally, business revitalization was supposed to be performed mainly through the early utilization of legal restructuring through systems such as the Civil Rehabilitation Law and the Corporate Rehabilitation Law, which were established as a legal reconstruction type. However, the current state of business revitalization in Japan was still centered on private arrangements, following the philosophy of the Composition (Peace Negotiation) Act. Specifically, there was still a strong tendency to revitalize businesses at the expense of financial creditors such as main banks.

Based on this uniquely Japanese system and the current situation, developing an institutional design centered on private organizations presented many challenges in terms of speed and other aspects. These issues had traditionally been examined by study groups within the Ministry of Economy, Trade, and Industry and the Business Revitalization Subcommittee of the New Growth Policy Subcommittee of the Industrial Structure Council, but institutional issues were said to need further specialized examination.

For this reason, the Industrial Revitalization Division of the Economic and Industrial Policy Bureau of the METI served as the joint secretariat with the Civil Affairs Bureau of the Ministry of Justice, and in June 2006, a business revitalization system study group comprised of experts (lawyers and academics) was established. Between June and August, the study group conducted intensive research and held a total of six study group meetings. The main issue was facilitating private reorganization and ensuring the continuity of both private and legal reorganization.

6.3 Business Revitalization System Study Group Report

The "Business Revitalization System Study Group Report," compiled in September 2006 (Gigyō Saisei Seido Kenkyū-kai 2006), made the following points.

Firstly, it considered the use of alternative dispute resolutions regarding creditor adjustments through the mediation or substitution function of business ("certified ADR") based on the Alternative Dispute Resolution Law (ADR Law), which came into effect in April 2007 to resolve issues related to the speed of the resolution of private arrangements.

The business value of a business operator entering a private reorganization procedure had already been damaged to a certain extent and the degree of damage would increase at an accelerating rate over time, so completing the procedures as promptly as possible was a major issue. However, under conventional practice, creditor adjustment, including the burden on the main bank,[15] takes time, creating a risk that the business value of the debtor could be damaged more than necessary.

The second issue was related to private reorganization bridge loans (pre-DIP financing), which were extremely important for the smooth progress of business revitalization. When shifting from private reorganization to legal reorganization, repayment was prohibited, like with other rehabilitation claims, and the rights became subject to change under the same conditions. For this reason, creditors hesitated to sponsor bridge loans during private arrangements, hindering private consolidation.

For this reason, to facilitate pre-DIP financing, the court could allow for rights different than those in the general claims for those that had been confirmed to meet certain requirements, such as certified ADR. This would make it possible to establish provisions to judge whether not doing so would harm equity.

The third issue was the use of DES as a method for debt reduction. Especially for SMEs, it was said to be important for financial institutions to identify the possibility of revitalization at an early stage, improve cash flow by methods such as rescheduling and interest rate reduction and exemption, and actively work on debt reduction through various methods, including debt waiver.

In addition, a method called "debt approach," in which regional revitalization funds discount and purchase receivables from financial institutions—including main banks and revitalize businesses from the standpoint of creditors—was already being used for the business revitalization of SMEs and the report considered it effective. In the future, it was predicted that these funds, including the regional SME revitalization one funded by the Organization for Small & Medium Enterprises and Regional Innovation, would be used for the business revitalization of local companies and SMEs.

6.4 *The 2007 and 2009 Revisions*

In July 2006, the Economic Growth Strategy Charter was formulated with the aim of obtaining sustainable economic growth through innovation and revitalizing the local economy. Toward the realization of this outline, the Industry Revitalization Law Amendment Bill was passed in May 2007 to promote the efforts of businesses to improve productivity through technological and business innovation and facilitate early business revitalization in the local economy.

The content of the law included (1) support for improvement in productivity in the service industry (e.g. special provisions in the Companies Act, taxation system, etc.), which accounts for 70% of employment and GDP and which is the core of the regional economy but is considered to have low productivity, (2) promotion of the utilization

[15] In the case of multiple financial institutions waiving claims, the main bank should agree to waive larger amounts of claims than other financial institutions would, consideration the degree of its involvement in the management of the company.

of intellectual property, and (3) facilitation of business revitalization of small and medium-sized enterprises in the region. In order to improve productivity, the bill planned to facilitate business revitalization by expanding the available measures, for example introducing management resources from outside and promoting business innovation by fusing resources from different fields. In addition, as a new mechanism for early business revitalization, it planned for the use of certified ADR for private reorganization procedures and the promotion of bridge loans.

The METI had formulated a new economic growth strategy in June 2006, but the economic environment had changed significantly since then due to soaring resource prices in the first half of 2008 and the global recession triggered by the subprime loan crisis. Based on this, the Ministry formulated a "follow-up and revision to the new economic growth strategy," which was approved by the Cabinet in September 2008 after incorporating measures from related ministries and agencies.

Against this background, the 2009 amendment aimed to utilize management resources such as materials, funds, intellectual property, and technology efficiently in order to restore the Japanese economy to a sustainable growth trajectory. The name of the law was also revised to the Act on Special Measures Concerning the Revitalization of Industry and Innovation in Industrial Activities. In addition, based on this revised law, the Innovation Network Corporation of Japan was established in 2009, with a 15-year timeframe, as a public–private investment fund that would support the commercialization of advanced technology and the reorganization of domestic companies using public funds.

7 Conclusion

This chapter examined the policy-making process of the industrial revitalization policies implemented by the MITI/ METI from the end of the 1990s to the mid-2000s in relation to changes in Japan's economy.

In Sect. 2, the policy-making process leading up to the enactment of the Industrial Revitalization Law of 1999 was examined. The catch phrase, "integrated revitalization of finance and industry," is often used when referring to the government's comprehensive deflation measures of October 2002, which later included the establishment of the IRCJ in April 2003, although similar concepts and policy ideas already existed before that. This goes back at least to the 1998 "Draft of Industrial Revitalization Plan" (formulated the following year in 1999), which was conceived as part of the emergency economic measures after the 1997–1998 financial crisis.

Initially, it was mainly meant to accept fiscal spending to create demand and included measures such as new industry creation and venture support based on conventional industrial policies, but owing to the requests of the Ministry of International Trade and Industry, the Economic Strategy Council, the Industrial Competitiveness Council, and the JBF, it eventually included special supply-side legal and tax incentives to encourage corporate business restructuring. The measures of this plan were embodied in the Industrial Revitalization Law, which was enacted in 1999.

In Sect. 3, the content and effects of the Industrial Revitalization Law were examined. Its content was centered around special legal system measures and tax incentives to support business restructuring. These special measures were implemented because the commercial code at the time provided uniform and strict procedures for organizational restructuring, which slowed down companies who wanted to restructure their business promptly in response to changes in the environment. The tax incentives included a reduction in the registration license tax. These measures would be further expanded with the 2003 revision of the law.

In Sect. 4, the policy-making process leading up to the revision of the law in April 2003 was described. In the comprehensive deflationary measures of October 2002, a new proposal to establish the IRCJ based on the "finance–industry integrated reconstruction" policies emerged and it was packaged with the Industrial Revitalization Law, which was then about to be revised. Initially, there was a conflict between the Ministry of Finance and the Ministry of Economy, Trade, and Industry regarding the establishment of the IRCJ, but plan was eventually based on the latter's proposal, which emphasized "market discipline" and focused on the strict disposal of non-performing loans and industrial revitalization.

In Sect. 5, the 2003 amendments to the law and the operation of the IRCJ were examined. The 2003 amendment added new options for different planning types for business restructuring, and also created an offsetting system for debt exemption gains, expanding legal and tax measures to support business restructuring. The IRCJ scheme worked well and the disposal of non-performing loans was completed by the mid-2000s.

One noteworthy characteristic of the industrial revitalization policy during this period was that the policy had expanded beyond the conventional framework of the Ministry of Economy, Trade, and Industry. In addition to communication with the Ministry of Justice regarding special exceptions to the commercial code, the law was gradually improved through the collaboration of the National Tax Agency and private organizations such as the Certified Public Accountants Association, the IRCJ as a public–private fund, and private experts such as lawyers and certified accountants from the IRCJ, allowing for the accumulation of business revitalization and company reconstruction know-how and the creation of human resources. This process was also meant to create a business revitalization market in Japan.

The next issue was institutional expansion related to the formation of the business revitalization market, which would, for example, speed up private reorganization procedures by establishing systems for local businesses and SMEs, improving productivity in low-productivity sectors such as the service industry, and promoting innovation. These issues were addressed in the 2007 revision, the 2009 revision, and the establishment of the Innovation Network Corporation of Japan (INCJ) and are mentioned as prospects in Sect. 6.

As described above, the Industrial Revitalization Policy has constantly evolved in response to the current challenges of the Japanese economy. In the short term, it responded to the demands of banks to dispose of non-performing loans and corporate excess debt, and in the medium- to long-term, it laid the foundation for building a more universal system that would lead to the formation of a business revitalization market.

"Promoting economic structural reform in consideration not only of the industrial side but also of the economic structure itself from both macro and micro perspectives," was set as one of the responsibilities under the jurisdiction of the Bureau of Economy, Trade, and Industry when the Ministry of Economy, Trade, and Industry was established. It can be said to have been realized through the process of policy-making related to the industrial revitalization policy.

References

Gigyō Saisei Seido Kenkyū-kai [Business Revitalization System Study Group] (2006) Gigyō Saisei Seido Kenkyū-kai Houkokusyo [Business Revitalization System Study Group Report] (September 2006).

Ishiguro N (2003) *Sanghō Saisei he no Senryaku: Genjyō, Seisaku, Kanren Hou-seido.* [*Strategies for Industrial Revitalization: Current Status, Policies, and Related Legislation*].

Kousei Torihiki Iinkai [Fair Trade Commission] (2003) 'Kigyō-Sangyō Saisei ni Kakaru Jian ni Kansuru Kigyō-Ketsugō Shinsa ni Tsuite no Kohyō ni Tsuite' [On the publication of "Regarding the Examination of Business Combinations in Cases Relating to Corporate and Industrial Revitalization"] (April 9, 2003).

Okazaki T (Tsūshō Sangō Seisaku-shi Hensan Iinkai [Committee for the Compilation of the History of International Trade and Industrial Policy] (ed.) (2012) *Tsūshō Sangyō Seisaku-shi: 1980–2000 (3) Sanghō Seisaku* [*History of International Trade and Industrial Policy: 1980–2000 (3): Industrial Policy*]. Keizai Sangō Chōsakai, Tokyo.

Shimizu M (2005) *Kantei Shudō: Koizumi Junichiro no Kakumei* [*The Prime Minister's Office Led: Junichiro Koizumi's Revolution*] Tokyo: Nihon Keizai Shinbunsya.

Tushō Sangyō Shō [The Ministry of International Trade and Industry] (ed.) (2000) *Wakariyasui Sangyo Katsuryoku Saisei Tokubetu Sochihō* [*Brief Explanation: Industrial Revitalization Special Measures Law*] Tokyo: Gyosei.

Watanabe J Takeda H (2021) *Nisen-nendai no Sangyo Saisei Seisaku* [*Industrial Revitalization Policies in the 2000s*] RIETI Discussion Paper Series 21-J-030. https://www.rieti.go.jp/jp/publications/dp/21j030.pdf.

Junko Watanabe is Professor of Economic History at Kyoto University and Faculty Fellow at RIETI. She has been involved in research on the economic policy history of MITI/METI for many years and has conduct-ed numerous interviews with bureaucrats. She has also conducted research on pre- and postwar Sumitomo Group and history of industry such as textile, coal mining and others.

Standards Administration Policy in Japan Between the 1980s and the 2000s

Satoshi Kawamura

Abstract This chapter considers the Japanese government's initiative for standards and certifications from a historical perspective to explore the significance of how and why it came to be seen as an important component of the nation's economic growth policy in the latter half of the 1990s. Back then, a slowdown in growth was beginning to become a norm of the Japanese economy and how to achieve economic growth emerged as a critical policy issue. The Japanese government had to grope for ways to ignite growth, while continuing to pursue deregulation to minimize government involvement. The Ministry of International Trade and Industry (MITI) was required to support innovative business activities. Having shifted away from its conventional industrial policy, the MITI was trying to find ways to support the development of business strategies by utilizing standards as a policy tool, recognizing that the standardization of competitive products can further enhance their value, a practice that had been in place for some time in other advanced economies. However, the government's initiative to promote standardization at an international level is still ongoing. Meanwhile, it has been found that the social significance of such standardization efforts will likely increase in the areas of welfare and environmental protection.

S. Kawamura (✉)
Josai University, Saitama, Japan

H. Takeda and J. Watanabe (eds.), *Rethinking Japanese economic policy at the turn of the 21st century*, Advances in Japanese Business and Economics 34,
https://doi.org/10.1007/978-981-97-5512-7_5

1 Introduction

[1]This chapter examines the significance of the standards administration policy from the late 1990s onward, which were emphasized as part of the economic growth policy based on historical thought. Economic growth arose as more important policy topic from the latter half of the 1990s when the blunting of economic growth began to become normalized. The Japanese government was forced to seek growth policies while being premised on deregulation limiting administrative involvement which had become established policy since the 1980s. While expecting competitive outcomes by strengthening the functions of markets, the government simultaneously sought for the Ministry of International Trade and Industry (MITI, which became the Ministry of Economy, Trade and Industry or METI following its reorganization in 2001) to support innovative business. MITI retracted the industrial policy and recognized the product-value-raising effects of standards that had already been adopted internationally. By promoting the trial and error method to support the creation of business strategies using standards, the administration of standards and conformity assessment was emphasized as a method of promoting economic growth while being subject to limited administrative involvement. However, this chapter brings to light that the adoption of international standards is still a developing field, and on the other hand that the social significance of standards policy may also increase in terms of welfare and environmental considerations. This chapter will mainly focus on the period from the 1980s through to around 2010.

Standards administration was examined by Minoru Sawai across a historical series of trade and industrial policies covering the period 1980 to 2000. However, since this compilation was carried out by separating into policy areas, it did not necessarily clarify the position of standards administration within the MITI policy as a whole (Sawai 2011, Chapter 6). Since standards administration was discussed after it was separated further into policy items, it is difficult to say that the policy stance for each period of time was clarified. The need to reconsider the issues posed by standards administration continue to remain.

Between the High-Speed Growth Period and the Stable Growth Period, MITI administration promoting industrial growth based on capital investment while providing incentives to companies by means of resource redistribution was the mainstream practice. Between the Stable Growth Period and the present day, in contrast, both government and business was distanced, and administrative involvement was limited (Odaka 2013, final chapter), thereby respecting the transparency of resource distribution more through the markets and increasing the freedom of business' actions. Economic growth has always been an important policy issue, but its seriousness has

[1] The original paper is as follows but is revised as necessary for this book. Satoshi Kawamura (2016) '1980 nendai-2000 nenndai ni okeru Kijyun Ninshō Gyōsei: Seisaku Kadai to shiteno Keizai Seichō to Seihinkachi-kojyo-shisaku no Tenkai' [The Japanese Government's Initiative for Standards and Certifications in the 1980s-2000s: Economic Growth as a Policy Goal and Improvement of Product Value] RIETI Discussion Paper Series 16-J-045. https://www.rieti.go.jp/jp/publications/dp/16j045.pdf.

increased, from the latter half of the 1990s onward when the blunting of economic growth began to become normalized. Expectations for MITI to support innovative companies began at around the same time as when further strengthening of market functions was found necessary.

Reflecting these changes in MITI's policy stance, the challenges facing standards administration pertained to the standardization of parts for the heavy industry in the 1960s and 1970s, the revision of standards with the aim of opening up markets against a background of trade friction in the 1980s, standardization in response to the development of the information communications industry and new materials, and the shift to an emphasis on international standardization activities in the late 1990s. This chapter highlights the fact that the importance of standards administration increased particularly since the late 1990s onward (Fujita and Kawahara 1998; Harada 2008; Izumi 2009; Chapter 4, etc.), because it was possible for a company to become a monopoly supplier and to expect to receive royalties if they promoted specification standards accompanying certain kinds of goods. It can be said that policies supporting the contribution of Japanese companies to international standardization was emphasized. In other words, this can be interpreted as a policy plan that recognizes the effects of standards that increase the value of a product, and that seek to increase the share of Japanese companies in the international markets by supporting for internationalization, which can be expected to lead to an increase in the gross domestic product (GDP). It is important to note that while the rise of deregulation theory reduced administrative involvement and the role of industrial policy was diminished, economic growth had to be considered an important aspect of policy, and thus the significance of the standards administration as an available growth policy increased. While the strengthening of the role of the market is obvious while considering the changes in issues faced by standards administration, I would like to focus on the characteristics of the era when economic growth was confronted by the difficult policy issue that economic growth is also the responsibility of the government and the emphasis placed on standards administration that as a result.

2 Industrial Standardization Methods and the Long-Term Plan for Industrial Standardization

For a long time, standards administration was under the jurisdiction of the standards department of the Agency of Industrial Science and Technology, an extra-ministerial bureau of MITI established in May 1949 (The following description refers to Odaka 2013, Chapter 5, Paragraph 1). The extra-ministerial bureaus were established to handle specialized fields, and the Agency of Industrial Science and Technology was "an engine for experimental research concerning science and technology for the mining industry" (Ibid., p. 247). Thereafter, the system of administration under the jurisdiction of the Agency of Industrial Science and Technology did not change even after organizational restructuring took place thrice in September 1952, April 1966, and July 1973. However, the reorganization of the central ministries in January 2001 saw the abolition of the Agency of Industrial Science and Technology and standards administration came under the jurisdiction of the Industrial Science and Technology Policy and Environment Bureau, which was an internal bureau.

The framework of major policy measures was based on the "Industrial Standardization Act" of June 1949 and on the long-term plans for industrial standardization that were formulated approximately once every five years following 1956 (The following description refers to, Advanced Industrial Science and Technology Department of Standards 1989, General Remarks). The Industrial Standardization Act rested on two pillars, the establishment of the Japanese Industrial Standards (JIS) for the official specification of standards and the operation of JIS mark system which aims at the production of JIS-compliant products by companies, improvements in technical production conditions, and the promotion of statistical quality control (*Ibid.*, p.1). The establishment of the JIS was intended to recognize standards publicly, while the operation of JIS mark system permitted the display of the JIS mark where companies declared that their products and manufacturing processes satisfied the JIS standards, and its display was restricted to standards within the JIS as specified by the government. The Industrial Standardization Act has been revised in line with the contents of the Long-Term Plan for Industrial Standardization. In its first revision in July 1965, processing techniques were added to the list of products that were subjects of the JIS mark system and JIS was added to the things to be considered by the national and local public bodies while making purchases. The second revision in April 1980 also extended the JIS mark to foreign manufacturers, the purpose of which was to solidify the principle of non-discriminatory operation of the basic standards certification system internally and externally based on the 1979 General Agreement on Trade and Tariffs (GATT) Standard Code coming into force, as well as to eliminate barriers to trade (Abe 2013, p. 477).

Table 5.1 summarizes the changes in the Agency of Industrial Science and Technology up to the Sixth Long-Term Plan for Industrial Standardization in 1986. It can be seen that the items in A were consistently considered an issue; however, if we take the view that this can be considered to accompany the mechanical industrialization, it ceases to be of fundamental importance from the 1970s onward. Moreover, it can be understood that issues B and C concluded their historical roles during the High-Speed Growth Period (1955–1973). Since the 1970s, the topics sought by the government ranged from D to G, which consisted of consumer protection, the environment, trade friction etc. In the late 1980s, topics assuming the development of the information communication industry began to be set (H).

Table 5.2 presents the industries in which the JIS standards were established. We can see that general machinery and chemicals occupied a large portion for half a century, followed by electronic devices, electric machinery and ships. On the other hand, textiles initially had a large share that fell gradually. It can be said that standards administration was primarily developed for the machinery and heavy chemical industries. Following the 1970s, the issues emphasized by the Long-Term Plans for Industrial Standardization had shifted (Table 5.1) and the establishment of standards in new fields began to be sought gradually. This is embodied by the slight increase in

Table 5.1 Trends in the long-term industrial standardization plans

	Area of focus	First 1956-	Second 1963-	Third 1967-	Fourth 1974-	Fifth 1981-	Sixth 1986-	Examples of setting and revising JIS standards
A	(1) Foundational and shared items for the strengthening and development of the industrial and technological bases (2) Strengthening the development potential of the industry (3) Ensuring compatibility and simplification	←	—	—	—	—	→	Metric coarse screw thread Mechanical drawing Manganese dry cell Measurement terms Nitrogen monoxide standard reference gas
B	(1) Export development (2) Strengthening the international competitiveness of the industry	←	—	→				Calipers Fluorescent lamps Watch testing methods Cigarette lighters
C	(1) Development of small and medium enterprises (2) Adapting to technological innovation		←	→				Wire rope Phillips screwdriver Ready-mixed concrete Hand cart
D	(1) Promotion of the development and rationalization of the industry (2) Ensuring safety and hygiene (3) Promotion of consumer protection			←	—	—	→	Anchors Ordinary rails Pressure vessel structure Gas stoves
E	(1) Pollution prevention and environmental protection (2) Promotion of resource and energy-saving measures				←	→		Solar water heaters for domestic use Automatic measurement of carbon monoxide in the atmosphere Methods for testing vehicle fuel consumption
F	(1) Improvements in the quality of people's lives (2) Product advancement and response to diversification (3) Improvements in medical care and welfare				←	—	→	General rules on sizing and labelling of existing clothing products General-purpose bicycles Steel office desks Aluminum alloy and steel sash electrocardiographs
G	(1) Ensuring consistency with international standards (2) Proposing to be an international standard				←	—	→	Automotive safety glass Cassette tape recorders Symbols for the coordinates and motion of numerically-controlled agricultural machinery Fitted kitchens Skis
H	(1) Establishment of a technological foundation in new technical fields (2) Promotion of information-related technologies						↔	Information processing terms (programming) A basic reference model for interconnectivity between open systems Setting general rules for modularizing industrial robots CAD drawing Solar cell modules General rules for passive components for optical transmission

Source: Advanced Industrial Science and Technology Standards Division ed., "Kōgyō hyōjunka no Ayumi — kōgyōhyōjunkahō shikō 40-shū nen —" [The Course of Industrial Standardization - The 40th Anniversary of the Industrial Standardization Law], Japan Standards Association, 1989, p.39.

the medical safety equipment and information fields since the 1990s onward. On the other hand, as shown in G in Table 5.1, issues that could not be captured by the establishment of the JIS and the operation of the JIS mark system began to emerge, namely trade friction countermeasures from the mid-1970s onward, and as indicated later, participation in international standardization activities from the mid-1990s onward.

3 The Response to Internationalization and the Development of the Internet and Communications Technology (ICT) Industry

3.1 The Sixth Long-Term Plan for Industrial Standardization: The Late 1980s

The Sixth and Seventh Long-Term Plans for Industrial Standardization in 1986 and 1991 emphasized new policy issues such as responding to internationalization and support for the development of the ICT industry and industries using new materials.

In the Sixth Long-Term Plan, the first issue pertained to the opening up of the Japanese market in response to the trade frictions that had begun to manifest from the late 1970s onward (The following description refers to, MITI Bulletin, July 13, 1985). In addition to allowing the inspection agencies of relevant countries to approve the display of the JIS mark by overseas factories that had already been approved to contribute to the expansion of imports from foreign companies that did not have a brand image in the Japanese market, it had the goals of making the JIS conform to international standards and of taking charge of the technical committee secretariat of the international conference deciding upon international standards.

The harmonization of standards that differed between countries originally emerged as a topic of international consideration because it was judged by developed nations that national standards based on independent market development could act as non-tariff barriers. After the Standards Code came into effect following the Tokyo Round in 1979, Japan was also forced to tackle the issue of internationalization. It focused on (1) respect for international standards and (2) the non-discriminatory internal and external operation of standards certification systems, and required (1) respect for international standards if they existed while setting official standards and (2) the recognition of the display of official standards for suppliers of foreign-made goods (Advanced Industrial Science and Technology Department of Standards 1989, pp. 11, 18–19). MITI recognized the display of the JIS mark by overseas manufacturers through a revision of the Industrial Standardization Act in 1980. Further, by revising the timeline for the periodic review of the JIS standards to match that of the International Organization for Standardization (ISO) from three to five years, the contents of the JIS standards began to be brought in line with international standards. The Sixth Long-Term Plan indicated that the operation of this framework would continue into the late 1980s as well.

Table 5.2 The number of JIS standards by field in the fiscal year prior to plan formulation

	1955		1973		1985		1990	
Civil engineering and construction	128	3%	333	5%	521	7%	532	6%
General machinery	480	**12%**	1,015	**14%**	1,184	**15%**	1,300	**16%**
Electronic equipment and electric machinery	356	**9%**	726	**10%**	825	**10%**	823	**10%**
Automobiles	103	3%	283	4%	341	4%	343	4%
Railways	58	1%	180	2%	221	3%	221	3%
Shipping	291	7%	485	7%	516	6%	528	6%
Iron and steel	140	4%	282	4%	312	4%	324	4%
Non-ferrous metals	171	4%	351	5%	347	4%	383	5%
Chemicals	1,134	**29%**	1,735	**23%**	1,591	**20%**	1,546	**18%**
Textiles	291	7%	319	4%	299	4%	310	4%
Mining	88	2%	225	3%	236	3%	220	3%
Pulp and paper	40	1%	102	1%	102	1%	95	1%
Ceramics	166	4%	219	3%	229	3%	247	3%
Daily Items	138	3%	220	3%	269	3%	269	3%
Medical safety equipment	104	3%	166	2%	220	3%	286	3%
Aviation	154	4%	178	2%	91	1%	107	1%
Information	0	0%	0	0%	0	0%	175	**2%**
Management systems	0	0%	0	0%	0	0%	0	0%
Other	106	3%	578	8%	674	8%	668	8%
Total	3,948	100%	7,397	100%	7,978	100%	8,377	100%

	1994		2000		2008	
Civil engineering and construction	440	5%	444	5%	559	6%
General machinery	1,271	**16%**	1,249	**14%**	1,598	**16%**
Electronic equipment, electric machinery	779	**10%**	1,064	**12%**	1,421	**14%**
Automobiles	318	4%	329	4%	363	4%
Railways	191	2%	182	2%	146	1%
Shipping	532	7%	480	5%	471	5%
Iron and steel	329	4%	357	4%	394	4%
Non-ferrous metals	401	5%	397	5%	406	4%
Chemicals	1,520	**19%**	1,748	**20%**	1,787	**18%**
Textiles	278	3%	223	3%	224	2%
Mining	202	2%	188	2%	167	2%
Pulp and paper	83	1%	61	1%	71	1%
Ceramics	250	3%	290	3%	351	3%
Daily Items	219	3%	175	2%	176	2%
Medical safety equipment	315	4%	349	4%	467	5%
Aviation	86	1%	87	1%	97	1%
Information	265	**3%**	428	**5%**	565	**6%**
Management systems	0	0%	24	0%	65	1%
Other	629	8%	666	8%	815	8%
Total	8,108	100%	8,741	100%	10,143	100%

Source: "Kōgyōgijutsuin nenpō" [The National Institute of Advanced Industrial Science and Technology Annual Report], annual edition. For 2008, METI Japan Industrial Standards Commission secretariat, "Nihonkōgyōhyōjunchōsakai nenji hōkoku 2008" [Japan Industrial Standards Commission Annual Report], p.8.

Information has been recorded since 1986.

Secondly, the response to new technologies and computerization was mentioned, in which it was viewed that "in fields of rapid technological progress, the promotion of the adoption of standardization from an earlier stage is important to increasing the efficiency of technological development and ensuring the mutual inter-operation of equipment and systems" (MITI Bulletin, July 13, 1985). The specific policies involved the "promotion of pioneering and flexible standardization" and the "reinforcement of Scientific Research." Both the opening of the Japanese market and the significance of the standards certification to support the development of new industries began to be explored.

These measures in response to the Sixth Long-Term Plan included promoting the setting of standards in new fields, the systematic review of existing standards, harmonization with international ones, the participation in international standardization activities and the expansion of technical cooperation in international standardization (The following description refers to, Advanced Industrial Science and Technology 1990). With regard to international issues, measures were developed to support the secondment of the staff to the ISO and the International Electrotechnical Commission (IEC) and to strengthen involvement in the international standards setting process. This was intended to reflect at least some Japanese standards in international standards in advance, in consideration for the labor of harmonization, because the official standards of countries began to respect international ones. The establishment, revision, and abolition of the JIS standards took place as shown in Table 5.2. Focusing on the trends in this period, it can be seen that "information" became an independent item in 1990 and the establishment of the JIS standards in this field began to be emphasized. While promoting standardization, the Agency of Industrial Science and Technology commissioned the private sector to research about standards, research in fields relating to new materials, information, and the robotics industry began to be promoted from 1985 onward.

3.2 The Seventh Long-Term Plan for Industrial Standardization: The Early 1990s

Although the Seventh Long-Term Plan for Industrial Standardization in 1991 stuck to the topics that were addressed in the sixth, a few new items were also added (The following description refers to, *MITI Bulletin*, June 14, 199). The basic focus of the plan was (1) "the internationalization of JIS, response to the ISO 9000 series and the promotion of further internationalization of JIS through active participation in international standardization activities," (2)"the implementation of standards setting as well as revision and abolition based on fundamental concepts such as ensuring international consistency, swift and flexible internationalization, and emphasizing users and consumers," (3) "active response to issues such as achieving a life of comfort and abundance, the promotion of the development and diffusion of new technologies, responding to global environmental issues, improving systems for the supply of standard reference materials, and the adoption of SI units," and (4) "the review of item designations in response to changes in the social situation, improving the efficiency of factory inspections, promoting the improvement of inspection systems and coordinated collaboration in order to ensure the efficient operation of the JIS mark system."[2]

Discussions on future policy measures continued even after the release of the Seventh Long-Term Plan. The response to the ISO 9000 series emerged as an issue in relation to trade friction. The ISO 9000 series adopted by the International Organization for Standardization (ISO) in 1987 were management system standards concerning quality control, and involved the standardization of workplaces such as offices (Eto 2007, p. 14). Since the private voluntary standard ISO 9000, which was instantly adopted around the world was considered as a factor affecting the competitive strength of companies, MITI promoted a project to introduce the ISO 9000 series into the JIS standards. Since the Industrial Standardization Act originally required the procurement of goods by national and local public organizations to respect the JIS standards, the Act required that national and local governments opt for JIS-certified goods while procuring goods. Therefore, new standards reflecting the ISO9000 series began to spread with the inclusion of goods and services demanded by the government. In November 1993, the Japan Accreditation Board (JAB) for Quality System Registration was established[3] together with the Ministry of Transport to promote the ISO 9000 series assessment and the registration body within Japan and to promote mutual recognition of standards with other countries (*MITI Bulletin*, November 15, 1993). Mutual recognition is the omission of examination and subsequent approval by one country where there are separate official standards between two countries, where the standards of one country are equivalent to those of the other.

Within the Seventh Plan, concrete policies continued to be examined even after the formulation of the plan with regard to achieving a life of comfort and abundance and responding to global environmental issues. The collection of data called a standards base, which constitutes the material for judging while deciding standards, had begun, targeting issues of (1) aging, welfare, and consumer fields, (2) cutting-edge technological fields, and (3) the global environmental field (*MITI Bulletin*, June 20, 1994).

Around the same time, and separate from the Seventh Long-Term Plan, guidelines were also presented, emphasizing a response to the aging society. The report from the "Livelihoods and JIS Special Committee" established in November 1990 as an organization within the Japan Industrial Standards Commission stated, "In the past, the JIS has been enacted mainly to contribute to industrial activities such as the rationalization of production, the streamlining of distribution, and improvements to the quality of industrial products, however, against a background of changing societal needs in recent years, efforts have been ongoing considering the rise in the aging population and the welfare society," and in continuing these efforts, pointed out the need to contribute to the harmonization of international standards and international

[2] "SI units" refers to the international metric system, the successor to the metric system.

[3] A public body that accredits audit certification bodies certifying companies to ISO 9000.

standardization activities together with the importance of establishing a standards base (METI Bulletin June 21, 1994).

From Table 5.2, it can be understood that while the total number of standards declined between 1990 and 1994, they increased in the non-ferrous metals, medical safety equipment, and ICT-related fields; further, JIS standards were beginning to be set in the new materials and new societal needs fields as well (The following description refers to, *Kōgyōgijutsuin nenpō*, Vol. 1, 1994, corresponding sections). While sponsored research themes focused on ICT-related and new materials-related fields, those relating to international standardization also began to come up. However, it was from the late 1990s onward that international standardization activities began to be given clear strategic significance; and moreover, the international harmonization of the JIS was progressing slowly, and only about 50% had been completed by the end of March 1995 (The Japan Standards Association (JSA) 1995, p.126).

As stated above, it can be seen from the Sixth and Seventh Long-Term Plans for Industrial Standardization and the policies grounded in each of those plans that until the early 1990s, (1) the response to trade frictions that emerged following the GATT Standards Agreement in 1979, (2) responses to new industries and new materials focusing on the ICT industry which were clarified from around the mid-1980s onward, and (3) responses to changing societal needs in the 1990s were considered as policy issues for standards administration. The significance of standards focusing on the machinery industry declined. New roles for standards certification that began to be explored from the 1970s emerged as issues (1)–(3) against a backdrop of trade friction issues, the development of the ICT industry, and the development of new materials, along with the transition to a domestic-demand driven economic structure with comfort and affluence as its slogan. However, compared to the responses to (1) and (3) where specific measures were sought by creating the JIS and operating the JIS mark system, with respect to issue (2), although the JIS standards increased in the field of information and some research began to be aimed at international standardization, if we compare this to the later time, regardless of whether they involve an official standard (de jure) involving the nation or a voluntary standard (de facto) based on the private sector, while emphasis was placed on the international competitive power of standards and the development of the ICT industry, there were few instances where this produced concrete policy. As we shall see next, the business community, which was acutely aware that standards had begun to dominate corporate management in the ICT field, was beginning to complain about the delays in administrative support.

3.3 The Evaluation of Policy by the Business Community

Books published in 1995 by the Japanese Standards Association, established in 1945, and complementing standards administration through projects such as the publication of the JIS standards table, summarize the situation at the time by drawing upon a survey of companies, as follows (The following description refers to, as above JSA

1995, pp. 72–73). In the ICT industry, because of the global scale of infrastructure construction and the rapid advancements in technological innovation, the task of standardization could not be concluded in the interests of a single country alone, and depending on the standard, these were capable of giving rise to situations that were more than capable of swaying companies' futures, so the importance of standards to Japanese companies in their international competitiveness was considered to have become extremely high. Issues to which the JIS framework cannot adequately respond such as the international consistency of standards, the timing of standards setting, and the handling of intellectual property rights have also arisen. There may have been a view suggesting that the role played by the private sector has expanded. However, it is not always the case that the significance of public standards has fallen; looking at the questionnaire for businesses introduced in the same book,[4] it appears that many companies had recognized the need for the prompt standardization of fields relating to new materials, the environment, and information. Stakeholders in the electronic equipment and electrical machinery industries took the view that "even amidst fierce competition, there ought to be areas where stakeholders can reach an agreement, such as naming, demonstrating performance, how evaluation is conducted etc.," and a new role was expected to be played by the government in coordinating between public standards and companies (Ibid., pp. 86–87).

The significance of standards was emphasized in particular for ICT-related industries and changes in the issues requiring harmonization with international standards were also highlighted. This was done not only with the aim of opening up the Japanese market against a background of trade friction, but also because it was believed that compliance with international standards (including de facto ones) was essential for market development with the emergence of global products centering on information-related devices (Ibid., p.95).

In relation to this, in response to the question of whether they felt the development of international standards had held Japan back, 62.2% of the general companies answered "no," while 37.4% responded saying "yes." Among the JIS factories, these figures were 87.4% and 12.6%, respectively. Although there were many respondents that said "no," a specific example of one that said "yes," stated that "the development of standards relating to the ISO 9000 series, the environment and to digital, has progressed in recent years." The reason for the delayed response was most often "the gathering of domestic opinions on the new and revised draft standards has been delayed," followed by "I did not attend the drafting meeting and so was unable to get them to accept the Japanese opinion" (Ibid., pp.100–101). Companies were faced with the problem of how to participate in the task of formulating international standards while rapidly gathering domestic opinions. Particularly in the information-related industry, because it began to be considered that once standardization began, it would thereafter affect the competitive strength of companies for a long time into

[4] The survey covered 247 companies and 1,501 JIS-mark-approved factories, the former covering 35 industries, the latter 15. The survey was conducted between January and February 1995 using a questionnaire sent in the post along with a request to complete the survey from the head of the standards department of the National Institute of Advanced Industrial Science and Technology and the President of the Japan Standards Association. Ibid., pp. 79–80.

the future, an involvement in the setting of either international voluntary standards (de facto) or official standards (de jure) was considered important.[5] Rather than responding to international standards in a way that opened up the markets passively so to speak, Japan's active involvement in the setting of international standards began to be considered important.

On the other hand, that there were many respondents in the same survey answering "no" to whether they had any experience of being held back by the development of international standards suggests that the role of the JIS in guaranteeing the technological strength of the mining and machinery industries had already declined as evinced by the changes in the key topics of the long-term plans for industrial standardization as identified above.[6]

As stated above, while it can be said that the significance of official standards in the mining and machinery industries had declined, new issues emerged for the business community, such as the creation and use of rapid and flexible standards by the private sector, the role of standards administration accompanying changing business structures, and means of participating in international standard-setting activities focusing mainly on the ICT industry. Based on the investigation in the previous section, although the government recognized the changing times felt by the private sector in the long-term plans for industrial standardization from one perspective, it was unable to formulate a concrete policy to convince the business community, and these issues remained.

---

[5] This point should be considered while capturing the characteristics of the ICT industry. A detailed examination is a topic for future research, however, from the 1980s onward, in the ICT field, and including home appliances, it is surmised that companies began to awaken to the standardization of not only technology and price but depending on the product, their specifications, in order to increase competitive strength and acquire market share. For example, in the home VCR market, competition to acquire market share was based on differences in specifications that could be called competing standards, VHS (JVC, Matsushita Electric Industrial, etc.) and Betamax (Sony etc.). By the late 1980s, the market share for Betamax had become negligible and the standard was retired (Yamada 2008). It is thought that the standardization of some standards for companies in the electronics industry in this period began to be viewed as affecting market competitiveness.

[6] As an indirect example, between 70 and 80% of the establishments used the JIS Mark labeling system as a criterion for purchasing products, but one-third did not use it as a guide, and many industries pointed out that "JIS standards are minimum standards rather than purchasing standards. Furthermore, about half of the respondents did not recognize the necessity of JIS mark when asked whether their business activities would be hindered without JIS mark when trading products, and in highly competitive fields such as automobile-related and information-related fields, In highly competitive fields such as automotive and information-related industries, the use of materials and parts that exceed JIS regulations has become commonplace. As above, see also The Japan Standards Association (1995, p. 94).

4 Promoting Deregulation and Defining Specific Responses to New Social Needs

4.1 The Impact of the World Trade Organization/Technical Barriers to Trade (WTO/TBT) Agreement

Through the GATT, a new standards agreement based on the results of discussions relating to the establishment and operation of the TBT (Agreement on Technical Barriers to Trade) Committee came into effect in January with the launch of the WTO in 1995 (as above Abe 2013, pp. 477–483). The contents of the arrangement referred to as the WTO/TBT Agreement were as follows: (1) the harmonization of standards and certifications with international standards, (2) the standardization of certification systems with international rules, and (3) the obligation to make efforts toward mutual recognition (MITI/METI journal [monthly] VOL.30 No.5, 1997). (2) required that the method of certification administration permitting the display of the JIS mark should come in line with international rules (guidelines offered by international organizations such as the ISO and IEC etc.). In 1996 the WTO's "Agreement on Government Procurement" entered into force, whereby member governments had to follow international standards if they used standards as a criterion while procuring goods and services (Izumi 2009, p. 130). In general, further respect for international standards was required and in this context this, the Agreement of Government Procurement had a great impact.

The WTO/TBT Agreement required the standardization activities of countries to be more international in accordance with the free trade system. As economic growth emerged as a topic of policy, standards administration had not lost sight of the importance of international standards in influencing the competitive strength of Japanese companies in foreign markets.

4.2 The Eighth Long-Term Plan for Industrial Standardization—The Late 1990s

The Eighth Long-Term Plan for Industrial Standardization compiled in 1995 was new in that it emphasized the promotion of deregulation, specific measures to respond to the development of the ICT industry, and the involvement in international standardization activities (The following description refers to, *MITI Bulletin*, January 6, 1995). Three new policy topics were presented: (1) in response to social needs, (2) in response to technological progress, and (3) in response to the development of the borderless economy. Specifically, (1) in response to social needs, the promotion of de-regulation, transition to an economic/social system emphasizing the principle of self-responsibility, consumer protection, and responding to an aging society such as medical welfare and environmental protections, were emphasized. (2) In response to technological progress, strategic standards were emphasized for corporate activities in fields with remarkable technical innovation and standardization linked to the collection of royalties by taking advantage of expanding the market share and intellectual property rights arose as an irreversible change. Moreover, it was judged that the success or failure of revenue collection from such rights depended on the adoption of products and services in the early stages. At the same time, emphasis was placed not only on the exclusive provision of standards, but also upon the interoperability and interconnectivity of standards that were geared toward a high-speed information society. Anticipating the ICT industry, de facto standards were set in the market and strategic management policies enabling a small number of companies to enjoy monopolistic benefits were supported on the one hand. However, on the other hand, the need for the consideration of policy among consumers and competitor businesses by opening up standards planning with appropriate royalties was also pointed out. (3) Participation in international standardization organizations was emphasized as a response to the development of the borderless economy. International standards were being decided by international standardization bodies such as the ISO and the IEC, which are in the private sector, but had begun to play an unrestricted official role. Therefore, democratic votes by each country were being used to select standards. But Because the European Union (EU) had a larger number of participating countries, EU regional standards had begun to become international standards because of their high versatility. If these were to be reflected in the WTO/TBT Agreement and thus become procurement criteria for participating countries, international market competition would be affected. Thus, participation in international standardization activities with a view to cooperate with other countries in the Asia–Pacific region became an issue.

Policies concerning deregulation continued to be formulated even after the publication of the plan. The report delivered by the Japan Industrial Standards Commission in December 1996 had a strong awareness of the impact of international standardization (The following description refers to, *MITI Bulletin*, December 25, 1996). As changes in recent years, the WTO/TBT Agreement states that "the importance of standards and certification policy for the facilitation of trade has increased greatly," and the definitive policy of the Eighth Long-Term Plan states that "reinforcing the role of the private sector and seeking their independent participation" were desirable. The report's examinations first spanned the state of the JIS, the JIS mark system second, and the promotion of international standardization activities last. Of these, for the first, in response to the growing emphasis placed on JIS in line with perspective (1) as shown in the plan above, "a basic policy was taken that stakeholders such as producers, including small and medium enterprises (SMEs), users, and consumers shall investigate the necessity or otherwise of whether or not a standard corresponds to a field important for the establishment of national standards, and whether or not it can transition to a private standard belonging to a business group etc., and based on such an investigation, it is appropriate to abolish standards that do not align with fields that are a priority for the establishment of national standards, or can be transferred to a private standard." Second, the "Industrial Standardization Act" was revised to call for the "introduction of a private certification body" and the "self-compliant display of undesignated products." On the other hand, the third emphasized financial assistance for international standardization activities and the harmonization of international standards with the JIS playing a national role. In response to the international issue of deregulation, together with strengthening the limits on administrative involvement, (first, second), on the other hand, it can be said that the point showing the third issue was shown by the increasing efforts of the administration in conducting international standardization activities.

4.3 *Revision of the Industrial Standardization Act*

The Eighth Long-Term Plan and the implementation of the above report were initially promoted through deregulation. The Industrial Standardization Act was revised in March 1997. The main points are: (1) to simplify and accelerate the procedures for the drafting of standards required for JIS registration, as well as revising the existing JIS standards from a zero-basis, to be carried out until 1999, and (2) to commission the private sector to carry out factory certification duties necessary for the display of the JIS mark, as well as to promote JIS self-conforming labeling (as above MITI/MRTI). With respect to (1), there were two routes for developing a standard: Article 12 applied by private groups and Article 11 where the cabinet minister responsible for the task would recognize the need for the standards; prior to the revision of the law, most provisions under Article 11 were considered for the simplification of procedures under Article 12 and for shifting the task of developing standards onto the private sector (as above, Eto 2007). For (2), the adoption of international rules was planned for and in cases where a private certification body was designated as a proxy for the administration, it was intended to accept foreign bodies actively and to satisfy the requirements of the WTO/TBT Agreement.[7] The reduction of administrative involvement based on the demands of era was also a form of deregulation in consideration of the WTO/TBT Agreement.

4.4 *Response to New Societal Needs*

Responses to new societal needs that had been viewed as an issue since the Seventh Long-Term Plan continued in the search for specific policy while reflecting the requirements of internationalized standardization. For example, in the context of welfare, according to the state of standards administration focusing on the elderly and disabled compiled by the Japan Industrial Standards Commission in June 1998 (The following description refers to, MITI Bulletin, June 24, 1998), the issues at that

[7] At the same time, this measure has also been viewed as broadening the scope of discussions about the acceptance of Japanese-developed standards by foreign countries.

point in time centered on efforts toward (1) the standardization of accessibility equipment, and (2) the standardization of common items. (1) emphasized on promoting research and development as well as adoption, and this was because "objective criteria for judgments concerning accessibility equipment are required, and further development of standardization and the promotion of international standardization are required of the JIS for accessibility equipment." However, because there are many types and these are custom-made for their users, by adopting the aim of creating interoperable goods as a basic principle while considering the needs of the elderly and disabled, cost-reduction effects were expected because of the advantages of scale while developing products that could also be used by healthy people as a result of the small size of the welfare equipment market. In order to ensure that the principle of interoperable goods was not limited to Japan alone but that it was also commonly recognized worldwide, it was decided that guides should be created and distributed widely to the ISO and the IEC.

In September 1998, the Japan Industrial Standards Commission Medical Safety Equipment Committee compiled guidelines on the standardization of medical equipment (blow, MITI Bulletin, September 16, 1998). The guidelines called for an end to the situation where even despite an exception being made that JIS-compliant medical equipment did not require approval under the Pharmaceutical Affairs Act, because of the rapid pace of technological progress in electronic devices, JIS-certification was delayed and the advantages in the Pharmaceutical Affairs Act were not being made use of. Furthermore, because the standardization of medical equipment was advancing internationally, Japan also made an issue of promoting active participation in international standardization activities and reflecting this in the JIS.

Also the same commission compiled a report concerning the standardization of occupational health and safety equipment in January 1999 (The following description refers to, *MITI Bulletin*, January 14, 1999). If we look among the points highlighted concerning the need for and the role of standards and specifically at the part in this report that discusses the relationship with mandatory regulations such as the Pharmaceutical Affairs Act, the use of worker health and safety equipment is obligatory under the Industrial Safety and Health Act, and the view was taken that the law could be supplemented by approving or disallowing the use of the JIS mark for this equipment. As in the case of medical equipment, this was a method whereby applying JIS to appropriate occupational health and safety equipment if the conditions were satisfied, the use of the equipment would be obligatory under compulsory labor regulations. The significance of the role of the JIS was greater from the perspective of product safety, however, in practice, as highlighted by the issues with medical equipment, prompt and appropriate standardization that was conscious of harmonization with international standards was a conspicuous issue. Thus, the operations of the JIS complementing mandatory regulations was also compatible with the notion of deregulation in that where privately-led standards maintained safety, they could be used as substitutes.

Among the efforts taken to address the issue of strengthening the so-called restrictions on the involvement of the government in such areas as market liberalization and deregulation, following the Seventh Long-Term Plan in 1991, the intent of standards administration which found significance in the fields of welfare, safety, and hygiene began to be connected to specific policy in the late 1990s.

4.5 *Results and Challenges*

The Seventh Long-Term Plan as well as the search for measures and policy guidelines developed in the late 1990s based on it yielded the following results. The establishment and revision or abolition of the JIS is as shown in Table 5.2, however, in this period, the zero-base review of the JIS standard in response to the revision of the Industrial Standardization Act established in 1997, as detailed above, continued to proceed based on the following perspectives. First, the creation of the JIS standards and their reform progressed by drawing on the perspectives of consumer protections, welfare for the elderly, and environmental protections, such as for example 31 conditions were set in the welfare field in 1998 in response to the Eighth Long-Term Plan (MITI, Annual Report, 1998, pp. 912–913). Moreover, the revision reflecting harmonization with international standards was emphasized, and following FY 1997, of approximately 8000 JIS standards, 2000 reflected international ones (ISO and IEC), and furthermore, work was taken forward by targeting the approximately 1,000 standards for which harmonization had not progressed (MITI, Annual Report, 1997, pp. 899–900).[8] However, harmonization took a long time. It was judged somewhat later in documents from 2005 that "excluding some exceptions, substantial harmonization is complete."[9] Besides this, with respect to deregulation, by FY 1999, about half of the proposals for new standards were based on Article 12 to promote initiatives in the private sector through the revision of the Industrial Standardization Act, and the limits on administrative involvement increased.[10]

As mentioned above, through policies based on the Eighth Long-Term Plan, the standards administration was first deregulated. Next, the JIS standards were revised based on three points, namely (1) the issue of new materials that had arisen since around the time of the Sixth Long-Term Plan, and (2) the new societal needs that had arisen since the Seventh Long-Term Plan, and (3) the additional aim of ensuring further international harmonization in response to the 1995 WTO/TBT Agreement. However, specific policies for international standardization activities focusing on the development of the ICT industry remained scarce, and the development of policies had to wait until the 2000s. Together policy issues responding to Japan's economic slowdown were prioritized, policies necessary for the business community to support

[8] Note that in the process of harmonization, there were international standards that had not been reviewed for a long time, or which were technologically inappropriate, and Japan is required to revise them.

[9] METI Standards Certification Unit, "*Kijun'ninshō seisaku ni okeru jigo hyōka-sho*" [Post-facto report on standards administration policy], December 13, 2006. WEB version, http://www.jisc.go.jp/jisc/data/soukai/soukai_12/soukai_12-5.pdf.

[10] Special Committee for the Investigation of Standardization for the 21st Century, "*Hōkoku-sho*" [Report], May 29, 2000. WEB version, http://www.meti.go.jp/report/downloadfiles/g00608aj.pdf.

the international competitiveness of Japanese companies in the ICT field had finally begun to take shape.[11]

5 Development of Strategic International Standardization Activities

5.1 Setting an International Standards Strategy

The setting of a long-term plan for industrial standardization once every five years concluded with the restructuring of government agencies in 2001. However, the necessity for long-term plans has been recognized thereafter, and around the time when the Eighth Long-Term Plan had reached its fifth year, new investigations were being made into relatively long-term policy. That policy was characterized by consideration for the limits of activities relating to international standardization. According to a government evaluation of the Eighth Long-Term Plan in May 2000, the importance of responding to the following four points was highlighted: (1) further advancement of deregulation, (2) international harmonization of JIS, (3) adoption of strategic international de jure standards from the perspective of strengthening industrial competitiveness, and (4) standardization considering consumer perspectives.[12] Of these, (1) deregulation emphasized the substitution of the mandatory regulations mentioned above and thus took up the task of setting of more flexible rules utilizing standards as a topic.

What should be noted is that in (3), standards decided by private international standards bodies (ISO, IEC) in practice functioned as public international standards, and for European companies "there are many examples of strategic adoption to gain competitive advantage by de jure standardization of their own standards," and it was viewed as important to "carry out strategic resource investment" in places where international standards are created aiming for academic-industrial collaboration. It was around this time that the administrative side clarified its intention to support the international standardization activities of the business community (Ogawa 2009).[13] The same intention also manifested where the report emphasized collaboration with intellectual property administration as a direction for the development of standards

[11] The Ministry of International Trade and Industry can be said to have had jurisdiction over the equipment-related industries relating to the ICT industry, though the ICT industry itself fell under the jurisdiction of the Ministry of Internal Affairs and Communications. This did not change until after the ministerial reorganization in 2001. I would like to leave the question of standards administration with jurisdiction over the ICT field split across two ministries as a topic for future investigation.

[12] Special Committee for the Investigation of Standardization for the 21st Century, "*Hōkoku-sho*" [Report], May 29, 2000.

[13] According to (Ogawa 2009, Chapter 4), the March 2006 Cabinet's Third Basic Plan for Science and Technology transformed it into strategic standards administration. However, it is safe to say that these guidelines were presented somewhat before this.

in the future. This focused on the review of the government reaction in response to the progress made by companies that had led international standards in claiming intellectual property rights.[14]

Recognizing this change in the environment, the Office of Standards and Certification of the METI's Industrial Science and Technology Policy and Environment Bureau, which was transferred to an internal bureau during the restructuring of government agencies as described above in the first paragraph of Sect. 1, compiled "*Hyōjunka senryaku*" [Standardization Strategy] in 2001 (The following description refers to, *METI Bulletin*, September 20, 2001). The overview of this "Standardization Strategy" addressed the following aspects: (1) "ensuring market harmonization and efficiency," (2) "promoting international standardization activities," and (3) "linking standardization policy and research and development policy." It included standardization strategies spanning across 27 distinct fields, of which the following were particularly important: (1) "Standardization of ICT," (2) "Development of environmental protection standards," (3) "Development of standards reflecting the perspectives of consumers, the elderly, and the disabled," and (4) "Development of standards for production and fundamental technologies for industry." The "Standardization Strategy" focused on the same perspectives that the planning evaluation from May 2000 above focused on, namely "creating international standards through Japanese leadership." Since then, a plan has been formulated annually based on the "Standardization Strategy" in lieu of the five-year plans that were used before. Even where they had not been drawn up formally, policies embodying this strategy were developed. The standards administration policy was presented this way between 2000 and 2010 (as above, Eto 2007).

5.2 Promoting International Standardization Activities

International standardization activities were promoted in the following manner. For example, though a measure had begun during the Eighth Long-Term Plan, the international standard "Guide for addressing accessibility in standards" (ISO/IEC Guide 71), proposed to the ISO by the Japan Industrial Standards Commission in 1998 came into effect in November 2001, and in April 2003 this ISO standard became a Japanese domestic standard (The following description refers to, *METI Bulletin*, April 16, 2003). Japan had led the development of this international standard, which was subsequently recognized as an ISO standard. This later became an official Japanese

[14] Intellectual property began to be emphasized by the government as a tool for strengthening the international competitiveness of Japanese companies because of the Intellectual Property Strategy Committee that was established as an internal bureau in February 2002. In the same year, the "*Chitekizaisan senryaku taikō*" [Strategic principles for Intellectual Property] was formulated, from which point the Patent Office that had jurisdiction over intellectual property sought to work together with standards and conformity assessment administration. Nakayama (2001, Chapter 1), Arai (2006) etc.

standard. Besides this, revised guidelines for international standardization activities were presented in June 2004, recognizing public–private activities and new materials as important fields (*METI Bulletin*, June 10, 2004). In the same month, sponsored research was commissioned to promote the standardization necessary for the creation of draft international standards. The state of public offerings was as shown in Table 5.3. Looking at June 17, 2004, the top four themes among public offerings were calls for "Implementing research and development necessary for the creation of draft international standards, by linking them to international standards, and strengthening the competitiveness of Japanese internationalization further, with the aim of contributing to the development of a country capable of sustainable development," and specifically pointed at strengthening strategic international competitiveness (*METI Bulletin*, June 17, 2004a). The two themes for June 17 were also calls that sought to emphasize the effects of achieving international competitiveness (*METI Bulletin*, June 17, 2004b). The public offerings in 2005 and 2006 also aimed at creating draft international standards.

Table 5.3 Calls for new commissioned research in 2004–2006

2004
1) Establishment of fundamental technology and standardization of low-temperature lead-free solder mounting
2) Standardization of information sharing systems for manufacturing use
3) Standardization of methods of testing microbial oxidation degradation
4) Standardization of free viewpoint television encoding systems
5) Standardization of cell production systems using industrial robots
6) Standardization of safety verification technologies for the hardware and software of electronically-controlled safety equipment
7) Standardization of performance evaluation testing methods of anisotropic (lotus type) porous metals
2005
1) Standardization of plastic recycling
2) Standardization of the safety and reliability of optical components and modules for high-quality optical transmission systems for the FTHT broadband era
3) Standardization of methods of testing the fracture characteristics of fine ceramics for rolling components
4) Standardization of methods of nanoparticle safety evaluation
5) Standardization of methods of evaluating the accuracy of non-contact three-dimensional measurement equipment
2006
1) Personal identification: standardization relating to the compatibility and interoperability of biometrics (fingerprints)
2) Standardization necessary for high-accuracy composition analysis of thin organic films
3) Standardization of accessible design technology
4) Standardization of methods of measuring thermal efficiency and hot water specification modes

Source For 1995 and 1996, applicable volumes of the "Tsūshōsangyōshō nenpō" [M ITI Annual Report], for all others, "Keizai sangyō kōhō" [METI Bulletin]

5.3 The Progress and Challenges of Deregulation

The promotion of deregulation accompanied by legal reform in 1997 was a policy that entrusted the administration of recognizing the display of the JIS mark to the private sector as described above. While the establishment and license of chartered organizations progressed based on this, errors began to arise in the JIS mark factory certification. For example, in January 2003, precast concrete products certified in December 2002 by the Japan Quality Assurance Organization (JQA) were found to include products that had been certified despite containing materials that had not been approved by the relevant JIS standards, and in June 2003, the Japan Quality Assurance Organization's operations were suspended for 90 days (*METI Bulletin*, February 18, 2003 and June 26, 2003).

These issues were judged as particularly likely to occur while certifying under ISO 9000 and ISO 140000 management systems. A report from July 2003 that was compiled by a special committee for the assessment of management systems standards and conformity that was established in 2002 expressed fear about the disadvantages of deregulation, saying that if there were companies with low awareness on obtaining certifications and if the private organizations entrusted with the administration of certification had weak investigative capabilities, the credibility of the standards would fall.[15] In response, in 2005, the scope of standardization was clarified "to prevent an organization from building a system in a way that excludes important environmental aspects when obtaining ISO 14001 certification, and then appealing as if all of the organization were certified" (*MITI Bulletin*, January 17, 2005). That being said, since similar administrative responses continued from 2005 to 2009, setting criteria to judge whether the quality and the environment have been standardized is difficult, and in cases promoting the commissioning of private organizations, the propriety of the examination and the applicability of judgment criteria have become issues.[16]

5.4 Results and Responses

The results of international standardization activities were as follows. In September 2002, the photocatalyst standardization committee was established within the Japan Fine Ceramics Association with support from METI, which intended to expand the market for photocatalysts, a new material; subsequently, the creation of draft JIS standards and their proposal to the ISO began (The following description refers to, *METI Bulletin*, January 29, 2004). Moreover, in October 2003, the Japanese proposal that the ISO ought to promote standardization in the field of methods of testing air purification was adopted, and in 2004, standards creation began. Japanese-led

[15] This has been pointed out as a "downward spiral." [METI Annual Report], 2003, p.268.

[16] For example, the creation of audit guides etc. *METI Bulletin*, August 7, 2008 and August 27, 2009 etc.

standardization in the field of air purification testing methods began to be investigated. However even as late as 2008, JIS standardization remained under investigation and was thus limited to domestic efforts; consequently, the results of the investigation were not reflected in international standardization activities as planned (*METI Annual Report*, 2008). The government also recognized that there were limits on international standardization activities since 2001, and guidelines compiled in December 2006 by the Intellectual Property Strategy Headquarters established within the cabinet in May 2003 titled "Comprehensive strategy for international standards" were forced to follow the 2001 "Standardization strategy," thereby reiterating the issue from five years earlier that Japan had to take the initiative in international standardization.[17]

Amidst these circumstances, the JIS standards for antimicrobial testing researched in Japan were approved as an ISO standard in 2007. This was the first case of international standardization without any modification of the JIS standard, and was described by METI as a "great opportunity for businesses with strengths in the antibacterial field" (*METI Bulletin*, October 15, 2007).

Although there was some awareness of the errors in deregulation, further progress was necessary. In the background of this development, the following aspects remained: (1) the recognition of the high significance of standards as a tool for strengthening industrial competitiveness, (2) the increased expectations for standards as an "information communication tool" in response to the diversification of consumer needs, and (3) the need for greater specifications of the deregulations promoted by the government as a whole (*METI Annual Report* 2001, and 2002, pp. 353–353). (2) was based on the perspective of needs corresponding to environmental protection, safety, the elderly, and the disabled, and because it took up the provision of information corresponding to the consumers' sense of values as a topic, it was intended as more proactive in promoting the substitution of safety indicators with the JIS mark. Thus, private-led standardization was considered effective in achieving goals (1) and (2), and was considered as consistent with the policy issues of (3). Item (3) was in response to the contents of a cabinet decision in March 2002 to "reform the implementation plan for administrative involvement in public-interest corporations." Its contents displayed the basic principle of moving away from the system of inspection and testing by public-interest corporations entrusted by the government to self-confirmation and self-security by companies.

The ongoing demand for deregulation came to fruition with the revision of the Industrial Standardization Act in October 2005. From the conventional method where the government specified the JIS standards that required the display of the JIS mark, it became possible to display it even without being a specified standard (The following description refers to, *METI Annual Report* 2005, pp. 239–242); conventional operations where the government specified consigned institutions to approve the display of the JIS mark had changed to a registration system, and the administrative involvement was restricted even further (Ibid., pp. 239–242). Consigned institutions were

[17] Intellectual Property Strategy Headquarters, "*Kokusai hyōjun sōgō senryaku*" [Comprehensive Strategy for International Standards], December 6, 2006. WEB version, https://www.kantei.go.jp/jp/singi/titeki2/kettei/061206.pdf.

recognized within Japan and overseas, and as of December 2008, 22 domestic institutions and 3 foreign institutions had been registered (METI Japan Industrial Standards Commission Secretariat 2008, p. 14). It has, however, been necessary to frequently create guidelines to continue to increase the reliability of audits. Even with the unmasking of these issues, it can be said that priority was given to the internal government judgment that current deregulation was insufficient to develop standards administration while taking advantage of the energy of the private sector and linking it to economic growth. On the other hand, although no specific policy was emphasized for the relationship between mandatory regulations and JIS standards, as of November 2008, 138 laws cited JIS standards as their technical standards (Ibid.).

6 Summary and Outlook

The role of the JIS in improving the competitive strength of the mining and machinery industries declined from the 1970s onward, and almost reached its expiry upon entering the 1990s. The standardization policy was emphasized again from the late 1970s onward for two reasons. First, the 1979 GATT Standards Agreement called for the review of each country's standards such that they would not establish non-tariff barriers. Second, in the 1980s, it became necessary to respond to the rise in trade friction and the development of the information and communications industry. In response to the recognition of the JIS mark for foreign businesses, the setting of official standards for new materials and new industries was promoted. However, the significance of official standards for new materials and new industries was not always clear, and so a questionnaire survey of the business community in the late 1990s highlighted the inadequacy in the administrative response. On the other hand, in the 1990s, the setting, revision, and abolition of the JIS standards introducing environmental and welfare perspectives emerged as a new topic.

The Eighth Long-Term Plan in 1995 primarily focused on deregulation relating to international harmonization and market liberalization as a response to the WTO/TBT Agreement that came into effect the same year, the issue of the active ongoing operation of JIS in the ICT, environment, and welfare fields was addressed, and emphasis also placed on policies utilizing the JIS for international competitive strength. It was around the time of the formulation of the 2001 "Standardization Strategy" that policies promoting Japanese leadership in international standardization began to be defined specifically. Although the importance of standardization of new materials and the ICT industry had already been highlighted, the response had been limited to a revision of the JIS standards. However, switching to the aim of ratifying standards through international organizations such as the ISO and the IEC, policy shifted to supporting the development of these companies and the competitiveness of Japanese companies by making the Japanese-developed standards as international standards. This was also influenced by the fact that the importance of international standards had increased with the "Government procurement Agreement" coming into effect in 1996 as part of the WTO/TBT Agreement. Standards administration since the 1980s onward had promoted a so-called "passive response" of diluting the originality of the JIS in response to trade frictions. However, specific policies dynamically bringing the results of research relating to standards adopted in Japan only appeared from around 2000. That said, there are many means to promote international standardization. Deregulation promoting the consignment of standards administration to private sector brought along errors in certification, etc., and the new direction began to reveal issues.

The change in standards administration in recent years to aggressively setting standards with internationalization as its main issue suggests the following. Looking at the policy method somewhat simplistically, trade and industrial policy from the High-Speed Growth Period through to the 1970s targeted industries to promote the renewal of facilities, and investment with the allocation of funding as an incentive. This was an industrial policy promoting rationalization, modernization, and the creation of new industries, and resulted in the contribution to economic growth (Hashimoto 2001, Chapter 6).[18] That said, amidst a policy shift toward market liberalization against a background of improving the efficiency of the energy industry and the protection of consumer interests from the 1970s and the trade frictions in the 1980s, policy methods targeting industry declined gradually. From the 1990s onward, economic growth through structural reform came to be viewed as a self-evident policy issue and policies contributing toward improving productivity, an important key to growth, became scarce. Emphasis was then placed on the logic that deregulation would give rise to economic growth.

These changes in policy methods can be attributed to the growth of fiscal deficit, the belief in values viewing Japanese economic activity as being of a different nature etc., but it can also be conjectured as being influenced by Japan's high-speed growth facing its limits and changes in its industrial structure. In other words, Japan' high-speed economic growth, in which investment in facilities for the machinery and heavy manufacturing industries maintained high levels of productivity, shifted to small batch production of many products from the late 1960s onward, thereby slowing productivity growth (Hirayama 2008; Takeda 2008), and increasing the importance of service industries like to raising the market value of goods. This manifested in the form of fads (Ishi 2004), conservatism, maintenance, standardization in recent years, and the creation of intellectual property rights based on such standards etc. (Ibid.). Furthermore, because these service industries were initially characterized by their productivity growth being very unlikely to be significant when compared to the machinery industry, the trend of slowing economic growth was strengthened by this shift in the industrial structure.[19] Accompanying this shift in the industrial structure to services, policies also shifted toward supporting not only the provision of investment for facilities, but also toward developing demand and increasing the

[18] Hashimoto's argument more accurately relates the efficacy of policy to an argument neglecting creative activities by private economic agents, highlighting the government's role.

[19] The gap in productivity between industries requires careful consideration. This is therefore a tentative interpretation. For now, let us consider the following perspectives. Hashimoto (2000, Sect. 3) and Takeda (2014).

value of products. In other words, it was a search for both the 1990s vision of policy expanding domestic demand (an emphasis on comfort and affluence etc.) influenced by the trade frictions of the 1980s, and for the international standardization activities from the late 1990s onward. Moreover, the shift in industrial structure to services, unlike the machinery and heavy manufacturing and chemical industries whose enormous capital investment costs were supported through policy, comparatively reduced the investment costs and government involvement as an investment provider[20]; so the new era policy approach was easily reconciled with deregulation theory.

With the collapse of the bubble economy and economic growth being emphasized as a policy issue, in the 2001 "Standardization Strategy," standards administration began to focus on supporting international standardization. This was because taking into account the limits of productivity growth and changes in industrial structure, as well as harmonization with the deregulation theory, the deliberate promotion of product standardization was thought of as linked to international market expansion.[21] In other words, the approach changed from industrial policy that fostered industry by allocating capital investment funding to one that resulted in economic growth in a somewhat roundabout way by supporting companies' autonomous innovation, and amidst these changes, standards administration would seem to have been given an important position as a growth policy adopted by the government. This direction again manifested in a 2006 strategy compiled by the METI to put the Japanese economy back on the path to economic growth as its population declined, where standards and conformity assessment administration supporting Japan in leading international standards was emphasized as part of several "Horizontal policies" to remove the industry framework (METI 2006).

However, even if the international standardization promoted by METI contributes to some kind of market expansion for Japanese companies and contributes to the economic growth by strengthening international competitiveness, it should not only be considered significant in this respect but also in that it may enable the rediscovery of the social significance of improvements to product value supported by standards administration. For example, standardization of sanitation may have an effect of representing the interests of consumers, as well as the effect of nurturing the perspective that even as a private money-making enterprise, the social act of supplying goods carries public significance. Moreover, the search by standards administration in recent years for the substitutability of welfare, environmental, and product safeties with JIS

---

[20] The allocation of funds to the development and rationalization of the machinery and heavy chemical industries during the high-speed growth period is significant. Following the stable growth period, the demand for investment in such fields declined, and as research has shown, the destination of such loans diversified and fragmented although a great deal of government finance was poured into ICT and into making improvements in transportation, see Uzawa and Takeda eds. (2009a, 2009b).

[21] However, even if a growth strategy using standards administration to secure overseas markets was possible, its efficacy would be limited while it ignored industrial characteristics. This is also true while making a standards corporate strategy. For example, Shintaku and Eto (2008) highlights the importance of standardization joining specific fields as part of corporate strategy. However, because it is not clear which industries are being assumed, it can be read that standardization is required in every industry and its promotion is a goal in and of itself.

standards in response to mandatory regulations can be considered significant for its revision of the public role of government even amidst the ongoing deregulation. While the examination of policy effects focusing on the subjective goal of strengthening international competitiveness and economic growth is important, at the same time, consideration from such a historical vantage point is also important. I wish to take up a detailed investigation of this point in the future.

Finally, let us briefly discuss the direction of standardization administration in recent years. In recent years, there seems to be an increasing number of discussions linking intellectual property rights to standardization in the hope of increasing market share, corporate profits, and ultimately economic growth.[22] This may be because strategic standard setting continues to grow in importance in the information and telecommunications industry. However, we must not forget that standards for goods and services have the potential to lead to market share, corporate profits, and economic growth only if we return to the viewpoint that they have public significance as well. It is important to place public significance at the top and consider private or national interests. It is also our issue for the future to examine how the government and information and telecommunications companies are responding to these recent intellectual property rights and standards.

References

Abe T ed. (2013) *Tsūshōsangyō seisaku-shi Vol.2, tsūshō-bōeki seisaku* [History of Trade and Industrial Policy Vol.2, Trade and Commerce Policy]. Research Institute of Economy, Trade and Industry.

Arai H (2006) *Chizai kakumei* [The Intellectual Property Revolution], Kadokawa ONE Theme 21

Eto M (2007) "Kōgyō hyōjunka seisaku no hensen to kijun'ninshō seisaku" [Transition to International Standardization Policy and Standards and Conformity Assessment Policy]. *Research and Technology Plan*, 22–1.

Eto M (2021) "*Hyōjunka Business senryaku taizen*" [Lodestat of Standardization]. Nihon Keizai Shinbun Publishing.

Fujita M and Kawahara Y (1998) *Kokusai hyōjun ga Nihon o hōi suru* [International Standards Surround Japan]. Tokyo: Nihon Keizai Shimbun, Inc.

Harada S (2008) *Sekaiichiba o seiha suru kokusai hyōjunka senryaku* [International Standardization Strategy to Conquer the World Market]. Tokyo: Tokyo Denki University Press.

Hashimoto J (2000) *Defure no shinkō o dō yomu ka* [Understanding the Advance of Deflation]. Iwanami Shōten Publishing.

Hashimoto J (2001) *Sengonihon keizai no seichō kōzō* [Post-War Japanese Economic Growth Structures]. Yuhikaku Publishing.

Hirayama T (2008) "Juyō kōzō to sangyō kōzō" [Demand and Industrial Structures]. In Haruhito Takeda ed., *Kōdo seichō-ki no nipponkeizai* [The Japanese Economy During the High-speed Growth Period], Yuhikaku Publishing.

Ishi S (2004) "Apareru sangyō to shōhi shakai—1950~1970-nendai no rekishi —" [The Apparel Industry and Consumer Society—A History of the 1950s-1970s]. *Socio-Economic History Society*, Vol. 70, No. 3.

[22] Recent studies that summarize examples of standardization that focus on the activities of companies include the following books (Eto 2021).

Izumi A (2009) *Hyōjun (sutandādo) no subete* [All of the Standards]. Research Institute of Economy, Trade and Industry.
Japan Standards Association (JSA)(1995) *Nihonkikakukyōkai 50-nen-shi—sangyō hatten to kōgyō hyōjunka*—[50 Years of the Japan Standards Association—Industrial Development and Industrial Standardization-]
Nakayama N (2001) *Tsūshōsangyō seisaku-shi*, Vol.11, *chiteki zaisan seisaku* [History of Trade and Industrial Policy, Vol.11, Intellectual Property Policy].
Odaka K (2013) *Tsūshōsangyō seisaku-shi Vo.1, sōron* [*History of Trade and Industry Policy, Vol.1, General Remarks*]: Tokyo: Research Institute of Economy, Trade and Industry.
Ogawa K (2009) *Kokusai hyōjunka to jigyō senryaku* [International Standardization and Business Strategy]. Hakutō Shobō Publishing.
Sawai M (2011) "Tsūshōsangyō seisaku-shi kyū sangyō gijutsu seisaku":*History of Trade and Industrial Policy Vol.9, Industrial Technology Policy.*
Shintaku J and Eto M eds. (2008) *Konsensasu hyōjun senryaku* [Consensus Standards Strategy], Nikkei Publishing.
Takeda H (2008) "Nihon no kō seichō keizai," [Japan's High-speed growth economy]. In Haruhito Takeda ed., *Kōdo seichō-ki no nipponkeizai* [The Japanese Economy During the High-speed Growth Period], Yuhikaku Publishing.
Takeda H (2014) *Datsu-seichō shinwa* [De-Mystifying Growth]. Asahi Shinsho Publications.
Yamada H (2008) *Defakuto sutandādo no kyōsō senryaku* [dai ni-han] [Competitive Strategy for de facto Standards [Second Edition]. Hakutō shobō publishing.
Uzawa H and Takeda H eds. (2009a) *Nihon no seisaku kin'yū I: kō seichō keizai to Nipponkaihatsuginkō* [Japan's Guidance Policy Finance—The High-speed Growth Economy and Japan's Development Banks].University of Tokyo Press.
Uzawa H and Takeda H eds. (2009b) *Nihon no seisaku kin'yū II: sekiyu kiki-go no Nipponkaihatsuginkō* [Japan's Guidance Policy Finance—Japan's Development Banks after the Oil Shocks]. University of Tokyo Press.

Government Reports, etc.

Advanced Industrial Science and Technology (AIST) Department of Standards ed. (1989) *Kōgyō hyōjunka no Ayumi—kōgyōhyōjunkahō shikō yon jū-shūnen —*" [The Course of Industrial Standardization—The 40th Anniversary of the Industrial Standardization Act]. Japan Standards Association,
METI ed. (2006) *Shin keizai seichō senryaku* [New Strategy for Economic Growth]. Research Institute of Economy, Trade and Industry.
METI Japan Industrial Standards Commission Secretariat (2008) "*Nihonkōgyōhyōjunchōsakai nenji hōkoku 2008*" [Japan Industrial Standards Commission Annual Report 2008]
Special Committee for the Investigation of Standardization for the 21st Century, "*Hōkoku-sho*" [Report], May 29, 2000.

Annual Reports, etc

MITI (various years) *Tsushōsangyōshō nenpō* [MITI Annual Report]
METI (various years) *Keizaisangōshō nenpō* [METI Annual Report]
MITI "*Kōgyōhyōjunkahō no kaisei to kongo no hyōjun gyōsei*" [Revision of the Industrial Standardization Act and Future Standards Administration], MITI/METI journal [monthly] Journal, Vol. 30 No. 5, 1997.

Advanced Industrial Science and Technology (AIST) ed. (various years) *Kōgyōgijutsuin nenpō* [The National Institute of Advanced Industrial Science and Technology Annual Report]

Tsusan-shō Kōhō [Official bulletin of trade and industry] (MITI Bulletin)/

July 13, 1985. "Kōgyō hyōjunka suishin chōki keikaku no sakutei ni kansuru hōkoku-sho matomaru" (Suishin chōki keikaku) [Summary report of the development of the long-term plan for industrial standardization]

July 13, 1985. "Kōgyō hyōjunka suishin chōki keikaku no sakutei ni kansuru hōkoku-sho matomaru" [Summary report of the development of the long-term plan for industrial standardization]

June 14, 1991. "Kōgyō hyōjunka suishin bumon betsu chōki keikaku no sakutei" [Setting the long-term plan for promoting industrial standardization by sector]

November 15, 1993. "Zaidanhōjin Nihon hinshitsu shisutemu shinsa tōroku nintei kyōkai no setsuritsu kyoka ni tsuite" [Concerning establishment permissions of the Japan Quality System Audit Registration Association]

June 20, 1994. "Nihonkōgyōhyōjunchōsakai hyōjun kiban kenkyū tokubetsu iin kaihōkokusho (sōron)" [Report of the Special Committee on Basic Standards Research by the Japan Industrial Standards Committee (General remarks)]

June 21, 1994. "*Nihonkōgyōhyōjunchōsakai kurashi to jisu tokubetsu iin kaihōkokusho*" [The circumstances of the Japan Industrial Standards Commission and JIS special committee report]

January 6, 1995. The National Institute of Advanced Industrial Science and Technology Standards Division, "Kōgyō hyōjunka no chōki-teki suishin hōsaku (dai hachi-ji chōki keikaku) no kentō ni tsuite" [About the examination of long-term measures to promote industrial standardization (the eighth long-term plan)]

December 25, 1996. "*Kokusai hyōjunka taiō no kyōka—nihonkōgyōhyōjunchōsakai tōshin—*" [Strengthening Responses to International Standardization—Report from the Japan Industrial Standards Commission]

June 24, 1998. Japan Industrial Standards Commission, "Kōrei-sha shōgaimono ni hairyo shita hyōjunka seisaku no arikata ni kansuru kengi (yōshi)—bariafurī shakai o mezashite—" [A Proposal for How Standardization Policy Should Consider the Elderly and Disabled (Summary)—Toward a Barrier-free Society]

September 16, 1998. Japan Industrial Standards Commission Medical Safety Equipment Division, "Iryō-yō kigu no kongo no hyōjunka no susumekata ni tsuite" [On How to Advance the Standardization of Medical Equipment in the Future]

January 14, 1999. Japan Industrial Standards Commission Medical Safety Equipment Division, "Roudou anzenyougu no kongo no hyōjunka no susumekata ni tsuite" [On How to Advance Standardization of Medical Equipment in the Future]

***Keizai-sangyō Kōhō* [Official Bulletin of Economy, Trade and Industry]**

September 20, 2001. Industrial Technology Environment Bureau Standards Certification Unit, "*Hyōjun-ka senryaku no sakutei ni tsuite—nihonkōgyōhyōjunchōsakai hyōjun bukai hōkoku—*" [On the formulation of Standards Unit Strategy - Report from the Japan Industrial Standards Commission Standards Subcommittee]

February 18, 2003. "Zaidanhoujin Nihon hinshitsu hoshō kikō ni yoru jisu māku kōjō nintei no sakugo ni tsuite" [On errors in the JIS-mark factory approval by the Japan Quality Assurance Organization (Incorporated Foundation)]

April 16, 2003. "Kōrei-sha shōgaimono e no hairyo kikaku no issō no kaihatsu sokushin—kokusai gaido nana jū-ichi o jisu-ka—"[Further promoting the development of standards considering for the elderly and disabled—Incorporating International Guide 71 into JIS]

April 16, 2003. "Shitei nintei kikan zaidanhoujin Nihon hinshitsu hoshō kikō ni taisuru gyōsei shobun ni tsuite" [On the administrative handling of the designated accreditation body (incorporated foundation) the Japan Quality Assurance Organization]

January 29, 2004. "Kōshokubai shiken hōhō no jisu seitei ni tsuite~kūki seijō-ka seinō shiken hōhō no jisu-ka~" [On establishing JIS standards for photocatalyst testing methods—JIS standardization of testing methods for air purification performance]

June 10, 2004. "Kokusai hyōjunka katsudō kiban kyōka akushon puran' ni tsuite" [On the "International standardization activity foundations reinforcement action plan"]

June 17a, 2004. "Heisei 16-nendo kijun'ninshō kenkyū kaihatsu jigyō oyobi shin hatsuden shisutemu chōsa kenkyū (hyōjunka chōsa kenkyū) ni kakaru itaku-saki no kōbo ni tsuite" [On the public offering to consignees concerning the 2004 standards certification research and development project and investigative research into new power systems (research into standardization)]

June 17b, 2004. "Heisei 16-nendo kijun'ninshō kenkyū kaihatsu jigyō-hi hojokin no kōfu-saki kōbo ni tsuite" [About the recipients of subsidies for the 2004 standards certification research and development project]

January 17, 2005. "Kankyō manejimento shisutemu jisu kikaku no kaisei tsuite" [On revisions to the JIS standards for environment management systems]

October 15, 2007. "Wagakuni no kōkin shiken hōhō ga kokusaihyōjunkakikō (aiesuō) kikaku to shite shōnin" [Japan's antibacterial testing method recognized as a standard by the International Standards Organization (ISO)]

August 7, 2008. "Manejimento shisutemu kikaku ninshō seido no shinrai-sei kakuho no tame no gaidorain' no kōhyō ni tsuite" [On the publication of guidelines for ensuring the credibility of the management system standards certification system]

August 27, 2009. "Manejimento shisutemu kikaku ninshō seido no shinrai-sei kōjō no tame no 'akushon puran (kōdō keikaku)' no kōhyō~shinrai-sei no takai aiso manejimento shisutemu kikaku ninshō seido o mezashite~" [Publication of an "action plan" for improving the credibility of the management system standards certification system—Aiming for the high-credibility ISO standards certification system for management systems]

Satoshi Kawamura is Associate Professor at Faculty of Economics Department of Economics, Josai University and Research Associate at RIETI. His research focuses primarily on the role of industrial policy in the mechanical and electrical industries in Japan. He has also written numerous articles on the small transport industry in pre- and postwar Japan. Additionally, he has recently developed an interest in consumer society and the music industry.

Changes in the Global Financial Environment Surrounding Japan in the 21st Century: Foreign Exchange Policy and International Financial Coordination

Kiyoto Ido

Abstract The two decades since 1990 have been a major turning point for Japan's economic and financial system. This chapter provides an overview of the evolution of its policy and position, focusing on changes in the international financial environment surrounding Japan. Three major shocks triggered the transition: (1) the "Bubble" brought about by the Plaza Accord and its collapse, (2) financial liberalization and the financial crisis that followed the burst of the bubble economy, and (3) the Asian currency crisis. Partly due to the appreciation of the yen after the Plaza Accord, Japanese companies relocated their production bases overseas and global supply chains developed. Japanese economic structure has become more committed to various regions of the world, especially in Asia. After the 1997–98 Asian currency crisis, financial cooperation among East Asian countries was established, in which Japan played a leading role. In 1999, the international financial coordination system was expanded from G7 to G20, and G20 began to discuss not only international financial crises but also a wide range of issues such as sustainable growth of the world economy. Japan's role was also increasing in this context.

1 Introduction

The twenty years from 1990 marked a momentous turning period for the economic and financial system of Japan, which had maintained high economic growth after World War II. This transition is attributable to three shocks. The first shock was the bubble economy led by the measures taken in response to the appreciation of the yen triggered by the 1985 Plaza Accord, and the burst of the bubble. The second shock was financial deregulation and the financial crisis that resulted from increases in non-performing loans in the recession that followed the collapse of the bubble economy. Thirdly, the Asian currency crisis, which began in Thailand in 1997, was a significant

K. Ido (✉)
Former Director-General of International Bureau, Ministry of Finance, Tokyo, Japan

H. Takeda and J. Watanabe (eds.), *Rethinking Japanese economic policy at the turn of the 21st century*, Advances in Japanese Business and Economics 34,
https://doi.org/10.1007/978-981-97-5512-7_6

event for the international environment around Japan. These shocks pressed Japan's economic and financial system to undergo structural reform. However, in a different light, it was an inevitable turning point for Japan to shift from a high economic growth system to a mature economy.

The subsections below will provide an outline of the three shocks and an overview of the structural change that they brought to the Japanese economy.[1]

1.1 The Bubble Economy and Its Collapse

In the 1980s, the US embraced "twin deficits," which called for a correction of the strong dollar. Hence, in 1985, the financial ministers of the G5 nations (Japan, US, UK, Germany and France) agreed to the Plaza Accord in New York to correct the strong dollar in coordination. Consequently, the Japanese yen rapidly appreciated and Japan lost its export competitiveness, pushing the economy into recession. Fiscal expansion and monetary easing measures were taken in response.

Furthermore in 1987, the G7 nations, comprising the G5 nations and Canada and Italy, adopted the Louvre Accord, which, for the purpose of stabilizing the dollar, had economies with trade surpluses commit to coordinated interest rate cuts while the US raised interest rates. As a result, given the insecurity of the Japanese economy, the Bank of Japan cut the official discount rate to historically low levels. The low interest rate encouraged excess money to inflow to stock market and real estate, thus developing an economic bubble.

However, controls on real estate lending were introduced as measures against the bubble and the official discount rate was raised for fear of inflation; and therefore, stock prices dropped in 1990, followed by land prices the following year, and the bubble burst. This was followed by a prolonged recession, with the yen remaining strong until 1995, and the Asian currency crisis provoking financial unrest in 1997. Also in the latter half of 1990s, the Japanese economy entered deflation, which continues today in Japan. The 1990s later came to be referred to as "the lost decade."

The appreciation of the yen following the Plaza Accord also changed industry. Firstly, companies coped with the strong yen by offshoring production and increased overseas production boosted intermediate and capital goods trade between Japan and East Asia thus forming crossborder supply chains. Secondly, financial institutions were also globalized to support these efforts. Furthermore, the development of the service economy called for increased competition and improved productivity in the service sector.[2]

[1] The author referred to Ito (2009) and Iwata (2011) in writing this chapter.

[2] Based on Saito (2017).

1.2 Financial Deregulation and Financial Crisis

In the post-war period, Japan took what is often referred to as the convoy system to protect the less competitive financial institutions in order to maintain the stable management of all financial institutions. However, as the bubble collapsed and the economy matured, the financial deregulation policy was announced in 1996 with an aim to activate the financial market through deregulation and to make Tokyo an international financial market that could compete on equal footing with New York and London. This is the so-called Japanese Big Bang, in which Japan attempted to deregulate and globalize the banking, securities and insurance industries, upholding the concepts of free, fair and global.

However, the burst of the bubble had generated enormous amounts of non-performing loans, which drove major financial institutions, such as Hokkaido Takushoku Bank and Yamaichi Securities, into bankruptcy; and therefore, resolving the non-performing loan issue and stabilizing the management of financial institutions became urgent priorities.

Given these circumstances, deregulation measures allowed for a wide range of business operations, including banking and insurance, to be conducted under a holding company. This led to the emergence of three megabanks, after rounds of integration and reorganization. In terms of monetary policy, the Bank of Japan Act was amended in 1998, strengthening its independence from the government. Furthermore, financial supervision functions were removed from the Ministry of Finance and housed in the newly established Financial Supervisory Agency, which became the Financial Services Agency in 2000, embracing policy planning functions as well.

1.3 Asian Currency Crisis

The East Asian region experienced high growth from the 1980s to the 1990s mainly driven by manufacturing and product exports, as the "THE EAST ASIAN MIRACLE" published by the World Bank in 1993 revealed to the world. ASEAN had come to lead international cooperation in industry. Furthermore, with the strong yen causing Japanese manufacturers to offshore their factories and Japan and China providing development assistance, ASEAN had fostered closer partnerships with Japan, China and Korea.

However, Asian financial markets were far from meeting international market standards, as most East Asian currencies were pegged to the US dollar and bond markets had yet to mature. Fiscal and monetary policy authorities advanced the deregulation of capital transactions while maintaining a dollar peg system and an anti-inflationary high interest rate policy; and therefore, they were challenged with the "open economy trilemma." Under such circumstances, the currency crisis that began in Thailand quickly spread to Indonesia, Malaysia and Korea.

In the chain of crises, these countries not only experienced economic stagnation but also faced a need for structural reform. Having succeeded in overcoming crisis through collaborative efforts among Japan, China, Korea and the ASEAN nations, the region has engaged in institutional cooperation under a framework known as "ASEAN Plus Three." These cooperative relations also helped Asian economies to avoid being exposed to critical damage in the Lehman collapse of 2008.

The ASEAN Plus Three Cooperation has been successful in terms of trade as well. The ASEAN Free Trade Area (AFTA) had been the sole FTA in the area, but after 2000, FTAs were concluded in succession between ASEAN nations and Japan, China and Korea. Japan has also concluded bilateral FTAs with many East Asian countries. And Japan and East Asian countries currently engage in negotiations on a Regional Comprehensive Economic Partnership (RCEP) with the participation of countries outside East Asia.

As described above, Japan faced a major turning period from the 1990s to the 2000s. East Asian countries recorded a high rate of growth that was referred to as the "East Asian Miracle" and became not only a major market for Japanese companies but also a promising offshoring destination for Japanese manufacturing hubs in the context of strong yen. In order to develop intra-regional trade networks and establish supply chains in Asia, a stable exchange rate and unified funding market and settlement system are essential. The Asian currency crisis that occurred at the end of the 1990s added momentum to advance the establishment of a financial system and regional financial cooperation.

This chapter will focus on changes in the international financial environment around Japan, discussing the evolution of foreign exchange policy, the Asian currency crisis and changes in the international financial cooperation regime.

2 Changes in the Foreign Exchange Policy

2.1 Overview

After World War II, the Japanese yen was pegged to the U.S. dollar at 360 yen. However, failing to prevent waves of hot money inflow triggered by the Nixon Shock in 1971, Japan experienced a rapid appreciation of the yen and shifted to a floating rate system in 1973. In 1964, Japan acceded to IMF Article 8 status and eliminated foreign exchange restrictions, but it required another twenty years to fully deregulate its foreign exchange market, with the liberalization in principle of foreign exchange and capital transactions in 1980, and the liberalization of cross-border transactions and foreign exchange operations in 1998.

Former US President Reagan, who took office in 1981, believed that if yen transactions could be liberalized, then the weak yen could also be corrected, and set up the Japan-US Yen-Dollar Committee in 1983, publishing a report in May the following year. On the other hand, from 1983 through 2002, the "internationalization of the yen" was repeatedly proposed in the Council on Foreign Exchange and Other Transactions and other forums. With an aim to turn Tokyo into an international financial market standing on equal footing with London and New York, the Foreign Exchange and Foreign Trade Control Law was amended, thus abolishing the authorized foreign exchange bank system and deregulated foreign exchange transactions between residents and nonresidents. This marked the beginning of the Japanese "Big Bang" financial regulatory reform aimed at developing a "free, fair and global" system.

Given these developments, interest rates were deregulated, access from foreign financial institutions to the Japanese market was improved, the firewall regulation separating banks, securities, and insurance were relaxed or abolished, the short-term money market was prepared, the euro-yen market was deregulated, and the Japan Offshore Market and the Tokyo International Financial Futures Exchange were established. However, the internationalization of the yen failed to make significant progress in both current transactions, including imports and exports, and capital transactions. The stagnant progress in growing out of dependence on the dollar can be attributed to several reasons: for example, (i) many Asian currencies were pegged to the dollar, and therefore it was more convenient from an accounting perspective for many countries to perform both money and trade transactions in dollars; (ii) while it is important that a currency can be conveniently managed, the options for investment in yen were at the time still limited both in quality and quantity, and thus there were few advantages in terms of product diversity and liquidity, and taxes; and (iii) international commodities, including crude oil, were all traded in dollars.

In this way, Japan gradually deregulated overseas and foreign exchange transactions, but after shifting to a floating rate system, its foreign exchange policy consistently focused on maintaining a stable yen market that reflected economic fundamentals and avoiding exchange rate fluctuation caused by speculation. This enhanced the predictability of corporate economic activities and limited impact on business.

The next section will first look at the long-term trends of the dollar-yen rate, then observe foreign exchange policy from the perspectives of foreign exchange intervention, its relationship with monetary policy, the real effective exchange rate and the balance of payment.

2.2 *Long-Term Trends of the Dollar-Yen Rate*

This section will first look at foreign exchange trends after Japan shifted to a floating rate system.[3] From 1977 to 1978, Japan ran large current account surpluses, but private capital flows were limited through exchange rate control. However, the 1980 renewal of the Foreign Exchange and Foreign Trade Control Act liberalized cross-border flows of private capital. In contrast, in the US, then President Reagan's so-called "Reaganomics," which involved tax cuts and increased fiscal spending, further boosted interest rates, which had already been raised as an anti-inflationary measure.

[3] Kuroda (2005a) and Kuroda (2005b) were referred to.

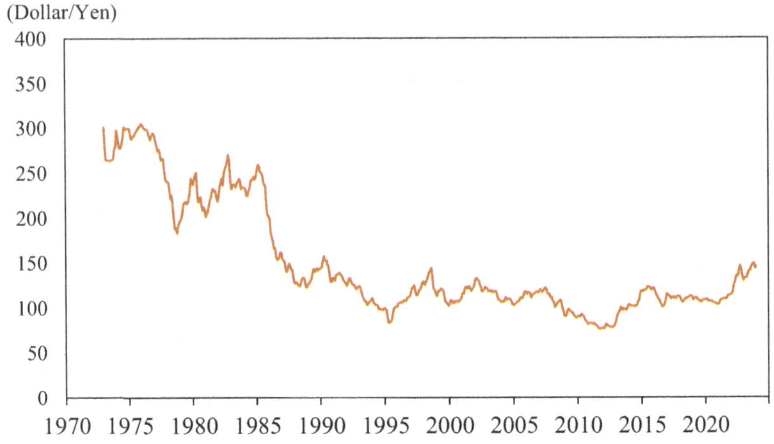

Fig. 1 Long-term trend of the dollar-yen rate (*Source* Bank of Japan, "Foreign Exchange Rates")

As a result, Japanese institutional investors increased investment in US Treasury bonds, strengthening the dollar.

In September 1985, at the Plaza Hotel in New York, the finance ministers of the G5 nations agreed that the dollar was overvalued, and thus the Plaza Accord was concluded in order to rectify the strong dollar. Japan then adopted a policy that would induce a stronger yen, which appreciated from 240 to 215 yen to the dollar. However, the yen continued to surge, and in 1987 the finance ministers of the G7 nations concluded the Louvre Accord at the Louvre in Paris to stabilize foreign exchange. Despite the conclusion of the Louvre Accord, the yen continued to appreciate for a while until the US consecutively raised its policy interest rate to counter the inflation induced by the bubble economy (Fig. 1).

However, in 1990, the US economy entered a recession and the US implemented a series of policy rate cuts. In contrast, even with the turn of the decade, the Bank of Japan was concerned that surging crude oil prices and a weak yen may trigger imported inflation and consecutively raised the official discount rate three times. After summer 1991, the Bank of Japan also shifted to lowering the policy rate, but because the US cut its rates at a faster pace, the interest rate differential between the US and Japan became smaller, to the extent that US and Japanese interest rates were transiently reversed. Consequently, the yen appreciated against the dollar once again, reaching a rate of 79 yen against the dollar in 1995, despite repeated attempts of intervention since 1993.

In January 1995, Rubin became US Secretary of the Treasury, and asserting that a "Strong Dollar Policy" would be in the interests of the US, laid more importance on capital transactions than on international trade transactions. As a result, the yen depreciated, reaching a dollar-yen rate exceeding 120 yen. Furthermore, in July 1997, the Asian currency crisis began in Thailand, and toward the end of the year, the Japanese financial market was also challenged with crisis, including the bankruptcy of Hokkaido Takushoku Bank and Yamaichi Securities, thus weakening the yen to as far as 150 yen in summer 1998. However, the Russian currency crisis that followed, affected by the Asian currency crisis, provoked the bankruptcy of LTCM; and therefore, carry trade, or procuring funds in currencies with a low interest rate and investing in currencies with higher yields, was abandoned. This involved, for example, buying yen, given its low interest rate, and investing in high-yield bonds denominated in Australian or New Zealand dollars, to capture the differential between the rates. The repurchasing of the yen, the funding currency, caused the yen to abruptly appreciate, pushing it up to 100 yen against the dollar in summer 1999.

Later from 2004 through 2007, the yen carry trade rose to the trend again. This effectively weakened the yen to a certain extent, increasing capital flows and moderating the appreciation of the yen provoked by the current-account surplus. However, it should be noted that in the long term, that this kind of money management will eventually unwind. After the financial crisis in 2008, given the US' quantitative easing policy, the Japanese yen became a "safe haven currency" and appreciated again. Furthermore, given the European credit crisis, beginning with Greece's credit issues, in October 2011, the yen marked a record high of 75 yen to the dollar. Speculations that insurance companies might sell foreign assets to procure funds in yen in order to pay the insurance on damages from the Great East Japan Earthquake also contributed to strengthening the yen.

After 2012, under Abenomics led by Prime Minister Abe, the new Governor Kuroda of the Bank of Japan aimed to pull Japan out of the prolonged recession by adopting a quantitative and qualitative easing policy (QQE), consequently depreciating the yen to 120 yen against the dollar.

2.3 Foreign Exchange Market Intervention

As aforementioned, Japan's foreign exchange policy is focused on maintaining a stable yen market that reflects economic fundamentals, but under a floating rate system, the market can deviate from economic fundamentals or become unstable due to exchange rate overshooting and psychological factors from drastic change in the financial or economic environment. In such cases, market interventions were performed to stabilize the market. Since Japan shifted to a floating rate system, the yen has followed an appreciating trend in the long term; and therefore, market interventions basically involved selling yen and purchasing dollars. From 2003 to spring 2004, in particular, massive market interventions were performed (Fig. 2).

Market interventions involve issuing foreign exchange fund bills and using the yen procured to purchase or sell yen and dollars. Interventions can be performed by one authority alone or in coordination with other G7 authorities. However, even in the case of a unilateral currency intervention, the intervention is basically performed based on close prior communications with the authorities of the counterpart country, as the measure will affect their currency value.

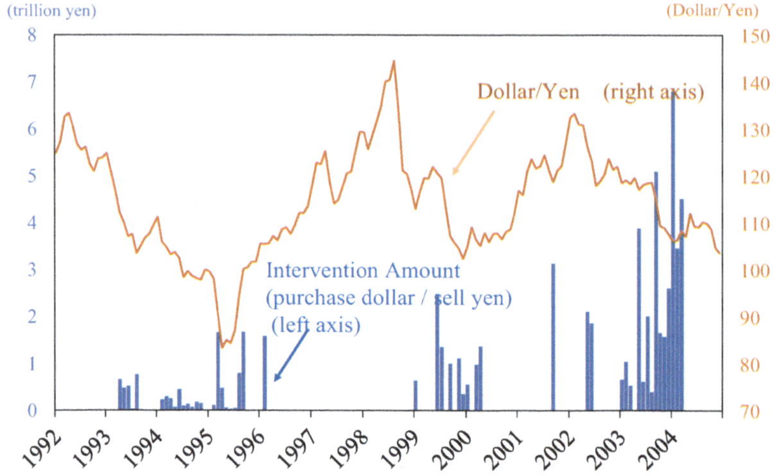

Fig. 2 The dollar-yen rate and foreign exchange market intervention (*Source*: Bank of Japan, "Foreign Exchange Rates"; Minstry of Finance, "Foreign Exchange Intervention Operations")

There are different ways to perform a foreign exchange market intervention. Other than purchasing and selling currencies, restricting capital transactions accompanying foreign exchange transactions, and "verbal intervention," or psychological persuasion by top officials of currency authorities, can also be effective. However, in the case of Japan, given the deregulation of the foreign exchange market in the 1990s, capital trade restrictions cannot be used to influence the foreign exchange market, and the impact of verbal interventions is unpredictable. Furthermore, with increased daily foreign exchange transactions, the effect of market interventions through the purchasing and selling of currencies has become limited. Methods of intervention include temporary massive money injection to convey the strong will of the authorities to the market and a series of small interventions that enshroud the authorities ("stealth interventions"). While there are divided views on which method is more effective, the outcome is largely dependent on the market situation.

Japan holds a significant amount of foreign reserves, standing at more than 1 trillion dollars. This is the result of continued current-account surpluses, as well as of market interventions. The necessity of holding foreign reserves is debated, but Japanese companies and financial institutions have received assistance of foreign reserves through JBIC, etc. when the Japan premium presented challenges in purchasing foreign currencies in the face of global financial crisis. Furthermore, during the Asian currency crisis, Japan was able to provide assistance to countries in crisis by using currency swap agreements. Based on these points, I believe that it is meaningful to maintain a certain amount of foreign currency reserves.

2.4 Monetary Policy and the Foreign Exchange Rate

Monetary policy is also closely linked to the foreign exchange rate. Changes in the interest rate differential between Japan and the US induced by changes in the monetary policies of the two countries affect the dollar-yen exchange. To present, interest rates have generally been higher in the US than in Japan; and therefore, financial tightening in the US and financial easing in Japan would widen the gap between interest rates in Japan and the US, pushing the market toward a strong dollar and weak yen (Fig. 3).

In recent years, with quantitative easing policies having become globally common, it has been debated that countries might be implementing monetary easing policies for the purpose of depreciating their own currency. However, it has been repeatedly confirmed at G7 and G20 Finance Ministers and Central Banks Governors' Meetings that the exchange rate should not be used to manipulate trade transactions or competitiveness, and that monetary easing can naturally be adopted as needed as a domestic economic policy.

Hence, the Ministry of Finance, the Financial Services Agency and the Bank of Japan need to coordinate closely not only because of the close link between monetary policy and the exchange rate, but also from the perspective that foreign exchange interventions affect the money supply. In addition to periodical meetings, consultations have come to be held as needed to address significant changes in the financial market.

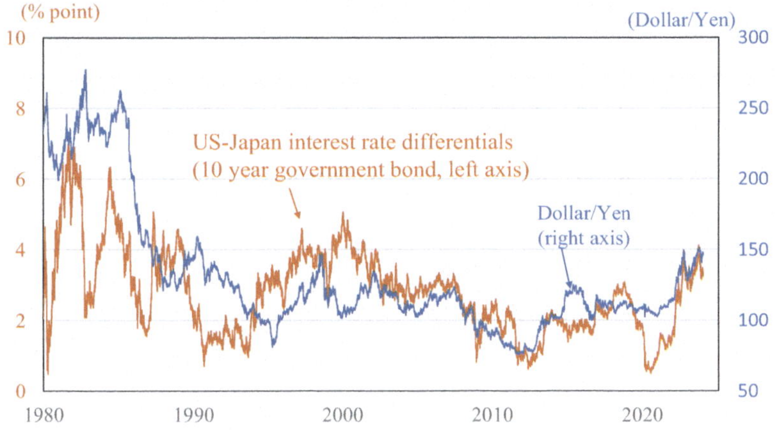

Fig. 3 The dollar-yen rate and interest rate differencials (*Source* Ministry of Finance, "Interest Rate"; FRB, "Foreign Exchange Rates," "Selected Interest Rates")

2.5 Real Effective Exchange Rate

The value of a currency, in the long term, is affected by price development. Focusing on purchasing power parity, the real exchange rate takes into account the rate of inflation.

Taking into account the difference between Japanese and American price developments, the real dollar-yen rate trend after 1973, when Japan shifted to the floating rate system, reveals that the US inflation rate being higher than that of Japan had been a contributing factor to a relatively strong yen. While trends are slightly different depending on whether the consumer price index (CPI) or producer price index (PPI) is used, the overall trend matches the nominal rate trend, in terms of the real purchasing power parity (Fig. 4).

The real effective exchange rate is the weighted average of the real exchange rate of the home currency against other currencies on the basis of trade weights (Fig. 5).

In terms of the real effective exchange rate, after shifting to a floating system, the yen has on the whole been strong, although it has been temporarily weak from time to time. After the Plaza Accord in 1985, in particular, it continued to surge until 1988. However, it depreciated during the Asian currency crisis and remained moderately weak until the financial crisis in 2008, when it resumed an appreciating trend again. Since 2013, when Governor Kuroda of the Bank of Japan adopted the quantitative and qualitative monetary easing policy, the yen has basically followed a depreciating trajectory.

When discussing industrial export competitiveness based on the real exchange rate, it should be noted that the indices used represent all prices. Real rates should

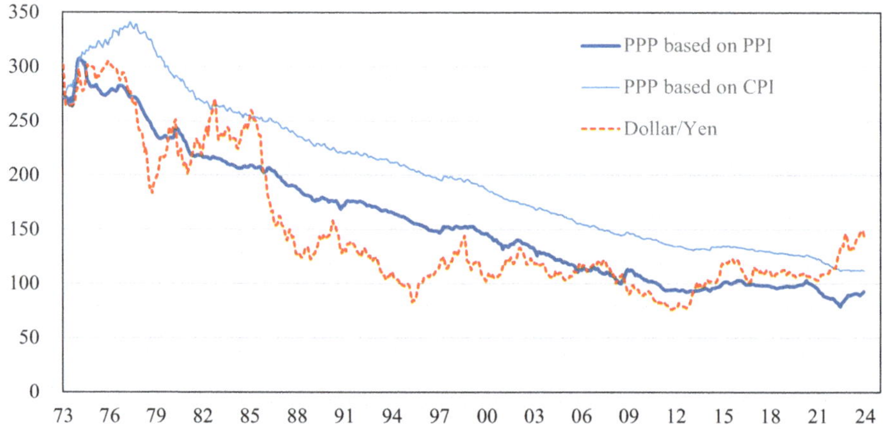

Fig. 4 The Dollar-Yen rate and purchasing power parity (*Source*: Bank of Japan, "Foreign Exchange Rates," "Corporate Goods Price Index,"; Ministry of Internal Affairs and Comunications, "Consumer Price Index"; Federal Reserve Bank of St. Louis (original data based on United States Bureau of Labor Statistics, "Consumr Price Index," "Producer Price Index"). *Note* PPP calculation based on 1973 average (1 dollar = 265.3 yen))

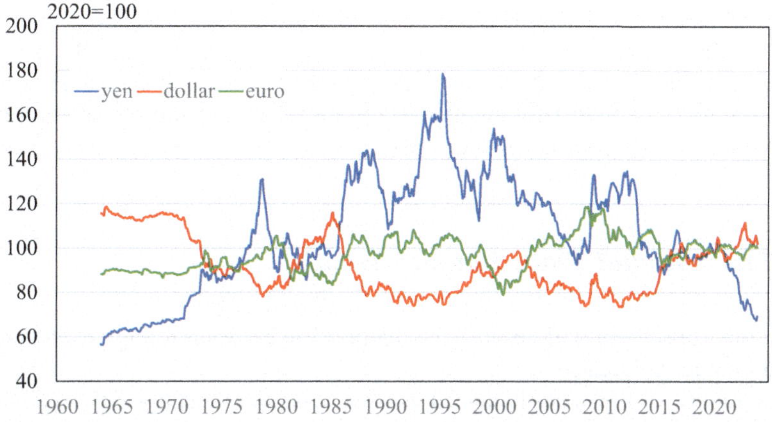

Fig. 5 Real effective exchange rate (*Source* BIS (Bank for International Settlements), "Effective exchange rates". *Note* Narrow base)

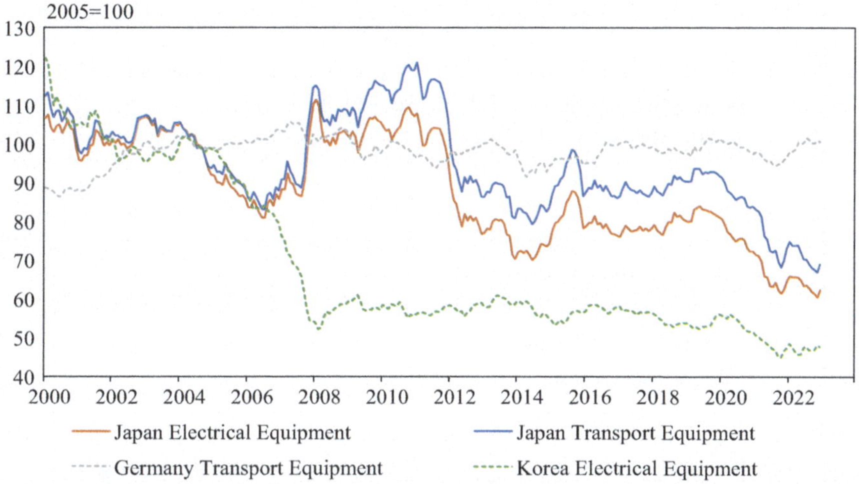

Fig. 6 Industry-specific real effective exchange rates (*Source* RIETI, "Industry-specific Real Effective Exchange Rates")

essentially be calculated by industry. The RIETI website provides industry-specific real effective exchange rates (iREER) (Fig. 6).[4]

This figure compares the real effective exchange rate for the electrical equipment industry in Japan and Korea and that for the transport equipment industry in Japan and Germany. The Japanese rate for electrical equipment has dropped by 30% from the

[4] RIETI "Industry-specific real effective exchange rates for 25 countries" https://www.rieti.go.jp/users/eeri/.

rate in 2005, but the Korean rate has become even lower, giving Korea a competitive advantage. In contrast, the Japanese rate for transport equipment has decreased by 10%, whereas the German rate has increased, giving Japan an advantage. However, it should be noted that the iREER should be used for bilateral comparison on condition that competitive export products are considered for competing importer countries.

2.6 *International Trade Balance Trends*

Finally, this subsection will observe the relationship between foreign exchange and international trade balance.

For a long time, Japan has balanced its current-account surplus with its financial-account deficits, thus making overseas investments using the foreign currencies gained from exports. In 2003, 2004 and 2011, when exceptional inflows of foreign money resulted in financial-account surpluses, large-scale foreign exchange interventions were performed, thus forming large foreign currency reserves.

In terms of the current account, for many years Japan's trade balance registered a surplus while service trade remained deficit. However, with the turn of the century, changes have been occurring in the structure of the current-account (Figs. 7 and 8).

Firstly, trade surplus has significantly decreased since the financial crisis in 2008. The introduction of Abenomics in 2012, in particular, significantly weakened the yen,

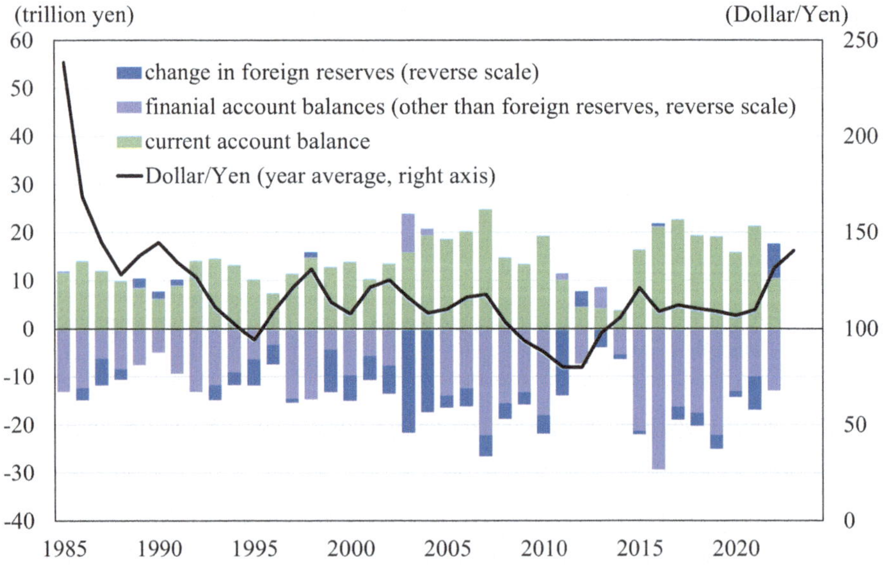

Fig. 7 Current account balance, Financial account balance, Foreign currency reserves (*Source* Ministry of Finance, Bank of Japan "Balance of Payments"; Bank of Japan, "Foreign Exchange Rates")

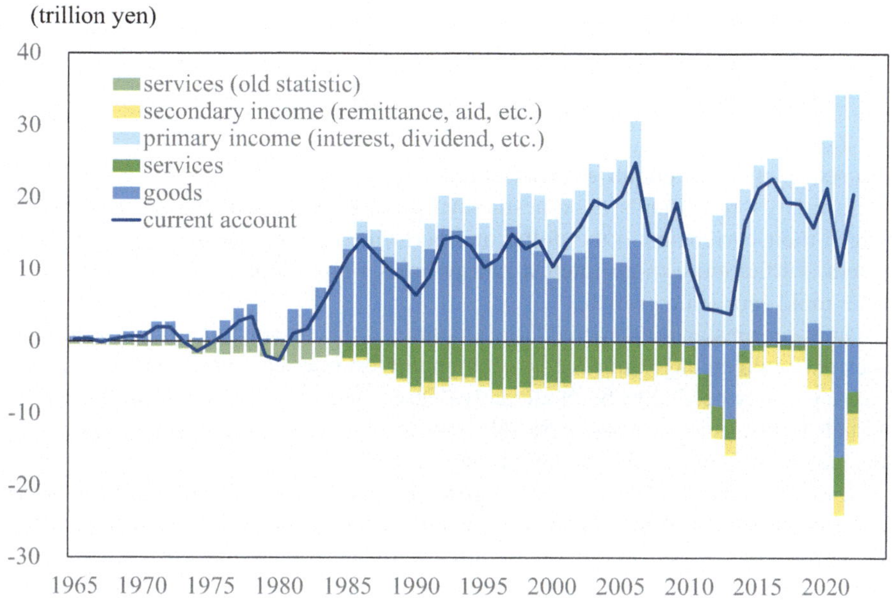

Fig. 8 Current account balance (*Source* Ministry of Finance, Bank of Japan, "Balance of Payments")

but the trade balance has yet to resume its former levels. This is attributable to the increased offshoring of production hubs by Japanese companies, and the rising rate of local procurement of parts, etc. Another factor is that exports from Japan are shifting to high-quality goods, including automobiles, for which it tends to be important in terms of maintaining brand value not to change the sales price in accordance with exchange rate trends.

Secondly, service deficits are shrinking, because tourism promotion policies have boosted inbound demand. Thirdly, the primary income balance has increased rapidly. The interests and dividends of investment in overseas projects and financial assets are increasing. This means that investment is producing larger income from overseas compared to exports, and hence indicates the maturity of the Japanese economy. Such changes should also be fully noted when observing future foreign exchange trends.

3 Asian Currency Crisis

3.1 Overview

East Asian emerging countries experienced a high growth rate of 7–8% in the 1990s, supported by foreign funds, as domestic savings were insufficient. However, countries pegged their currencies to the dollar and performed interventions to maintain this system. Furthermore, high interest rate policies were adopted to control inflation under rapid economic growth.

These circumstances attracted large amounts of short-term dollar funds as foreign investors could manage their funds at a high interest rate without exchange rate risk. Exchange rates needed to be moderately depreciated in order to control the inflow of such funds, but countries were reluctant to take action for fear that once they devalued their currency the market might plunge.

However, in the late 1990s, the US registered significant current-account deficits as the US economy recovered, and it turned to the "strong dollar policy." Given the dollar peg system, East Asian emerging countries were challenged with currencies appreciating in tandem and consequently lost export competitiveness, spreading among foreign investors, a sense of insecurity regarding East Asian emerging economies in general. As a result, funds rapidly flowed out of the region and currency values could no longer be maintained by intervention; and therefore, currencies plunged. Short sales of currencies by institutional investors, mainly hedge funds, fueled such trends.

The Asian currency crisis that started in Thailand in 1997 spread to neighboring countries. After hitting Indonesia and Korea, it went on to affect Malaysia and the Philippines. Monetary turmoil later prevailed across emerging economies and lead to the Russian crisis in 1998 and the Brazilian currency crisis in 1999.

The Asian currency crisis is attributable to a "double mismatches" provoked by domestically financing medium- to long-term investment in the home currency using overseas short-term funds in foreign currencies. Countries were challenged with the trilemma of open economy, with foreign exchange transactions being freely performed amid a policy environment that called for foreign exchange policies based on exchange rates pegged to the dollar and high interest rate policies to prevent domestic inflation.

3.2 Background of the Asian Currency Crisis

In the 1990s, Thailand offered preferential treatment to foreign capital in terms of taxes and foreign exchange management; and therefore, tremendous amounts of short-term funds flowed in from overseas, contributing a growth rate of around 9%. However, the US' "strong dollar policy" pushed the Thai baht up and slowed exports, thus stagnating economic growth. In 1996, Thailand recorded trade deficits for the first time, making foreign investors anxious of Thailand's economic growth, and in 1997, Thailand found itself under increasing pressure to devaluate the baht. The Thai central bank attempted to prop up the baht by buying baht, but in vain. In July, the Thai baht shifted to a floating rate regime.

Thailand then requested assistance of the IMF, which called for a structural reform package that would reverse the country's fiscal deficit and current-account deficit, control inflation, and implement financial reform as conditionality. However, the Thai economy had already entered recession and the austerity policy aggravated the situation.

In contrast, the Japanese government, in response to Thailand's request for assistance, hosted the Friends of Thailand Meeting in August 1997. The meeting, attended by major East Asian countries, the World Bank, and the Asian Development Bank, decided on an unexpected amount of more than 17 billion dollars in assistance. Later, the Japanese and Thai finance ministries engaged in consultations on the IMF package and other ways to support Thailand. Being one of the few Asian countries not colonized in the history, Thailand was reluctant to have its economy controlled by an IMF package. I had tête-à-tête meetings with Finance Minister Thanong concurrently with the plenary meetings, and we were finally able to reach agreement on concrete measures, including assistance from Japan.

The currency crisis that occurred in Thailand spread to Indonesia, which had also been enjoying high growth. Indonesia had sufficient foreign currency reserves, embraced no trade balance issues, and was experiencing moderate inflation. The Indonesian authorities had also been cautious of inflows of dollar funds, but was reluctant to lower the interest rate for fear of abrupt outflows of funds. However, after the Thai currency crisis, the authorities widened the rupiah's exchange rate band, thus increasing pressures to devalue the currency, leaving Indonesia with no choice but to shift to a floating rate system. Furthermore, the rupiah plunged due to the large amount of debts outstanding. The fact that the authorities lacked precise information of the debts held by private companies caused more confusion in the market than necessary. The debt amounts reported to us by the authorities also rapidly increased day after day.

Indonesia requested assistance of the IMF in October 1997, but the program that IMF made conditional exacerbated the Indonesian economy, as was the case in Thailand. The IMF then had little acknowledgement of the double mismatch issue involving the mismatch with the maturity structure of Indonesian corporate debt and the currency mismatch. It also drove many financial institutions into liquidation, arousing unnecessary confusion to the financial market, as viewed by some. As a result, relations between the Indonesian government and the IMF worsened, and these developments triggered political turmoil in Indonesia.

Korea's economic fundamentals were not as poor as those of other East Asian countries, but Korean financial institutions and private companies had borrowed large sums from abroad in foreign currencies, with some loans guaranteed in effect by the government. Therefore, when the currency crisis spread to Korea, Japanese and Korean authorities would check every day for foreign currency reserves that could be used freely. In the end, Korea requested IMF assistance, but as many other countries, was required to reduce fiscal deficit and to tighten the money supply. Furthermore, many private banks were brought under government control. As a result, the economic situation worsened beyond necessity, arousing strong criticism toward the IMF. For example, people sold "IMF lunch boxes" in the streets in protest against the hard lives that were being forced upon them.

Vietnam was fortunately not directly affected by the Asian currency crisis, but in response to a request for assistance from the Vietnamese government, Japanese delegation engaged in talks with then Deputy Minister of the Ministry of Planning and Investment on supporting economic structural reform in Vietnam. Back then, strong sense of reluctance towards economic liberalization still prevailed within the Party and the Vietnamese government, but we persistently negotiated with the cooperation of the resident office of World Bank, until we could finally reach agreement on deregulating imports, auditing state owned enterprises according to international standards, and fostering small and medium sized companies.

3.3 New Miyazawa Initiative

Japan had already adopted a floating rate system and was not exposed to direct impact of the currency crisis, but companies and financial institutions with operations in Asia were greatly affected. Japanese companies started offshoring in the late 1980s, when the yen was strong, in order to acquire competitiveness, and capital liberalization trends in Asia facilitated investment. Financial institutions increased their presence in Asia, supporting the offshoring of these companies.

Given the close economic relations between Asian countries and Japan, then Finance Minister Miyazawa decided to provide assistance to countries suffering the Asian currency crisis, commenting that "we are on the same boat," despite being challenged with financial crisis at home. In October 1998, he announced the New Miyazawa Initiative, a thirty billion dollars financial rescue scheme to help countries in crisis overcome their economic difficulties and to stabilize the international financial and capital markets. The New Miyazawa Initiative comprised fifteen billion dollars of medium- to long-term funds to be provided as Export–Import Bank of Japan (JEXIM) and ODA yen loans and fifteen billion dollars of short-term assistance provided using foreign currency reserves. The short-term assistance was loaned to countries in crisis through foreign currency reserve swaps in order to fund market interventions to maintain currency values.

Later, the Japanese Ministry of Finance collaborated with the IMF, the World Bank, and the Asian Development Bank to offer assistance through medium- to long-term loans and to concurrently support the authorities of Thailand, Indonesia,

Malaysia, Korea, and Vietnam in formulating economic reform plans. These economic reform plans helped countries faced with crisis make rapid economic recovery and successfully implement economic structural reform.[5]

3.4 *Efforts in Economic and Financial Cooperation in East Asia*

At the dawn of crisis, it was believed that the East Asian crisis had occurred as a result of the economic structure of each country dependent on foreign capital and exports, as well as foreign debt of the governments, and that it could be solved by following the conventional way of applying the IMF economic program. However, as the crisis spread to other Asian and emerging economies, it was revealed that the crisis had been caused by short-term debts that private financial institutions and companies had borrowed from overseas to perform the investments required for economic growth, and that it was of a different nature from past Latin American crises attributable to fiscal and trade deficits. Furthermore, countries were challenged with the trilemma of international finance, as countries had implemented monetary policies tailored to country-specific circumstances and had liberated capital transactions both domestically and internationally, while the exchange rate was still in effect pegged to the dollar. Hence, it became gradually clear that the crisis was a new "twenty-first century-type of crisis" that not only required emergency loan assistance more urgently and in larger amounts for countries in crisis to recover confidence, but also called for the monitoring of short-term capital flows and coordination with private financial institutions.

The IMF faced criticism that it tried to resolve the crisis by using conventional fiscal tightening and financial austerity policies without fully understanding the issue prevailing in Asian countries, and thus exacerbated the economic situation. Furthermore, large amounts of financial support measures were required in order to facilitate the refinancing of short-term foreign debt, but the IMF had yet to bear such functions. This led to the IMF reform, and in 1997, the Supplemental Reserve Facility was newly set up with no credit limit. Since the IMF had shown that it lacked enough understanding of the Asian economy, distrust in the organization prevailed among countries that experienced the crisis, and Japan would often serve as an in-between for the IMF and Asian countries.

Countries that experienced the currency crisis adopted new policies, including shifting to a floating rate system (abolishment of the dollar peg), strengthening financial supervision, and increasing foreign currency reserves. Furthermore, I believe that

[5] The rescue scheme for medium income debtor countries that then Finance Minister Miyazawa proposed at the Toronto summit to rescue Mexico, which faced a foreign debt crisis in 1988 was called the first "Miyazawa Initiative." The assistance scheme proposed in response to the Asian Currency crisis ten years later is known as the "New Miyazawa Initiative."

the unforeseen amount of assistance announced at the Friends of Thailand Meeting in August 1997 was a representation of partnership in Asia that built momentum for the establishment of a regional financial assistance framework in East Asia.

4 Development of International and Regional Financial Coordination

4.1 Overview

After World War II, the GATT/IMF regime has globally led discussions on international trade and finance. However, the twenty-first century brought in regionalism, which emerged alongside globalism. For example, the 1997 Asian currency crisis could not be addressed by IMF alone, and a currency and financial cooperation regime comprising ASEAN, Japan, China and Korea was formed. Furthermore, in the area of trade, the 1999 WTO ministerial meeting failed to agree on the launching of a new round, and the Doha Round that was finally launched in 2001 ended unsuccessfully in 2008, increasing bilateral and inter-regional EPA/FTA negotiations.

However, in the global financial crisis triggered by the financial crisis in 2008, global frameworks such as the G20, the G7 and the IMF contributed to resolving the situation. Such frameworks are indeed necessary when large amounts of money are required on a global scale. However, in the euro crisis that later started in Greece, while the IMF did play a certain role, the EU and the ECB led the region in handling the situation. That leads me to the conclusion that the future will require global frameworks and regional frameworks to join forces as required by the circumstances.

This section will first look at the IMF, the establishment of which was decided at the conference held in Bretton Woods after World War II, and then at developments in financial cooperation in the East Asia region that emerged in the Asian currency crisis. In conclusion, it will discuss how the international cooperation regime has changed from a G7-led regime to one centered on the G20 framework.

4.2 International Monetary Fund (IMF)

The International Monetary Fund is a specialized organization of the United Nations established in December 1945. Its establishment was decided at the United Nations Monetary and Financial Conference held in Bretton Woods for discussing the postwar economic recovery; and therefore, the IMF and the World Bank, whose establishment was also decided at the conference, are collectively referred to as the Bretton Woods regime.

In the 1980s, the IMF provided loans to Latin American and African countries that were challenged with debt crises. The IMF observed such crises to be a result of temporary liquidity shortage, and attached structural adjustment policy conditionalities to the loans. That is, the IMF called for structural reform, including fiscal balance improvements through austerity policy, current-account balance improvements by devaluing currencies, and economic deregulation.

In the Asian currency crisis in 1997, the IMF also rescued Thailand, Indonesia and Korea, but these IMF rescue packages came to be questioned in various discussions that followed. This led to later reviews of the IMF-supported lending packages.

Firstly, the IMF attempted to address the Asian crisis using strategies such as fiscal austerity and monetary tightening measures as it had historically done in solving conventional fiscal deficit and international trade deficit crises, but this caused an even larger credit crunch, thus aggravating the economic situation in each country.

Secondly, the Asian currency crisis was different from conventional debt crises in that it was not an issue of economic fundamentals, but a credit crisis that included private debts and involved rapid capital outflow. Therefore, an urgent rescue measure was called for in order to recover confidence in the international market, but IMF packages required a long time to formulate.

Thirdly, the crisis spread quickly to neighboring countries, to the extent that the amount of funds required was too large to be covered by the conventional IMF rescue framework.

The short-term assistance proposed by Japan to use fifteen billion dollars of its foreign currency reserves was not actually executed, but the announcement of its intention to offer support effectively contributed to confidence recovery in the market. Based on such discussions, the conditionalities for IMF assistance have been reviewed and the IMF can now provide immediate assistance in large amounts.

4.3 Regional Financial Cooperation in East Asia

In contrast, the Asian currency crisis encouraged East Asian countries to develop a regional financial cooperation framework. At an international conference held in Manila in November 1997, countries agreed on the "New Framework for Enhanced Asian Regional Cooperation to Promote Financial Stability," known as the "Manila Framework," under which programs for cooperation in various areas would be considered.

At the APEC summit meeting in November 1998, Japanese Prime Minister Obuchi and US President Clinton announced the "Asian Growth and Recovery Initiative—AGRI," an initiative led by Japan and the US, joining forces with international financial institutions and supporting nations, to provide assistance for economic stabilization and growth recovery in countries impacted by the currency crisis. In April 1999, a follow-up meeting was held, co-chaired by Under Secretary Geithner of the US Treasury and I, then Deputy Director General of the Japanese Ministry of Finance. The Asian Development Bank, the IMF, and the World Bank were joined by representatives of the private sector to discuss multilateral and bilateral financial initiatives to support economic growth recovery.

In November 1999, the ASEAN Plus Three agreed on "enhancing self-help and support mechanisms in East Asia through the ASEAN+3 Framework." This later crystalized into the Chiang Mai Initiative adopted in May 2000.

4.4 Asian Monetary Fund Initiative

Given the unexpected amounts of assistance that many countries offered to Thailand at the Friends of Thailand Meeting, the Japanese Ministry of Finance tried to propose an Asian Monetary Fund initiative. This was based on the judgment that because IMF funds were not enough to resolve the Asian currency crisis and many Asian countries were unhappy with its response, the Asian region needed a regional financial organization to complement the IMF. This organization would, like the IMF, conduct surveillance of the economic situation in each country for the economic and financial stability of the Asian region and provide financial assistance in the face of crisis.

Many countries, including ASEAN members and Korea, supported the initiative, but China was hesitant to agree. Furthermore, the US, wishing to maintain its presence through the IMF, strongly opposed to the initiative from the perspectives of redundancy with the IMF and moral hazard; and therefore, the vision was not realized.[6]

4.5 Asian Currency Unit Initiative

Naturally, after the Asian currency crisis, currency policy coordination in East Asia was intensively discussed. One of the topics of concern was stabilizing the exchange rate among Asian currencies. Volatility can be effectively prevented by engaging in close discussion on country-specific economic situations through the surveillance process and by performing policy coordination as required. These ideas were later incorporated in AMRO (ASEAN+3 Macroeconomic Research Office).

A second topic was introducing a currency basket or a common currency unit. The Asian Currency Unit initiative was debated over three years from 2006 in a task group under the ASEAN+3 Finance Minister Meeting. The initiative originated in the idea of introducing a framework similar to the eurozone to the East Asian region, but discussions failed to make much progress, given skeptic views both within and outside East Asia, as well as the large economic gaps and regional system differences among countries in the region. It took Europe, a highly homogenous region both historically and economically, fifty years to introduce a common currency; and therefore, we must look to the far future if such an initiative is to be realized in the East Asia region. It was also difficult to immediately introduce a currency basket, because while a currency basket should essentially be composed only of freely tradeable currencies, few currencies other than the yen were freely tradeable in Asia.

---

[6] Based on Asian Capital Market Research Workshop ed. (2018), etc.

4.6 Chiang Mai Initiative

After the 1980s, loaning foreign currencies, including the dollar, through bilateral swaps to assist a country challenged with a trade deficit crisis became a widely accepted way to resolve currency crises. The Chiang Mai Initiative, agreed upon at the ASEAN+3 Finance Ministers Meeting held in Chiang Mai in 2000, enabled such swap schemes to be executed at any time under a regional framework.

The initiative started as a network of bilateral currency swaps agreements using foreign currency reserves, but it was multilateralized in 2010. Countries agreed on common procedures for decision-making among swap authorities, enabling the prompt execution of swap transactions. The total size of the initiative has currently expanded to 240 billion dollars.

From the perspective of ensuring repayment, swaps could in principle only be executed based on agreement on the IMF program, but agreement with the IMF required much time; and therefore, ten percent of the assistance could be executed before agreement on the program. In response to calls to raise this ratio to endorse efficient support, it has currently been raised to 30%, with the enhancement of surveillance functions by AMRO, as described below.

4.7 Asian Bond Market Initiative

One of the most significant factors of the Asian currency crisis was that private companies had relied on foreign currency-denominated funds for the investment funds required for economic growth. It was a financial crisis provoked by currency and maturity mismatches that occurred as a result of financing short-term funds procured in foreign currencies by Asian financial institutions as long-term investment funds in local currencies.

Hence, in order to facilitate the use of funds pooled within the region for intra-regional investment, the region needed a means of direct financing through the bond market, in addition to loan financing. Furthermore, as individual markets in each country were small, the ASEAN+3 Finance Ministers Meeting in 2003 agreed on the Asia Bond Market Initiative (ABMI), with an aim to foster a bond market in the Asian region featuring efficiency and high liquidity. Working groups were established to address the issuance of bonds denominated in local currency by international organizations and multinational corporations, the development of a rating system, a settlement system, information communications, etc. Detailed discussions were conducted on: 1) establishing the Asia Bonds Online web portal to communicate information on the bond market; 2) establishing a forum for standardizing market practices and coordinating regulations in order to develop a unified region-wide market; and 3) establishing a Credit Guarantee and Investment Facility to support the issuance of bonds denominated in local currency. In particular, the Credit Guarantee and Investment Facility (CGIF), established in the Asian Development Bank with initial capital contributions of 700 million US dollars, has gradually produced results since its first project in 2013 and has increased its capital to 1,200 million US dollars as of the end of 2017.

4.8 ASEAN+3 Macroeconomic Research Office (AMRO)

The ASEAN+3 process was launched with the participation of the heads of Japan, China and Korea in the ASEAN summit meeting in 1997, amid the Asian currency crisis, to discuss regional cooperation in East Asia. The ASEAN+3 Finance Ministers Meeting has played an important role in economic and financial cooperation in the East Asian region, establishing the Chiang Mai Initiative in 2000 and AMRO in 2011.

AMRO was established in April 2011 in Singapore as an organization to conduct surveillance and analysis of the ASEAN+3 region and to support the implementation of the Chiang Mai Initiative. It became an international organization in 2016 with Japanese members constantly in senior management, beginning with the second Director, Yoichi Nemoto.

The Chiang Mai Initiative is a scheme to provide assistance in the face of a currency crisis, and initially did not bear functions to prevent currency crises. Hence, the ASEAN+3 Economic Review and Policy Dialogue was integrated with the Chiang Mai Initiative in order to enable surveillance for the prevention of currency crises. This development allowed the Chiang Mai Initiative to take precautionary measures, hence enabling the integrated undertaking of currency crisis prevention and management.

To be more specific, AMRO is mainly responsible for the early discovery of risk in the ASEAN+3 regional economy and advising improvement measures. When the Asian currency crisis occurred, Indonesian and Korean private companies shouldered large amounts of debt from fund procurement from overseas, but the authorities were not aware of the situation until the crisis broke out, thus complicating crisis response; and therefore, it was decided that the macroeconomy and international capital transactions would be placed under constant surveillance.

The development of such functions served to ensure repayment of swap arrangements under the Chiang Mai Initiative; and this enabled the larger swap amounts (the IMF delink portion) to be available prior to agreement on the IMF program.

In this way, tools similar to the functions of the IMF have been developed under the framework of macroeconomy surveillance conducted by AMRO and financial support under the Chiang Mai Initiative. However, the surveillance process has yet to be organically incorporated in the financial assistance framework. AMRO holds promise for future development.

4.9 G7

In the 1970s when the world was challenged with the oil crises, the French President proposed a summit meeting, and the first meeting was held in 1975 in Rambouillet with six attendees (the G7 nations less Canada). Canada joined the following year, forming the Group of Seven, and the G7 summit meeting became an annual event. With the end of the Cold War in 1991, Russia eventually became a member and the group came to be known as the G8. However, given the 2014 Crimean crisis, it has returned to being the G7.

The G7 was originally launched as a process for finance ministers to address policy coordination regarding currency policy. It started as the G5, with Japan, the US, the UK, Germany and France. Therefore, even after it developed into the G7, there were times when currency policy would be discussed among the G5 nations prior to the G7 meeting, as the intention was to discuss international currency policy among the five countries that issued international currencies. Since international currencies should intrinsically be equivalent to those included in the IMF's special drawing right (SDR) basket (then, the Japanese yen, the US dollar, the pound sterling, the German mark and the French franc), the composition of the G5 was appropriate. However, in 1996, the euro replaced the mark and the franc, and the Chinese yuan Renminbi joined the SDR basket in 2016 (although it has yet to become fully freely tradeable).

4.10 From the G7 to the G20

The Asian currency crisis heightened awareness that discussions on international capital markets required not only the participation of the G7 nations but also that of emerging countries. Hence, in 1999, the G20 meeting was launched as a conference among finance ministers and central bank governors of twenty countries. Following the financial crisis in 2008, the G20 summit meeting was also launched, giving the G20 regime a leading role in international economic and financial coordination, in addition to the conventional G7/G8 regime.[7]

Until then, the G7, launched in 1975, had led global economic discussions, but as the BRICs nations increased their economic power, a framework engaging emerging countries was called for. Prior to the G20, the expanded G7 meetings with the participation of emerging economies, such as China and India, had attracted more attention.

It was natural for the G7 to expand to the G20 as a forum for discussions on global economy. However, given the participation of twenty countries with diversified economic situations, it is more challenging than it was in the G7 regime to reach agreement on concrete policies. During the G7 era, many communiques were published, each consisting of a few pages, but now a communique can run for several tens of pages. Furthermore, a G20 Finance Minister and Central Banks Governors'

---

[7] Based on Asakawa (2015), etc.

meeting is a gathering of not only the finance ministers and governors from each country but also heads of international financial institutions; and therefore, there are more than fifty speakers. It is undeniable that even a meeting running for one and a half days would be insufficient for thorough discussions. From this perspective, the role of the G7 is being re-acknowledged in the areas of currency issues and economic crisis response. In contrast, many other areas, such as cyber security and environment, are better addressed under the G20 framework. Closer cooperation between the G7 and G20 regimes will need to be sought in the future.

5 Conclusion

Almost twenty years have passed since Japan's financial crisis, triggered by the burst of the bubble economy, and the Asian currency crisis. These two decades have seen significant changes in foreign exchange policy, the Asian financial system, and international coordination regimes. In conclusion, this section will address the current situation and challenges.

5.1 Relationship Between Foreign Exchange Policy and Trade, and the Tokyo Global Financial Market

In recent years, the relationship between foreign exchange and monetary policy and improvements in transparency of foreign exchange policy have been on the agenda of G20 and G7 meetings. This is because monetary easing policies have been continued over a long period of time in developed countries, increasing their impact on the foreign exchange market. While G7 countries have disclosed data on their foreign exchange reserves and interventions, many G20 countries, especially emerging countries, have yet to disclose sufficient data.

There has been agreement at G20 meetings to date that monetary policy should be implemented in accordance with domestic economic needs and not for the purposes of the foreign exchange market. Since 2012, when Governor Kuroda of the Bank of Japan assumed his position under Abenomics, Japan has implemented large-scale quantitative monetary easing policies in order to pull itself out of deflation. As a result, the yen has depreciated substantially against the dollar. However, the trade surplus, which drastically shrunk after the financial crisis in 2008, has not returned to previous levels despite a weak yen. While the main factor behind this phenomenon is increased offshoring, another contributing factor is that the sales price of many of Japan's leading exports, including automobiles, are not frequently changed to meet with foreign exchange trends from the viewpoint of maintaining market reliability.

Furthermore, the US has strongly asserted that it would introduce currency provisions in trade agreements including FTAs, and has included currency provisions in the United States-Mexico-Canada Agreement (USMCA). Also under the TPP, from which the US finally withdrew, agreement has been reached on currency in a side letter. Disclosure of interventions, for example, are also included in these currency provisions. In all cases, currency policy should essentially be discussed at Finance Ministers and Central Bank Governors' Meeting and should not be included in trade agreements, as discussed at G20 Finance Ministers and Central Bank Governors' Meetings.

Furthermore, we have seen new developments in the globalization of the Tokyo financial market. A reason for this may be that there is an emerging need to support companies from a financial dimension, as Japanese companies become increasingly globalized, expanding on overseas investment, including offshoring production. Also, as aforementioned, Japan recently embraces an income surplus that exceeds has been the trade surplus; and therefore, we need to consider our national strategies from the standpoint of a "mature creditor nation." With the establishment of a Tokyo Global Financial Center constituting a pillar of Tokyo's National Strategic Special Zone scheme, the Tokyo Metroplitan Government proposed the "Global Financial City, Tokyo" Vision in November 2017. A global financial center would require financial institutions and human resources with the abilities and experience, and under Abenomics, we can expect to be able to utilize American and European financial institutions and human resources. If the Tokyo market can develop as a global financial center, then we might be able to see developments in the stalled internationalization of the yen in the future.

5.2 Evolution of the Asian Financial System

For twenty years since the Asian currency crisis, Asian emerging countries have implemented policies to increase resilience. As their current accounts turned surplus, they have increased their foreign currency reserves to ten months of import cover. Furthermore, the issuance of bonds denominated in local currency under the Asian Bond Market Initiative is slowly but steadily on the rise. In terms of foreign exchange policy, countries have shifted from a dollar peg system to a floating rate system because the currency peg caused an abrupt inflow of foreign funds. However, Chinese currency, with its large influence on other emerging countries, still puts its currency, in effect, subject to the influence of the dollar. Therefore, the region is still under some impact of the dollar exchange rate.

On the other hand, developments in the financial market and financial globalization have generated new issues. First, US monetary easing has caused the dollar interest rate to drop, boosting the issuance of US dollar-denominated bonds by companies in emerging countries. Also, the development of local bond markets and the liberalization of capital transactions have increased securities investment from abroad; and therefore, foreign holders account for a growing ratio of government bonds. Furthermore, under a floating rate system, foreign exchange interventions and domestic monetary control should be appropriately combined for foreign exchange stability.

For example, if a central bank performs a local currency-selling intervention to counter increased capital inflow, the money supply will increase. Then buying operations will lead to sterilization, without which the exchange rate will be affected. Hence, in order to increase resilience against capital flow, close coordination between foreign exchange policy and monetary policy should ideally be enhanced, in addition to developing a short-term financial market.

While countries develop their markets, bilateral government-level cooperation is also being sought. For example, Japanese and Chinese authorities are establishing a yuan clearing bank and advancing talks on a yen-yuan currency swap agreement. Japan and India are also enhancing their currency swap agreement.

As the author has seen, after the Asian currency crisis, Asian emerging countries did not suffer significant confusion in the financial crisis in 2008, as they had the ASEAN+3 (Japan, China and Korea) framework for regional cooperation, as well as domestic and bilateral schemes. It is clear that the stabilization of the foreign exchange market through policy coordination, and developments in the regional bond market and regional settlement system have significantly contributed to the establishment of intra-regional trade and production networks; and such efforts need to be continued.

5.3 Recent Trends in International Coordination Regimes

After World War II, the global financial coordination has been guided by a monetary system featuring the US dollar as the key currency and the Bretton Woods regime led by the IMF and the World Bank. However, in terms of development assistance, international financial institutions for regional development were established in the 1960s: the Inter-American Development Bank for the Latin America region, the African Development Bank and the Asian Development Bank. In terms of trade, since WTO-based multilateral trade negotiations became stalled, many FTAs and regional free trade agreements were concluded in the 1990s. As aforementioned, Asia has also established an regional financial cooperation regime, inspired by the Asian currency crisis. The European Central Bank was established when the euro was introduced in 1999. Regional coordination regimes are likely to increase in the future, but global regimes will also be necessary in order to address global crises and for global system advancements. It will become important to develop close and efficient relationships between global and regional coordination regimes.

The G20 summit will be held in Japan in June 2019. The G20 meetings were initially launched to address international financial crises and currency policies, but they currently cover a wide range of discussions transcending financial issues for sustainable and inclusive global economic growth. For example, the Finance Minsters' process will address several pillars: risks and challenges faced by the global economy; enhancing growth power; socioeconomic structural change induced by globalism and technology innovation. "Risks and challenges faced by the global economy" will address the issues of an aging population that Japan is challenged with ahead of other countries, and "enhancing growth power" will cover discussion of high-quality infrastructure investment and debt-trap issues in low-income countries. Japan has contributed to the economic development of East Asia through large amounts of economic assistance and highly advanced technological support, and is expected to maintain its strong leadership. "Socioeconomic structural change induced by globalism and technology innovation" will include international taxation, such as digital taxation, and cryptoassets, or virtual currencies. As aforementioned, the G20 embraces efficiency issues, but it is also true that it is the only forum today where global discussions on the issues mentioned above take place. The future of the G20 is promising.

References

Asakawa M (2011) Kokka Zaisei Hatan he no Taiou [Addressing National Financial Collapse] *Financial Review*, January 2011.

Asakawa M (2015) Atama wo Yawarakaku Suru Koto [Flexible thinking] *Finance*, September 2015.

Asian Capital Market Research Workshop ed. (2018) *Kan-Minami-Shina-kai, Chiiki-kinyū, Shihon-shijou* [*Pan-South China Sea, Regional Finance, Capital Market*]. Japan Securities Research Institute, Tokyo.

Ito M (2009) *Baburu/Defure-ki no Nihon-Keizai to Keizai-Seisaku 3: Kokusai Kankyou no Henka to Nihon Keizai* [*The Japanese Economy and Economic Policy during the Bubble/Deflation 3: Changes in the International Environment and Japanese Economy*] Keio University Press, Tokyo.

Iwata K (2011) *Baburu/Defure-ki no Nihon-Keizai to Keizai-Seisaku - Wareware ha Nani wo Manandanoka-* [*The Japanese Economy and Economic Policy during the Bubble/Deflation – What Lessons were Learned?*] Economic and Social Research Institute, Tokyo.

Kuroda H (2005a) *Zaisei Kinyuu Seisaku no Seikou to Shippai* [*The Success and Failure of Fiscal and Monetary Policies*]. Nippon Hyoron Sha, Tokyo.

Kuroda H (2005b) *Tsūka no Kōbō* [The Rise and Fall of a Currency]. Chuō-Korōn Shin-sha, Tokyo.

Saito J (2017) Japan's Economy and Policy in a Global Context: Postwar Experience and Prospects for the Twenty-First Century. *Postwar Japan*, CSIS.

Kiyoto Ido worked at the Ministry of Finance (MOF) and was primarily engaged in international issues. After joining the MOF, he served in several executive positions in the Inter-American Development Bank and the Embassy of Japan in Washington, DC, USA. During the 1997–1998 Asian currency and economic crisis, he cooperated with and assisted Asian countries. After leaving the MOF as Director-General of the International Department, Mr. Ido worked at the Bank of Japan as Executive Director and at the Institute for International Economic Studies as Vice Chairman.

Monetary Policy in Japan: A Review of the Heisei Period

Wataru Takahashi

Abstract This chapter discusses Japan's monetary policy during the Heisei Period (1989–2019), an era of roughly 30 years that included the boost and bursting of the bubble economy and the subsequent deflationary period. In addition to a review of unconventional monetary policies that began about 20 years ago, it also will shed light on discipline of monetary policy, inflation targeting, and the relationship to fiscal policy. Lastly, it will discuss the independence of the Bank of Japan, recommending that the Bank of Japan demonstrate proactive independence based on its constitutional independence. The present monetary policy, Quantitative and Qualitative Monetary Easing (QQE), has struggled to achieve the target. This is mainly due to the stagnated growth potential of the economy. Discipline of monetary policy is a way that manage monetary policy while making the best use of market mechanism and minimizing the size of central bank asset. Although central banks have traditionally emphasized these disciplines, unconventional monetary policy could be the process to loosen the discipline of monetary policy. Japan is a typical. As an independent agency, central bank is expected to check government economic policies from her standpoint of non-political and longer viewpoint in order to revive the Japanese economy.

1 Introduction

The main purpose of this chapter is to review Japan's monetary policy over the past 30 years. Following the bursting of the stock-market bubble in 1989 and the bubble in the real-estate market a little later, Japan's economy was forced to deal with the repercussions of these over the period until the early 2000s, and then with the challenges of decreased growth potential due to a shrinking population of labor.[1]

[1] While this slowdown in the Japanese economy is referred to generally as deflation, the term deflation is not necessarily apt, since it emphasizes only the decrease in the inflation rate on the surface. The fundamental cause of the economic slowdown is lower growth rates.

W. Takahashi (✉)
Osaka University of Economics, Osaka, Japan

H. Takeda and J. Watanabe (eds.), *Rethinking Japanese economic policy at the turn of the 21st century*, Advances in Japanese Business and Economics 34,
https://doi.org/10.1007/978-981-97-5512-7_7

This slump in the Japanese economy has generally been attributed to deflation. But this may not always be appropriate. The more important problem of the economy is a decline in the potential growth, and deflation is considered to be just one of the symptoms. During this period, the Bank of Japan was relaunched as an independent central bank under 1998 amendments to the Bank of Japan Law. A look back at the Bank of Japan's policies over the 25-year period beginning in 1998 shows that the path of seeking recovery for Japan's economy was a difficult one. It can be compared to "uncharted waters."

This chapter will discuss the Bank of Japan's policies over the 30-year Heisei Period; particularly the 20 years of unconventional policy centered on the latter part of this period, as, in part, a process of relaxation of the discipline of monetary policy. Japan's economy was one of the first in the world to experience developments such as the bubble in the latter part of the 1980s and the unconventional monetary policy that began in 1999 with the zero-interest-rate policy. Accordingly, in Sect. 2, this chapter will incorporate a new perspective on issues related to the 1980s bubble economy. Section 3 will discuss 25 years of unconventional monetary policy from the perspectives of the discipline of monetary policy and adoption of inflation targets. Section 4 will assess the four unconventional monetary policies implemented during these 25 years, based on the perspectives discussed in Sect. 2. Section 5 and 6 will discuss Japan's unconventional monetary policy in connection with fiscal policy and independence. Section 7, in lieu of a conclusion, will touch on the path in which Japan's economy should move forward.

2 The Bubble Economy of the Latter 1980s

2.1 The Process of the Formation and Bursting of the Bubble

As the history of developments prior to the Bank of Japan's adoption of unconventional monetary policy, this section will review the formation and bursting of Japan's bubble economy in the latter part of the 1980s.

Many have identified the coordination of monetary and fiscal policies resulting from the September 1985 Plaza Accord as the initial spur behind the formation of the bubble economy. Accordingly, where we will begin by reviewing the process of the formation and bursting of Japan's bubble economy in light of developments in monetary and fiscal policy.

Although the appreciation of the yen following the Plaza Accord exceeded initial intentions, at that time Japanese business continued export competition through improving product quality. As a result, despite massive increases in the value of the yen rectification of trade imbalances did not proceed to the extent that had been expected by the governments of the U.S. and Japan.[2] In response to these situations,

[2] The "J Curve" effect was considered to be one reason why export qualities did not decrease despite the increasing value of the yen on international currency markets.

the Japanese government was forced to correct trade imbalances through increasing imports instead of restraining exports alone,[3] and this led to even more expansionary monetary and fiscal policy. The US external deficit was structural due to macro savings shortage due to the expansion of fiscal deficit under the Reagan administration. It would not be easy to rectify the structural imbalances of disparities between Japan and the U.S. through monetary and fiscal policy. For the Japanese government, rectification of trade imbalances became an international commitment, and it was expected that expansionary monetary and fiscal policy would continue for a considerable period until prospects for their reconciliation were apparent in the market. In terms of monetary policy, a major contributing factor behind the formation of the bubble economy in Japan was the presence of expectations that policies of low interest rates would continue over the long term, rather than the low level of interest rates itself.

Policies that further promoted the formation of the bubble were the decreases in official discount rates under the February 1987 Louvre Accord, the enactment by the Japanese government in May of a large-scale supplementary budget, and the postponement of interest-rate increases in response to Black Monday in October. As a result of the expansionary policies implemented through then and improving "terms of trade" due to the high yen, in 1987 economic conditions already had begun to improve (even under the government's official definition of the business cycle, the recession spurred by the high yen, which had begun in June 1985, ended after 17 months in November 1986, when the 51-month bubble, which lasted until February 1991, began). While it is difficult to confirm economic improvements econometrically at the time they occur, a lengthy rise in long-term interest rates is apparent beginning in early 1987, and this was seen as a sign of an improving economy in the financial markets.[4] While large-scale economic stimulus measures had been pledged in the February 1987 Louvre Accord, the lowering of the official discount rate in February and the massive JPY6 trillion supplementary budgets in May spurred an overheating, rather than a recovery, of the economy. In addition, while the Bank of Japan was believed to be watching for a chance to raise interest rates as the economic recovery trend became clear, it is thought that Black Monday in October caused it to miss this opportunity. The collapse of share values on the New York Stock Exchange on Black Monday is thought to have been spurred by earlier interest-rate increase in West Germany. Accordingly, Japan postponed its own interest-rate increases out of concern that they would lead to a breakdown of international cooperation, and ultimately it was not until May 1989 that rates in Japan rose.

The bubble in Japan is believed to have burst at the end of 1989 in the stock markets and in 1990 in real-estate markets. The fundamental cause of the collapse

---

[3] In its Monthly Report, the Bank of Japan points out that while the U.S. economy has a structure that makes it easy for imports to increase, the Japanese economy has one that makes it difficult for exports to decrease.

[4] In its Monthly Report, the Bank of Japan points out that in early 1987, when an increase in long-term interest rates was apparent on the financial markets, signs of economic improvement also were apparent.

of the bubble economy was a reversal of expectations of rising asset values. Asset markets differ from conventional goods and services markets in that in that rising prices lead to expectations of increases in asset values leading to growth in demand. This increased demand spurs further price increases. But once prices have fallen, the market begins to expect further decreases in prices, leading to an oversupply that spurs further price drops. This reversal of expectations is often caused by monetary policy. During the period of the bubble economy, monetary policy resulted in continued decreases in interest rates and led the markets to expect low interest rates to continue afterward as well. But these expectations were bought to a sudden end when interest rates were increased. Japan's official discount rate was increased three times in 1989 (in May, October, and December), twice in 1990 (in March and August), and once in 1991 (in July). In addition, in March 1990 the Ministry of Finance introduced restrictions on real-estate lending by banks. As a result of these factors, Japan's economic bubble collapsed.

2.2 Changes in the Theory of Economic Bubbles

The preceding section summarized the formation and bursting of Japan's bubble economy from the perspectives of monetary and fiscal policy. However, since that time there has been a number of theoretical developments regarding the explanation of Japan's bubble economy.

Theoretically, the bubble was explained first as reflecting the background of low-interest-rate policies that had continued since the Plaza Accord. Certainly the true cause of the bubble was the dominance of expectations that low-interest-rate policies would continue over the long term, as outlined above.

But attention subsequently focused on the behavior of financial institutions that contributed to the bubble, such as rapid increases in real-estate lending. As financial deregulation progressed, Japan's banking sector experienced intensification of competition under less strict regulation, and this brought about decreases in profit margins. In addition, their previous main customers of large enterprises increasingly raised funds from the capital markets,[5] relying less on borrowing from banks, and as they sought new customers the banks inclined heavily toward real-estate lending. It would not be possible to explain Japan's extraordinary bubble as being a product of low interest rates alone in the absence of this excess lending by the banking sector.

The most comprehensive theoretical explanation of the bubble was provided by Okina et al. (2001). Analyzing comprehensively contributing factors such as policy, the behavior of financial institutions, and taxation, they argue that the additional social psychological factor of swelling expectations in Japan's society at that time played a major role in the formation of the bubble. If one focuses on the perspective of bubble as resulting from group behavior, then it should be important to point

[5] Behind the increase in fund-raising on the capital markets by major firms was the possibility of raising funds on the capital markets at low interest rates due to the bubble.

out that it was caused by interdependent group judgments, rather than independent judgments by individuals.

While at first most saw the collapse of Japan's bubble economy and financial institutions' subsequent problems with bad debts as issues peculiar to Japan, they later would come to be understood as more universal issues as attention focused on the similarities to the 2008 global financial crisis that followed the collapse of Lehman Brothers. Hattori et al. (2009) analyze Japan's bubble with a focus on these similarities.[6] They focus on the fact that the bubble arose in response to domestic supply of foreign liquidity through activated international capital flow under financial deregulation.[7] They also focus on the fact that the route of such supply of liquidity was through an inflow of funds in which sectors other than the traditional banking sector performed financial intermediating functions. For example, in the case of the subprime loan crisis in the U.S. it can be pointed out that funds flowed into the U.S. as financial instruments generated by U.S. investment banks and other "shadow banks" were purchased by financial institutions in Europe and elsewhere. At the time of Japan's bubble as well, trading companies and other non-banking-sector actors deposited funds raised from issue of bonds overseas with domestic banks in large-scale deregulated-interest-rate deposits. Faced with swollen deposits, banks increased real-estate lending in search of opportunities to invest the deposited funds.

After presenting this analysis, Hattori, Shin, and Takahashi raise doubts about the way financial regulations focus solely on traditional financial sectors. Finance always tends to expand activities beyond existing financial sectors, and this not only improves economic welfare but also can lead to new risks.

Hattori, Shin, Takahashi also focus on the way the bubble arose from the group behavior of banks, pointing out the importance of regulating group behavior. At the time, the Bank of Japan conducted "window guidance" to restrict banks' volumes of lending. "Window guidance" was considered old-fashioned policies to supplement interest-rate policies at a time in which interest rates did not fluctuate freely due to various regulations that still remained in place. Since interest-rate deregulation also had advanced in the latter half of the 1980s, the Bank of Japan believed that "window guidance" had decreased in importance. In fact, it considered restraint of competition. For this reason, in the latter half of the 1980s it left decisions on target lending amounts under "window guidance" to the banks themselves. But since there remained the conventional "egalitarian" manner, each bank set high targets these actually had the unintended effect of spurring competition to increase volumes of lending, furthering the formation of the bubble. "Window guidance" was abolished during the first half of the 1990s, citing as the reason the fact that they involved too many negative effects. However, Hattori, Shin, Takahashi suggest that if "window guidance" had been managed properly at the time, then it might have been possible to restrain the

[6] Hattori et al. (2009) was chosen as a recommended paper by the European Central Bank.

[7] Bruno and Shin (2013) points out that a similar picture arises from monetary easing in advanced economies in the 2010s. In particular, he has warned that companies in emerging economies are increasing their overseas funding similar to the situation in Japan in the 1980s. In order to respond to this situation, he points out the importance of macroprudential policy, as well as the importance of monitoring quantitative indicators such as money supply to monitor financial stability.

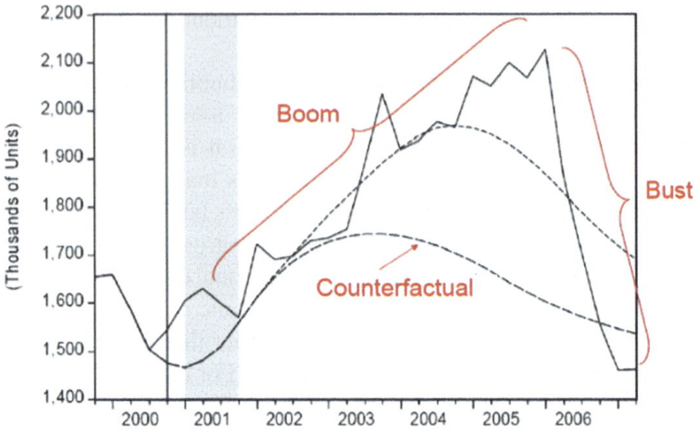

Fig. 1 The boom-bust in housing starts compared with the counterfactual (*Source* Taylor [2008, p. 5] and his Blog, https://economicsone.com/)

formation of the bubble. Quantitative regulations on banks, such as liquidity restrictions and other examples of contemporary macro prudence, are making a comeback. Restrictions such as restraints on "window guidance" is justified at a time in which rational individual behaviors can have irrational effects through group behavior.

Lastly, let's consider the argument that a bubble cannot be explained entirely through economic theory. Fig. 1 illustrates John Taylor's analysis of the subprime crisis (Taylor 2008). Taylor argues that it was the low-interest-rate policies of then-Fed Chairman Alan Greenspan that led to the U.S. housing bubble that resulted in the subprime crisis. He shows empirically that if the Fed had, in accordance with his proposed "Taylor Rule," raised interest rates at an earlier stage, then such a large bubble would not have formed.

Figure 1 depicts trends in U.S. housing starts during the years 2000 through 2006, when the subprime bubble formed in the real-estate market. The uppermost line shows the trend in actual housing starts. The overlapping curved line shows Taylor's estimates of housing starts from an econometric model based on actual interest rates. This empirical model shows that the bubble formed in the housing market because actual interest rates were low. The lower dashed curve (counter-factual) shows estimated figures if interest rates had been increased earlier in accordance with his proposed Taylor Rule. This empirical model suggests that if the Fed had managed monetary policy in accordance with the Taylor Rule, then the bubble would have been much smaller. However, even Taylor didn't mention, what attracted my attention in this Figure is the relation between the slashed curve line estimated using actual interest rates and the actual trend in housing starts. The estimates of this model show smoothly rising and falling trends in housing starts, symmetrical over the four-year period of the two years leading up to the peak in 2004 and the subsequent two years. The estimates show that housing starts, which stood in 2002 at approximately 17 million homes, rose to a peak in 2004 of 20 million homes and then decreased in a smooth line back to 17 million homes in 2006. But the actual data show that housing starts increased over the three years from 2002 to 2007 and then fell over the one-year period from 2007 to 2008. Thus, the period in which they fell was shorter than the one in which they increased. In other words, the bubble actually swelled at a gradual pace and then collapsed rapidly. What's more, while the increase was one of 4 million homes, from 17 to 21 million homes, the decrease was a sudden one of 6 million homes, from 21 to 15 million. Thus, while housing sales rose at a pace of 1.3 million homes over three years, they fell suddenly by 6 million homes in one year. Such a rapid, large-scale drop cannot be explained by economic theory alone. The phenomenon of a bubble is not yet understood fully by economic theory and econometric estimation. Since our knowledge of bubbles is lacking, surely we need to look at them with some humility. During the 1990s, the Japanese economy would tread the difficult path of recovery from the damage caused by the collapse of such a bubble.

For the Japanese economy bubble in the late 1980s, at first, a significant fiscal and monetary easing due to international cooperation as a factor has been emphasized, gradually, are also important factors such as changes in bank behavior in addition to that due to financial liberalization. This shows theory has been recursively developed by experience.

Despite the subsequent development of theory, theoretical and empirical elucidation of the bubble is still insufficient. In addition, a point that has not been pointed out in the past was the implementation of a conventional expansion policy without recognizing structural changes in a situation where the high growth period was over, growth potential declined and the financial structure changed. There is also a problem. This was also the result of an improper response that addressed the long-term issues of structural issues, focused exclusively on short-term fiscal and monetary policy. Policy management in the bubble era has brought about major challenges in the face of increasing uncertainties that the economic structure has changed significantly. Should we actively adopt bold policies to eliminate uncertainty, should we deal with uncertainty carefully, and should be aware of the long-term consequences that are not necessarily explicit. These policy issues have remained unchanged for about 30 years since then, and what should be taken as a guideline when there is not enough theoretical clarification.

In the 30 years after the burst of the bubble, monetary policy was burdened by the economic recovery as structural growth policy progressed slowly due to the decline in the potential growth rate. Financial liberalization in the midst of changes in the financial structure led to the search for a new regulatory regime after paying the high price of banking crisis.

3 Japan's Unconventional Monetary Policy

3.1 The Discipline of Monetary Policy[8]

In this section, Japan's unconventional monetary policy will be discussed from the relationship between "traditional monetary policy discipline" and "inflation targeting." "Inflation targeting (mainly since the 1990s)" is a discipline in monetary policy framework along with "gold standard system (from the nineteenth century to the middle of the twentieth century)" "fixed exchange rate system (Bretton Woods system: 1944 to 1971)" "monetary target (mainly the 1970s and 1980s).

By contrast, "traditional monetary policy discipline" is a more practical discipline for monetary operation, such as a determination of interest rate, a transaction of financial asset by a central bank. As expressed in the description of a central bank as the lender of last resort, its position is that of the monopoly supplier of short-term funds. In guiding market interest rates, it is desirable that the central bank do so while minimizing its exclusive supply of short-term funds in order to respect the functioning of the markets. To ensure that prices of long-term assets reflect market expectations, it is desirable that the central bank limit its transaction to short-term assets as much as possible, to avoid impeding this process. Furthermore, since it is desirable that risk premiums on private-sector assets be evaluated by the markets, it is preferable that the central bank buys and sells only risk-free government bonds.[9]

In sum, it is desirable that the central bank control the shortest-term interest rates through buying and selling short-term government bonds to the minimum extent possible, leaving to the markets evaluation of interest rates on private-sector assets (i.e., evaluation of credit premiums) and evaluation of long-term interest rates (i.e., evaluation of term premiums). This is the ideal form of the discipline of a central bank.

The central bank is in the position of a monopoly supplier of central bank credit, the most credible liquidity, as expressed by the term "Lender of Last Resort." In order to respect market functions while inducing market interest rates, it is desirable to induce interest rates by minimizing short-term funding and reducing the negative effects of monopolies. Also, in order to respect the market mechanism, it is desirable that long-term asset pricing reflects market expectations, so the central bank should limit trading to short-term assets as much as possible so as not to impede it. Furthermore,

[8] "Discipline" here is synonymous with "anchor", which is often used in policy management. In the history of monetary policy, "gold parity" was the anchor under the gold standard, and the exchange rate was the anchor under the fixed exchange rate system. In the 1970s, developed economies were destabilized by stagflation, a combination of inflation and recession. One reason for this is the shift to the floating exchange rate system and the loss of anchors. The inflation targeting can be said to be an anchor following the gold standard system and the fixed exchange rate system.

[9] Traditionally, the fundamental principle of a central bank was one of discounting bills (real bills) issued through sale of traded commodities (the Real Bill Doctrine). However, today the orthodox view calls for buying and selling only government bonds through open market operations (Bills only policy).

it is desirable for private assets to be assessed for risk premiums in the market, so central banks should only buy and sell risk-free government bonds.[10]

Central banks have a self-perception that "the central bank is in the market." This is very different from a government economic agency. The reason behind this is that utilizing market mechanisms in the above-mentioned direction will increase the efficiency of the economy and nurture the potential of growth. This is widely shared by economic scholars. It is also true that maintaining monetary policy discipline contributes to the soundness of the central bank's finances, but monetary policy discipline reflects the central bank's view of the market and the economy.

From the standpoint of monetary policy discipline, it is advisable to observe traditional discipline and cautiously conduct policies in situations where uncertainty is high. On the other hand, if market functions and economic functions are impaired, it is desirable to have an aggressive and bold policy that gives priority to the recovery of those functions and temporarily breaks discipline. This can be distinguished from normal discipline and emergency response, but it is not easy to distinguish between them in practice. Japan's non-conventional policy can be summarized as a process of gradually relaxing discipline, taking into account two standpoints.

3.2 *Japan's Case*

The Bank of Japan has implemented various unconventional monetary-easing policies in succession.

From the perspective of discipline of monetary policy, policies can be organized into the process of gradual relaxation of discipline in the following order: (i) zero-interest-rate policies (February 1999–August 2000), (ii) quantitative-easing policies (February 2001–March 2006), (iii) comprehensive-monetary easing policies (October 2010–April 2013), and (iv) quantitative- and qualitative-easing policies (QQE: March 2013 and later). The Bank of Japan has made sacrifices to prioritize macroeconomic recovery and impede the market functions of the short-term money market and the government bond market while advancing non-conventional monetary policy. In addition, the Bank has increased potential risks related to the Bank of Japan's financial soundness by accumulating long-term government bond, private debt, etc.

[10] Purchase of assets involving increases in banknotes is justified when allocating it to purchase of long-term government bonds. This is because a permanent increase in banknotes means an increase in long-term debt, and responding to this increase in debt with an increase in short-term government bonds would have the undesirable effect of increasing turnover of short-term government bonds. This is the reason for the practice of term matching through responding to an increase in long-term debt with the purchase of long-term assets (long-term government bonds). At the same time, it would be undesirable for purposes of term matching if the volume of long-term government bonds held were to exceed the balance of banknotes. This is why central banks such as the Bank of Japan and the Fed follow the so-called "banknote rule" of keeping the value of government bonds held to no higher than the balance of banknotes issued.

The first of these, a zero-interest-rate policy, is, put bluntly, a scheme by which the central bank responds to demand for short-term funds through an interest rate of zero, achieving discipline in the supply of short-term funds through supplying an amount corresponding to the necessities of demand. The next policy category of quantitative-easing policies involves aspects of distorting the natural relationship between supply and demand as the central bank decides on a supply target without regard for demand.[11] As such, it also involves the aspect of creating demand as the bonds subject to open-market operations gradually grow longer-term. Indeed, the average remaining term of government bonds held by the BoJ at the time, which was roughly four years, was considerably shorter than the average of 7.5 years under the quantitative- and qualitative-easing policies of today. In addition, at first it proved relativity easy to reach quantitative expansionary targets under quantitative-easing policies because there was strong demand for short-term funds in the form of precautious demand while fragility in the financial system continued. Financial fragility was resolved around 2003, when the Payoff was lifted (the deposit insurance changed from unlimited to limited guarantee). For this reason, the phenomenon of undersubscription, in which the amount of the bid offered is lower than the amount of the bid tendered, occurred frequently in open-market operations at the time of ending quantitative-easing policies. This reflects the market principle of respect for natural supply and demand in that the final bid price is determined by demand, and at that point discipline still was maintained. The next policies implemented, comprehensive-easing policies, stepped out of the bounds of traditional discipline by involving purchase of assets in excess of those purchased under quantitative easing and purchase of equities through exchange-traded funds (ETFs) in addition to private-sector bonds. However, at the same time they also incorporated disciplinary measures such as maintaining a fixed margin in excess of short-term market interest rates and employing conceptually different accounts for purchases of long-term government bonds and private-sector bonds through quantitative easing, as the Asset Purchase Program. These were intended to avoid dysfunction of short-term financial markets. The main intention of establishing the Asset Purchase Program was to position unconventional monetary policy as clearly an emergency measure. This both disciplined unconventional monetary policy and expanded the margin for its implementation.

The quantitative- and qualitative-easing policies (QQE) implemented through now can be described as policies that intentionally break down this discipline. They merged the Asset Purchase Program established under comprehensive easing with

[11] In general, even if the central bank switches the target of policy manipulation from interest rates to quantity, the supply–demand relationship in the market should not be distorted. The central bank would achieve quantitative targets through freer fluctuation in short-term interest rates than under interest-rate targets. However, under the restrictions of a zero interest rate policy, such fluctuation in interest rates is not possible, and as a result market functions are distorted because the central bank intervenes more in the markets, for example by decreasing long-term interest rates through buying longer-term assets or reducing credit premiums on private-sector assets by buying such assets, in order to realize its quantitative target.

the general account and, through rapidly increasing purchases of long-term government bonds, broke the banknotes rule that had been maintained through the stage of comprehensive-easing policies, as well as massively increasing amounts purchased of instruments such as ETFs and J-REITs. In addition, through yield-curve control, which corrected negative-interest-rate policies, the forward guidance that had identified achievement of inflation targets as the condition for release from large-scale purchases of assets was revised to an inflation-overshooting commitment, under which the BoJ committed to continue asset purchases to some degree even after achieving inflation targets.

As discussed above, the traditional monetary policy discipline has continued to relax under the Bank of Japan's non-conventional monetary policy. This became particularly noticeable after the QQE, with the Bank of Japan's long-term government bond balance increasing from approximately 90 trillion yen at the beginning of 2013 to approximately 450 trillion yen in the middle of 2018. The Bank of Japan holds more than 40% of the outstanding balance, and JGBs have become scarce in the market. As a result, the Bank of Japan often lends JGBs necessary for market transactions. In addition, the Bank of Japan's share of ETFs is up to 70% on a stock basis, and there are concerns that the market function will be hindered. Furthermore, it has been pointed out that the negative interest rate policy that has been implemented since February 2016 has deteriorated the bank's business condition and hindered the financial intermediary function, which has hindered the monetary easing effect itself.

In addition, the author would like to discuss forward guidance that is widely used in non-conventional policies and surprise policies that are also characteristic after quantitative qualitative easing from the aspect of monetary policy discipline.

The Forward Guidance is a policy adopted by the Bank of Japan for the first time in the world since the adoption of the zero interest rate policy in 1999, and it enhances the monetary easing effect through expectations by promising to continue the monetary easing policy in the future. This policy complements the interest rate policy that has fallen into the zero interest rate constraint by promising future monetary easing. Among non-conventional monetary policies, the effect of forward guidance is actually a relatively effective policy that has the effect of lowering long-term interest rates through expectations. On the other hand, the evaluation is subtle in terms of monetary policy discipline. Even in traditional monetary policy, rule based monetary policy enhances the predictability of interest rate policy and affects long-term interest rates through the effects of expectations. This is rather a policy that respects market mechanisms. However, the forward guidance adopted in non-conventional policies has discretionary aspects that are not based on rules and can distort market functions.

Another distinguishing disciplinary feature of QQE is that of "surprise": the possibility of implementing policy without announcing it in advance. Since the "rational expectations revolution" in economics, enabling the market to form expectations in advance through rule-based monetary policy had been considered an appropriate way to strengthen policy effects. In contrast, QQE sought to strengthen policy effects through the element of surprise, by implementing policy changes with no prior notice. QQE is policy that stress control of market expectations. Presumably this element of surprise was judged to be necessary in order to effect a sudden change in deeply rooted deflationary expectations in the market. But this is a highly experimental approach, and it is likely to be difficult to control expectations in the desired direction after they have been changed through such a surprise change in policy. In addition, as seen when negative interest rates were adopted, an element of surprise may lead to confusion. For this reason, it can be said that it is not necessarily easy to judge whether this method of surprise has been a success or a failure.

In addition to the above, in implementing unconventional monetary policy the Bank of Japan also began to accept asset-backed securities (ABS) and asset-backed commercial paper (ABCP) as security and to make them subjects of its operations as well as commencing policies to encourage bank lending to specific industries, such as lending to support the foundations of economic growth. While acceptance of ABSs is justified on the grounds of market development and correcting for market failures, arguing that the central bank should promote the development of the underdeveloped ABS market and correct for banks' excessively atrophied attitude toward lending to support the foundations of economic growth, it must be noted that if these were to go too far then the central bank would be stepping into areas that traditionally should be left to the market mechanism.

3.3 Regarding Inflation Targeting

As mentioned above, inflation targeting have the aspect of policy discipline following the "gold standard," "fixed exchange rate system," and "monetary target." But for the Bank of Japan's monetary policy, "adopting inflation targets" has long been a difficult issue.

To the BoJ, which got a new start in 1998 as an independent central bank, this became an issue of great concern, and one also related to the issue of the Bank's independence. During the 1990s, the central banks of a number of developed countries—New Zealand, Australia, Canada, and Great Britain—adopted inflation targeting as a framework for monetary policy. Most of these cases were supported by economic theory such as Debelle and Fisher (1994), and governments, legislators, and other political actors took part in deciding on numerical values of inflation targets (goals of monetary policy), leaving decisions on levels of short-term interest rates to achieve these targets (instruments of monetary policy) to the central banks. Thus, goals and instruments were separated and the central bank was given only instrument independence, not goal independence. In the case of the BoJ, the establishment of this framework is ambiguous, and its adoption involved at least three issues.

The first issue concerned the fact that originally inflation targeting was a framework for controlling inflation and were not expected, even in theory, to be used to overcome deflation. As seen in the model of Rogoff (1985), considered a classic of central-bank independence, basically monetary policy to control inflation should be entrusted to a central bank that has a conservative approach to inflation, rather than to politicians (government and legislatures) who would prefer inflation. This is why there were fundamental doubts about the efficacy of inflation targets to combat deflation.

Second, in the countries where inflation targeting were adopted, they were adopted after the central bank had earned a degree of trust based on a track record of having been able already to control inflation through its policies. The BoJ lacked a track record of having realized its target inflation rate through either zero-interest-rate policies or quantitative-easing policies.

Third, even when actually setting inflation targets, there were questions about the specific percentage rate to target. While a standard inflation target in most developed countries was 2%, past data showed that the average inflation rate in Japan was much lower than those in Europe and United States. For this reason, it was considered likely to be difficult to achieve a 2% inflation target. On the other hand, there were concerns that setting a low inflation target would promote revaluation of the yen due to international differences in inflation rates.

Under the conditions outlined above, the BoJ's course in setting inflation targets was an irregular one. While under zero-interest-rate policies and quantitative-easing policies inflation rates were mentioned as conditions for release of these policies—worded, for example, as, "until deflationary concerns have been overcome" (1999) or "until the rate of inflation in consumer prices remains at or above zero with stability" (2003)—it was not a clear and specific goal. With regard to the setting of numerical goals, in 2000 the BoJ announced its thinking on price stability but was dismissive of setting numerical goals, arguing that "it would be difficult to express goals in numerical figures." But as political pressure later increased in connection with release of quantitative easing and passivity in monetary policy, in 2006 it announced that its nine Policy Meeting members had reached an understanding on medium- to long-term price stability in the form of a target inflation rate in the 0–2% range, in 2009 it clarified this further by identifying as its goal an inflation rate of 1% (the median value in this range of 0–2%) and avoidance of a negative rate, and in 2010 it identified as the conditions for release of its comprehensive easing policy the achievement of the state described in this understanding on medium- to long-term price stability. However, in January 2013, in joint statement of Bank of Japan and Government, an inflation target of 2% was adopted. This meant that the goal of 1% indicated in 2010 had suddenly been increased to 2%. However, at the time no specific timing was indicated for achievement of this goal.

The BoJ's non-straightforward path in adoption of inflation targets can be described as being problematic in terms of consistency of monetary policy. The fact that, despite changing circumstances, the Bank of England maintained its initial 2% inflation target is regarded highly as having stabilized inflationary expectations. But considerable doubts remain as to whether or not the BoJ was able to achieve its inflation targets in light of the differences between an inflationary economy and a deflationary one and the severe instability in the financial system.

In addition, in the 2009 document "Clarification of the Understanding of Medium- to Long-term Price Stability," the BoJ both mentioned inflation targets and pointed out the importance of inspection of financial imbalances. It emphasized these points again in a January 2013 joint statement with the government. As Shirakawa (2021) points out, as seen in the global financial crisis monetary policy focused solely on achieving inflation targets could lead to overlooking the signs of developments such as the formation of an economic bubble, as risk awareness decreases under conditions of economic stability.

While the BoJ has been subjected to severe criticism for its delay in adopting inflation targeting, at the same time doubts have arisen about the appropriateness of the current framework of inflation targeting. It is highly possible that the BoJ's caution about adopting a policy of inflation targeting in fact may turn out to have been justified.

The current Bank of Japan's inflation targeting is questionable as a monetary policy discipline that will stop the expansion of monetary easing. It has set a goal of 2%, which is difficult to achieve, and have postponed the timing of achievement.[12] This raises concerns that can stick to unattainable goals and can protract monetary easing. This is also the result of assigning monetary policy, which is essentially a short-term policy, to the long-term structural problem of declining growth potential. For this reason, it can be said that future risks are increasing compared to current results. The success or failure of the Bank of Japan's inflation targeting will be judged by policy change when the goal is expected to be achieved, but it is promoting the loosening of discipline under the current situation. As non-conventional policies are lengthened, there is an opinion that it will become "New Normal." In future monetary policy, it is important to carefully evaluate the advantages and disadvantages objectively.

See Nakaso (2017) regarding the background of unconventional monetary policy. Figure 2 reviews Japan's unconventional monetary policy as described by Nakaso.

4 History of Japan's Unconventional Monetary Policy

In the previous section, the Bank of Japan's monetary policy was discussed from the perspective of "relaxation of monetary policy discipline." There, I tried to discuss it rather conceptually. However, the fact that this discipline was actually loosened is the result of the transition of non-traditional monetary policy in line with changes in the economic situation. In this section, the Bank of Japan's monetary policy will be discussed in chronological order in line with changes in the economic situation.

[12] As of December 2013, Japan's CPI inflation has already exceeded the target of 2% for about two years, but this is due to the rise in international commodity prices and the weaker yen, and the Bank of Japan is still cautious to judge that inflation will continue to reach the target.

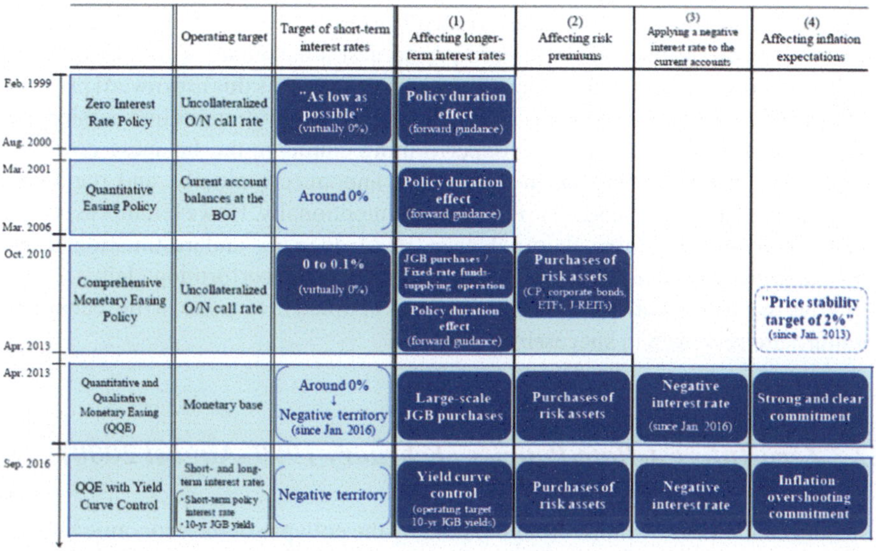

Fig. 2 Transition of BoJ's monetary policy (*Source* Nakaso [2017])

4.1 *History Prior to Adoption of Unconventional Monetary Policy*

With hindsight, the bubble's macroeconomic damage to the Japanese economy can be summarized as involving the following three excesses: excess debt, excess capital investment, and excess employment. These three excesses were considered to reflect abnormal growth in borrowing, capital investment, and employment during the bubble period. But later, these came to be seen as excesses that accompanied the distorted growth of the Japanese economy—i.e., the transition from an economy characterized by rapid growth to a slow-growing one—unrelated to the bubble, and adjusting for these excesses remained a challenge to the Japanese economy in the form of deflation even after responding to the bubble was completed around 2003.

The true issue in the Japanese economy over these 30 years was a decrease in its potential growth, which led to deflationary conditions in the economy. In the area of policy decisions, since this decrease in potential growth had not been recognized accurately, the drafting of policies to restore growth was delayed, and the setting of goals that were beyond the actual abilities of the economy meant that they would be difficult to achieve.

Adjustments for these three excesses can be summarized as stock adjustments, in the form of balance-sheet adjustments. It would become clear later that balance-sheet adjustments involved a very complex and difficult process. Let's consider debt adjustments as an example. Excess debt led to excess nonperforming claims. Since adjusting for such excess debt all at once would result in considerable damage to businesses, adjustment is conducted gradually over time. But if adjustment takes time, then over that time the downward pressure of adjustments would continue to be felt, resulting in continued poor business performance. As this downward pressure continues to be felt on the economy as a whole, the economy remains in recession and new nonperforming claims arise. Nonperforming claims in the Japanese economy proved to be much higher than the estimates announced initially, and regulators were criticized as having underestimated them intentionally. However, this aspect of dynamism in nonperforming claims also was involved in this underestimation, as the adjustment process later led to the appearance of new nonperforming claims.

Below, the unconventional monetary policies adopted in response to the economic downturn are reviewed in succession.

4.2 *Zero-Interest-Rate Policies (February 1999–August 2000)*

Amid the economic downturn brought about by the collapse of the economic bubble, the Bank of Japan successively lowered interest rates. While in addition to the after-effects of the collapse of the bubble the economy also was impacted by the April 1997 increase in the consumption tax rate (from 3 to 5%), instability in the financial system, as symbolized by the bankruptcies of major financial institutions in 1997 and 1998, became a very important issue in terms of monetary policy. A loss of trust in Japanese financial institutions made it more expensive to raise foreign currency, and the Japan premium, charged to Japanese financial institutions when raising dollars from financial institutions overseas, increased as trust in Japanese financial institutions fell.

Amid continuing strong pressure toward balance-sheet adjustments, the effects of monetary policy decreased markedly. The BoJ's official discount rate fell nine times from its 1990 level of 6% to a level of 0.5% in 1995. As the progress of financial deregulation strengthened the functions of short-term money markets, during the first half of the 1990s the BoJ shifted its goals from the official discount rate, one regulated interest rate, to short-term interest rates that move freely with market supply and demand. However, amid balance-sheet adjustments and increasing fragility in the financial system, the economic stimulus effects of falling interest rates lessened, and in September 1999 the BoJ finally began to adopt a zero-interest-rate policy. Interest rates were again constrained by the zero interest rate barrier and its unconventional monetary policy started.

A zero-interest-rate policy has more of an impact than a simple reduction in interest rates. A zero-interest-rate policy means that the Bank of Japan has committed to supplying funds to ensure that interest rates in the short-term money market will average zero. At the time, when confidence in the financial system was unstable financial institutions with lower levels of creditworthiness were charged a risk premium on borrowing in the money markets. But under a zero-interest-rate policy resulting in an average money market rate of zero, even financial institutions with poorer credit are guaranteed to be able to raise funds at a zero interest rate. This was a strong effect

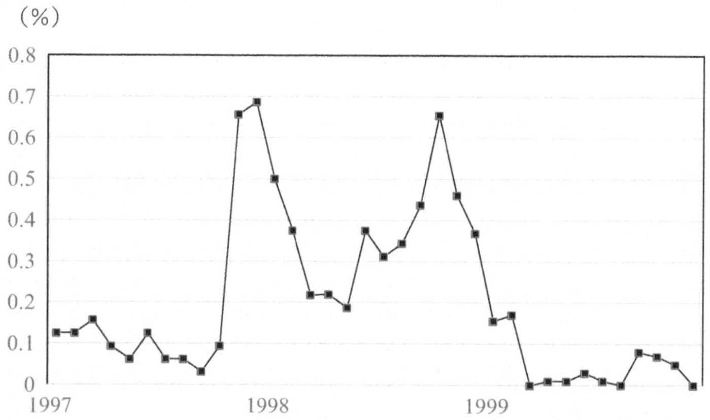

Fig. 3 Japan premium (*Source* Bank of Japan, Japan premium (Time series data) Accessed online at https://www.boj.or.jp/statistics/stop/premium/index.htm, on February 20, 2024)

of the policy. It succeeded in eliminating the Japan premium that had continued to be charged, without decreasing, on dollars raised by Japanese financial institutions even as interest rates had decreased (Fig. 3).

4.3 Quantitative-Easing Policies (March 2001–March 2006)[13]

In response to the impact of the shock occasioned by the collapse of the tech bubble in the U.S. (2000), the BoJ decided to adopt quantitative-easing policies that identified as the policy goal BoJ current-account balances rather than short-term market interest rates. While this policy prolonged the zero-interest-rate policy by providing financial institutions with the funds they needed under a zero interest rate, it was able to demonstrate results based on its announcement alone, as the supply of more funds than necessary pushed up the amount of the goal. In fact, the current account balance goal that began at JPY5 trillion was revised eight times in pursuit of these announcement effects, rising to JPY30-35 trillion. In addition, in foreign-exchange markets the increase in the monetary base resulting from the BoJ's rising current account balance led to devaluation of the yen, since the view prevailed that, as exemplified by the Soros Chart, exchange rates were determined by the volume of the monetary base. As a result, the understanding spread that the intervention by the Ministry of Finance through purchasing dollar funds to induce devaluation of the yen was sterilized amid an increase in the monetary base.

[13] See Bernanke (2009) for the differences between Japan's QE policy and the QE policy implemented in the United States after the Lehman Shock. The US QE policy is similar to Japan's Comprehensive Monetary Policy (2010–2013) and QQE (2013–).

Whatever the case, at that time the Japanese economy recorded an economic recovery, driven by increased exports backed by economic expansion overseas in particular driven by the historical rapid growth of the Chinese economy and the low value of the yen on international currency markets, and at the same time the Koizumi government implemented financial revitalization policies through injection of public funds into troubled financial institutions, under what was known as the "Takenaka Plan." As a result of these measures, the hoped-for stabilization of the financial system was almost achieved, and in April 2003 the Payoff was lifted. While since the start of zero-interest-rate policies in 1999 Japan's monetary policy had supplied liquidity in large volumes in pursuit of the dual goals of economic recovery and financial-system stability, the achievement, to a degree, of the goal of financial-system stability meant that it no longer would be the priority goal of monetary policy. As the financial crisis lurks and the precautional liquidity demand of financial institutions declines, the effect of quantitative easing policies on liquidity provision will gradually decline.

Assessments of the economic recovery spurred by devaluation of the yen at this time are split. While an economic recovery was achieved through increases in exports and in capital investment, it also can be argued that this led to a swelling of inefficient investment premised on a low yen. In fact, at this time productivity grew only slightly despite the increase in capital investment and some of newly built factories in this period became idle later.

4.4 Comprehensive Monetary Easing (October 2010–April 2013)

After the economic downturn spurred by the global financial crisis, the BoJ again adopted unconventional monetary policy, in the form of comprehensive monetary easing. A characteristic of this policy is the way the portion of the unconventional monetary policy corresponding to quantitative easing was established in the form of the Asset Purchase Program. In addition, a positive margin was retained in the guidance goal for short-term interest rates, at 0–0.1%. This reflected consideration for avoidance of an extreme decrease in the money market transactions as had been seen under zero-interest-rate policies and quantitative easing.

While ultimately the Asset Purchase Program would grow to about JPY100 trillion, it was distinguished among the policies of BoJ Governor Shirakawa, who had implemented comprehensive easing, in that it was a multifaceted policy that extended beyond the scope of traditional monetary policy. First, in response to increasing instability in corporate finance since the financial crisis, the BoJ purchased CP (Commercial Paper) and corporate bonds and eased the conditions for securing BoJ open-market operations using private-sector bonds. These measures were described as the credit-easing portions of unconventional monetary policy. At the same time, the BoJ viewed the fundamental problem behind Japan's deflation as a decrease in growth potential. For this reason, it implemented growth policies as monetary policy, albeit on an exceptional basis. As the Fund-Provisioning Measure to Support Strengthening the Foundations for Economic Growth, it implemented a scheme to provide long-term, low-interest financial backing for lending by private-sector banks to fields considered necessary for growth, including healthcare.

This understanding of lowering growth as the essence of the Japanese economy's deflationary issues is quite accurate judgement.[14] This meant that there were limits to the effects that monetary policy could have on resolving deflation. Also, at this time Japan's financial system had regained its soundness, and the necessity of supplying liquidity through quantitative easing had lessened. The turmoil in the international financial market following the Lehman shock caused problems in foreign currency liquidity, which was addressed by the establishment of a swap network between central banks. However, during this period, the European banking crisis occurred in parallel with the global financial crisis, and the yen was bought to avoid risk, resulting in a sharp appreciation of the yen and increasing monetary easing pressure on the Bank of Japan. While the BoJ responded by increasing the purchases of the Asset Purchase Program through comprehensive easing, since quantitative easing in Europe and the United States increased even more, the monetary easing in Japan by the Asset Purchase Program was criticized as being too little, too late.

The most difficult evaluation of the policy of the Shirakawa governor era was that if the Bank of Japan adopted a larger quantitative easing more quickly in response to the U.S. quantitative easing after the Lehman shock, the appreciation of the yen was suppressed. The first quantitative easing in the United States, QE1, was adopted in November 2008, while the Bank of Japan's comprehensive easing was adopted approximately two years later. However, many central banks, including the Bank of Japan, thought that the quantitative easing policy was rather a financial stabilization policy and had little effect on the convenyional economic recovery. In fact, in the US, QE1 was focused on restoring the function of the mortgage bond market, which was malfunctioning at that time. The FRB itself did not use the term QE (Quantitative Easing) but the term "LSAP: Large Size Asset Purchase". Chair Bernanke also emphasized the differences from the Bank of Japan's quantitative easing policy with a "Credit Easing (CE)" policy. On the other hand, in the Japanese economy at that time, the problem of financial system was once resolved, and it was judged that the need for credit easing was small. The market focused on the volume of US QE, which had a major impact on the asset market. Given the impact on exchange rates, it may be argued that the Bank of Japan should make a major quantitative easing in line with US policy. However, the difference between domestic and foreign interest rates is also a major determinant of foreign exchange. Even if US interest rates declined, Japanese interest rates were already at zero. Under these circumstances, it was doubtful how much the appreciation of the yen would be corrected by the Japanese quantitative easing policy.

---

[14] Shirakawa (2012b) points out that "the gradual decline in potential growth is a major cause of moderate deflation by lowering future income expectations and reducing spending."

The government of Prime Minister Abe, which took office in December 2012, was critical of the BoJ's monetary policy and had pledged publicly to change BoJ monetary policy even before securing power. The Liberal Democratic Party strengthened political pressure on the BoJ, including the suggestion of amendment of the Bank of Japan Law. In response, in January 2013 the BoJ and the government adopted an inflation target of 2% through a joint statement.

4.5 Quantitative- and Qualitative-Easing Policies (QQE)

The quantitative-easing policies (QQE) that began in April 2013 were bold policies that were described as a new dimension of easing, declaring as their goal the achievement of the Abenomics inflation target of 2% through doubling the monetary base in two years. These policies have a strong nature of being the antithesis of the BoJ's previous policies. First of all, on the subject of deflation they reflect the belief that it would be possible to realize inflation simply through growing the monetary base, without touching on the issue of economic growth. To do so, they acted to influence people's expectations through implementing large-scale monetary easing all at once, based on the belief that a bold measure to overturn people's expectations for the future was essential in order to turn around deflationary expectations in one fell swoop. This differs greatly from the BoJ's argument during the term of Governor Shirakawa, which was that elimination of deflation and related changes in deflationary expectations were one and the same with strengthening economic growth. They also combined the separate account of the Asset Purchase Program, under which quantitative easing had been implemented through then, with the general account. This too was intended to make it easier to affect people's expectations by simplifying the policy framework and making it easier to understand. Greeted with surprise, this policy of quantitative and qualitative easing had a strong impact on asset prices such as stock prices and exchange rates. This was a natural outcome, since changes in expectations have a strong effect on asset prices.

The innovative aspect of QQE is that the policy is highly dependent on expectation control. The effects of monetary easing will be diminished if the interest rate does not decrease even if the volume increases. In the quantitative and qualitative easing policy, emphasis is placed on the policy effect that the real interest rate falls due to rising inflation expectations. In QQE, it committed a quantitative expansion that could be described as anomalous, but this aimed more at controlling expectations than the quantitative expansion itself.

While the enactment of QQE spurred temporary increases in both inflationary expectations and the rate of inflation, the 2% inflation target still has not been achieved a decade later. The BoJ has cited as reasons behind this failure to achieve its target the reaction to the April 2014 increase in consumption tax and falling crude-oil prices. But this contradicts the traditional arguments by the economists, so-called reflationary school, who provide the theoretical support for quantitative and qualitative easing. Those adherents had argued that inflation was determined by the relationship between total demand and total supply, and that trends in individual prices such as tax rates and oil prices were unrelated to inflation rates. For this reason, citing changes in the consumption tax rate or crude-oil prices as causes of policy failure was counter to their own earlier arguments.

While in addition to the initial simple quantitative monetary easing intended to spur inflation by expanding the monetary base another measure, that of increasing the amount of assets purchased, was adopted in October 2014, the BoJ was forced to revise its policies as easing policies became more long term, exceeding the initial target period of two years. In January 2016, while still maintaining the expansion of the monetary base, a negative-interest-rate policy was adopted by applying a negative interest rate to a part of current account deposit. Thus, the interest rate was added to the target of manipulation through a negative-interest-rate policy. At a time when a lengthening of the term of quantitative and qualitative easing was anticipated, an increase in the amount of long-term government bonds purchased would invite a decrease in not only short-term but also long-term interest rates. This would cause considerable harm to the earnings of private-sector banks. Even if short-term policy interest rates are negative, private banks cannot pay negative interest on deposits. At the same time, the interest rates on lending charged by private banks fell due to the impact of the decrease in long-term interest rates. As a result, private banks' profit margin in the form of the difference between interest rates on lending and on deposits contracted. BoJ Governor Kuroda also was aware of the "reversal rate" issue,[15] through which a flattening of the yield curve due to an excessive decrease in interest rates would lessen the effects of monetary easing. In September 2017, the BoJ switched to a policy of yield-curve control, targeting a short-term interest rate of –1% and a long-term interest rate of roughly 0%. The target of manipulation shifted from the previous quantitative target of the monetary base to the interest target of the yield curve. This is aimed at working positively for banking business by securing profit margins created by the difference between long and short interest rates.

In 2017, the goal of expanding the monetary base became more flexible, and the pace of an annual increase of JPY80 trillion lessened. At the same time, the BoJ has maintained its expansionary policy for the quantitative target, as an instrument for realizing a future economic recovery. Probably this reflects an awareness of the need to continue to maintain a route to inspire inflationary expectations—and in particular, to secure influence on asset prices such as exchange rates and stock prices—through expansion of the quantitative target. Even so, at present the quantitative target no longer is a priority goal. Also, since April 2018 the BoJ has not mentioned a period for achievement of its inflation target.

In order to secure flexibility in monetary policy, in October 2018 the BoJ switched to a policy that took the form of providing considerable breadth for fluctuation in long-term interest rates. This is seen as a tolerance for increases in domestic long-term interest rates as interest rates overseas are rising in general.[16]

---

[15] For reversal rate, see Brunnermeier and Koby (2023).

[16] The Bank of Japan's long-term interest rate control has become more flexible, with the initial target of 0% now allowed to rise to 1% as of December 2013.

While quantitative- and qualitative-easing policies got their start as antitheses of previous BoJ policies, the strategy of achieving an inflation target of 2% through bold quantitative easing involving a breakdown of previous policy discipline has not yet succeeded. It would appear as if the BoJ has fallen into "the trap of the 2% inflation target," as it has no choice but to continue policies of easing in perpetuity as long as there is no prospect of achievement of this target.

Even though bold monetary easing has not achieved its goal, one success that can be identified is that of contributing to a long standing recovery even modereate. However, the fact must not be overlooked that at this time global economic conditions are favorable, centered on the U.S., and the Japanese economy has enjoyed the positive effects of such global economic conditions. While Iwata (2018), a influential scholar who is an adherent of reflationary policy as well as a former Deputy Governor of the BoJ, identified as reasons for the BoJ's failure to meet its inflation targets external factors beyond the BoJ's control, such as a worsening of economic conditions due to the effects of the increase in consumption tax and falling oil process, at the same time it cannot be denied that the economic recovery over this period was due to the external factor of favorable global economic conditions—also external to the BoJ's monetary policy. In addition, at present the side effects of quantitative- and qualitative-easing policies are intensifying. The main side effect is the distortion of fiscal discipline discussed below. However, even an easing of discipline of monetary policy and discipline of fiscal policy would not be problematic if growth potential, the biggest challenge to the Japanese economy, were to be strengthened. A more important issue is the fact that even though discipline of monetary policy and fiscal discipline have been eased, the central issue of the growth potential of the Japanese economy has not improved at all.

5 Relationship to Fiscal Policy

5.1 Trends in Fiscal Policy

Until the period of rapid economic growth in the mid-1970s, Japan's fiscal policy had maintained balanced budgets, not permitting fiscal deficits to continue over the long term. Later, the Japanese government continuously issued deficit-financing government bonds beginning in 1975, to cover revenue shortfalls accompanying the increase in social security expenditures intended to realize a welfare society as well as low revenues due to a slowdown in economic growth in the latter half of the 1970s.[17] However, even during this period the Ministry of Finance, the ministry responsible for the budget, continued to argue for a long-term balanced budget. In addition, the fixed exchange-rate system that prevailed until 1971 imposed a rule that

[17] Under Japan's Public Finance Act, issue of government bonds is an exception. While deficit-financing government bonds were issued for a while after being legalized in 1965, the government later refrained from issuing them, and their full-fledged issue only began in 1975.

required a tightening of monetary and fiscal policy if the current-account deficit were to increase. Until the amendment of the Bank of Japan Law in 1998, the Bank of Japan was under the strong control of the government. Even so, it was able to make decisions on monetary policy in relative independence because of this principle of a balanced budget under the fixed exchange-rate system.

During the 1980s, the budgetary authorities sought means of fiscal reconstruction such as the introduction of consumption tax, under conditions of widening fiscal deficits. However, in the bubble economy of the late 1980s fiscal revenues raised up, and in the first half of the 1990s the government ceased issuing deficit-financing government bonds. This strengthened the argument for implementing fiscal reconstruction during an economic expansion, such as the bubble economy, instead of implementing steady fiscal reconstructing efforts, and it weakened subsequent fiscal-reconstruction efforts.

However, with the bursting of the bubble economy measures taken in response to the economic downturn shifted beginning in the mid-1990s from increasing fiscal expenditures to a steady increase in fiscal deficits, with increased issue of government bonds. The year 1997 was an epochal one for Japan's monetary and fiscal policy. In terms of monetary policy, the Bank of Japan Law was amended, and the amended law was enacted in the following year. At the same time, in terms of fiscal policy a consumption tax was introduced, and the Fiscal Structure Reform Act,[18] intended to strengthen fiscal discipline, was passed. As seen in the European Union's adoption in the Maastricht Treaty of balanced finances as a condition of accession to the Euro and Britain's adoption of a rule calling for a balanced budget along with amendment of the Bank of England Act under the Blair government, balanced budget was a necessary condition for central bank independence, and it is worth noting that in Japan too a similar balanced-budget bill was passed, although not necessarily for purposes of securing the independence of the Bank of Japan. However, in Japan's case the balanced-budget bill was abandoned in the following year due to the economic slowdown and financial crisis that followed the adoption of consumption tax in 1997, and no balanced-budget act has been passed since then. Reflecting such circumstance, since 1997 Japan's fiscal deficits have swollen further.

With regard to fiscal reconstruction, while in 2006, under the Koizumi government, a goal was identified of making primary balance of the budget surplus by FY2011, the target for achievement of this goal has been postponed repeatedly. In 2010, the target was postponed to FY2020, and in 2018 it was postponed again to FY2025. While the Japanese government has strived to restrain expenditures through means such as keeping down increases in public-works project expenditures, expenditures increased with growth in social-security costs accompanying the progressive ageing of Japan's population and other factors. However, in 2012 the second Abe administration eased restraints on fiscal expenditures for purposes including renovation of aged social infrastructure. Expenditures increased after that as well, due

[18] The Fiscal Structure Reform Act called for reducing the fiscal deficit, which stood at 5.4% of GDP in 1997, to no more than 3% of GDP by 2003 and reducing issue of deficit-financing government bonds to zero.

to measures such as expansion of social security across all generations. Behind this change in policy is the idea of shifting from previous policies that gave too much emphasis to restraining expenditures toward contributing to an economic expansion through increasing fiscal expenditures, and shrinking fiscal deficits through the resulting increase in tax revenues. However, a look at the results shows that while tax receipts have increased with the economic recovery, economic growth is below targets, and as a result the resolution of fiscal deficits has been put off.

5.2 Relationship to Monetary Policy[19]

While in 1989, at the time the bubble burst, the general account budget stood at approximately JPY60 trillion, by 2019 it had increased to over JPY100 trillion. As a result, the fiscal deficit too has increased from approximately JPY10 trillion to approximately JPY40 trillion over this 30-year period, and the amount of government bonds issued also increased, from approximately JPY6 trillion to, at one time, approximately JPY50 trillion. (It stands today at approximately JPY35 trillion.) As a result, the balance of public debt also increased, from approximately JPY200 trillion to approximately JPY900 trillion. However, interest expenses, which constitute the costs to the government of issuing government bonds, now stand at only about JPY9 trillion, compared to JPY10 trillion 30 years ago. The reason why interest expenses have not increased despite the increase in the balance of government bonds issued is because the interest rate on government bonds has decreased, from about 6% 30 years ago to about 1% today. This massive decrease in the interest rate is the most important reason why interest expenses have not risen.

While this was not necessarily intentional, the decrease in interest rates due to large-scale monetary easing does involve an aspect of permitting an increase in issue of government bonds. Put another way, a central bank must be cautious about increasing interest rates because such an increase could swell fiscal deficits. When such fiscal conditions have a strong influence on monetary policy, it is referred to as “fiscal dominance”. Japan today is in a state of “fiscal dominance.” In addition, a policy that central banks keep artificially low long-term interest rates is called “financial repression.”[20] “Financial repression” was once discussed in the context of promoting investment for economic growth in developing economies, but it has recently been discussed in the context of reducing fiscal costs. The current situation in Japan is the state of “financial repression” as well as “financial dominance”. In

[19] Shirakawa (2012a) discusses fiscal policy in relation to monetary policy and financial system policy.

[20] Regarding QQE, focusing on the aspect of financial repression, it is criticized that the fiscal expansion due to financial repression has created distortions in resource allocation and has not improved the growth potential inherently.

particular, as noted below under the restrictions of a zero interest rate monetary policy must be managed as one with fiscal policy. How a central bank can demonstrate its leadership under such conditions is an issue related to central-bank independence.

6 Relationship to Independence[21]

6.1 The Independence Trap

The Bank of Japan's unconventional monetary policy has been criticized as being unnecessarily conservative until the adoption in 2013 of quantitative- and qualitative-easing policies. In the early years, Cargill et al. (1997) argue that from its start as an independent central bank the Bank of Japan was caught in the "independence trap." Orphanides (2018) argues that, had the Bank of Japan set an inflation target of 2% from the start, it probably would have been able to implement more proactive easing policies.[22] Orphanides also points out that the elimination by the 1998 Bank of Japan Law of provisions on government supplementation of the Bank of Japan's losses could have caused the BoJ to be hesitant to purchase large volumes of government bonds.

However, this assumes that if the Bank of Japan had implemented policies like its current policy of QQE easing 20 years ago it likely would have achieved its 2% inflation target. But what the experience of the past 20 years, and in particular of the ten years of QQE, suggests is that it would be difficult to achieve the 2% inflation target through monetary policy alone. In an economy in which growth expectations are decreasing because there is no prospect of sustained economic growth through an increase in potential growth, businesses are wary of increasing wages and product prices, and it is difficult to achieve expected inflation as well as increases in inflation. Put in more intuitive terms, companies are wary of raising prices if they do not expect sales figures to increase.

[21] The independence of the central bank was strengthened legally in the late 1990s by the establishment and revision of the Central Bank Law in the UK, Europe and other countries. However, the discussion at that time was mainly focused on the independence of monetary policy aimed at restraining inflation, and, as in the UK, monetary stability policy was separated from the central bank. Purified as a single-purpose institution for monetary policy, it became "independence of monetary policy = independence of central banks." Later, especially after the financial crisis, the economic situation became deflationary, non-traditional monetary policies such as quantitative easing were taken, and financial stability policy such as macroprudential policy were delegated (re-delegation). The environment surrounding the central bank has changed greatly. Takahashi (2021) tries to discuss the independence of the central bank in a new environment.

[22] Fujiwara et al. (2007) have adopted more aggressive monetary policy since the early 1990s, taking into account the inertia of inflation, using the Bank of Japan's large macroeconomic model (JEM). They have concluded that they have been able to support inflation and growth to some extent. However, the effect is limited, and it seems that the whole picture of long-term stagnation in the 1990s could not have been changed.

Accordingly, a look at trends in Japan's potential growth rate shows that potential growth has fallen continuously over the past 30 years. Even during the past ten years, in which QQE began under Abenomics, the potential growth rate has not exceeded 1%. While Abenomics included plans for fiscal reconstruction under the assumptions of a nominal economic growth rate of 3% and a real rate of 2%, its goals—including its inflation target of 2%—have not been achieved.

While the adherents of reflationary policy who supported Abenomics expected to be able to realize an inflation rate of 2% through growth in the monetary base, seeing inflation as a monetary phenomenon, their argument ignored the potential growth rate. Probably it would be more apt to say that the reason the Japanese economy has been so slow to break free from deflation is due to a failure to increase potential growth rather than to overly conservative monetary policy on the part of the BoJ.

6.2 *Proactive Independence*[23]

In a broad sense, today's central banks are independent presences within government (the system of governance of a nation). Independent powers within a system of governance are in a tense relationship of mutual checks and balances. This is the concept of the constitutional separation of powers in which independent powers are established within the government.[24] Since at present government has the authority to

[23] In economics, regarding the independence of central banks, "the goal independence" that a central bank itself sets monetary policy objectives (for example, target inflation rate) and "instruments independence 'or operational independence" that a central bank itself control monetary policy instrument variables (short-term interest rates, etc.). Even in the case of an independent central bank, in a democratic society, it is not appropriate to be completely free from political control, and it is widely believed that monetary policy goals should be determined with politics involved (Debelle and Fischer 1994). The issue of political pressure discussed in this chapter is "political independence (PI)", and it is generally related to "goal independence". It also related to "instruments independence" because it can affect the monetary operations. In economics, studies such as indexing "political independence" are being conducted. In the previous studies, "political independence" was determined by: (1) the appointment of officers such as governors and policy committees by the government, (2) the term of officers and policy committees (more than 5 years), and (3) It is indexed by paying attention to the attendance of government officials at committee and (4) adjustments when opinions differ from the government. As a result, in addition to Japan, the UK is also categorized as the least politically independent central bank. In addition to these factors, the author believes that independence from fiscal policy is important as a factor for measuring political independence. The author believes that there are certain limits to study that focuses on such institutional aspect and indexes it. In extreme cases, the law (Central Banking Law) can also be changed by politics. After all, even if there is a good system, there is an aspect that good behavior that actually respects independence is more important. The actual situation is not fully reflected in the index that focuses only on systems like previous studies.

[24] The author has discussed the importance of central bank independence from a constitutional standpoint (Takahashi 2021). As for the central bank's monetary policy, there is an undemocratic nature of unpopular policy, as seen in the metaphor "taking out a punch ball in the middle of a party". The constitution is based on liberalism (constitutionalism) to protect fundamental human rights that cannot be violated by democracy. Central bank independence is based on this liberalism. The right

appoint central bankers as well as the authority to approve budgets and other matters, even though independent decision-making is guaranteed for monetary policy, central banks tend to avoid political conflicts in general. In addition, the legislature has the authority to amend laws governing the central bank. For this reason, central banks also tend to avoid conflicts with legislatures. The Abe government today has an absolute majority in parliament. Memories still are fresh of the ruling Liberal Democratic Party putting political pressure on the BoJ from 2012 to 2013 by suggesting amendment of the Bank of Japan Law, as noted above. This political situation is in contrast to the UK. According to Mr. Brown (former finance minister and former prime minister) who promoted the amendment of the Bank of England Law, the Labour Party said that the independence of the central bank would not be a political issue in the general election in the amendment of the Bank of England Law in 1997.[25] He also stated that the Bank of England was dissatisfied during the 2007–2009 financial crisis but respected its independence and did not profess dissatisfaction at all.

In the previous sections, it has been discussed that the Bank of Japan's non-conventional monetary policy has changed reflecting economic situations, and monetary policy discipline has been loosed. This is also largely due to increased political pressure. The Bank of Japan, which relaunched as an independent central bank in 1998, has relaxed traditional monetary policy discipline while reversing independence. In January 2013, the inflation target was raised from 1 to 2%, which is reported as a result of accepting political involvement in setting targets under political pressure.[26] As mentioned above, if the target of 2% is an excessive target setting based on the economic potential, the discipline of the inflation target will not function, and it will be assumed that the situation will lead to unrestrained relaxation. Economics argues that the central bank's independence should be differentiated into "goal independence" and "instrument independence," but the Japanese case is a counterexample to the claim that "goal independence" should be left to politics.

If we refer to central-bank independence that avoids conflict with politics as "passive independence," then under passive independence a central bank would refrain from proactive statements in areas outside its own responsibility of monetary policy. But surely this is not the form expected of a central bank within a system of constitutional separation of powers.

---

to pursue happiness in Article 13 of the Japanese Constitution is a typical basic human right. The central bank's mission will be to ensure free economic activity through the smooth function of the market economy. The central bank should actively demonstrate independence to achieve this mission.

[25] Gordon Brown's remarks at the Bank of England (2017). The Labour Party said that it was considering giving independence to the Bank of England from around 2015, but this was for the sake of medium- to long-term economic stability and said it was not a political issue.

[26] Negotiations between the government and the Bank of Japan when raising the inflation target in January 2013 cannot be confirmed by official records of the government or the Bank of Japan. This is reported by journalists who have carefully accumulated interviews with those involved. From the perspective of accountability, it is desirable that this process be clarified by official records of the government and the Bank of Japan.

The reason for an independent central bank charged with monetary policy is to enable it to plan policy from a medium- to long-term perspective based on a different point of view than that of the government.[27] In addition, under the current zero-interest-rate conditions in particular the effects of monetary policy and fiscal policy are demonstrated in unison. Under such conditions, the mission of the central bank is likely to be one of thinking about fiscal and monetary policies together from a medium- to long-term perspective. Since of course fiscal policy itself is the government's responsibility, coordination of monetary policy and fiscal policy might extend no further than statement of opinions by the central bank. It is worth listening closely to the proposal by Balls et al. (2018)[28] in Britain, which faces similar conditions, for the Bank of England to issue open letters to the Chancellor of the Exchequer periodically on the state of the nation's fiscal situation.[29] The growth strategy is definitely the most important issue in Japan, and the central bank is required to express its opinions appropriately.

Furthermore, under current conditions the central bank also has important responsibilities in the area of financial stabilization policy, not just monetary policy. While of course this too is a policy implemented in cooperation with the government, it is expected that the central bank, in light of its closer position than the government's to the financial markets and its more medium- to long-term perspective, would serve in a planning and advising role regarding policy.

It is not the case that the Bank of Japan has refrained from commenting on the medium- to long-term issues faced by the Japanese economy over the past 20 years. For example, BoJ Governor Shirakawa pointed out repeatedly that the essential factor behind the deflationary issues in the Japanese economy was a decrease in the potential growth rate. But such arguments were attacked from the political side as signs that the Bank of Japan was being reluctant to massive monetary easing. For the Bank of

---

[27] AT the time of the BoJ's centennial in 1982, Governor Haruo Maekawa cited the famous words "the leader of wild geese" by Yukichi Fukuzawa, a great thinker in the Meiji period, to describe the norms of Bank of Japan. It can be considered an apt description of the role of the Bank of Japan within Japanese society:

"When a group of wild geese are pecking for food, there is one goose who higher up the neck. It's the leader whose role is wary around." (Yukichi Fukuzawa, 1874)

This description of the role of a central bank likened to a leader of wild geese is an apt expression of the strong independence of a central bank with its eye on the medium and long term.

[28] Balls et al. (2018) argues that monetary policy needs to be coordinated with fiscal policy under zero interest rate constraints. And in order to maintain the independence of the central bank, the central bank's initiative requires the coordination of monetary policy and fiscal policy. If the fiscal policy deviates from the coordination, the central bank will send an open letter indicating the desired corrective measures for the macro policy.

[29] Brown points out that the central bank and the government need to cooperate in the financial stabilization policy. And it proposes to introduce an open letter system so that underlap does not occur rather than overlap of both. On the other hand, it was a mistake that the Bank of England criticized the fiscal policy that turned to be expansional during the financial crisis. And commenting on areas where the central bank does not hold direct responsibility criticizes it as a threat to independence. Balls proposed an open letter because monetary and fiscal policies would have to be coordinated under zero interest rates, but his views differ from Brown, who together promoted the independence of the Bank of England in 1997.

Japan to perform its essential role as an independent central bank, there is a need for an understanding of the meaning of constitutional independence under which the BoJ should make statements proactively on an equal footing with the government. Under a constitutional framework, politicians too should understand that theirs is a relationship of constructive tension with the Bank of Japan and it is natural that they might be subject to criticism. Surely the independence of the Bank of Japan should be demonstrated and established as "proactive independence" in which opinions are exchanged on an equal footing with the government.

7 Concluding Remarks

While the Bank of Japan has been a world pioneer in implementing unconventional monetary policy in the Japanese economy, which has been faced with the challenges of slow economic performance since the economic bubble burst 30 years ago, many have questioned its responsibility for monetary policy in light of the long time it has taken to address the economy's greatest challenge of overcoming deflation. However, the experience of the past 20 years would seem to suggest that there are limits to the effects of monetary policy, and that the issue cannot be resolved without a recovery in medium- to long-term growth potential.

Relaxing monetary and fiscal policy discipline may increase future risks. Despite the large-scale policy, the potential growth potential, which is the economic ability, has not increased. Current policies are poor in terms of cost and potential risks. Objective evaluation is necessary. Ambitious economic goals can add to these negative effects. Given the current situation, it will also be necessary to review the goals to be more realistic.

Is it not the case that what Japan has lacked over the past 20 years is medium- to long-term vision? It also would seem that the position of the Bank of Japan, which traditionally has the power to draft medium- to long-term policy, has not been taken advantage of sufficiently.

While the Japanese government over the past 20 years has worked out a growth strategy centered on deregulation, its results have been felt only at a microeconomic level, and it has not contributed sufficiently to building up potential growth.

Probably a better approach to a growth strategy would be to proceed proactively with economic integration with nearby Asian states. In 2010, the Japanese economy was overtaken by the Chinese economy in terms of GDP, and today China's GDP has grown to about 2.5 times the size of Japan's. In terms of per-capita GDP as well, Japan has been overtaken by the economies of Singapore and Hong Kong. The Japanese economy has not capitalized successfully on Asia's growth potential. Economic integration would improve productivity in the Japanese economy by promoting competition among firms while advancing horizontal specialization within the region.

Fortunately, the past 30 years also has been a period in which the Bank of Japan has strengthened its partnerships with Asian central banks. In the 1990s, the Bank of

Japan established a policy-dialogue forum with Asian central banks. Together with Asian central banks, it established and invested in the Asia Bond Fund, an investment trust for Asian bonds intended to serve as a catalyst for the growth of Asian bond markets. In its relations with China as well, in 2001 the Bank of Japan and the People's Bank of China concluded an agreement on currency swaps between the yen and the renminbi. This was China's first swap agreement. Traditionally, economic relations with China have advanced separately from politics. However, recently politics has begun to interfere in economic relations as well, and progress on economic relations with Asia and China appears to have come to a relative standstill. Has not this fact become an impediment to the progress of the Japanese economy?

What is important for the Japanese economy is to increase potential growth by improving productivity. Both improvements in the effects of monetary policy and progress on fiscal reconstruction are conditional on increases in potential growth. The Bank of Japan can demonstrate its true power through drafting medium- to long-term policies to address issues such as this. It needs to demonstrate the vision of a central bank separate from political standpoints, in areas including the building of ties with Asia.

References

Balls E, Howat J and Stansbury A (2018) "Central Bank Independence Revisited: After the Financial Crisis, What Should a Model Central Bank Look Like?" Harvard Kennedy School Mossavar-Rahmani Centre for Business and Government Associate Working Paper No. 67.

Bank of England (2017) "Independence—20 years on" Accessed online at website of Bank of England, https://www.bankofengland.co.uk/events/2017/september/20-years-on, on February 20, 2024. (last access date).

Bernanke B (2009) "The crisis and the policy response: a speech at the Stamp Lecture, London School of Economics 2009" Accessed online at website of Bank of England, https://www.federalreserve.gov/newsevents/speech/bernanke20090113a.htm, February 20, 2024 (last access date).

Brunnermeier M and Koby Y (2023) "The Reversal Interest Rate" *American Economic Review* 113.

Bruno V and Shin H (2013) "Capital Flows, Cross-Border Banking and Global Liquidity" Working Paper 19038, National Bureau of Economic Research.

Cargill T, Hutchinson M and Ito T (1997) *The Political Economy of Japanese Monetary Policy*, MIT Press

Debelle G and Fisher S (1994) "How Independent Should a Central Bank Be?" in Fuhrer J ed. Goals, Guidelines, and Constraints Facing Monetary Policymakers, Federal Reserve Bank of Boston Conference Series No. 38, Federal Reserve Bank of Boston.

Fujiwara I, Hara N, Hirakata N, Kimura T, Watanabe S (2007) "Japanese Monetary Policy during the Collapse of the Bubble Economy: A View of Policymaking under Uncertainty" Bank of Japan, *Monetary and Economic Studies, Institute for Monetary and Economic Studies*, 25(2).

Hattori M, Shin H and Takahashi W (2009) "A Financial System Perspective on Japan's Experience in the Late 1980s" IMES Discussion Paper Series, No. 2009-E-19. Institute for Monetary and Economic Studies, Bank of Japan.

Iwata K (2018) "Japan's Economy and Monetary Policy" Speech at a Meeting with Business Leaders in Oita (January 31, 2018) Accessed online at website of Bank of Japan, https://www.boj.or.jp/en/about/press/koen_2018/ko180131a.htm

Nakaso H (2017) "Evolving Monetary Policy: The Bank of Japan's Experience" Speech at the Central Banking Seminar Hosted by the Federal Reserve Bank of New York (New York, October 18)]. The Bank of Japan (October 19, 2017).
Okina K, Shirakawa M and Shiratsuka S (2001) "The Asset Price Bubble and Monetary Policy: Japan's Experience in the Late 1980s and the Lessons" Bank of Japan Monetary and Economic Studies 19. Institute for Monetary and Economic Studies, Bank of Japan.
Orphanides A (2018) "The Boundaries of Central Bank Independence: Lessons from Unconventional Times" Bank of Japan Monetary and Economic Studies 36. Institute for Monetary and Economic Studies, Bank of Japan.
Rogoff K (1985) "The Optimal Degree of Commitment to an Intermediate" *Quarterly Journal of Economics*, 100.
Shirakawa M (2012a) "The Importance of Fiscal Sustainability: Preconditions for Stability in the Financial System and in Prices" April 21. Accessed online at website of Bank of Japan, https://www.boj.or.jp/en/about/press/koen_2012/ko120422b.htm, on February 24, 2024. (last access date)
Shirakawa M (2012b) "Demographic Changes and Macroeconomic Performance: Japanese Experiences" *Bank of Japan Monetary and Economic Studies* 30. *Accessed online at website of Bank of Japan, https://www.boj.or.jp/en/about/press/koen_2012/ko120530a.htm, on February 24, 2024. (last access date)
Shirakawa M (2021) *Tumultous Times: Central Banking in an Era of Crisis*, Yale University Press.
Takahashi W (2021) "Central Bank Independence in a Changing Environment" In Matsubayashi K, Nakamura T, Aoki K and Takahashi W, *Monetary Theory in the Age of Uncertainty*, Chapter 2 pp. 13–42, Springer Briefs in Economics and Kobe University Social Science Research Series, Springer.
Taylor J (2008) *Global Financial Warriors; The Untold Story of International Finance in the Post-9/11 World*, W.W. Norton & Company.

Wataru Takahashi is Professor at Osaka University of Economics and Research Fellow at Kobe University. After joining Bank of Japan, he became Director-General at Institute for Monetary and Economic Studies through a career in various departments and study abroad at Oxford University. He has taught at several universities and has been involved in various finance-related research projects.

Policy Discussions on Output Gaps in Japan During the 1990s

Takeshi Tashiro

Abstract The output gap, also known as the gross domestic product (GDP) gap, has long served as a guiding principle in economic policymaking. In Japan, it played a significant role in economic policy discussions from the late 1990s to the early 2000s. Nevertheless, its usefulness for real-time policymaking was a subject of debate. This chapter aims to provide an examination of the controversies surrounding the output gap during the aforementioned period. Upon thorough review and analysis, several noteworthy observations emerge regarding this debate. Firstly, these discussions delved into the complexities of output gap measurement and sought to uncover the true reasons behind economic recessions. Secondly, over the years, other advanced economies have drawn insights from Japan's experience. In Europe, a campaign known as the "Campaign Against Nonsense Output Gap" aims to scrutinize the dependability of the output gap in policymaking and policy evaluations. Given the shared challenges faced by advanced economies, the lessons from Japan's historical economic policy debates hold valuable significance and deserve ample attention.

1 Introduction

The output gap, also known as the gross domestic product (GDP) gap, has long served as a guiding principle in economic policymaking. In Japan, it played a significant role in economic policy discussions from the late 1990s to the early 2000s. Nevertheless, its usefulness for real-time policymaking was a subject of debate. These discussions delved into the complexities of output gap measurement and sought to uncover the true reasons behind economic recessions. Over the years, other advanced economies

The author thanks Keita Oikawa, Adam Posen, and Junko Watanabe for the comments. The views expressed in the paper are solely those of the author and do not represent the views of the organizations to which the author belongs.

T. Tashiro (✉)
Research Institute of Economy, Trade and Industry, Tokyo, Japan

Peterson Institute for International Economics, Washington D.C., United States

H. Takeda and J. Watanabe (eds.), *Rethinking Japanese economic policy at the turn of the 21st century*, Advances in Japanese Business and Economics 34,
https://doi.org/10.1007/978-981-97-5512-7_8

have drawn insights from Japan's experience. In Europe, a campaign known as the "Campaign Against Nonsense Output Gap" aims to scrutinize the dependability of the output gap in policymaking and policy evaluations. Given the shared challenges faced by advanced economies, lessons learned from Japan's historical economic policy debates hold great significance and deserve ample attention.

2 The Campaign Against Nonsense Output Gap

The trustworthiness of output gap estimates in policymaking has been a subject of debate among advanced nations. Beginning in early 2019, Robin Brooks, Chief Economist at the Institute for International Finance, spearheaded the "Campaign Against Nonsense Output Gap" (CANOO) (Brooks and Basile 2019a, b, c). This campaign challenges the validity of output gap estimates, particularly concerning the Eurozone peripheries, asserting that these estimates made little sense due to the lack of inflationary pressure before the pandemic and the failure to reflect actual economic growth performances.

The estimation of the output gap in European countries is conducted by different entities such as the European Commission, the Organisation for Economic Cooperation and Development (OECD), and the International Monetary Fund (IMF). Prior to the pandemic, as highlighted by Brooks, the European Commission reported positive output gaps in Spain and Portugal, suggesting that demand exceeded supply in those regions, even though Germany's output gap was slightly negative, indicating that actual GDP fell short of potential GDP. In light of Germany's notably faster growth compared to Spain and Portugal over the past decade, Brooks and Basile (2019a) emphasized that these estimates failed to capture the actual situation. They further expounded in Brooks and Basile (2019b) on the concept of "bending down" potential GDP, elucidating that potential GDP estimates closely track past economic growth averages, thereby automatically "bending down" potential growth when economic activity remains weak for extended periods. Nevertheless, this sluggish economic growth might have resulted from a tight macroeconomic policy, regardless of whether potential growth shifted downward. Brooks and Basile (2019c) proposed an alternative approach allowing for sustained GDP contraction during a downturn but assuming a positive albeit reduced trend growth thereafter. Their findings indicated that output gaps in the Euro periphery were twice as large as the consensus estimates.

Additionally, Brooks and Basile (2019c) utilized the Phillips curve for a further "common sense" test, comparing widely used unemployment gap estimates with core inflation. The Phillips curve, which illustrates the inverse relationship between unemployment rates and the corresponding increases in inflation rates, did not hold across advanced economies. Furthermore, Brooks and Basile (2019c) pointed out that given low inflation levels with similar labor market slack, structural unemployment estimates in the Euro periphery seemed disproportionately high. The core issue lies in the fact that structural unemployment estimates did not decline as actual unemployment rates decreased. Belgium, Spain, and Portugal exhibited similar unemployment gaps, despite significant variations in their unemployment rates. Fundamentally, price pressures displayed disparities, with Belgium's core inflation being nearly three times that of Spain. This observation aligns with the analysis of the substantial output gaps that persisted in the Euro periphery.

In response to this campaign, Adam Tooze of Columbia University highlighted that the primary issue lies in the statistical methods employed to disentangle the trend and cyclical components of the labor market (Tooze 2019). He proposed that potential output estimates are heavily grounded in historical experience. Furthermore, these estimates are intrinsically linked to the actual economic performance. In addition, if the performance is subpar, the potential output bends mechanically downward.

Several economists have acknowledged the varying degrees of these estimates. For instance, Darvas (2019) demonstrated that the estimates exhibit substantial disparities among three organizations. However, Heimberger (2021) suggested that the European Commission's model for estimating output gaps tends to generate a procyclical bias, raising concerns about the necessity for public discourse and potential improvements in fiscal rules post-COVID-19 crisis.

Meanwhile, Barkema et al. (2020), three economists at the IMF, uncovered a notable negative skew in the historical record of global output gap estimates. They also identified a positive albeit limited correlation between output gap estimates and slack. Based on these findings, they stressed the importance of exercising continued caution when relying on output gaps for real-time policymaking and policy assessments.

The output gap, which partially guides policy decisions, has recently faced widespread criticism with regard to its theoretical basis and practical utility.

3 What Is an Output Gap?

An output gap indicates the difference between the actual output and the unobservable potential output. The controversy surrounding these seemingly "nonsense output gaps" is intricately linked to the definition of potential output, its growth trajectory, and the precision of its estimation. Potential output is essentially a supply-side constraint on production. From the vantage point of a production function, the output gap serves as a metric for gauging economic stagnation or the underutilization of production resources, including labor. Similarly, additional demand is interpreted as an output level sufficient to create inflationary pressure, and is instrumental in shaping monetary policy. Output gap estimates are produced by governments, central banks, and international organizations, such as the OECD and IMF, as well as economists.

In Japan, the government (the Cabinet Office[1]) and central bank (the Bank of Japan [BOJ]) produce output gap estimations using the following approaches:

- The Cabinet Office defines potential output as the GDP level achieved using the average input of capital and labor. It also delineates the GDP gap as the ratio of the differences between actual and potential output to the potential output level (Yoshida 2017).
- The BOJ characterizes the output gap as "…the economic measure of the difference between total demand as an actual output of an economy and average supply capacity smoothed out for the business cycle — namely potential GDP — in the goods and services market of the nation. The potential growth rate is the annual rate of change in potential GDP. In factor markets, the output gap expresses the differential between labor and capital utilization rates and their average past levels" (Kawamoto et al. 2017).

Each of these methodologies has evolved over time. The present estimation methods are distinguished by their assessment of potential GDP based on the average supply resource input. They further remove the influence of business cycles and estimated the potential GDP by assuming that production factors followed historical trends. Nevertheless, a caveat arises: When an economy experiences a substantial shock, gauging economic activity in relation to potential becomes challenging. One potential factor contributing to this challenge is the intricacy of distinguishing trends and cycles. In addition, the measurement of structural changes from average inputs is not entirely precise. CANOO addresses these measurement challenges that have been highlighted in Japan's economic policy discourse since the 1990s.

4 Japanese Output Gap Estimates from the Late 1990s to the Early 2000s

4.1 Current Output Gap Estimations

Figure 1 illustrates two output gap estimates for Japan. The government and BOJ estimates show a gap of approximately 3% between 1998 and 2002. The output gap was positive in the mid-1990s. By contrast, the BOJ estimated a positive output gap, whereas the Cabinet Office estimated a negative gap around 2000. Regarding recessions, the output gap in the 1990s was not as substantial as it was during the 2007 global financial crisis and 2020 COVID-19 crisis.

Figure 2 presents the output gap estimates produced by international organizations (IMF and OECD). According to the OECD estimates, a constant negative output gap has existed since 1997. By contrast, the IMF estimated that almost no output gap

[1] In the 2001 central government reform, the Japanese government consolidated various departments, including the former Economic Planning Agency, to establish the Cabinet Office. Prior to the reform, the Economic Planning Agency was responsible for producing output gap estimates.

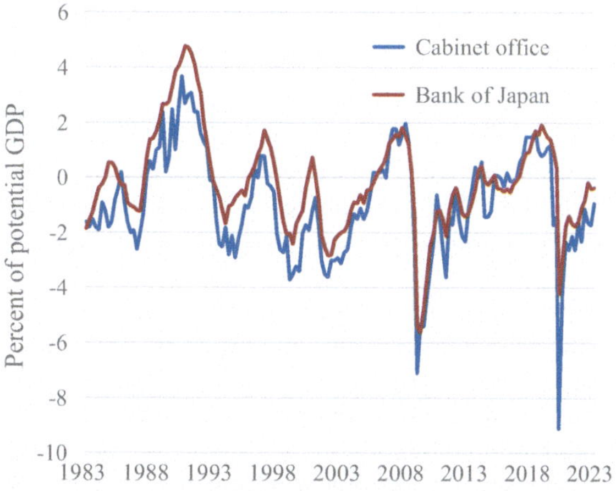

Fig. 1 Japan's output gap estimates (Japanese Government and BOJ) (*Source* Cabinet Office "GDP Gap and Potential Output Growth Rate"; Bank of Japan "Output Gap and Potential Growth Rate" [Data accessed on February 25, 2024])

existed around 2000. In terms of size, the OECD estimated a negative output gap of 3% around 1999. However, IMF estimates were not as large during that period.

Similar to the estimates for Eurozone countries, Japan's output gap estimates exhibit significant variations among these organizations. Such discrepancies in the estimates partly stem from differing views on potential GDP. Different methodologies yield different output gap estimations. If potential GDP is assessed as the average supply capacity, the negative output gap during a recession tends to be moderated. In contrast, the negative output gap tends to be more pronounced when potential output is estimated as the level of output an economy can produce at a constant inflation rate, even when inflation is weak but the capacity is relatively well utilized.

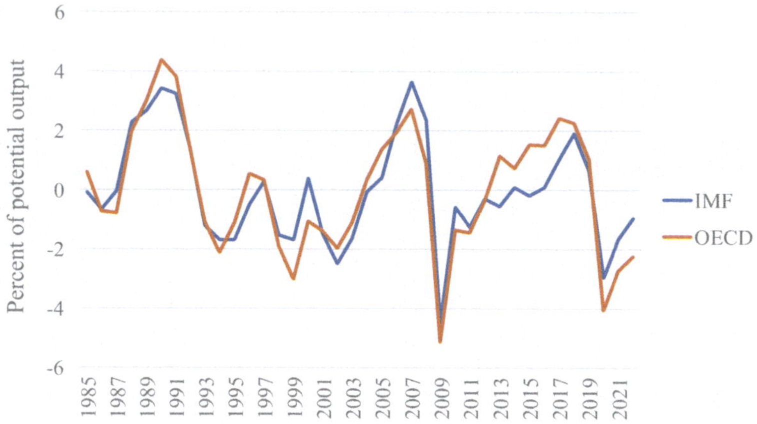

Fig. 2 Japan's output gap estimates (IMF and OECD) (*Source* IMF, *World Economic Outlook Database*, October 2023; OECD, *Economic Outlook*, No. 114 [November 2023])

4.2 Japan's Output Gap Estimates Back Then

How were Japan's output-gap estimates made in the late 1990s and early 2000s? As Japan entered a recession in the early 1990s, the government reported negative output gap estimates. The Economic White Paper published in 1993 recognized the recession and stated, "The GDP gap reached its peak in the January–March 1991 period, then rapidly declined, and turned negative in the April–June 1991 period. Subsequently, the negative output gap continued to widen October-December 1992." The 1997 White Paper evaluated the negative output gap had narrowed in 1994, partly because of the economic recovery that began in 1993. However, the country experienced a severe financial crisis in 1997. According to an Economic White Paper published in 1998, the negative output gap widened because of the recession that started in the latter half of 1997.

However, the usefulness of output gap in economic policy was questioned. The 2000 White Paper warned about the disadvantages of implementing discretionary policies to close the output gap owing to measurement issues. The White Paper indicated that when growth shifted downward, potential growth rate was likely overestimated. Furthermore, it mentioned the risk that an economy operating at full capacity would save inefficient resources.

4.3 Relationship with Other Indicators of Slack

Some economic indicators are related to the output gap. When the output gap narrows, inflationary pressure emerges. The output gap widens during high unemployment periods. Figure 3 illustrates the relationship between the structural unemployment rate and output gap in pre-pandemic Japan. Using structural unemployment rate and output gap data published by the OECD, we can discern that the relationship between the output gap and structural unemployment rate is not always straightforward. However, since the 1990s, the structural unemployment rate has been deteriorating. Despite the economic recovery and a tight labor market (resulting in a positive output gap), structural unemployment has remained high.

The Cabinet Office once estimated the structural unemployment rate to be approximately 4% and considered unemployment due to structural factors, rather than cyclical unemployment, as an issue (Annual Report on the Japanese Economy and Public Finance 2002). This Annual Report suggested the need for labor market reform. More recently, the BOJ estimated a continuous decline in the structural unemployment rate. As of April 2018, the structural employment rate was in the mid-2% range, which is lower than the OECD estimate. According to the BOJ's estimates, a major factor contributing to labor market improvement could be tight labor market conditions, thanks to economic recovery rather than the elimination of structural problems, signifying the challenge of distinguishing the cyclical from the trend. Additionally, the BOJ explained that the structural unemployment rate differs from

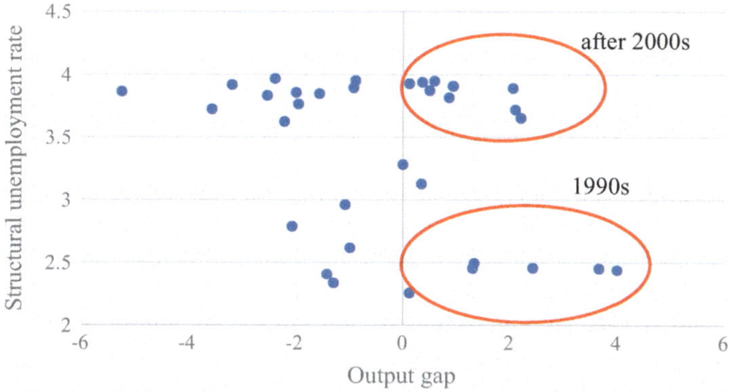

Fig. 3 Output gap and structural unemployment (OECD estimation) (*Source* OECD, *Economic Outlook*, No. 106 [November 2019]. *Note* The equilibrium unemployment rate, as a percentage of labor force is used as the structural unemployment rate)

the non-accelerating inflation rate of unemployment. However, this raises a question about its adequacy in explaining the weakness of inflation at very low unemployment rates. The actual unemployment rate could further decline. Therefore, the endeavor to approach the "true" output gap through real-time estimations presents a formidable task and should be undertaken with a degree of uncertainty.

5 How Output Gap Estimates Have Been Used in Japan's Policymaking

5.1 Economic Stimulus Debate in the Late 1990s

These output gap estimates were used for economic policymaking from various perspectives. In this section, we examine the output gap estimates by reviewing the statements at the Diet. Some argued that the official output gap was underestimated, whereas others disagreed, pointing out that the size of the stimulus should not be determined by the size of the output gap. Moreover, there was a disagreement over the "true" output gap, and these output gap estimations guided Japan's economic stimulus debate in the late 1990s.

In 1993, as the Japanese economy entered a recessionary phase, one Ministry of Finance official made a statement in the Diet, emphasizing that the size of the economic stimulus should not be solely determined by the output gap. In 1997, independent economists presented GDP gap estimates, ranging from 20 to 30 trillion yen (4–6% of GDP) during a Diet session. Another official from the Economic Planning Agency addressed the Diet, indicating an output gap of approximately 3%, as per the OECD. The Ministry of International Trade and Industry estimated the output gap to be approximately 18 trillion yen, which is roughly 3.5% of GDP. While acknowledging the existence of the output gap, Taichi Sakaiya, Chief of the Economic Planning Agency, stressed the importance of addressing structural issues.

In 1998, Prime Minister Keizo Obuchi acknowledged the challenge of accurately measuring the output gap. Nonetheless, he emphasized the government's commitment to taking all necessary measures, recognizing that the economy would not recover without narrowing the output gap. Prime Minister Obuchi emphasized the need for a supplementary budget. In 2000, the Finance Minister Kiichi Miyazawa expressed uncertainty about the size of the output gap.

In 2001, Heizo Takenaka, the Minister of State for Economic and Fiscal Policy, specified that the output gap was approximately 3–4% of GDP, as shown in the Annual Report on the Japanese Economy and Public Finance. He also highlighted that the decline in demand aligned with the decline in potential growth and supply capacity. Takenaka concluded that fine-tuning to fill the GDP gap through fiscal policy had not been implemented in other countries and should be avoided because it would lead to an expansion of the budget deficit.

Although the government acknowledged the existence of a negative output gap, debates persisted regarding whether filling the gap was a wise course of action. The government's reluctance to address the gap partly stemmed from the belief that structural factors contribute to economic stagnation. This debate on economic policy revealed diverging opinions about the appropriate response, ranging from fiscal reform to fiscal stimulus and structural reform. Low assessments of potential growth and small output gap estimates justify fiscal reforms to ensure sustainability and stimulate reforms. However, larger output gap estimates were used to argue for stimulus packages.

5.2 Views from the Outside

Several economists outside the government, particularly foreign economists, heavily criticized the Japanese government's response to the recession. They condemned the conservative estimates of Japan's output gap and the government's unwillingness to take necessary measures to boost the economy.

Krugman's criticisms are particularly noteworthy. In his study on Japan's liquidity trap, Krugman (1998) argued that the estimates of Japan's output gap were too conservative. If these estimates accurately reflected the situation, Japan's potential growth rate would have sharply declined. Specifically, the OECD estimate was notably low at 1.2%, which resulted from updating the estimates of normal working hours and worker productivity in a manner that reinterpreted cyclical factors as structural trends. Krugman suggested that Japan's output gap in 1998 should have been more than 8%. He emphasized the underestimation of the output gap and stressed the importance of policies that support demand.

Echoing Krugman (1998), Posen (1998) estimated a large output gap for Japan and questioned the rapid decline in potential growth in his book, *Restoring Japan's*

Economic Growth. He argued that structural factors alone could not explain the stagnation in economic growth. Furthermore, in 2001, Posen (2001) argued that discussions on Japan's economic potential were unduly pessimistic in their assessments. He proposed active macroeconomic policies and structural reforms that consider a more realistic assessment of potential growth.

In 2002, an article titled "Japan's Lost Decade" in the British newspaper *The Economist* highlighted that the OECD's estimate of Japan's output gap was only approximately 3%, which implied a significant decline in when considering the accuracy of the OECD estimate. The newspaper suggested that if the potential growth rate had remained unchanged, the output gap would have been 18%.

These economists and the newspaper criticized Japan's policy inaction and overly cautious macroeconomic response. Notably, Japan had the lowest growth rate among G7 nations during the 1990s. Conversely, the implementation of proactive policies later led to an economic turnaround, underscoring the importance of avoiding excessively cautious macroeconomic approaches.

6 Conclusion

What lessons be learned from this recurring debate? The ongoing discourse on the reliability of output gap estimates underscores the necessity for prudence when employing output gaps for real-time policymaking. These gaps should be utilized in conjunction with various indicators, such as inflation, and structural changes, including labor participation status, should be considered. Another crucial lesson is the significance of retrospection into Japan's economic debates from the 1990s. The output gap controversy that Japan grappled with during this period is now surfacing in other countries, notably in Europe and the United States. Insights gleaned from Japan's historical economic debates carry considerable value, especially in light of the common challenges confronting advanced economies. Japan's past experiences can provide pertinent perspectives on the issues currently affecting advanced economies worldwide. Enhanced knowledge exchanges between Japan and the rest of the world have the potential to refine economic policymaking and assessments, thereby driving improvements in both realms.

References

Barkema J, Gudmundsson T, and Mrkaic M (2020) "What Do We Talk About When We Talk About Output Gaps?" IMF Working Paper, WP/20/259.

Brooks R and Basile G (2019a) "Campaign against 'Nonsense' Output Gaps (CANOO)". Global Macro Views. Institute for International Finance, May 23, 2019.

Brooks R and Basile G (2019b) "Nonsense Output Gaps" Global Macro Views. Institute for International Finance, May 30, 2019.

Brooks R and Basile G (2019c) "Nonsense Output Gaps and the Phillips Curve" Global Macro Views. Institute for International Finance, June 6, 2019.

Darvas Z (2019) "Uncertainty Over Output Gap and Structural-Balance Estimates Remains Elevated." Bruegel, June 17, 2019. *Accessed online at: https://www.bruegel.org/blog-post/uncertainty-over-output-gap-and-structural-balance-estimates-remains-elevated, on February 25, 2024.

Heimberger P (2021) "Keynes, the Output Gap and the EU's Fiscal Rules" *Notes on Macro Policy Debates*. *Accessed online at: https://wiiw.ac.at/philipp-heimberger-s-1138.html on February 25, 2024.

Kawamoto T, Ozaki T, Kato N, and Maehashi K (2017) "Methodology for Estimating Output Gap and Potential Growth Rate: An Update" Bank of Japan, *Reports & Research Papers*, May 2017.

Krugman P (1998) "It's Baaack: Japan's Slump and the Return of the Liquidity Trap" *Brookings Papers on Economic Activity*, 2: 1998.

Posen A (1998) *Restoring Japan's Economic Growth*. Columbia University Press.

Posen A (2001) "Recognizing Japan's Rising Potential Growth" NIRA Economic Viewpoint 2001 Winter.

Tooze A (2019) "Output Gap Nonsense" *Social Europe*, June 30, 2019. *Accessed online at: https://www.socialeurope.eu/output-gap-nonsense, on February 25, 2024.

Yoshida M (2017) "A New Methodology for Estimating GDP Gap and Potential Output in Japan" Cabinet Office, DP/17-3.

Takeshi Tashiro is Consulting Fellow, Research Institute of Economy, Trade and Industry, and Nonresident Senior Fellow, Peterson Institute for International Economics. His research focuses on fiscal policy, financial crises, and Japan's long stagnation. He is a coauthor of "Fiscal Policy Options for Japan" (with Olivier Blanchard), "Does Reserve Accumulation Crowd Out Investment?" (with Carmen Reinhart and Vincent Reinhart), and "Japan's Exorbitant Privilege" (with Kenneth Rogoff).

Redefining the Path to Economic Recovery and Prosperity: Keidanren, the Consumption Tax, and the Lost Decade of the 1990s in Japan

W. Miles Fletcher III

Abstract This chapter examines the dynamics of the "lost decade" of the 1990s in Japan by analyzing the major role of Keidanren (The Federation of Business Organizations) in advocating the raise in the national consumption tax rate from 3 to 5% in 1997. Some observers blame this action for halting an incipient recovery from an extended period of economic stagnation since 1990, throwing Japan into another recession, and hence contributing to the nation's deflationary doldrums that continue today. This chapter traces the changing attitudes of Keidanren toward the consumption tax, from adamantly opposing proposals for introducing it in the late 1970s to zealously advocating it in the mid-1980s, accepting its passage in 1988 at the rate of 3%, and supporting an increase to 5% in the middle of a severe economic downturn. The main motivation was to achieve long term goals of balancing the national budget and funding increased services for a rapidly aging population, but this approach took the risk of hampering the shorter-term goal of economic recovery.

1 Introduction

This chapter aims to elucidate some of the causes of the extended period of economic stagnation in Japan during the "lost decade" which began in 1990 after the demise of the "bubble economy" of the late 1980s. Amid the many commentaries on this topic, this project contributes to the discussion through a specific case study that will examine the role and motivations of the Japanese business community as represented

---

The author would like to thank Professors Haruhito Takeda, Peter von Staden, and Junko Watanabe for their comments on earlier drafts of this study. The author would also like to note that it builds on the analysis presented in his article, "Dreams of economic transformation and the reality of economic crisis in Japan: Keidanren in the era of the 'bubble' and the onset of the 'lost decade,' from the mid-1980s to the mid-1990s in Japan," *Asia Pacific Business Review*, Volume 18, No. 2 (April 2012), pp. 149–165.

W. M. Fletcher III (✉)
Department of History, The University of North Carolina, Chapel Hill, NC, USA

H. Takeda and J. Watanabe (eds.), *Rethinking Japanese economic policy at the turn of the 21st century*, Advances in Japanese Business and Economics 34,
https://doi.org/10.1007/978-981-97-5512-7_9

by Keidanren (Keizai Dantai Rengōkai, The Federation of Economic Organizations) in promoting the decision to increase the national consumption tax (shōhizei) in 1997. Observers have often cited Keidanren, whose membership centers on large corporations, as the most prominent and powerful business group in Japan.[1]

The raising of the consumption tax and its role in the dynamics of the "lost decade" merit attention for several reasons. As the melodramatic term "lost decade" suggests, the sudden drop in Japan's economic growth in the early 1990s shocked observers. In a figurative instant the Japanese economy fell from the status of being an international superstar to that of a failure. Accordingly, analysts switched from examining the reasons for Japan's economy being, in the words of sociologist Ezra F. Vogel, "Number One" to wondering what had gone wrong. In this context, some observers have blamed the raising of the consumption tax from three percent to five percent in 1997 for stalling an incipient recovery of the economy that began in 1996. Fumitoshi Takahashi, a specialist on comparative economic policy, explains dispassionately that in Japan "the peak of economic recovery following the collapse of the bubble [in 1990] was in March 1997; relapses in the economic indicators began in April following the consumption tax increase." More dramatically, historian Jeff Kingston calls the raising of the consumption tax the "height of folly" that "stifled a fragile recovery" (Vogel 1979; Takahashi 1999, p. 92; Kingston 2013, p. 26; Garside 2012, pp. 116–119; Kuttner, Iwaisako, and Posen 2015, p. 28).[2] Probing the reasons for the government enacting this tax hike when the economy was still so vulnerable is important.

In recent years, increasingly mellow views of the "lost decade" have, one could argue, increased its significance. Because Japan's economic growth remained low except for just a few years in the early 2000s, one could glumly argue that by the 2010s the "lost decade" as a unique debacle had entered its third decade. Japan, though, avoided high levels of unemployment and remained one of the most affluent nations in the world. Moreover, much of the rest of the developed world, especially since the Great Recession of 2008, suffered from sagging economic growth. As one foreign journalist opined a decade ago, "Japan had a genuinely lousy 1990s. But it turns out that, relative to other rich countries, the last decade has not been quite so bad." (Pilling 2014, p. 120). Indeed, the Japanese economy had not imploded. Hindsight suggests that Japan had the honor of first confronting the type of prolonged economic slump that would later affect other economically advanced nations, such as the United States and members of the European Union. This perspective makes the Japanese case less distinctive but more relevant to the experiences of other nations in recent decades.

The business community deserves attention, because it has played a crucial role in the formation of national economic policy, including the enactment of the increased

[1] In 2002 Keidanren (Keizai Dantai Rengōkai, The Federation of Economic Organizations), merged with Nikkeiren (Nihon Keieisha Dantai Renmei, The Japan Federation of Employers' Organizations) to become the Japan Federation of Economic Organizations (Nihon Keizai Dantai Rengōkai).

[2] Shigeki Morinobu spreads blame in arguing that several developments, including the raise in the consumption tax, caused the recession in 1997. See Morinobu (2000, pp. 93–94).

consumption tax in 1997. Hence, examining the development of Keidanren's stance on the consumption tax has major implications for understanding the economic dynamics of the era of the "lost decade," especially what many analysts agree was the failure of government officials to recognize quickly the extent of the economic crisis that developed rapidly in the early 1990s and to react boldly to it. As suggested above, the main problem centered on an asset bubble that resulted from steady economic growth during the late 1980s that helped fuel soaring markets for stocks and for real estate. When the Bank of Japan raised its basic interest rate in 1989 and 1990 to try to bring an orderly end to the bubble, both markets declined sharply over the next few years. As many observers have noted, the government then eschewed strong fiscal or monetary initiatives. For example, Kenneth Kuttner, Tokuo Iwaisako, and Adam Posen emphasize the government's reluctance to adopt aggressive policies of fiscal stimulus or quantitative easing and its failure to coordinate the expansionary fiscal and monetary policies that officials did adopt (Kuttner, Iwaisako, and Posen 2015, pp. 31–33). Masazumi Wakatabe concurs that the government did "too little, too late" in terms of monetary policy in the 1990s and even afterwards. He contends that the Japanese economy did not begin to recover from its stagnation until Prime Minister Shinzō Abe launched a determined program of quantitative easing after 2012 (Wakatabe 2015, pp. 18–19, 137–139). Keiichirō Kobayashi stresses the inability of Japanese executives and government officials to deal with financial institutions' rapidly growing portfolios of non-performing loans until the collapse of several banks in 1998 forced decisive action (Kobayashi 2015, pp. 40–43).

The reasons for the timid responses of officials and executives need further exploration, particularly in terms of the views and influence of the business community as manifest in the positions taken by Keidanren. To date, other influences have received more emphasis. Wakatabe underlines the impact of certain ideas circulating among the policy-making elite. He argues that first a "policy trap" ensnared government officials who in the early 1990s feared that a surge in government spending would create another asset bubble. He stresses even more the growing dominance among Japanese economists of proponents of the "structural reform" of the private sector that would center on deregulation and an increase in companies' efficiency. In his view, these economists deflected officials' attention from expansionary monetary policies that would have been much more effective (Wakatabe 2015, pp. 21–28 and Chapter 3). Kobayashi blames the failure of officials and executives in financial firms to tackle the problem of non-performing loans on their desire to avoid controversy and to protect their vested interests in the status quo. Kuttner, Iwaisako, and Posen mention "institutional inertia" as an influence on national economic policy in general (Kobayashi 2015, p. 41; Kuttner, Iwaisako, and Posen 2015, p. 32). Marie Anchordoguy contends that the postwar Japanese system of "communitarian capitalism," which prized economic stability and orderly competition, inhibited a rapid and forceful response to the economic challenges that emerged in the early 1990s (Anchordoguy 2005, pp. 28–34).

The role of the business community in attempting to comprehend and respond to the nature of Japan's economic crisis after 1990 has not totally escaped notice. Anchordoguy credits "big business" with helping the economic ministries, the

Ministry of Finance (MOF) and the Ministry of International Trade and Industry (MITI), alter communitarian norms, but she does not examine the role of the organized business community in influencing specific national policies (*Ibid.*, p. 34). Kobayashi and Wakatabe hint at some influence by the business community on national economic policies, as they each briefly mention that in 1993 Gaishi Hiraiwa, the president of Keidanren, chaired a taskforce appointed by the prime minister that issued a report urging deregulation and structural reform (Wakatabe 2015, p. 27; Kobayashi 2015, p. 44). Neither scholar, however, elaborates on the Federation's policy proposals or role in making national policy.

This case study will show the impact that Keidanren had on tax policies as vital components of a national economic strategy. The group played a crucial role in first opposing the implementation of a consumption tax in the late 1970s, then supporting its introduction a decade later, and subsequently advocating increases in it. This change resulted from a shifting view of the economic challenges facing Japan which gradually led to a new strategy for recovery from an economic downturn. Rather than aim at an immediate recovery through expansionary fiscal and monetary policies, Keidanren began to advocate that the government should place at least an equal priority on restoring healthy national finances. Keidanren's prescriptions for the tax system and the economy in general by the 1990s thus began to contain contradictions that worked against setting a clear priority on the nation's rapid economic recovery. Ultimately, its proposals emphasized a reduction of government debt as essential to economic prosperity. Its views thus helped inhibit a robust fiscal and monetary response to the downturn in the economy after 1990.

2 Origins of the Campaign for a Consumption Tax, 1977–1979

Comprehending the influence that Keidanren could wield on tax policy and the changes in its thinking during the 1980s and 1990s requires an understanding of the emergence of the issue of the consumption tax and its implementation. In the late 1970s pressure for a new source of revenue, such as a consumption tax, stemmed from shocks to the Japanese economy early in that decade.[3] Prior to that point, Japan had experienced almost two decades of double-digit economic growth spurred by the circumstances of an undervalued yen, a stable exchange rate, and low prices for raw materials. This situation, as is well known, began to change when President Richard M. Nixon of the United States in 1971 ended the postwar "Bretton Woods" system of fixed exchange rates for currencies by decoupling the value of the dollar from gold. One motive was to promote American exports and trim burgeoning trade deficits with nations, such as Japan. As expected, the dollar immediately began to lose value against the yen. By 1973 the yen had strengthened from 360 to the dollar to 265. In that year, this "Nixon Shock" was followed by the first "oil shock" when members

[3] Much of the analysis below is based on Takeda (2009, Chapter 14).

of the Organization of Petroleum Exporting Countries (OPEC) began to reduce the overall production of crude oil and embargo the export of oil to certain nations. OPEC's aim was to pressure other nations, especially the United States, to moderate their policies of support for the state of Israel during the October War of that year. The price of oil jumped from $2.65 per barrel in January 1973, to $11.65 twelve months later. Concerned about a possible downturn in the economy, the Japanese government abandoned the balanced budget policy that it had followed since the early 1950s in order to use deficit bonds to increase spending. Consumer prices rose quickly, reaching an inflation rate of 10% per year in 1972 and 20% in 1974. The national government's total debt ballooned from 2.9 trillion yen in 1970 to 70 trillion yen in 1980. That burden loomed as a major problem for Japanese officials in the Ministry of Finance (MOF).

Masataka Ōkura, the head of the Tax Bureau at the ministry, kicked off the campaign for a consumption tax in early 1977 by arguing to a committee in the Upper House of the Diet that rebuilding public finance would require both a boost in the corporate tax and enactment of a consumption tax. This was the first attempt at substantial tax reform in Japan since the Allied occupation that ended in 1952. Frequent references by proponents to the use of the Value Added Tax (VAT) in Western Europe suggested that its adoption by members of the European Community (now, the European Union) served as a model and inspiration. The ministry aimed, Ōkura explained, at achieving "zero" issuance of national deficit bonds by 1980. Tax revenue would therefore have to increase by almost 14% each year. Increasing the personal income tax, which provided 38% of all revenue, was "politically and socially impossible" because it already imposed a heavy burden on the people (*Yomiuri*, March 23, 1977). Next, the Government's Tax System Research Council (Seifu no Zeisei Chōsakai/Zeichō), a consultative group to the prime minister, took up the issue. By the late summer its subcommittees reported that a rise in taxes was feasible: "For the income tax and the corporate tax the level of the [tax] burden is fairly low in international comparison; there is room to raise taxes…" In regard to a consumption tax, the problems of placing a heavy burden on people with a low income and of sparking inflation "[were] not decisive difficulties." Moreover, a general consumption tax could immediately produce "many trillions of yen" (*Yomiuri*, August 31, 1977). A few weeks later, the entire Zeichō affirmed that the government could consider raising the income tax and the corporate tax as well as creating a consumption tax. The Committee recognized that the new tax would generate controversy because of determined opposition from one sector (*ichibu*) since "the burden for the low-income stratum (*teishotokusha sō*) would increase" (*Yomiuri*, September 14, 1977).

Meanwhile, the Ministry of Finance continued to lobby for the new tax. Noting that deficit spending now provided 29.9% of the national budget, one vice minister exclaimed that the government must not break the "30 percent wall." Soon, he claimed, the government would have to issue bonds to redeem previous ones that were coming due (*Ibid.*). Leaders of the ministry announced that they supported the implementation of a consumption tax during the next year, in 1978, even while details of the proposal—such as the tax rate, exemptions, and procedures for applying the tax at different stages of distribution—remained to be worked out (*Yomiuri*, September 22, 1977). A delay would only worsen the crisis in public finance.

Opposition to the new tax soon emerged. As expected, political parties opposing the governing Liberal Democratic Party (LDP) objected to the consumption tax as a "mass levy" that would hurt low-income earners (*Ibid.*). Within the business community nine groups representing wholesalers and retailers complained that a general consumption tax would dampen consumption by raising the prices of goods (*Yomiuri*, September 23, 1977). A report by the Tax System Committee of Keidanren emphasized that the government needed to focus on economic recovery by restoring the rate of utilization of manufacturing capacity from 76 to 90%. This task would take two or three years, and until then "planning the recovery of the economy [had to] be the most important current policy topic." "Rebuilding public finance [was] possible" only when the economy was "riding on the road of stable growth." Intriguingly, the Committee cryptically left open the possibility for considering a general consumption tax in the future because of the rapid aging of Japanese society (Keidanren, Zeisei Iinkai, September 27, 1977, pp. 1–2). Meanwhile, the powerful Ministry of International Trade and Industry (MITI) took a similar stance. It opposed a rapid adoption of the new tax by stating that "it [was] necessary to investigate cautiously whether or not the introduction of a general consumption tax [was] desirable as a means" of "securing a source of revenue," because it would "deepen the recession." (*Yomiuri*, October 7, 1977). This resistance helped ensure that a final proposal did not develop until the fall of 1978. Meanwhile, the MOF ended up having to yield on the budget. Facing strong pressure from "economic circles" for increased spending that would stimulate economic growth, the budget indeed broke the 30% barrier in 1978 (*Yomiuri*, December 12, 1977).

This temporary defeat seemed to fortify proponents' resolve to enact a consumption tax in 1979. They now aimed to eliminate the government's dependence on deficit bonds by the mid-1980s, a goal that would require increased revenue of ten trillion yen per year (*Yomiuri*, July 19, 1978). In September, the Government's Tax System Research Council issued its final draft. This proposal would levy a flat rate of five percent on sales of goods at different stages of processing to generate three trillion yen per year. In a concession to small enterprises, the proposal exempted firms whose annual sales fell below a certain limit from paying the tax (*Yomiuri*, September 5, 1978). Earlier in the year, members of the Council had broached the idea of designating the consumption tax to fund social welfare services in the hope of building more support for the measure. The MOF, however, had balked at creating "a source of funding with strings attached" (*Yomiuri*, May 25, 1978). In September, the Zeichō explained that the consumption tax would be collected as a "general tax" but would "in reality have a hidden meaning as a tax for social welfare services and would be appropriated in a prioritized manner related to the expansion of the administration of social welfare services" (*Yomiuri*, September 5[a], 1978). In the 1980s, proponents of the consumption tax would emphasize its potential contribution to social welfare services in a rapidly aging society.

At this point representatives of the most important business organizations came out against the consumption tax. As reported by the *Yomiuri*, a meeting of vice-chairmen of Keidanren produced expressions of concern about the adverse influence of the new tax on business conditions. These business leaders acknowledged the goal of balancing the national budget but believed that "when considering the order of priorities it is most essential at the present time to have Japan's national economy riding on a path of stable growth by achieving a growth rate of 7 percent...for the next year too it is necessary to continue an economy led by public finance." Makers of consumer goods such as Hirokichi Yoshiyama, the president of Hitachi, were especially opposed to levying a consumption tax (*Yomiuri*, September 5[b], 1978). Worries about a stalled economic recovery prompted three major business groups—Keidanren, the Japan Chamber of Commerce and Industry (JCCI), and the Japan Association of Corporate Executives (Keizai Dōyūkai)—to issue a formal joint protest against a rapid enactment of a general consumption tax even if deficit bonds would end up providing 37% of revenue in 1979 (*Yomiuri*, September 27, 1978). Noting that the strategy of expanding the government's fiscal stimulus had yet to increase "private demand," the Tax System Committee at Keidanren called for greater efforts in that direction for at least one or two more years. Its report argued that "if [we] ignore the normalization of the economy as a whole and advance the restoration of public finance impatiently, the economy will stagnate and bring about results that contradict the restoration of public finance." As before, the Committee's report ended with a vague concession that if Japanese decided at some time in the future that they needed to raise taxes, a "cautious investigation of which taxable items to choose would be necessary" (Keidanren, Zeisei Iinkai, September 27, 1978, p. 1). Comments from MITI officials affirmed the need, from its perspective, to maintain a strong economic growth rate, which they predicted might slip to an annual rate of four percent from the current level of five percent growth in 1978, far from the ministry's target of seven percent growth (*Yomiuri*, November 21[a], 1978). In response to this pressure, the MOF prepared for 1979 a national "budget to stimulate business conditions" that would rise by 16.6 percent to [expenditures of] 40 trillion yen and require deficit spending to supply 40 percent of the budget" (*Yomiuri*, November 21[b], 1978).

Late in 1978 Minister of Finance Tatsuo Murayama announced his intention to introduce legislation for a consumption tax in 1979 in order for it to start in January 1980. He argued that if Japan continued to increase employment "only through public finance" it would collapse (*Yomiuri*, November 21[c], 1978). Shortly afterwards Prime Minister Masayoshi Ohira, who had forged a career in the MOF before entering politics, pledged to enact a consumption tax in 1980 (*Yomiuri*, December 19, 1978). He consistently maintained that a general consumption tax was essential to rebuilding public finance, which he identified as the main task in managing the economy (*Yomiuri*, June 6, 1979). Resistance to the consumption tax, however, ultimately forced the LDP to change its tune, especially as national elections for the Lower House approached in early October 1979. As the *Yomiuri* newspaper noted in late September, the prime minister's comments on the consumption tax had "toned down." After boldly promising to implement the new levy, his rhetoric had become more cautious. He began talking about "'creating a forum to debate the general consumption tax'" and to investigate "alternative plans" (*Yomiuri*, September 26, 1979). Finally, he announced the end of efforts to implement the tax (*Yomiuri*, September 27, 1979). Even so, the LDP barely managed to maintain a majority of seats in the Lower House.

Holding only a slim majority of seats in the Lower House both before and after the election, the LDP did not feel confident about pushing through a consumption tax. Beyond the expected hurdle of the Japan Socialist Party and other opposition political parties, the two main economic ministries had split on the issue, as MITI rejected MOF's initiative in order to encourage strong economic growth. Moreover, many members of the business community, from small businesses to large corporations, expressed doubts. Success would not occur until the government and the business community achieved a measure of unity in support of the measure.

3 Keidanren: Developing a New Perspective on the Economy and Public Finance

After its disappointing results in the election of 1979, the LDP understandably shied away from the issue of the consumption tax. In fact, the Lower House of the Diet passed a resolution specifically noting the failure of the proposal for a consumption tax and asserting that the "rebuilding of public finance should not depend on a general consumption tax." The cabinet of Prime Minister Zenkō Suzuki adopted a policy of "fiscal reconstruction without a tax increase" (Takeshita and Hirano 1993, pp. 41–42; Hori 2005, pp. 79–80). This strategy sought to restore public finance by cutting expenses through downsizing the government, a process termed "administrative reform." Accordingly, Suzuki in early 1980 appointed Toshio Dokō, the retiring chairman of Keidanren, to chair the Second Temporary Council on Administrative Reform. When it submitted its final report in 1983, Prime Minister Yasuhiro Nakasone pledged to enact its proposals. The most extensive reforms centered on privatizing three large government corporations—Japan National Railways, Nippon Telephone and Telegraph (NTT), and the Tobacco Monopoly. The Diet passed legislation to accomplish this goal in 1985 (Takeda 2009, pp. 300–314).

In this context, Keidanren's strategy for restoring public finance and ultimately the group's attitude toward the consumption tax began to change. After 1978, Keidanren's Tax System Committee (Zeisei Iinkai) initially hardened its opposition to possible tax raises of any type. Dropping all mention of a future consideration of new taxes, including a consumption tax, the Committee's reports concentrated on opposing increases in the corporate tax, a measure that the Ministry of Finance started to champion in the wake of the government's failure to create a consumption tax. That the government in 1980 raised the corporate tax rate by two percent and in 1984 by 1.3% along with boosts in the liquor tax and levies on other specific commodities alarmed Keidanren.[4] The Tax Committee countered by arguing that raising the corporate tax would only hinder the international competitiveness of Japanese firms while increasing the public deficit by dampening economic growth. The Committee pointed out that the administration of President Jimmy Carter in the United States and nations in Western Europe were, in fact, cutting corporate taxes. Far from raising the corporate tax, the Japanese government should be lowering the rate and follow the example of Western nations in creating a "policy tax system" that provided financial incentives to lighten their firms' tax burden through expanding their investments in equipment and research.[5]

Meanwhile, within Keidanren a new concern arose. Members perceived that because the standard policy in an economic downturn of inducing economic growth through fiscal expansion was not working as well as expected, Japan was entering a period of low economic growth that would require novel remedies. A long report of the Economic Research Committee (Keizai Chōsa Iinkai) introduced this incipient shift in perspective in early 1979. The report expressed disappointment in the nation's economic performance since the "oil crisis" of 1973. The report characterized the period since then as a "long-term recession (chōki fukyō)" because annual economic growth had rebounded but had not exceeded five percent. Japan was slipping from a period of "high growth (*kō seichō*)" to an era of "middle growth (*chū seichō*)." This pattern prompted doubts as to whether the emphasis on fiscal policy had reached its limits of effectiveness, as budget deficits had accumulated for the national government and decreasing profits for companies had slowed their investment in equipment and research. Future growth, therefore, had to depend not on public works or exports, as in the past, but on strengthening the private sector and expanding domestic private demand (*Keidanren*, Keizai Chōsa Iinkai, January 23, 1979, pp. 1–4). Members foresaw that in the near future deficit spending would have to continue, but in the longer term the nation had to "plan the thorough implementation (*tettei*) of cheap government." Intriguingly, the report added a vague reference to the need for new revenue: "To restore public finance, the need for an increase in general tax income is recognized" (*Ibid*., p. 10).

A year and a half later, one vice-chairman of Keidanren, Kaneshige Hasegawa of Sumitomo Chemical Industries, elaborated on these ideas at a forum on fiscal policy and tax policy. Citing cuts in the corporate tax enacted by President Jimmy Carter in the United States as well as tax reductions implemented by Prime Minister Margaret Thatcher in Britain, Hasegawa boldly proclaimed that in the United States and Europe "the type of thinking of [Sir John Maynard] Keynes was disappearing" as developed nations shifted away from Keynes's emphasis on using fiscal pump-priming to revive an economy in a recession and moved toward an "economy [based on] the new

---

[4] *Ibid*., pp. 303 and 311; Hori (2005, p. 80); *Keidanren Review on Japanese Economy*, No. 85, February, 1984, pp. 2–3; and Keizai Dantai Rengōkai (ed.) (1999, pp. 309 and 318). This study discusses in some detail the struggle between Keidanren and the MOF during the early 1980s over the corporate tax rate (see pp. 307–325).

[5] For example, see *Keidanren*, Zeisei Iinkai, December 3, 1979, pp. 1–2, and October 28, 1980, pp. 1–2.

economists' stress on supply." Noting the 1979 report of the Economic Research Committee, Hasegawa argued that "prosperity centered on a free private economy had to plan for [a transition] from a type [of economic prosperity] led by public investment as in the past to economic prosperity centered on private investment." He specifically recommended emulating new policies in the United States and Western Europe, such as reducing the corporate tax rate and providing tax incentives for firms to invest more money in equipment and research. Echoing the 1979 report, he also urged Japanese, "as the first step toward restoring public finance to realize cheap government, carry out administrative reform, reduce government expenditures, and implement rationalization." As a subsequent step, he called for raising "indirect taxes" as they would be borne widely by the people and were, he claimed, most neutral toward affecting different sectors of the economy. He predicted that in the future the introduction of a general consumption tax was inevitable (*Keidanren*, Keizai Kōhō Sentā, 1980, pp. 6, 8–10, 12, and 19).

In early 1983 a lengthy report from the Economic Research Committee placed its previous insights about the advent of a new economic era into a broader historical context. Committee members explained that Japan was no longer dealing with just cyclical recessions but with a basic shift in the global economy. Economic growth in all developed nations had slowed from an average of five percent per year in the 1960s to no more than a one percent annual rate during the past three years. Meanwhile, in many nations the unemployment rate and the inflation rate had increased (Keidanren 1983, p. 2). The roots of inflation and hence economic stagnation, according to the report, lay in the 1960s, when social welfare services, government administration, and the tax burden expanded while wages rose with escalating prices for goods. The resulting suppression of companies' profits dampened firms' desire to invest in equipment and "seized the dynamism of the private sector" as "raising productivity became difficult." The slowdown in economic growth caused a crisis in public finance because of the fall in tax revenue (*Ibid.*, p. 3). In sum, the authors argued that "[b]ecause the various systems [in place] since the period of high growth have been left in place despite changes in the [economic] situation, the economic stagnation of developed nations has come from very deep problems that have arrived at an impossible stage." The report noted that some nations, "beginning with America and Britain," were "starting to grope toward implementing basic policies to break [this] deadlock…through severing the vicious cycle of the rise of wages and prices, reducing public expenses by reconsidering social welfare services, and by abolishing and moderating the government's regulations to realize a small government" (*Ibid.*, p. 4).

In the eyes of the Economic Research Committee Japan shared the same woes as other developed nations. Even though the nation's recent economic performance surpassed that of the United States and Western European nations, Japan's economic growth had fallen from an annual rate of 10% in the 1960s to only 3% in the early 1980s. Moreover, the Japanese faced mounting trade friction over increasing surpluses in foreign trade, especially with the United States, and a dramatic worsening of public finance where "the dependence of the national budget on bonds continue[d] at a high level of 30 percent not seen in [other] developing nations." Hence, the authors feared that "strong inflationary pressure [was] lurking" (*Ibid.*, pp. 5–6).

To adjust to these challenges, the Committee urged that Japan soothe trade friction by liberalizing imports and prevent the pernicious effects of inflation by reforming public finance. In this regard, cutting expenses still took priority over raising taxes. In particular, the report stressed that the corporate tax, which the government had managed to raise twice in recent years, "had reached the highest level from an international perspective." The authors worried that if Japan did not re-energize its private sector, it might fall behind: "Japan's enterprises are now highly regarded for their flexibility and international competitive power. However, if, as mentioned before, policies in America of prioritizing the dynamism of enterprises and their efforts are realized by the end of the 1980s, the reversal of competitive power between us and them could even occur" (*Ibid.*, pp. 9–14). The omission of any reference, no matter how vague, to creating or raising any "indirect" taxes fit the stance of the Tax System Committee in opposing any increase in taxes.

During the early 1980s reports of the Tax System Committee maintained its strategy of "rebuilding public finance without raising taxes." Believing that Japan had entered a protracted era of lower economic growth, members proposed that "the driving force for overcoming this [problem] is to utilize (*hakki suru*) private energy," primarily through tax cuts. In order to decrease taxes, the government had to reduce expenses. As political pressure mounted in the mid-1980s for the government to slash the individual income tax, the Tax Committee resolutely opposed compensatory raises in other taxes, such as the corporate tax and sales taxes on selected products (See *Keidanren*, Zeisei Iinkai, November 24, 1981, pp. 1–2; December 7, 1982, pp. 1–2; October 12, 1983, pp. 1–2; and Keidanren, September 25, 1984, pp. 1–4). The reports did not even mention the possibility of instituting a general consumption tax.

In early 1986, however, the public strategy of Keidanren changed abruptly to support the creation of a general consumption tax. A long report issued in the name of the entire Federation explained several reasons for this shift in attitude. One reason was that although five years of preparing budgets under the policy of "restoring public finance with no tax raises" had some success in privatizing government corporations and "freezing general expenditures," "the expansion of national bonds and the crisis of public finance had deepened still more." The national debt had grown from 56 trillion yen in 1979 to 143 trillion yen in 1986. Interest payments equaled 20% of expenditures by the national government (Keidanren, March 26, 1986, pp. 2–3).[6] Moreover, with the rapid aging of the society, the demand for public funding of services was bound to expand (*Ibid.*, p. 2). On the other hand, raising taxes would be difficult. Individual taxpayers felt that the burden of the income tax was too heavy because of its severely progressive character, with rates rising in fifteen brackets from 10.5% to 70% despite a comparatively equal distribution of income in the

---

[6] For a chart showing the growth of the Japanese government's debt from 1965 to 1999 see Zeisei 5, Kōsai zankō ruizō, in Morinobu (2000, p. 554).

society. Large portions of the report examined complaints about the operation of the income tax and ways to reform it (*Ibid*., pp. 2, 4, and 7–8). In addition, businesses felt aggrieved at recent boosts in the corporate tax of 2% in 1981 and 1.3% in 1984. Keidanren argued for a repeal of these measures as a step toward restoring Japanese firms to an "equal footing" with overseas competitors, many of whom were benefiting from lowered corporate taxes (*Ibid*., pp. 2–3, 7, and 10–12).[7] The refrain became that Japan needed a reformed "tax system in which the people would widely and thinly bear the burden" (*Ibid*., pp. 2 and 5–8). Simply put: if the strategy of reducing public expenses had reached its limit of effectiveness, Japanese had to focus on enhancing revenue not by increasing current levies but by introducing a new tax (*Ibid*., p. 6).

The leaders of Keidanren decided that the main solution to the nation's fiscal problems would be a general consumption tax, because it would produce a lot of revenue and help distribute the burden of taxes more fairly. "If the unfairness and irrationality of the current tax system are to be reformed and the Japanese people demand a large-scale expansion of public finance to support an increase in benefits and a large reduction of the income tax, a re-examination of the tax system including revision of the ratio between direct and indirect taxes will be inevitable." Furthermore, "if [we] correct the unfairness and irrationality inherent in the current income tax, corporate tax, and indirect taxes, as a result in many cases fairness and justice will be guaranteed in regard to the people bearing the [tax] burden widely and thinly." The report concluded with an exhortation for the Japanese to investigate carefully the advantages and disadvantages of introducing a new indirect tax (*Ibid*., 16–17).

Although the public announcement of Keidanren's shift in direction in regard to the consumption tax seemed abrupt, this change had been developing for some time. As discussed above, reports of the Tax System Committee in 1977 and 1978 mentioned the possibility that in the future Japanese might have to consider new taxes to pay for increased services to a rapidly aging society. The Economic Research Committee took a similar stance in early 1979. In 1980 Vice-Chairman Kaneshige Hasegawa viewed the introduction of a consumption tax as inevitable. Meanwhile, economic developments also closed off other options for restoring public finances. In the late 1970s the failure of fiscal expansion to jumpstart a high economic growth rate above five percent per year, which leaders of Keidanren viewed as an unsatisfactory result, and to boost tax revenue had led to the strategy of balancing the budget through slashing expenditures without saddling the private economy with tax hikes. By 1986 the leaders of Keidanren viewed that approach as a failure, because the nation's annual economic growth remained below five percent and the government's debt continued to rise. In addition, they perceived that, aside from the long-term obligation to fund more services for the elderly in the future, an urgent strain on the budget was arising from political pressure exerted by opposition parties in the Diet for cuts in the individual income tax (Takeshita and Hirano 1993, pp. 50–54 and 68–70).

---

[7] During the early 1980s Keidanren and the Ministry of Finance engaged in a lengthy and heated dispute about the international ranking of corporate taxes in Japan. The MOF emphasized that Japan's national corporate tax rate was relatively low, but Keidanren claimed that if calculations included local taxes Japan's corporate rate was the highest in the world.

In fact, the boost in the corporate tax rate in 1984 resulted from the government's decision to produce more revenue to fund a cut in the income tax. Realizing that the corporate tax was vulnerable to further pressure to produce more revenue, leaders of the Federation wanted to provide an alternate source of new funding. They argued as well that the new tax would be fairer by spreading the burden of paying taxes more widely. In brief, by 1986 the leaders of Keidanren observed that neither the old Keynesian solution of fiscal pump-priming nor the new supply-side approach of trying to slash public expenditures had been able to restore a balanced budget for the national government. Only a new stream of revenue would enable the government to reform perceived deficiencies in the tax system and meet demands to provide essential services.

4 The Second Try

Starting in the mid-1980s, the second attempt to institute a consumption tax again sparked a major political struggle. Proponents dubbed the proposed levy a "sales tax" (*uriagezei*), perhaps to distance it from the failed push for a consumption tax in the late 1970s. This time, Keidanren helped initiate the campaign, when in late September, 1986, Eiji Suzuki, the chairman of the Federation's Tax System Committee, hand delivered to Prime Minister Yasujirō Nakasone a report supporting a "Japan style of VAT" (Value Added Tax) shortly after its approval by the Board of Directors of Keidanren (*Yomiuri*, September 25, 1986).

Affirming the main conclusions of its interim report in March, Keidanren declared the need for a cut in both the personal income tax and the corporate tax and the introduction of an indirect tax, such as a consumption tax. Such measures would bring needed relief to the main body of individual taxpayers and to companies. The new levy, essential to funding tax cuts, would help to reduce the national deficit and spread the burden of paying for government services. The measure could usher in a new economic era: "What is demanded by basic reform of the tax system is that [we] reconsider the strains and distortions of the tax system that have accumulated over thirty years since the recommendations of [Carl S.] Shoup [during the Allied occupation of Japan] from the viewpoint of fairness, impartiality, simplicity, and [economic] vitality as well as an international [perspective] and expect new developments of economic society."[8] As opposition mounted, the Federation remained steadfast in its backing. In February 1987, Vice-Chairman Gaishi Hiraiwa emphasized the general goal of adjusting the ratio of direct and indirect taxes: "If [we] think of the future, [we] must implement the sales tax" (*Yomiuri*, February 26, 1987).

If Keidanren, as the representative of large corporations in Japan, now believed in the economic need for a sales/consumption tax, small and medium enterprises continued to oppose the measure. Noboru Gotō, chairman of the Japan Chamber of Commerce and Industry (JCCI), explained to the governing Liberal Democratic Party

[8] Keidanren (September 24, 1986, p. 1). See also, Keizai Dantai Rengōkai (1999, p. 623).

(LDP) his determined opposition to a sales tax. He worried that it would become, in effect, an "'enterprise tax'" because "'excessive competition'" among small firms would prevent their raising prices to accommodate the tax. Moreover, he cynically predicted that the government could easily raise the tax after its introduction and "checks on the swelling of public finance will vanish" (*Yomiuri*, September 18, 1986).

Undoubtedly aware of opposition to a new tax and mindful of the failure of the proposal seven years beforehand, the Government Tax System Research Council tread lightly in its report of October 1986. It endorsed a "Japan style value added tax" in principle but did not set forth any details. The Council concluded only that "'it is not possible to plan a solution to [Japan's fiscal] problems with an expansion of the current form of individual consumption taxes'" in which the sale of some goods, such as *sake*, were each taxed at different rates and others were not taxed at all. The report also stressed the need for reform of the income tax to help the typical white-collar worker (*sarariman*). For example, the government could reduce the highest personal tax rate from 70 to 50% and the total number of tax brackets from 15 to six (*Yomiuri*, October 21, 1986).

When the LDP proposed an Outline for Reform of the Tax System in December that included a sales/consumption tax along with cuts in the income tax and the corporate tax, Gotō of the JCCI affirmed his opposition to the consumption tax as a leader of an organization representing small and medium enterprises: "I have a feeling that [the tax reform] is opening the window for a raise in taxes." He noted, as well, a lack of a "sufficient consensus" to support the measure in "distribution circles" and "manufacturing circles" (*Yomiuri*, December 24a, 1986).[9] A few months later dislike of the proposal induced a rare instance of collaboration between two groups usually at opposite ends of the political spectrum, when leaders of the National Federation of Textile Industry Workers' Unions (Zensen Dōmei) and the Japan Chain Store Association (JCSA) met to discuss cooperation to "advance a movement to smash the sales tax from the standpoint of each [organization] as a common problem of labor and management." (*Yomiuri*, February 19, 1987). The Japan Department Store Association (JDSA) announced its strategy of freezing its monetary contributions to the LDP and of lobbying individual members to switch sides unless the party agreed to drop the proposal for a sales tax (*Yomiuri*, February 25, 1987).

Two days later, a "Grand Meeting of a Consumers' and Citizens' Rally convened to protest the sales tax." As the *Yomiuri Newspaper* reported, "at this first national meeting of consumer groups" in the Hibiya Concert Hall in Tokyo approximately 10,000 people from 302 organizations participated. The latter included the well-known Housewives Association (Shufuren) and the Japan Consumers Cooperative Federation (Nihon Seikyōren) (*Yomiuri*, February 27, 1987). Just a few days later at Meiji Park in Sendagaya more than 70,000 citizens joined the March 1st Meeting to Smash the Sales Tax and the Bad Changes to the Tax System (*zeisei kaiaku*). The participants represented over one hundred groups of artists, housewives, workers,

[9] The proposed rate was five percent (*Yomiuri*, January 30, 1987).

and small businesses. Speakers emphasized the regressive nature of the proposed tax reforms, because people with low incomes would not benefit much from tax cuts and they would pay more taxes through the sales tax (*Yomiuri*, March 2, 1987).

Still, Prime Minister Nakasone vowed to push through the tax reform. Conceding that advocating a raise in taxes shortly before nation-wide local elections posed a challenge, Nakasone asserted that tax reform was essential to "open up the future of Japan's economy." The LDP could not just consider its own political interests, he explained, but the party had to carry out its "destiny." In grandiose fashion he invoked the examples of previous Japanese leaders who had made unpopular decisions for sake of the long-term welfare of the nation. For example, he compared himself to Foreign Minister Jutarō Komura who in 1905 during the Russo-Japanese War had provoked riots in Tokyo by accepting lenient terms for Russia in a peace treaty in order to end the conflict. Nakasone also cited the example of Prime Minister Nobusuke Kishi whose determination in 1960 to ram through the Diet a revised Mutual Security Treaty with the United States had triggered massive protests from opponents of any military cooperation between the two nations (*Yomiuri*, February 11, 1987).

In any event, Nakasone's political *bravado* did not work. The results of the local elections in the spring of 1987 for the LDP were weak enough to embolden the leaders of opponents, such as the Japan Chain Store Association and the Japan Department Store Association, to interpret the party's poor showing as expressing the "'will of the people'" on the topic of the proposed sales tax and to call for its withdrawal (*Yomiuri*, April 14, 1987).[10] At a large rally in Hibiya Park organized by opposition parties Diet representatives wore headbands vowing to "Smash the sales tax." Speakers demanded not only that Nakasone abandon the sales tax but also that he resign. At a subsequent rally for "the unheard voices of the salaryman" the prime minister continued to call for "reform of the tax system for the twenty-first century" (*Yomiuri*, April 18, 1987). As doubts about the sales tax spread within the LDP, however, Nakasone had to concede defeat.

The overall campaign for an overhaul of the tax system, however, would persist. As Eiji Suzuki, the chairman of the Tax System Committee of Keidanren, maintained, "'there [was] no change in the need for reforming the ratio between direct and indirect taxes and for a new indirect tax.'" Significantly, in early May the four major business groups, including the JCCI, agreed to "tackle together the creation of a plan for a new type of indirect tax" (*Yomiuri*, April 24, 1987, and May 8, 1987). JCCI chairman Gotō revealed that discussions had already begun. This development indicated that in the future the business community would take a more unified stand in support of the consumption tax. Not surprisingly, the next effort would succeed.

[10] On the results of the local elections, see Takeshita and Hirano (1993, p. 116).

5 Success at Last: Passing the Consumption Tax in 1988

The third effort to pass a consumption tax began in the fall of 1987 with a proposal from the LDP's Tax System Research Council headed by Sadanori Yamanaka. Tying in with the perspective that Keidanren adopted in the early 1980s, this report accepted the notion of the development of a new economic era that mandated novel responses, namely the "future arrival of an aging society and the further internationalization of economic society." In order to achieve a "'society of people's welfare and long life'" Japan had to "sweep away the feeling of unfairness regarding the people's taxes." The government had to spread the burden "widely and thinly" and "realize a tax system that can support society based on mutual cooperation between generations." In recalibrating the ratio between direct and indirect taxes the new system had to balance taxes on income, consumption, and financial assets. Cuts in the income tax should relieve the "heavy pressure on the taxes of the main body of income earners (*chūken shotokusha sō*)," while lowering the corporate tax would make Japanese firms more competitive in the international arena (*Yomiuri*, October 12, 1987). Two months later, Prime Minister Noboru Takeshita announced that he would aim to implement a consumption tax in the fall of 1988.

The government did try to accommodate at least some of the complaints of small enterprises. In this regard, the stance of MITI toward the consumption tax changed significantly. Whereas in the late 1970s MITI had joined Keidanren in staunchly opposing the tax, this time the cabinet asked the ministry, as an important agency of the government, to cultivate support for the new tax in various industries. Hence, even if MITI officials held little enthusiasm for the tax, their strategy shifted to attempting to blunt some of the potentially harmful effects of the tax rather than to resist it entirely. For example, MITI sought to assuage some concerns of small enterprises by successfully lobbying for a temporary exemption to the Anti-Monopoly Law to allow managers of small enterprises to meet to discuss together the implementation of price increases that the new levy would necessitate (*Yomiuri*, December 24b, 1986; February 5, 1987; February 2, 1987; February 6, 1987; June 25, 1988; July 9, 1988; July 12, 1988).

In June, Yamanaka outlined the LDP's official proposal. Prime Minister Takeshita pledged to "risk the fate of his political power on this issue." The government sought to curry popular support for a value added tax of three percent by including a large tax cut exceeding 5 trillion yen by simplifying brackets for the income tax and lowering the corporate tax from 42% to 37.5%. Indeed, the tax reductions would exceed the gains in revenue from the consumption tax (*Yomiuri*, June 15, 1988; July 29, 1988). Despite continued criticism from opposition parties, the legislation with some changes passed in December, to the cheers of Keidanren. Chairman Saitō noted dryly that the tax had been a "pending proposal for many years for the people." Eiji Suzuki, now chairman of the Japan Employers Association, claimed that the changes were "essential for [Japan's economic] soft landing in the twenty-first century." Takashi Ishihara, representing the Japan Association of Corporate Executives, called the reforms "epochal in the history of the tax system" (*Yomiuri*, December 25, 1988).

6 The Significance of Enacting the Consumption Tax

While previous accounts of the enactment of a consumption tax have emphasized the role of the MOF in promoting the measure, the Japanese business community, especially Keidanren, played a crucial role. By the mid-1980s the Federation had become an active proponent. Moreover, the consumption tax passed the Diet only after the *business community (zaikai)* united to at least some degree behind the new levy, as evident in the endorsement, with or without specific conditions, by the four most prominent business groups. The JCCI, which represented small businesses, showed the least enthusiasm,[11] but it succeeded in exacting substantial concessions in return for its grudging support. Hence, the proposed rate for the consumption tax fell from five percent to three percent and the exclusion of very few items from the levy simplified its administration. The measure, however, did exempt very small enterprises with annual sales of less than 30 million yen from the administrative and financial burdens of paying the tax. Finally, the LDP's decision to combine a substantial cut in the income tax with the consumption tax helped to counter arguments that the new levy would dampen consumption (*Yomiuri*, June 15, 1988).[12]

While citing foreign models in backing a "Japanese style of indirect tax," Keidanren developed a distinctive version of the doctrine of neoliberalism that was emerging in the United States and Britain. Just as the introduction of the consumption tax in Japan drew inspiration from the earlier enactment of a VAT (Value Added Tax) by members of the European Economic Community (later, the European Union), the policies and rhetoric of Presidents Jimmy Carter and Ronald Reagan in the United States and Prime Minister Margaret Thatcher in the United Kingdom influenced Japanese business leaders in terms of stressing the goal of re-invigorating the private sector by downsizing government. As mentioned above, reports produced by Keidanren and statements by individual leaders after 1979 referred to these economic policies. Accordingly, Chairman Yoshihiro Inayama explained that "an example is set for us to follow by British Prime Minister Margaret Thatcher who asks for sacrifice from the people and with a firm resolve pursues the goal of revitalizing the British economy" (*Keidanren Review of Japanese Economy*, No. 78, December 1982). While working toward "administrative reforms" that would shrink government, Keidanren, though, chose not to argue for a reduction in the overall tax burden. Instead, holding true to the goal of moving toward a balanced budget, the Federation advocated a regressive indirect tax in order to fund reforms that would moderate the progressive character of the income tax in Japan and take a modest step toward liberating the

---

[11] Ironically, executives from large corporations often led the JCCI. For example, Noboru Gotō was the president of the Tōkyū Company, which operated a chain of major department stores. Rokurō Ishikawa served as president of the Kajima Company, a large construction firm. His father became the first president of Keidanren in 1948.

[12] The Japan Socialist Party (JSP), however, calculated that the regressive character of the combined tax reforms increased as family income decreased, because families with a modest income would not benefit much from the planned cuts in the income tax but would have to pay the consumption tax on goods purchased (*Yomiuri*, June 25, 1988).

private sector from what members viewed as an unfairly high corporate tax.[13] Business leaders framed these measures in a historical context of responding to sweeping changes in the economy and society—in particular, the aging of Japanese society and the "internationalization" of the economy with the attendant intensification of international competition in trade. This perspective would continue to shape Keidanren's views, even as it confronted a persistent slump in economic growth in the 1990s.

7 The Campaign for Raising the Consumption Tax in the First Lost Decade

As the leaders of small and medium enterprises had feared, it did not take long for a campaign for raising the consumption tax to begin, even as the economy headed quickly toward a downturn. Such was the strength of Keidanren's new convictions and determination. As mentioned above, in 1989 the Bank of Japan started to increase its prime interest rate to rein in speculation in the stock market and the real estate market. After the prime rate had more than doubled by August 1990, the stock market fell sharply and the real estate market started to decline. Overall economic growth slowed (Takeda 2009, p. 339; Tiberghien 2014, p. 39). Although the government was successfully ending its dependence on national deficit bonds (*Yomiuri*, May 8, 1993), Keidanren once more raised the issue of the need to boost tax revenue and to lessen the burden of direct taxes as a vital economic concern.

To Keidanren the structure of taxes remained a crucial issue. While the Federation's major report on the tax system for 1992 offered several reforms, the centerpiece was clearly raising the consumption tax. According to the report, a major specter hanging over the nation was the rapid aging of society, which would reach its peak in 2020, when the "rate of burden for the people [would] rise to 53.5 percent" (*Keidanren*, Keizai Dantai Rengōkai 1992, p. 1).[14] Companies and the bulk of employees were already laboring under tax rates that were comparatively high. As the aging of society increased citizens' demands for services, the government would have to find new sources of revenue while acting to energize the economy. The report noted that "[i]n the three years since the introduction of the consumption tax, it has become part of the people's life" and predicted that "[i]t is inevitable that [we] will make as our basic tax system a consumption tax through which the people will divide the burden widely and thinly." Raising the rate would require a "sufficient consensus of the people" and had to be combined with a "large reduction in the corporate tax and the income tax" (*Ibid.*, p. 1).

[13] Keidanren was not entirely consistent on the issue of "small government." In September 1986, Eishirō Saitō, as president of the Federation, called for an increase in national construction bonds to stimulate "internal demand." See *Yomiuri*, September 12, 1986. Even if such demands became less frequent afterwards, Keidanren consistently advocated increased government spending for research and development to benefit companies.

[14] In other words, at that point, individual taxpayers would be paying over 50% of their income to the government and companies would be paying over 50% of their profits to the government.

In November 1993, the Government Tax System Research Council, headed by Keio University Professor Hiroshi Katō, released a preliminary report calling for a reduction of five trillion yen in the income tax for the "'main body'" of taxpayers and a hike in the consumption tax from three percent to a range of five to seven percent. The goal would be to realize a "fair and energized aging society" in which "members of society would share the burden widely" to provide a "stable structure for tax revenue." Despite clear signs of slowing economic growth, the Council insisted on the principle of replacing revenue lost through tax cuts, which might stimulate the economy, with new funds from another source (*Yomiuri*, November 20[a], 1993). The report added a new wrinkle by including a proposal for a local consumption tax of one percent whose revenue would go to local governments.

Responses somewhat reflected old battle lines. Gaishi Hiraiwa, as chairman of Keidanren, commented that he "could understand" the need to link a reduction in the income tax with a rise in the consumption tax. Kōsaku Inaba, chairman of the JCCI, agreed with the "basic ideal" of "evening out" the tax burden between generations of an aging society but he did not think that the government should investigate raising the consumption tax until an economic recovery had started. Otherwise, as he commonsensically pointed out, the raised consumption tax would simply throttle a recovery by cancelling out any expansion of consumer spending induced by the cut in the income tax. Tadahiro Sekimoto, president of the large electronics manufacturer NEC and president of the Japan Electrical Machine Industry Association, welcomed reductions in the income tax to aid recovery (*Yomiuri*, November 20[b], 1993).

Raising the consumption tax also attracted international attention, as the American government took an interest in the issue. After the government Council's interim report became public President William J. Clinton in November 1993 sent a letter to Prime Minister Morihiro Hosokawa to advise that increasing the consumption tax should not negate the effects of the cut in income taxes. Painfully aware of the continuing large deficits that the United States continued to run in its trade with Japan, American officials were urging the Japanese government to stimulate economic growth in order to expand the market for American exports. Enacting a consumption tax would lead to an opposite result by dampening demand. In response, the prime minister avoided any specific commitments on the issue while pledging in general terms to concentrate on encouraging Japan's economic recovery (*Yomiuri*, November 20[c], 1993).

Early in 1994 a consensus on tax policy began to emerge between the business community and the Japanese government on implementing a hike in the consumption tax only after a cut in the income tax. At a press conference, leaders of the four main business groups agreed on the need for an early tax cut, although they split on the timing of the tax raise. Chairman Hiraiwa of Keidanren, and Chairman Masaru Hayami of the Japan Association of Corporate Executives advocated designating in relevant legislation a specific date for upping the consumption tax following the tax cut. Inaba from the JCCI and Takeshi Nagano, chairman of the Japan Employers Association, however, favored postponing even the discussion of a raise until the implementation of the tax cuts (*Yomiuri*, January 6, 1994).

Several business leaders advocated prudence in raising the consumption tax. There was no reason, they thought, to rush into action. Tadahiro Sekimoto from NEC backed a "large cut in the income tax" but cautioned that a rapid enactment of a higher consumption tax could exert a "'bad influence on the psychology of consumers and invite political confusion.'" He suggested that one should not "'think in a rigid way'" about the connection between the two taxes but one should view them as in a "flexible relationship as if they are connected by a rubber cord." Fearing that the economy was reaching a point of crisis in which "the bottom might drop out," Ken'ichi Suematsu of the Sakura Bank backed a delay in boosting the consumption tax because the government could use deficit bonds for revenue until the tax increase took effect. Yoshinari Yamashiro of NKK (Japan Iron and Steel) stated flatly that the "only option was to enact an income tax cut first with deficit bonds as a funding source." He conceded that raising the consumption tax was important in the long term to revise the ratio between direct and indirect taxes, but he asserted that "it is impossible to accomplish together [both] a tax cut as a policy for improving business conditions and tax reform aimed at [coping with] the arrival of an aging society." Tetsurō Kawakami, the president of the large Sumitomo Bank, opposed the tax cut, because "the expectations for [expanding] consumption are small and [the cut] goes against [the goal of restoring] public finance to health." He insisted that if the government enacted the planned cut in the income tax, the consumption tax would have to rise to a rate of 7% within 15 months to compensate for lost revenue (*Yomiuri*, January 23, 1994).

Both Kawakami and Yamashiro raised important issues about the contradictions in the proposed strategy of pursuing the dual goals of stimulating the economy in the short term and effecting changes in tax policy in order to solve longer-term problems. At a basic level, their point was that the strategy of reducing some taxes while raising others ran the risk of accomplishing neither the goal of stimulating the economy nor of increasing revenue to deal with anticipated expenses in the future. In any event, the MOF clearly stated that it would resist efforts to implement an expansionary fiscal policy. Finance Minister Hirohisa Fujii announced bluntly that he would "'absolutely not permit the incontinent (*tarenagashi*) [use of] deficit bonds. (Doing so) would leave [a legacy of] shame for future generations.'" Other MOF officials emphasized that a measure to enact tax cuts first would have to "specify the period for raising the consumption tax" (*Yomiuri*, February 2, 1994). MITI announced its full support for this stance by declaring jointly with the MOF the need for a raise in the consumption tax only one year after cuts in the income tax because of the need to raise revenue to fund services for an "aging society" (*Yomiuri*, January 14, 1994).

Gradually the major players regarding this issue inched toward agreement on a detailed proposal. In June the Government Tax System Research Council, headed by Katō, and the Ruling Parties Tax System Reform Council each issued reports that "recognized" the need for a "rise in the consumption tax above the decrease in the income tax" in order to support an aging society (*Yomiuri*, June 22[a], 1994). Although the report of the government's Council did not specify a rate for the consumption tax, Katō explained members' general opinion that "it [was] necessary to raise the rate [of the consumption tax] to more than seven percent" in order to "'progress toward a net increase in taxes (in order to create a source of funding for welfare programs)" (*Yomiuri*, June 22[b], 1994). In July, the ruling coalition formed a Governing Parties Tax Reform Project Team headed by Ichirō Hino of the Japan Socialist Party (JSP). The JSP, despite having been a bitter and once powerful rival of the LDP from 1955 through the 1980s, had joined a coalition with the LDP in 1993. The socialists had staunchly opposed the consumption tax since the 1970s but in their weakened state could now only hope to moderate the impact of the tax (*Yomiuri*, July 20, 1994).[15] Meanwhile, a meeting of the LDP's Tax System Research Council reached several conclusions: "1) regarding the contentious issue of a raise in the consumption tax, to manage the increase and decrease in taxes together [in a way] that will specify at the same time a tax cut [as well as a tax increase] in a proposed law related to reform of the tax system, 2) to make the period of a hike in the consumption tax [start in] April 1997, two years after [the tax cut], 3) [to make] the scale of the increase and of the decrease in taxes the same amount" (*Yomiuri*, September 2, 1994). Shortly afterwards, the three ruling parties—the LDP, the JSP, and Sakigake—agreed to split the proposed income tax cut into two levels, a "permanent reduction (*kōkyū genzei*)" and an "annual fixed reduction (*tannendo no teiritsu genzei*)." The aim of this approach, which the JSP and Sakigake advanced, was to encourage the government in two years to keep only the "permanent" tax cut and to reduce the size of the corresponding raise in the consumption tax (*Yomiuri*, September 11, 1994).

Two weeks later the three governing parties agreed on a plan. In April 1997, the consumption tax would rise from three percent to five percent, although the rate could be reconsidered six months beforehand. The cut in the income tax in 1995 would take a "two-level form" in which a reduction of 3.5 trillion yen would be "permanent" and a reduction of two trillion yen would be "fixed" through 1996, at which point the "fixed" portion of the cut could end. To mitigate the impact of the consumption tax on more vulnerable members of society the government would make temporary payments to elderly recipients of pensions. In addition, the lowest bracket of the income tax with a 20% rate would expand from those earning a maximum annual income of six million yen to those earning up to nine million yen. The plan touted the goal of "advancing three reforms together—[reform] of the tax system, administrative reform, and [reform] of [funding] welfare services." Accordingly, the proposed changes would re-adjust the ratio of direct and indirect taxes, promote decentralization by allotting one fifth of the projected five percent rate of the consumption tax to local governments, and provide funding to "prepare for an aging society with few children." Because designating a portion of the new revenue to local governments proved popular with local chambers of commerce, this provision may have mitigated opposition to the consumption tax from the JCCI (*Yomiuri*, September 23, 1994; September 15, 1994). Minister of Finance Masayoshi Takemura expressed a desire to raise the consumption tax in 1996 if business conditions permitted, but Minister of

[15] The other member of the ruling coalition was the Sakigake political party.

Foreign Affairs Yōhei Kōno advocated caution in response to pressure from American officials on the Japanese government to stimulate the domestic economy to boost imports (*Yomiuri*, September 18, 1994; September 21, 1994). In November 1994, the Diet passed the plan for raising the consumption tax and reducing the individual income tax.

The Federation continued to press for further reforms of the tax system, including measures specifically to aid large corporations. A proposal approved in October made clear that the "revision of the ratio of direct and indirect taxes ha[d] not occurred sufficiently" and set out a strategy of continuing to pursue a "reconsideration of the ratio of direct and indirect taxes as a central topic of drastic reform of the tax system" in order to "respond to an aging society and international harmonization [in economic matters]." Other issues meriting "reconsideration" included the rate of the consumption tax, fiscal reform, a "vision for welfare services," and reduction of the comparatively high corporate tax. The Federation also argued for a reduction of the land tax, which in a case of unfortunate timing the government had enacted in the early 1990s in order to cool off the speculative market in real estate that had emerged in the late 1980s. The tax now imposed a heavy burden on owners since land prices had deflated (*Keidanren shūhō*, 1994, No. 2236, pp. 4–10).[16] When Federation Chairman Shōichirō Toyoda met with Prime Minister Tomo'ichi Murayama nine months later in 1995 he lamented that "our economy is in a severe situation in which a collapse of business conditions is feared." First on Toyoda's proposed list of reforms were tax measures—lowering the corporate tax and the income tax and abolishing the land tax (*Keidanren kurippu*, 1995, p. 7).

Despite the new emphasis on deregulation and administrative reform aiming at a smaller government, the leaders of Keidanren recognized the benefits of government aid. While urging the enhancement of "efforts of the people to help themselves and the dynamism of the private sector," leaders advocated the expansion of a system of reserve funds for helping banks deal with non-performing loans (*Keidanren shūhō*, 1994, No. 2236, pp. 4 and 7). While meeting with Prime Minister Murayama, Toyoda recommended increased public works and, in regard to "managing the problem of non-performing loans, setting drastic policies for a solution, including the introduction of public finance" (*Keidanren kurippu*, 1995, No. 13, p. 7).

In the fall of 1995 Keidanren pressed its case on tax reform. Reducing the corporate tax was an "urgent issue" for "restoring dynamism to the Japanese economy" (*Keidanren kurippu*, 1995, No. 20, p. 1). While Japan needed to "raise the portion of taxes on consumption to correct the government's excessive dependence on direct taxes, the real tax burden for enterprises should be on an internationally equal footing," especially as enterprises were "in an era of mega-competition in which firms aggressively advance[d] abroad." Japan's high corporate tax rate could even cause domestic firms to move overseas. Insistence that the corporate tax had to fall at least to the level of the American rate of 40% became a constant refrain, along with expanded deductions to encourage research and development as well as new

[16] For further information regarding Keidanren's views on the issue of the land tax, see Keizai Dantai Rengōkai (1999, pp. 636–638).

industries. According to the Federation, the land tax was at the very least too heavy for some industries in some regions (Keidanren, 1995, pp. 1–4).

An internal discussion of issues produced even more strident comments. One executive lamented that in 1995 indirect taxes at the central and local level provided only 25% of revenue for the national government, whereas in Europe they provided 40% of revenue. He noted that the Japanese consumption tax would rise from three percent to just five percent, whereas European rates for similar taxes varied from 15 to 25%. Japanese firms paid 49% of their profits as taxes to the government compared to a range from 33 to 34% in the United States. Moreover, in 1995 there were four workers in Japan to support each citizen over age 65, but in 2020 that ratio would be only two to one. Another executive proposed that the consumption tax should increase to 15%, while yet another suggested the radical goal of a 50/50 ratio of direct to indirect taxes (*Gekkan Keidanren*, December 1995, pp. 8–11). The discussants noted as well that the high corporate tax rate might account in part for the low level of foreign investment in Japan (*Ibid.*, pp. 13–14).

Keidanren's response to what it now recognized as a dire economic crisis for the nation brought out more starkly the contradictions in its approach. While supporting increased government spending to rescue banks from their non-performing loans, the Federation advocated lowering the corporate tax and increasing the consumption tax. This strategy aimed to rescue Japan's public finances in the long run, but it would immediately shift some of the tax burden from companies to ordinary citizens. Moreover, attempts to balance cuts in some taxes and raises in others were unlikely to stimulate the economy. Recognition of these contradictions came in the outline of a ten-year plan to reform public finance that would gradually limit the rise of public expenditures, lower the ratio of public expenditures to the gross domestic product, and reduce the use of long-term bonds. The plan proclaimed: "to realize again a prosperous and dynamic economic society [we] must first accept suffering.'" Japanese society had to adopt a "spirit of first pain, then recovery" (*Keidanren kurippu*, No. 46, December 26, 1996, pp. 8–9). It seemed that most of the pain suffered for improving the common welfare would hit common citizens while the tax burden on corporations would diminish without providing a noticeable stimulus to the economy, certainly in the near term.

From the fall of 1994 to the fall of 1996, the government fended off several challenges to its pledge to increase the consumption tax. As the date for the change neared, the large Isetan Department Store and business groups representing the automobile and petroleum industries expressed worries about the impact of the tax raise on dampening consumption. Ministry officials, however, reacted quickly by pointing out that the government needed the consumption tax to fund at least some of the permanent cuts in the income tax that were already in effect and to begin to close the gap between the government's overall expenses and its revenue. In June, 1996, the Tax System Research Councils of both the government and the LDP each endorsed raising the consumption tax to five percent (*Yomiuri*, June 21[a], 1996; June 21[b], 1996; June 22, 1996). Looking further ahead, the LDP under Prime Minister Ryūtarō Hashimoto released a draft of "'The Hashimoto Vision.'" It advocated cuts in the corporate tax and the income tax and touched on the "possibility of raising the consumption tax" again (*Yomiuri*, July 02, 1996). Still, statements by two opposition parties, the New Progressive Party (Shinshintō) and Kōmeitō, signaled a new movement in the Diet to freeze the consumption tax (*Yomiuri*, August 20, 1996; September 7, 1996).

Meanwhile, Keidanren's campaign for lowering the corporate tax encountered resistance. The Government Tax System Research Council decided to take up the issue. Its approach, however, of raising funds to compensate for cuts in the overall tax rate by eliminating firms' deductions for creating "reserve funds" for employees' annual bonuses and for their retirement packages sparked strong opposition from the business community. The Government Council then decided to delay its report until the spring of 1997, well after the scheduled nationwide election for the Lower House in October 1996 (*Yomiuri*, September 13, 1996; September 14, 1996).

The increase in seats in the Lower House which the LDP won in that election helped ensure that the ruling coalition cabinet would stick to its commitment to raise the consumption tax. While beating back a formal proposal from the New Progressive Party to keep the current rate in place for three years, Prime Minister Hashimoto invoked the need for more revenue to meet critical social needs: "'the consumption tax is a response of the tax system to the structural changes of the advance of an aging society. Following the law, [we] must implement (the raise from April of next year)." He remained convinced that the negative effects of the tax boost would be relatively minor. "Private demand,'" he predicted, "will increase its firmness; as for the economy, the movement of recovery will continue. Raising the consumption tax will influence the economy but not the basis of the road to recovery of business conditions." He thus hoped that the economic effects of upping the consumption tax would in the short term not be too bad and would lay the foundation for further recovery. The LDP, though, showed some sensitivity toward the optics of adding to the tax burden of ordinary citizens while reducing taxes for wealthy corporations. Members of the LDP Tax System Research Council observed that "while waiting for the raise in the consumption tax next spring it is best not to touch other matters that can cause problems." "When increasing a mass tax such as the consumption tax, cutting taxes only for business makes no political sense" (*Yomiuri*, December 9, 1996; December 13, 1996). The Council decided to postpone any changes in the corporate tax until 1998 (*Yomiuri*, December 19, 1996).[17]

8 Conclusion

Keidanren and the business community played a central role in bringing about the controversial hike in the consumption tax in 1997, just as they had done in the rejection of the consumption tax in 1979 and in 1987 and in its enactment in 1989. The MOF had initiated the campaign for the consumption tax in 1977 but gaining approval from the business community turned out to be crucial. Opposition from both large and small enterprises helped throttle the tax in the late 1970s, and a split in the

[17] The government did lower the corporate tax rate in 1999 and 2000. See Keidanren (2002, p. 7).

business community between Keidanren and the Japan Chamber of Commerce and Industry had doomed the measure in 1987. By then Keidanren had decided to support the consumption tax, as other strategies—a period of fiscal expansion followed by a period of fiscal restraint—failed to meet lofty expectations. In the 1980s business leaders were disappointed that annual economic growth rates did not surpass five percent and that, although officials gradually reduced the government's reliance on deficit spending, they could not eliminate it. Moreover, the Federation perceived the need for a new stream of tax revenue to fund expanded social services for a rapidly aging population and to accommodate political pressure to slash individual income taxes. In addition, a new source of revenue would forestall attempts to increase the corporate tax rate and thus help keep Japanese firms competitive with rivals in other nations.

As noted above, some business leaders by the mid-1990s criticized Keidanren for pursuing contradictory goals. It was in the short-term trying to stir the economy from several years of lethargy through advocating the lowering of the income tax rate for individuals and decreasing the corporate tax rate. At the same time the Federation justified boosting the consumption tax to restore the nation's public finances so that it could meet long-term obligations to support an aging population. Proponents knew that raising the consumption tax would temporarily dampen economic growth, but they thought that the longer-term gain would outweigh the short-term "pain."

Keidanren's support for the consumption tax demonstrates that a preoccupation with long-term goals can create contradictions in national economic policy during an economic slump. In particular, the Federation's concern for the long-term goal of restoring public finance interfered with the immediate goal of effecting economic recovery. The possibility of this result should not have been a surprise, because in the late 1970s Keidanren had opposed the introduction of a consumption tax by arguing that economic recovery had to precede a successful effort to balance the budget of the national government because premature efforts toward that end could stifle an economic recovery and thus worsen a fiscal crisis by lowering the flow of revenue to the government. Indeed, raising the consumption tax in 1997 hampered economic growth and may even have helped undermine the achievement of the long-term goal of balancing the budget to the extent that contributing to the persistence of the nation's economic slump helped cause a decline in the government's revenue.[18]

Still, over the next two decades the Federation persisted in advocating the same strategy toward the economy and taxes. Bemoaning the continuing stagnation of the economy, a report issued in late 2008 emphasized the need for an "emergency comprehensive policy" to make the social welfare system sustainable, restore the national budget to fiscal health, and promote economic growth. "From now on, along with supporting the social welfare system for all people, to maintain and strengthen the vitality of the economy, the establishment of a tax system that balances [revenue

---

[18] Christian Broda and David E. Weinstein show that government revenue, which had stabilized for three years, did decrease for three years after 1997, recovered, and then declined again. See Broda and Weinstein (2005, pp. 49–51, especially Fig. 2.1). See also, Wright (2002, p. 49, Fig. 3.2), and Noble (2012, pp. 63–65).

from] each aspect of consumption, income, and financial assets is demanded" (Nihon Keizai Dantai Rengōkai, October 2, 2008, p. 1). Increasing the consumption tax assumed a central role in these proposals. It was "essential to supply the expansion of social welfare expenditures through the consumption tax" in order to end the overreliance on "direct taxes" and to "distribute the burden [of supporting social welfare] among people of the generations that currently make up society as much as possible without postponing the burden for future generations [to bear]" (*Ibid.*, p. 5).

A consumption tax would have other benefits. Revenue from it would be more stable than revenue from direct income taxes. Because a consumption tax would not affect exports, it would not lower Japanese firms' competitiveness on the global market. Without offering evidence, the Federation asserted as well that compared to alternative levies the consumption tax would have the "most neutral influence" on different sectors of economic activity. More controversially, the report stated that because everyone would pay a consumption tax for items that they purchased it would not target "specific people (*tokutei no mono*)" (*Ibid.*, p. 6). This argument obviously overlooked the common belief that without special provisions the impact of a consumption tax would be regressive, because usually people who are less well-off spend a higher percentage of their income on purchases of goods. In fact, the report itself obliquely recognized this unequal impact in justifying a cut in the income tax for middle-and-low-income earners by noting that "it was necessary to plan a mitigation of the burden of a raise in the consumption tax" for them. Meanwhile, the Federation recommended "at least a five percent raise" in that tax, i.e. a doubling from five to ten percent (*Ibid.*, pp. 8–9).

Keidanren continued to insist on lowering the corporate tax rate in order to enhance the international competitiveness of Japanese companies. Successfully "creating a sustainable tax system in an aging society based on raising the consumption tax" would not be enough to spur economic growth: "…[O]n the other hand if [we] neglect a response of the tax system to rapidly developing globalization including the BRICs, our nation's development will be uncertain." The report elaborated, "the greatest topic is the response to the competition among some other nations to lower the real corporate tax rate." Noting that in the European Union the average corporate tax rate was 28% compared to 40% in Japan, the report argued that "quickly lowering the real corporate tax rate is the main topic of the [needed] drastic reform of the tax system" (*Ibid.*, pp. 9–10).[19] Business leaders feared that the lower corporate tax rates levied on foreign competitors on the world market would enable them to produce goods at lower cost and make foreign nations more attractive as locations for companies, even Japanese firms.

While Keidanren's perception of the development of an economic crisis had intensified by 2012, its prescription for a cure remained basically the same. A pamphlet that the Federation published that year advised that continuing economic lethargy put Japan in danger of losing its "international presence" and its status as a leading nation: "confronting the harsh reality of being in a crisis of falling from the ranks of advanced

---

[19] The term BRICs refers to emerging and then rapidly growing economic powers, such as Brazil, Russia, India, and China.

nations, [we] are raising [the issue] that [we] must consider the path to take" (Nihon Keizai Dantai Rengōkai, May 15, 2012, pp. 2–3). One new item in the prescription was government aid to rebuild the northeastern region of Japan's main island (Tōhoku) after the devastating Great Eastern Japan Earthquake and the resulting tsunami in March 2011 as this aid could become a "triggering charge (*ibakuzai*) for economic growth" (*Ibid.*, pp. 22–23).[20] A brief paragraph of one sentence toward the end of the report also hinted at an acceptance of an expansionary monetary policy by suggesting succinctly that the government should set a goal of an annual inflation rate of one percent in order to combat deflation (*Ibid.*, p. 34). As before, however, Keidanren emphasized the need for slashing the corporate tax rate further to compete with other nations in attracting investment. Japan had to cut the corporate rate to the 20-percent range to match the rates of neighboring nations (*Ibid.*, pp. 24–25).[21]

As one might expect, the report endorsed legislation for substantial increases in the consumption tax to 8% in 2014 and 10% in 2015. While the justification for this stance continued to stress the necessity to pay for increasing social welfare expenditures, the report took care to explain more fully the advantages of increasing revenue through this type of tax. Additional revenue for the government was now essential for the recovery of the national economy. If the national debt continued to grow, economic stagnation would continue, because doubts among the current generation of workers about the future of the social welfare system would cause them to restrict their consumption in order to save for their old age. Raising the consumption tax was preferable to other levies, because it would "not obstruct the formation of capital" within Japan and thus hinder economic growth or reduce the number of available jobs. True, the authors admitted, raising the consumption tax in April 1997 had "resulted in a worsening of business conditions," but "the drop in household expenditures had been temporary, and what had the most significant influence on reducing economic growth were extraneous causes [such as] the Asian currency crisis later [that year] and a series of bankruptcies of financial institutions" (*Ibid.*, pp. 12–13, 28, and 32). Keidanren predicted that "by the mid-2020s" the consumption tax would have to rise to the "upper part of the 10-percent range (*10% dai kōhan made*)" in order to fund social welfare benefits for the "baby boomer generation (*dankai sedai*)" (*Ibid.*, p. 33).[22] To counter that bracing prediction, the report ended this section on an optimistic note that professed an increasingly firm belief in the centrality of fiscal reform for the nation's economic health. "With the sustainability of the systems of public finance and social welfare being guaranteed, for the first time the unease of the people and business about the future will be removed; individual consumption and [companies'] investment in equipment will become active and will become linked to sustainable growth" (*Ibid.*).

---

[20] Picking up on a theme developed previously, as noted above on pp. 15, 29 (Footnote 83), and 38, the report also endorsed increased government spending to enhance scientific and technological innovation. See *Ibid.*, pp. 21 and 25–26.

[21] According to Keidanren, a reform of the tax system in 2012 had lowered the corporate tax rate by 5%. Then, to help pay for recovery after the Great Eastern Japan Earthquake, the government had added a special corporate tax for three years as a supplementary tax.

[22] Baby boomers were those born within several years after the end of World War II.

Although some aspects of Keidanren's economic and tax strategy had changed, support for the consumption tax and working toward a balanced national budget remained top priorities along with economic recovery. After the devastating earthquake and tsunami of 2011, the Federation understandably backed increased government spending for Tōhoku's economic recovery. In addition, the report of 2012 recommended a mildly expansionary monetary policy. More predictably, though, the need to balance the national budget by raising the consumption tax took priority along with the cuts in the corporate tax rate. The dilemma, however, remained that the dampening of demand by the increased consumption tax would counteract the economic stimulus provided by the corporate tax cut as well as expansionary fiscal and monetary policies and would fail to restore either strong economic growth or the nation's fiscal health.

References

Secondary Works

Anchordoguy M (2005) *Reprogramming Japan: The High Tech Crisis Under Communitarian Capitalism*. Cornell University Press.

Broda C and Weinstein D (2005) "Happy News from the Dismal Science: Reassessing Japanese Fiscal Policy and Sustainability," in Ito T, Patrick H, and Weinstein D, ed., *Reviving Japan's Economy*. Cambridge, MA: The MIT Press.

Garside W (2012) *Japan's Great Stagnation: Forging Ahead, Falling Behind*. Cheltenham, UK: Edward Elgar.

Hori H (2005) *The Changing Japanese Political System: The Liberal Democratic Party and the Ministry of Finance*. New York and London: Routledge.

Keizai Dantai Rengōkai (ed.) (1999) *Keizai Dantai Rengōkai gojū nen shi*. Tokyo: Keizai Dantai Rengōkai.

Kingston J (2013) *Contemporary Japan: History, Politics, and Social Change since the 1980s*. Chichester, West Sussex, and Malden, MA: Wiley-Blackwell.

Kobayashi K (2015) "The Two 'Lost Decades' and Macroeconomics: Changing Economic Policies," in Funabashi Y and Kushner B, ed., *Examining Japan's Lost Decades*. Abingdon: Routledge.

Kuttner K, Iwaisako T, and Posen A (2015) "Monetary and Fiscal Policies during the Lost Decades," in Funabashi Y and Kushner B, ed., *Examining Japan's Lost Decades*. Routledge.

Morinobu S (2000) *Nihon no shōhizei: Dōnyū, kaisei no kei'i, to jūyō shiryō*. Osaka: Nōzei Kyōkai Rengōkai.

Noble G (2012) "Japan's Economic Crisis: More Chronic than Acute," in Bong Y and Pempel T, ed., *Japan in Crisis: What Will It Take for Japan to Rise Again?* New York: Palgrave Macmillan.

Pilling D (2014) *Bending Adversity: Japan and the Art of Survival*. New York: The Penguin Press.

Takahashi F (1999) "Manipulations Behind the Consumption Tax Increase, The Ministry of Finance Prolongs Japan's Recession," *Journal of Japanese Studies*, Vol. 25, No. 1, Winter 1999.

Takeda H (2009) *Nihon Keizai no Jikenbō: Kaikoku kara Baburu Hōkai made*. Tokyo: Nihon Keizai Hyōronsha.

Takeshita N and Hirano S (1993) *Shōhizei seido seiritsu no enkaku*. Tokyo: Gyōsei.

Tiberghien Y (2014) "Thirty Years of Neo-liberal Reforms in Japan," in Lechevalier S ed., *The Great Transformation of Japanese Capitalism*, trans. by Stockwin J. Abington and Oxon: Routledge.

Vogel E (1979) *Japan as Number One: Lessons for America.* Harvard University Press.
Wakatabe M (2015) *Japan's Great Stagnation: Lessons for the World.* Palgrave Macmillan.
Wright M (2002) *Japan's Fiscal Crisis: The Ministry of Finance and the Politics of Public Spending, 1975-2000.* Oxford: Oxford University Press.

Opinions, Policy Statements, Proposals, and Reports Produced by Keidanren

Available Online at the Library of Keidanren in Tokyo, Japan

Keidanren, Keizai Chōsa Iinkai, January 23, 1979, "Nihon keizai no genjō to chūkiteki kadai"
Keidanren, Keizai Kōhō Sentā, 1980. Dainanakai Keidanren fuoramu, Zeisei no arikata o kangaeru (September 25, 1980)
Keidanren (1983) "1980 nendai o tōzuru Nihon keizai no kadai—Antei keizai to kigyō katsuryoku no hakki o motomete"
*The copy of this report that the author read in the Library of the Faculty of Economics at The University of Tokyo does not indicate the date of publication, but an authoritative source explains that the Economic Research Committee of Keidanren compiled the report and issued it on February 22, 1983 (See Keizai Dantai Rengōkai, 1999,p. 275.) The copy of the report in the Library of the Faculty of Economics at The University of Tokyo was donated on August 15, 1984.
Keidanren, September 25, 1984. "Genkō zeisei no sho mondai to kongo no hōkō"
Keidanren, March 26, 1986. "Gyōzaisei kaikaku to zeisei no konpon kaikaku ni tsuite—chūkan hōkoku to teigen"
Keidanren, September 24, 1986. "Zeisei konpon kaikaku to 62 nendo zeisei kaisei ni kansuru iken"
Zeisei Iinkai, September 27, 1977. "Kongo no zaisei un'ei to zeisei no arikata ni kansuru kenkai"
Zeisei Iinkai, September 27, 1978. "Kongo no zeisei no arikata ni tsuite no kinhonteki na kangaekata"
Zeisei Iinkai, December 3, 1979. "Wagakuni keizai no tōmen suru kadai to zeisei kaisei ni kansuru iken"
Zeisei Iinkai, October 28, 1980. "Kigyō katsuryoku no hakki to kongo no zeisei no arikata ni kansuru kenkai"
Zeisei Iinkai, November 24, 1981. "Gyōzaisei kaikaku to kongo no zeisei no arikata ni kansuru iken"
Zeisei Iinkai, December 7, 1982. "Tōmen no zeisei mondai ni kansuru kinhonteki kangaekata"
Zeisei Iinkai, October 12, 1983. "Zeisei o meguru tōmen no sho mondai to kongo no hōkō"
Keizai Dantai Rengōkai (September 22, 1992) "Heisei 5 nendo zeisei kaisei ni kansuru kenkai"
Keidanren (October 11, 1995) "Zeisei kaisei ni kansuru teigen"
Keidanren (February 19, 2002) "Zeisei bappon kaikaku no arikata ni tsuite"
Nihon Keizai Dantai Rengōkai (October 2, 2008) "Zei, zaisei, shakai hoshō seido no ittai kaikaku ni kansuru teigen: anshin de katsuryoku aru keizai shakai no jitsugen ni mukete"
Nihon Keizai Dantai Rengōkai (May 15, 2012) "Seichō senryaku no jikkō to zaisei saiken no dankō o motomeru: Genka no kiki kara no dakkyaku o mokushi shite"

Articles in Periodical Publications of Keidanren, such as Gekkan Keidanren (Keidanren Monthly), Keidanren Kurippu *("Keidanren Clip")*, Keidanren Review, Keidanren Shūhō *(*Keidanren Weekly*)*

Gekkan Keidanren, December 1995, "Korekara no Nihon ni fusawashii zeisei o kōchiku suru"
Keidanren kurippu, No. 13 (July 13, 1995). "Keizai kasseika ni muke, jikkō aru daitan na kinkyū keizei taisaku no jisshi o motomeru"
Keidanren kurippu, No. 20 (November 9, 1995). "Kigyō no zei futan no keigen ni yoru keizai kasseika ga fukaketsu"
Keidanren kurippu, No. 46, December 26, 1996 "Zaisei minshushugi no kakuritsu to nōzei ni ataisuru kokka o mokushi shite"
Keidanren Review of Japanese Economy, No. 78, December 1982. "Priorities Defined for National Economy"
Keidanren Review of Japanese Economy, No. 85, February 1984. "Business to Foot Bill for FY '84 Income Tax Cut"
Keidanren shūhō, No. 2236 (October 31, 1994). "Rainendo zei, zaisei un'ei ni kansuru kenkai' o kengi"

Yomiuri Shinbun (Yomiuri)

*All references to articles in the *Yomiuri Shinbun* (Yomiuri newspaper) are from the Yomidasu Rekishikan database available at the library of Duke University in Durham, NC. Unless otherwise indicated, the citations are to the Tokyo morning edition.

1977

March 23. "Zōzei, hashira wa ippan shōhizei, fukakachizei fukume"
August 31. "Shōhizei dōnyū nanten nai, zeichō bukai hōkoku"
September 14. "Shotoku, hōjin zōzei no yochi, fukōhei zesei ga fukaketsu"
September 22. "Ippan shōhizei, rainendo jisshi no ikō, Ōkurashō shunō hajimete jiki shimesu"
September 23. "Ippan shōhizei ni ryūtsū gyōkai mōhanpatsu"
October 7. "Ippan shōhizei no sōki dōnyū, tsūsan wa kyōkō hantai"
December 12. " Ippan shōhizei 54 nendo ni dōnyū, Zeichō tōshin meiki"

1978

May 25. "Ippan shōhizei wa 'fukushizei' ni"
July 19. "Ippan shōhizei 5% uchi ni, Zeiritsu medo hajimete meigen"
September 5[a]. "'Ippan shōhizei' de zeichō saishū an"
September 5[b]. "Zaikai 'shōhizei' ni hantai"
September 27. "Ippan shōhizei no sōki dōnyū, Zaikai 3 dantai ga hantai"
November 21. "Seichō 4% dai ni"
November 21. "Ōkurashō ga kihon hōshin: kibō 40 chō en nose ka"

November 21. "Ōkurashō wa shōhizei dōnyū o uttae"
December 19. "Shushō 55 nen jisshi katameru, Tsūjō kokkai ni teishutsu mo"

1979

June 6. "Shōhizei no rainendo dōnyū shushō futatabi kyōchō"
September 26. "Shōhizei' yureru Ōhira hatsugen"
September 27. "Yosan hensei, hageshiku minaoshi, hōjinzei 3% appu"

1986

September 12. "Saitō Keidanren kaichō no kensetsu kokusai zōhatsu hitsuyō no kenkai shimesu"
September 18. "Shinkei kansetsuzei de seifu zeichō no 4 an ni Nisshō ga zenmen hantai Jimin ni ikensho"
September 25. "Nihonkei fuka kachi zei no dōnyū"
October 21. "Shinkei kansetsuzei wa 'Nihonkei' ga nozomashii, Ittaika wa dekizu/Seifu zeichō saishū tōshin katamaru"
December 24. "Zaikai, Shinzeisei ni fukuzatsu na hannō, Hōjin genzei hyōka, Uriagezei wa hihan"
December 24. "Uriagezei de keiki dō naru'

1987

January 30. "Zeisei kaikaku san hōan (Shotokuzeihō, uriagezeihō, sozei tokubetsu sochihō) no yōshi"
February 2. "Uriagezei dōnyū e jimin, Tahōmen sakusen, PR hisshi no kōbō"
February 5. "'Shikai' uriagezei, Tsūsan no kunō fukashi, Honne shiritsutsu gyōkai settoku e"
February 6. "Uriagezei dōnyū kakaku tenka, Dokkinhō de rūru tsukuri, Shitauke, chūshō no 'hogo' e"
February 11. "Uriagezei no jimin zenkoku kaigi, Nakasone shushō ga netsuben 'aete kachū no kuri o hirō"
February 19. "Uriagezei no funsai de gōi / Zensen Dōmei to Chēnsutoa Kyōkai"
February 25. "Jimin e no konkin 3000 man'en o tōketsu, Uriagezei dōnyū de, Hyakkaten kyōkai"
February 26. "'Shōrai kangaete ima uriagezei no jisshi o'/Hiraiwa Keidanren fukukaichō"
February 27. "Uriagezei hantai ni ichi man nin sanka, Zenkoku Shōhisha Dantai Renrakukai no shimin kekki taishūkai" [Evening Edition]
March 2. "Uriagezei hantai shūkai hiraku, Rōdō dantai yobikake, Meiji kōen ni nana man nin"
April 14."'Shikai' tōitsusen jimin haiboku keizaikai, Nao uriagezei ronsō Ōkurashō ni wa sekinin tsuikyū ron"
April 18. "Uriagezei 'Hibiya no jin,' yatō ga hantai shūkai, Nakasone san suishin taikai de iyoku hyōmei, Tokyo tō"
April 24. "'Chokkan zesei' wa hitsuyō/Uriagezei no 'haian' de zaikai hannō"
May 8. "Shinkei kansetsuzei no kōsō zukuri, Zaikai yon dantai ga kyōdō de, Nisshō mo ashinami"
October 12. "Jimintō no zeisei kaikaku hōshin yōshi"

1988

February 24. "Ippan shōhizei hitei no kokkai ketsugi ni kōsokuryoku wa nai/Saitō Keidanren kaichō"
April 5. "Nisshō mo shinkei kansetsuzei mitomeru, Hikazei nashi o jōken ni jimin zeichō no iken chōshū de hyōmei" [Evening Edition]
May 28. "Chēnstoa kyōkai, Shinkei kansetsuzei ni 'jōkentsuki sansei' e, Seifu jimin ni shitsumon o yōi"
May 31. "Jimin zeichō, Shinkei kansetsuzei de gyōkai chōshū o kaishi hantai, kaizen yōbō aitsugu" [Tokyo Evening Edition]
June 15. "Shōhizei 3%, Genzei 5 chō 6,000 oku en, Jimin ga zeisei kaikaku taikō kettei, Ronsen rinji kokkai e"
June 25. "Seifu no zeisei kaikaku an, Nenshū 856 man ika wa zōzei, Teishotokusō ni funtanzō/Shatō shikisan"
June 25. "Shōhizei kakaku tenka no enkatsuka o jimin zeichō nado ni yōsei e/Tsūsanshō"
July 9. "Gen, jūyū kanzei no teppai yōkyū, Tsūsanshō ga Ōkurashō, Jimintō to chōsei e"
July 12. "Shōhizei tenka karuteru fusoku, Hō shikkō to dōji jisshi, Zei tekiyō ni wa yūyo kikan mo"
July 29. "3% shōhizei dōnyū wa kyūmu, Shinmei sasage torikomu, Takeshita shushō ga shoshin hyōmei ensetsu" [Tokyo Evening Edition]
December 25. Shōhizei seiritsu, 'Kakiteki' to zaikai ga kangei"

1993

May 8. "Zeishū fusoku, Akaji kokusai rongi ga fujō mo, 'Chokusetsuzei tayori' no yowami, Shotoku genzei no yukikata bimyō ni"
November 20[a]. "Genzei, shōhizei age ittai de, seifu zeichō 'kongo no zeisei' chūki tōshin, chūkensō no futan keigen"
November 20[b]. "Seifu zeichō chūki tōshin –zaikai, shōhizei age ni sanpi"
November 20[c]. "APEC Hosokawa Kurinton kaidan, ken'an yamaseki, jitsumu tōgi e"

1994

January 6. "'Keiki kaifuku wa jūgatsu irai'—genzei sōki jisshi motomeru, keizai 4 dantai shunō ga kyōdō kaiken"
January 14. "Zōgenzei ittai shōri, Ōkura to Tsūsan ga 'kyōdō sensen,' Kōreika shakai e no kikkikan ga haikei ni"
January 23. "Fukyōka no konmei, Seiji wa ima nani o subeki ka, Keizeikai no ronkyaku 5 shi ni kiku"
February 2. "Zaigen tanpo no nai genzei, Tsuyoku kensei/Fujii Ōkurashō"
June 22. "Shōhi zeiritsu wa seiji handan ni, Seifu zeichō ga tōshin, Yotō zeisei kaikaku kyō no hōkoku o teishutsu"
June 22. "Shōhizei wa '7% ijō ga taisei,' Katō kaichō ga kaiken de akasu"
July 20. "Zeisei kaikaku wa zōgenzei ittai de shingi, Yotō sho kaigō de kakunin"
September 2. "Shōhizei hikiage wa 2 nen ato, Zōgenzei ittai shōri de Jimintō zeichō hōshin" [Evening Edition]
September 11."Shotoku genzei 'nikaitate' ni seido kaisei to tannendo kiteiritsu kumiawase, Yotō hōshin"
September 15. "Chihō shōhizei no dōnyū mondai, kakuchi shōkō kaigisho nado ga taido o nanka"

September 18. "Chihō shōhizei sōsetsu e chōsei, Chōzei, kokuzeichō itaku de, Takemura Ōkurashō ga hyōmei"
September 21. "Shōhizei age 97 nen 4 gatsu, Yotō 3 tōshu, Genzei 3 nen senkō de gōi, zeiritsu nado saikyōgi"
September 23, 1994. "Shōhizei 97 nen 4 gatsu kara 5%, Seifu yotō, Zeisei kaikaku taikō o kettei"

1996

June 21[a]. "Shōhi zeiritsu hikiage, Sangyōkai ga kōjin shōhi no hiekomi kennen"
June 21[b]. "Shōhizei 5% kakutei, Zōshū nen 4 chō 4,000 oku en, Fukureagaru kokusai, Akaji anaume ni tōku"
June 22. "21 hi kettei shita shōhi zeiritsu ni kansuru gōi bunsho no yōshi"
July 02. "Jimin Hashimoto bishion gen'an zenyō, Hōjinzei, Shotokuzei sage, Shōhizei hijū fuyasu," [Evening edition]
August 20. "Rinji kokkai, Raigetsu kaikai no yōkyū e, 'Shōhizei' 'Okinawa' o shingi/Shinshintō"
September 7. "Kōmei ga shōhizei appu no hantai ikenshoan o tōgikai ni teishutsu"
September 13. "Seifu zeichō kyō saikai, Hōjinzei sage ga shōten, Jitsugen semaru keizaikai, Shōhizei wa senkyō ni eikyō mo"
September 14. "Seifu zeichō saikai, Shōhizei sueoki ron hihan, Chūki tōshin, toshiake irai"
December 9. "Jimin zeichō, zeisei bappon kaisei sakiokuri e, Kentō no kikan mijikaku, Shōhi zeiritsu age mo eikyō"
December 13. "Shōhi zeiritsu sueoki hōan hiketsu, 'raishun kara 5%,' kakutei e/Shūin tokubetsu i"
December 19. "Rainendo zeisei kaisei taikō kettei, Shōhizei 5%, Tokubetsu genzei uchikiri, Kokumin futanzō 7 oku en"

W. Miles Fletcher III is Professor Emeritus in the Department of History at the University of North Carolina at Chapel Hill. Much of his research has focused on the role of business organizations in the modern Japanese economy. His publications include *The Japanese Business Community and National Trade Policy, 1920–1942* (University of North Carolina Press, 1989) and a volume co-edited with Peter W. von Staden, *Japan's Lost Decade: Causes, Legacies and Issues of Transformative Change* (Routledge, 2013).

Name Index

H. Takeda and J. Watanabe (eds.), *Rethinking Japanese economic policy at the turn of the 21st century*, Advances in Japanese Business and Economics 34,
https://doi.org/10.1007/978-981-97-5512-7

Subject Index

Note about the Index: English translations of Japanese laws may vary from chapter to chapter. In many cases there is no official English translation, even by the government. There is also a difference in notation between "Act" and "Law", which should be read as such.

H. Takeda and J. Watanabe (eds.), *Rethinking Japanese economic policy at the turn of the 21st century*, Advances in Japanese Business and Economics 34,
https://doi.org/10.1007/978-981-97-5512-7

The manufacturer's authorised representative in the EU is Springer
Nature Customer Service Centre GmbH, Europaplatz 3, 69115 Heidelberg,
Germany. If you have any concerns regarding our products, please
contact ProductSafety@springernature.com

Printed and bound by CPI Group (UK) Ltd, Croydon, CR0 4YY
01/10/2026
02225961-0011